From Ralph
5/94

Geography
Maps
Anthropology
Recreation

FOURTH EDITION

D0529027

$\times$ S-

T_n

16/3/

The additions and changes in Class G adopted while
this work was in press will be cumulated and
printed in List 183 of
LC Classification—Additions and Changes

Library of Congress Cataloging in Publication Data

United States. Library of Congress. Subject
    Cataloging Division.
    Classification, Class G.

    First ed. published in 1910 by the Classification
Division of the Library of Congress.
    1. Classification—Books—Geography.   2. Classifica-
tion—Maps.   3. Classification—Books—Anthropology.
4. Classification—Books—Folk-lore.   5. Classifica-
tion—Books—Manners and customs.   6. Classification—
Books—Sports.   7. Classification, Library of Congress.
I. United States. Library of Congress. Classification
Division. Classification. Class G: Geography,
anthropology, sports, and games.   II. Title.
Z696.U5G   1976   025.4'6   76–4560
ISBN 0–8444–0209–5

PREFACE

This fourth edition of the Class G schedule is not a total revision, although there are numerous spot revisions throughout the various subclasses. It incorporates all additions and changes made after the 1953 publication of the third edition and before March 1975.

The atlas and map section of Subclass G has been thoroughly overhauled, not only through the adaptation of modern terminology but also in the realignment of jurisdictions to reflect the current political situation. An additional innovation is the introduction of maps to illustrate these alignments and to serve as an index to this section of the subclass. The instructions for applying the tables of subdivisions used in classifying maps have been restated for greater clarity. The Ethnology section of Subclass GN has also been extensively revised with numerous topics introduced into the schedule for the first time and new relationships established between topics.

Where complete revision is neither possible nor desirable we have attempted to improve the schedule by: restating captions in modern terminology and eliminating obsolete expressions; regrouping and aligning topics to create an arrangement conforming more to current categorization; simplifying and clarifying instructions to catalogers in the form of notes; expanding the system of references between related topics; and providing an expanded index.

Edward J. Blume
Chief, Subject Cataloging Division

William J. Welsh
Director, Processing Department

SYNOPSIS

G	GEOGRAPHY (GENERAL). ATLASES. GLOBES. MAPS
GA	MATHEMATICAL GEOGRAPHY. CARTOGRAPHY
GB	PHYSICAL GEOGRAPHY
GC	OCEANOGRAPHY
GF	HUMAN ECOLOGY. ANTHROPOGEOGRAPHY
GN	ANTHROPOLOGY
GR	FOLKLORE
GT	MANNERS AND CUSTOMS (GENERAL)
GV	RECREATION. LEISURE

G   GEOGRAPHY (GENERAL)

100.5-108.5	Toponymy
	Including gazetteers, geographic names
	and terms
140	Great cities of the world
141	Historical geography
142	Aerial geography
149-180	Travel. Voyages and travels (General)
155-180	Travel and state. Tourist trade
200-336	History of discoveries, explorations,
	and travel
369-503	Special voyages and travels
521-539	Adventures, shipwrecks, buried treasure, etc.
540-550	Seafaring life, ocean travel, etc.
575-890	Arctic and Antarctic regions
905-910	Tropics (General)
912-922	Northern and Southern Hemispheres

ATLASES

1000.3-1000.5	Atlases of the moon, planets, etc.
1001-1046	World atlases
1050-1052	Northern and Southern Hemispheres
1053	Tropics
1054-1055	Polar regions
1059-1061	Maritime atlases (General)
	By region or country
1100-1779	America. Western Hemisphere
1105 1694	North America
1110-1114	Greenland
1115-1193	Canada
1200-1534.24	United States
1535-1537	Caribbean area
1540-1542	Latin America (General)
1545-1549	Mexico
1550-1594	Central America
1600-1694	West Indies
1700-1779	South America
1780-2799	Eastern Hemisphere. Eurasia, Africa, etc.
1791-2082	Europe
2110-2193	Union of Soviet Socialist Republics
2200-2444	Asia
2445-2739	Africa
2740-2799	Australasia
2800-3064	Oceans (General)
3100-3102	Antarctica
3122	Atlases of imaginary, literary and
	mythological regions
3160-3182	GLOBES

OUTLINE

G   MAPS

3190-3192	Celestial maps
3195-3199	Moon
3200-3202	World
3210-3222	Northern and Southern Hemispheres
3240-3241	Tropics
3250-3251	Temperate Zones
3260-3272	Polar regions
	By region or country
3290-5668	America. Western Hemisphere
3300-5184	North America
3380-3384	Greenland
3400-3612	Canada
3690-4383	United States
4390-4392	Caribbean area
4410-4763	Mexico
4800-4884	Central America
4900-5184	West Indies
5200-5668	South America
5670-9084	Eastern Hemisphere. Eurasia, Africa, etc.
5700-6966	Europe
7000-7342	Union of Soviet Socialist Republics
7400-8198.54	Asia
8200-8904	Africa
8950-9084	Australasia
9095-9794	Oceans (General)
9800-9804	Antarctica
9900-9980	Unlocalized maps

GA   MATHEMATICAL GEOGRAPHY

51-87	Surveys (General)

CARTOGRAPHY

109	Aerial cartography
.5	Cadastral mapping
.8	Statistical mapping
110-115	Projection
125-155	Map drawing, modeling, printing, reading, etc.
192-197.3	Collections of maps, globes, etc. Map libraries
260-288	Globe making. Globes
300-325	World maps, general atlases, etc.
341-1776	Maps. By region or country

OUTLINF

GB   PHYSICAL GEOGRAPHY

400-649	Geomorphology. Landforms. Terrain
447	Climatic geomorphology
448	Slopes
450-460	Coasts
461-468	Reefs
471-478	Islands
500-555	Mountains. Orography
561-649	Other natural landforms: Floodplains, caves, deserts, dunes, etc.
651-2998	Hydrology. Water
	Ground and surface waters
980-992	Watersheds. Runoff. Drainage
1001-1199.8	Groundwater. Hydrogeology
1201-1598	Rivers. Stream measurements
1601-1798.9	Lakes. Limnology
2401-2598	Ice. Glaciers. Ice sheets
2601-2798	Snow. Snow surveys
2801-2998	Hydrometeorology
5000-5030	Natural disasters

GC   OCEANOGRAPHY

63	Oceanographic expeditions
65-78	Underwater exploration
83-87.6	Submarine topography
96-97.8	Estuarine oceanography
100-103	Seawater
109-149	Chemical oceanography
150-181	Physical oceanography
150-155	Density
160-177	Temperature
177.6-181	Optical oceanography
190-190.5	Ocean-atmosphere interaction
200-376	Dynamics of the ocean
205-226	Waves
228.5-228.6	Ocean circulation
229-296.8	Currents
297-299	Water masses and oceanic mixing
300-376	Tides
377-399	Marine sediments
401-881	Oceanography. By region
1000-1023	Marine resources. Applied oceanography
1080-1581	Marine pollution. Seawater pollution

GF   HUMAN ECOLOGY. ANTHROPOGEOGRAPHY

51-71	Environmental influences on man
75	Man's influence on the environment
101-127	Settlements
125	Cities. Urban geography
127	Rural settlements. Rural geography
500-895	By region or country

OUTLINE

GN ANTHROPOLOGY

49-296	Physical anthropology. Somatology
51-59	Anthropometry
62.8-263	Human variation
	Including growth, physical form, skeleton, nervous system, skin, etc.
269-279	Race (General)
280.7	Man as an animal. Simian traits versus human traits
281-289	Human evolution
282-286.7	Fossil man. Human paleontology
296	Medical anthropology
301-673	Ethnology. Social and cultural anthropology
357-367	Culture and cultural processes
	Including social change, structuralism, diffusion, etc.
378-395	Collected ethnographies
397-397.5	Applied anthropology
	Cultural traits, customs, and institutions
406-442	Technology. Material culture
	Including food, shelter, fire, tools, etc.
448-450.7	Economic organization. Economic anthropology
451-477.7	Intellectual life
	Including communication, recreation, philosophy, religion, knowledge, etc.
478-491.7	Social organization
492-495	Political organization. Political anthropology
495.4-498	Societal groups, ethnocentrism, diplomacy, warfare, etc.
502-517	Psychological anthropology
537-673	Ethnic groups and races
550-673	By region or country
700-875	Prehistoric archaeology

GR FOLKLORE

72-79	Folk literature (General)
	Including folktales, legends
81	Folk beliefs, superstitions, etc. (General)
100-390	By region or country
	By subject
430-487	Folklore relating to private life
	Including dreams, love, children, nursery rhymes, etc.
500-615	Supernatural beings, demonology, fairies, ghosts, charms, etc.
620-635	Cosmic phenomena
650-690	Geographical topics
700-860	Animals, plants, and minerals
865-874	Transportation, travel, commerce, etc.
880	Medicine. Folk medicine
890-910	Occupations
931-940	Signs and symbols

OUTLINE

GT   MANNERS AND CUSTOMS (GENERAL)

170-474	Houses. Dwellings
485	Churches and church going
500-2370	Costume. Dress. Fashion
2400-3390	Customs relative to private life
	Including children, marriage, eating
	and drinking, funeral customs, etc.
3400-5090	Customs relative to public and social life
	Including town life, court life, festivals,
	holidays, ceremonies of royalty, etc.
5220-5285	Customs relative to transportation and travel
5320-6720	Customs relative to special classes
5320-5680	By birth, rank, etc.
5750-6390	By occupation

GV   RECREATION. LEISURE

181.35-181.55	Recreation leadership. Administration
	of recreation services
182-182.5	Recreational areas and facilities. Recreation
	centers
191.2-200.6	Outdoor life. Outdoor recreation
191.68-198.9	Camping
199-199.6	Hiking. Pedestrian tours
199.8-200.3	Mountaineering
200.4-200.5	Orientation. Wilderness survival
200.6	Water oriented recreation
201-555	Physical education and training
346-350	School and college athletics. Intramural and
	interscholastic athletics
401-433	Physical education facilities. Sports facilities
	Including gymnasiums, athletic fields,
	playgrounds, etc.
435-436.5	Physical measurements. Physical tests, etc.
450	Nudism. Sunbathing
460-555	Gymnastics. Gymnastic exercises
	Including calisthenics, heavy exercises,
	acrobatics, etc.
561-1198.995	Sports
711	Coaching
712-725	Athletic contests. Sports events
733-734	Professionalism in sports. Professional
	sports (General)
735	Umpires. Sports officiating
743-749	Athletic and sporting goods, supplies, etc.
750-770	Air sports: Airplane flying, kiteflying, etc.
770.3-840	Water sports: Canoeing, sailing, yachting, etc.
840.7-857	Winter sports: Ice hockey, skiing, bob-
	sledding, etc.
861-1017	Ball games: Baseball, football, golf, etc.
1020-1034	Automobile travel. Motoring
1040-1060.2	Cycling. Bicycling. Motorcycling
1060.5-1098	Track and field athletics
1101-1150.6	Fighting sports: Bullfighting, boxing,
	fencing, etc.

OUTLINE

GV   RECREATION. LEISURE

561-1198.995   Sports - Continued
1151-1190   Shooting. Archery
1195-1198.995   Wrestling
1199-1570   Games and amusements
      1201.5   Hobbies (General)
1203-1218   Children's games and amusements
1218.5-1220.7   Toys
1221-1469   Indoor games and amusements
1232-1299   Card games: Poker, patience, whist, etc.
1301-1311   Gambling. Chance and banking games
1312-1469   Board games. Move games
                          Including chess, go, checkers, etc.
1470-1511   Parties. Party games and stunts
1491-1507   Puzzles
1541-1561   Parlor magic and tricks
1580-1799   Dancing
1800-1860   Circuses, spectacles, etc.
                        Including rodeos, waxworks, amusement
                          parks, etc.

GEOGRAPHY (GENERAL)

For geography and description of individual countries, <u>see</u> D-F
For mathematic geography and cartography, <u>see</u> GA
For physical geography, <u>see</u> GB

1	Periodicals. Serials
	<u>Societies</u>
2	International
3	United States
4	Canada
5	Mexico. Central America. West Indies
6	South America
7	Great Britain
8	Czechoslovakia
9	Austria
10	Hungary
11	France
13	Germany
	Including West Germany
14	East Germany
15	Greece
17	Italy
19	Belgium
21	Netherlands (Holland)
23	Russia
.5	Poland
24	Finland
25	Scandinavia
27	Spain
28	Portugal
29	Switzerland
31	Balkan States
32	Turkey
33	China
35	India
36	Pakistan
.5	Bangladesh
37	Indochina
39	Japan
41	South Africa
43	Egypt
45	Algeria
47	Tanzania
49	Other African (not A-Z)
51	Australia
53	New Zealand
55	Pacific islands
56	Congresses
	<u>Collected works (nonserial)</u>
	Cf. G1594, Collections of voyages
58	Several authors
59	Individual authors

62	Addresses, essays, lectures
63	Dictionaries. Encyclopedias
64	Directories
	<u>Geographers</u>
65	Geography as a profession
	Biography
	Cf. D-F, History
	G200+, Explorers
	GA198, GA407, GA473, etc., Cartographers
67	Collective
69	Individual, A-Z
	e. g. .A2 Adamus Bremensis
	.B35 Barkov, Aleksandr Sergeevich
	.B4 Behaim, Martin
	.H2 Hakluyt, Richard
	.P4 Petermann, August
	.R4 Rennell, James
	.R6 Ritter, Karl
	.T55 Tillo, Aleksei Andreevich
70	<u>Philosophy. Relation to other topics. Methodology</u>
	Cf. GA, Mathematicl geography
	Relation to economics. Economic geography, <u>see</u> HF1021+
	Relation to history. Historical geography, <u>see</u> G141
	Relation to geopolitics, <u>see</u> JC319+
	Relation to religion, <u>see</u> BL65.G4
	Relation to sociology, <u>see</u> HM36
	Special methods
.2	Electronic data processing
.25	Network analysis
.28	Simulation
.3	Statistical methods
.4	Remote sensing
	Cf. G142, Aerial geography
	TR810, Aerial photography. Photographic
	interpretation
71.5	Geographical perception
	<u>Study and teaching. Research</u>
72	Periodicals. Societies. Serials
73	General works
74	General special
.5	Fieldwork
75	Home geography
76	Audiovisual aids
	Textbooks, <u>see</u> G125+
.5	By region or country, A-Z
77	Schools. By place, A-Z
	<u>Museums. Exhibitions</u>
.8	General works
78	By region or country, A-Z
	Under each country:
	.x General works
	.x2 Special. By city, A-Z

<u>History of geography</u>
     Cf. G200+, History of voyages of discovery

80	General works
81	General special
	Cf. GN476.4, Primitive geography
82	Ancient and medieval
	Including Chinese

<u>Ancient</u>
     Cf. DE23+, Classical geography

83	Dictionaries. Encyclopedias
	Modern authors
84	General works
86	General special

<u>Classical authors (Greek and Roman)</u>

87.A1A-Z	Collections
.A3A-Z	Selections, extracts, etc.
.A6-Z	Individual authors, A-Z

       Under each:
        (1) Texts
             For original Greek and Latin texts, <u>see</u> PA
               except where authors write on geography
               only or texts are accompanied by
               translations or commentaries interpreting
               geography
             Cf. subdivisions (2) and (3) below.
        (2) Translations
             Including texts with translations
             For Latin translations, <u>see</u> PA if Greek
               texts class there; for translations into
               lesser known languages, <u>see</u> the language
        (3) Commentaries. Criticism
             Including texts with commentaries
             For textual criticism, <u>see</u> PA

e. g.	.D5-7	Dionysius Periegetes
		Orbis terrae descriptio
	.D5-59	Greek texts (chronologically)
		Translations
	.D6	Latin. By date
	.D61-69	Other languages (alphabetically)
	.D7	Commentaries. Criticism
	.S86-95	Strabo
		Geographica
	.S86	Greek texts. By date
	.S87	Greek and Latin texts. By date
	.S875	Selections (Greek). By editor
		Translations
	.S88	Latin. By date
	.S9	English. By date
		Including Greek and English
	.S91-94	Other languages (alphabetically)
		e. g. .S92 German. By
		translator
	.S95	Commentaries. Criticism

<pre>
              History of geography
                  Ancient - Continued
                      Sources and ancient authors other than Greek and Roman
87.5   Modern works
   .7   Texts with translations
88   Voyages
   .5   Special regions, A-Z
                            Including works of geographical interest not provided
                            for in D-F
                      Medieval to 1600/1650
                          Modern writers
89   General works
   .5   General special
90   Early writers (including Oriental) other than those in
                            G91-95
91   Early Christian
92   Viking age
93   Arabic geographers
94   Other later ("Scholastic") to 1420/1492
95   15th-16th centuries (1420/1492 to 1600/1650)
                            For discovery of seaway to India, see G280+
                      Modern, 1600/1650-
96   General works
                            For treatises, see G113+
97   17th-18th centuries
98   19th century
99   20th century
                      Geographical myths, folklore, etc., see GR650+; GR940
                  Toponymy
100.5   General works
                      Gazetteers
                          For gazetteers of individual continents and countries,
                            see D-F
101   Through 1800
102   1801-1870
103   1871-1974
   .5   1975-
                  Geographic names (Universal)
                          For geographic names of individual continents and
                            countries, see D-F
104   Periodicals. Societies. Serials
   .5   Polyglot lists
                        By language
                            Including reports of national boards and commissions
105   English
106   Other languages, A-Z
107   Latin
                  Geographic terms
   .8   Periodicals. Societies. Serials
   .9   General works
108   By language, A-Z
                            e. g.   .F7 French
                                    .G3 German
                                    .R9 Russian
   .5   Special topics and terms, A-Z
                          .C3 Cardinal points
   .7   Geographical location codes
</pre>

109	Tables. Distances, geographical positions, etc.
110	By region or country, A-Z
	Latitude and longitude, see QB224.5+
	General works, treatises, and advanced textbooks
	General systematic works
113	1450-1600
	Ptolemy revised, Solinus, Franck, etc.
114	1601-1800
115	1801-1974
116	1975-
	Compends
120	Through 1700
121	1701-1870
122	1871-1974
123	1975-
	Textbooks
	Cf. GB51+, GB55, Textbooks in physical geography
125	Through 1870
126	1871-1970 Octavos
127	1871-1970 Quartos (25 cm.+)
128	1971-
129	Outlines. Syllabi
131	Examinations, questions, etc.
133	Juvenile works
	Pictorial works
136	Through 1830
137	1831-1870
138	1871-1974
.5	1975-
140	Great cities of the world
	Including capitals of the world, great streets of the world, etc.
141	Historical geography
	For individual countries, see D-F
	For individual oceans, seas, etc., see GC401+
	For polar regions, see G575+
142	Aerial geography
	Cf. TR810, Aerial photography. Photographic interpretation
	Travel. Voyages and travels (General)
	Cf. GT5220+, Customs relative to travel
149	Periodicals. Societies. Serials
	Cf. G154, Travel agencies and clubs
	GV1027, Automobile clubs
.5	Congresses
	Traveling instructions
	Cf. G597, Polar expeditions
	Q116, Scientific expeditions
	RA783.5, Travel hygiene
.9	Early works through 1800
150	1801-1974
151	1975-
153	Guidebooks, prospectuses, etc.
	Class catalogs of audiovisual material in .Z9A-Z
	Cf. GV1024+, Automobile roadguides
	HE2727+, Railway guides
	HE9768, Air travel guides

Travel. Voyages and travels (General) - Continued

154	Travel agencies and clubs
	Cf. HF5686.T73, Accounting
	Biography of travel agents, publicists, etc.
.49	Collective
.5	Individual, A-Z

Travel and the state. Tourist trade
  Including tourist travel promotion, statistical surveys, etc.
  Cf. RA638, Immunity and immunization

155.A1A-Z	General works
.A2-Z	By region or country, A-Z
	Including regulations, requirements for entry, economic studies and reports, etc.
.5	Vocational guidance
156	History of travel and touring
.5	Special topics, A-Z
	.C5 Church and travel
	Education and travel, see LC6681
	.Y6 Youth travel

Travel and etiquette, see BJ2137+
Collected works (nonserial)

159	Through 1700
160	1701-1800
161	1801-1950
162	1951-1974
163	1975-
175	Juvenile works
180	Addresses, essays, lectures

History of discoveries, explorations, and travel
  For discovery of and exploration and travel in an individual country, see D-F
  For voyages to the East Indies, 1498-1761, see DS411
  For polar voyages, see G575+
General works, see G80
Juvenile works, see G175

200	Collective biography

By period, see G82+
By nationality
  For records of individual voyages, see G370+
  For travels in individual countries, see D-F
  For polar exploration, see G575+
American

220	Collected works (nonserial)
222	History
	Biography of explorers and travelers
225	Collective
226	Individual, A-Z
228	Austrian
	Chinese, see G320+
230-236	Dutch[1]
240-246	English[1]
250-256	French[1]
260-266	German[1]
268	Hungarian

[1] Divided like G220-226

GEOGRAPHY (GENERAL)

<u>History of discoveries, explorations, and travel</u>
        By nationality - Continued

270-276	Italian[1]
	Japanese, <u>see</u> G330+
277	Jewish
.5	Polish
	Portuguese and Spanish
	Cf. E110+, Discovery of America
278	Collected works (nonserial)
279	History
280-286	Portuguese[1]
	Cf. DP583, Portugal, 1385-1580
	Spanish
287	Collected works (nonserial)
288	History
	Biography
.8	Collective
289	Individual, A-Z
	Romanian
	Biography
.5	Collective
.52	Individual, A-Z
290-296	Russian[1]
300-306	Scandinavian[1]
310-316	Swiss[1]
320-326	Chinese[1]
330-336	Japanese[1]

<u>Special voyages and travels</u>
    Ancient, <u>see</u> G88
    Medieval

369	General works
370	By explorer or traveler, or if better known, by name
	of ship, A-Z
	e. g. .M2 Mandeville, Sir John. Itinerarium
	For anonymous metrical version,
	Boke of Mawndevile, <u>see</u>
	PR2065.B57
400-401	1400-1520[2]
	For voyages to America, <u>see</u> E101+

<u>Modern, 1521-</u>

419-420	Circumnavigations (Expeditions)[2]
	Cf. Q115+, Scientific expeditions
	R687, Medical expeditions
439-440	Tours around the world[2]
445	Flights around the world
	Cf. TL721, Special historic flights (Aeronautics)
	<u>Travels in several parts of the world</u>
	General works
460	Through 1800
463	1801-1949
464	1950-1974
465	1975-

---

[1]
  Divided like G220-226
[2]
  Divided like G369-370

Special voyages and travels
Modern, 1521-
Travels in several parts of the world - Continued
468   Pictorial works
         Juvenile works, see G570
470   America and Europe
475   America, West Indies, Africa
477   America and the Pacific
478   Atlantic to the Pacific (and vice versa) via Cape
            Horn
480   America and Asia
490   Europe and Asia. Africa and Asia. Europe and Africa
         Tropics (General), see G910
         Polar regions, see G575+
492   Arctic regions and Africa, Europe, etc.
         Northern Hemisphere, see G916
         Southern Hemisphere, see G922
500   Islands
            Cf. D-F, Description and travel
               GB471+, Physical geography
               VK798+, Pilot guides
503   Isolated areas
    Walking. Tramping. Pedestrian tours, see GV199+
    Backpacking, see GV199.6
    Mountaineering, see GV199.8+
    Adventures, shipwrecks, buried treasure, etc.
        For official reports of shipwrecks, see VK1250+
521   Periodicals. Societies. Serials
522   Philosophy. Motivation
      Biography of adventurers, see CT9970+
525   General works
        Including nonserial collected narratives
530   Individual narratives
        Including sailors' yarns
        For wrecks of special vessels, assign Cutter for
          the name of vessel. For accounts of individual
          treasure sites, see CJ153 or D-F
      Beachcombing
532   General works
        By region or country
        United States
.4   General works
.5   By region or state, A-Z
.6   Other regions or countries, A-Z
      Pirates, buccaneers, etc.
        For works limited to one region or country, see
          D-F, e. g. DT201+, Barbary corsairs; F2161,
          Pirates in the Caribbean
535   Collective
537   Individual, A-Z
539   Filibusters. Soldiers of fortune
        For works limited to one region or country, see
          D-F

<u>Seafaring life, ocean travel, etc.</u>
         Cf. GR910, Folklore of the sea
            VK149, Nautical life

540	General works
545	Whaling voyages
	Cf. SH381+, Whale fishery
	Merchant vessels, <u>see</u> G540
549	Men-of-war. Cruises (in time of peace)
	Cf. V720+, Naval life and customs
550	Passenger life
	Cf. GV710.5, Deck sports and games
555	Voyages touching unidentified places
	e. g. Lost islands
	Cf. GN751, Atlantides
560	Imaginary voyages
	Cf. GR650+; GR940, Geographical myths and folklore
	HX806+, Utopias
570	Juvenile voyages and travels

ARCTIC AND ANTARCTIC REGIONS

Including exploration, history, description, travel

<u>Polar regions</u>
    Including both poles

575	Periodicals. Societies. Serials
576	Collected works (nonserial)
578	Congresses
580	History
	Biography
584	Collective
585	Individual, A-Z
	e. g. .A6 Amundsen, Roald
	.B8 Byrd, Richard Evelyn
	.E6 Ellsworth, Lincoln
587	General works
590	Popular works
593	General special
	Including jurisdiction, sovereignty, etc.
595	Addresses, essays, lectures
597	Instructions for polar exploration
	Including equipment, hygiene, etc.
599	Aircraft for polar exploration

<u>Arctic regions. Arctic exploration</u>

600	Periodicals. Societies. Serials
601	Collected works (nonserial)
606	General works
608	Popular works
610	Pictorial works
614	Juvenile works
.5	Addresses, essays, lectures
615	General special
	Including theory of north-polar exploration, etc.

Arctic and antarctic regions
  Arctic regions. Arctic exploration - Continued
    History of exploration

620	General works
623	Early through 1800
625	19th century
626	20th century
627	1945-
630	Exploration. By nationality, A-Z

        e. g. .A5 American
              .D9 Dutch

    Biography

634	Collective
635	Individual, A-Z

        e. g.   Franklin, see G660+
             .P4 Peary, Robert Edwin
             .R3 Rasmussen, Knud Johan Victor
             .S7 Stefansson, Vihjalmur

639	Northeast and Northwest Passages

Western Hemisphere
  Northwest Passage

640	General works
650	Special expeditions (Sea and land). Narratives. By date

    Franklin Search
      Including biography of Sir John Franklin

660	General works
662	General special
665	Narratives. By date
670	Expeditions. By. date

Eastern Hemisphere
  Northeast Passage

680	General works
690	Narratives. By date
700	Expeditions. By date

Special regions
  American Arctic regions
    Greenland

725	Periodicals. Societies. Serials
730	Collected works (nonserial)

    General works. Description

740	Through 1821
742	1822-1900
743	1901-
750	Social life and customs

      Cf. E99.E7, Eskimos

760	History

    Biography

761	Collective
762	Individual, A-Z
765	Local, A-Z

        e. g. .K5   King Christian X Land
            .P4   Peary Land
            .S35 Scoresby Sound

770	Other regions, A-Z

    For Canadian Arctic regions, see F1090.5
    e. g. .S6 Smith Sound

Arctic and antarctic regions
   Arctic regions. Arctic exploration
      Special regions - Continued
         Norwegian Arctic regions
           Including Svalbard

778	General works
780	Spitsbergen
782	Jan Mayen Island
785	Bear Island. Bjørnøya
787	Other islands, etc., A-Z
	e. g. .H6 Hope Island
	Barents Sea
790	General works
800	Novaya Zemlya
810	Franz Josef Land

Siberian Arctic regions. Laptev Sea, East Siberian Sea

820	General works
825	New Siberian Islands
827	Severnaya Zemlya
830	Wrangel Island
839	Other islands, etc., A-Z

Antarctic regions. Antarctic exploration

845	Periodicals. Societies. Serials
846	Collected works (nonserial)
850	Voyages. By date
855	Dictionaries. Encyclopedias
860	General works
863	Juvenile works
	Museums. Exhibitions
864	General works
865	By region or country, A-Z
	Each region or country subarranged by author
870	History
	Biography
874	Collective
875	Individual, A-Z
	e. g. Byrd, see G589.B8
	.S35 Scott, Robert Falcon
876	Addresses, essays, lectures
877	General special
878	Jurisdiction, sovereignty, etc.
890	Special regions, A-Z
	e. g. .A4 Terre Adélie
	.B4 Beardmore Glacier region
	.C45 Chilean areas
	Graham Land, see .P3
	.P3 Palmer Peninsula
	Cf. F3031, Falkland Islands
	.Q4 Queen Maud Land
	Tropics (General)
905	General works
907	General special
910	Special voyages and travels
	Northern Hemisphere
912	General works
914	General special
916	Special voyages and travels
	Southern Hemisphere
918	General works
920	General special
922	Special voyages and travels

ATLASES

For history and description of atlases, <u>see</u> GA

<u>Atlases of the moon, planets, etc.</u>
    Class here atlases of the moon, planets, etc. which
      record topographic data resulting from exploration
      by manned or unmanned space vehicles
    Cf. QB595, Photographs, maps, drawings of the moon
        QB605, Photographs, maps, drawings of the planets

1000.3–.32	Moon[1]
.5	Individual planets or moons (other than Earth's moon), A- e. g. .M3 Mars

    <u>World atlases</u>
      <u>By period</u>

1001	Ancient and medieval before 1570
1005	Ptolemy
	Modern, 1570–
	1570–1800
1006	Ortelius
1007	Mercator
1015	Others
1019	1801–1975
1021	1976–

      <u>Atlases of facsimiles</u>

1025	Compilations from various sources
1026	Reproductions of single world maps in atlas form
	Including collections of world maps of a single cartographer
1028	Cities of the world
1029	Islands of the world

      <u>By subject</u>

1030	Historical atlases
	Cf. G2230+, Bible atlases
1033	Ancient
1034	Medieval
1035	Modern
1036	Discoveries, explorations, and travel
1037	World War I
1038	World War II
1046	Other subject atlases
	Subdivided by Table IV, pp. 210-223
	For maritime atlases, <u>see</u> G1059+

    Western Hemisphere, <u>see</u> G1100+
    Eastern Hemisphere, <u>see</u> G1780+

---

[1] For subdivisions, <u>see</u> tables, pp. 206-223

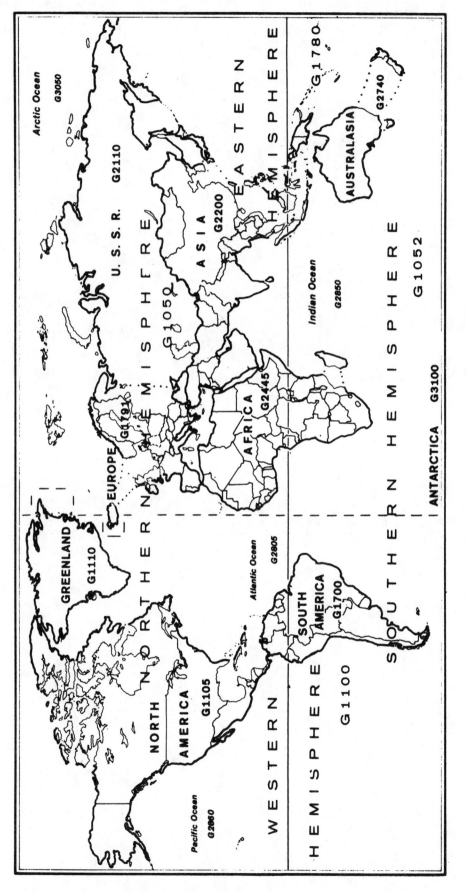

Pacific Ocean
G2860

WESTERN HEMISPHERE G1100

GREENLAND G1110

NORTH AMERICA G1105

NORTHERN

Atlantic Ocean G2805

SOUTH AMERICA G1700

SOUTHERN HEMISPHERE G1052

EUROPE G1791

HEMISPHERE

AFRICA G2445

AFRICA

ANTARCTICA G3100

Arctic Ocean G3050

U.S.S.R. G2110

G1052

ASIA G2200

EASTERN HEMISPHERE

Indian Ocean G2850

G1780

AUSTRALASIA

G2740

Hemispheres, Continents and Oceans

ATLASES

1050	Northern Hemisphere
1052	Southern Hemisphere (Map, p. 13)
1053	Tropics. Torrid Zone
1054	Polar regions. Frigid Zones
1055	Arctic regions
	Cf. G3050+, Arctic Ocean
	Antarctic regions, see G3100+
	Maritime atlases (General)
	For oceans (General), see G2800+; for individual
	oceans, see G2805+
1059	Early through 1800
1060	1801-1975
1061	1976-
	By region or country[1]
1100-1102	America. Western Hemisphere
1105-1107	North America
1107	Regions and natural features, etc., A-Z
	e. g. .G7 Great Lakes
	.R58 Rio Grande Valley
	.S3 St. Lawrence River
1110-1114	Greenland
1115-1117	Canada
1120-1122	Maritime Provinces
1125-1129	Nova Scotia
1130-1134	New Brunswick
1135-1139	Prince Edward Island
1140-1144	Quebec
1145-1149	Ontario
1150-1152	Prairie Provinces
1155-1159	Manitoba
1160-1164	Saskatchewan
1165-1169	Alberta
1170-1174	British Columbia
1175-1179	Yukon
1180-1184	Northwest Territories
1185-1189	Newfoundland
1190-1193	Labrador
1195-1197	Saint Pierre and Miquelon Islands

----

[1]

For subdivisions, see tables, pp. 206-223

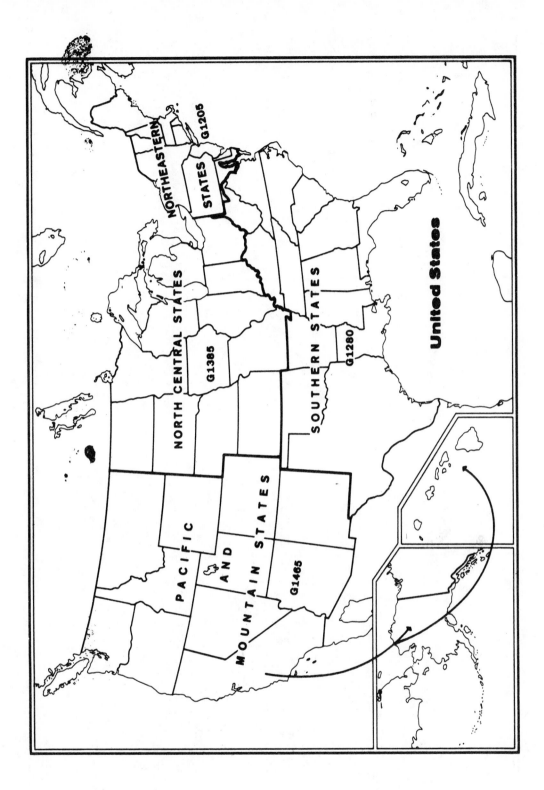

United States

NORTHEASTERN STATES

G1205

NORTH CENTRAL STATES

G1385

SOUTHERN STATES

G1280

PACIFIC AND MOUNTAIN STATES

G1465

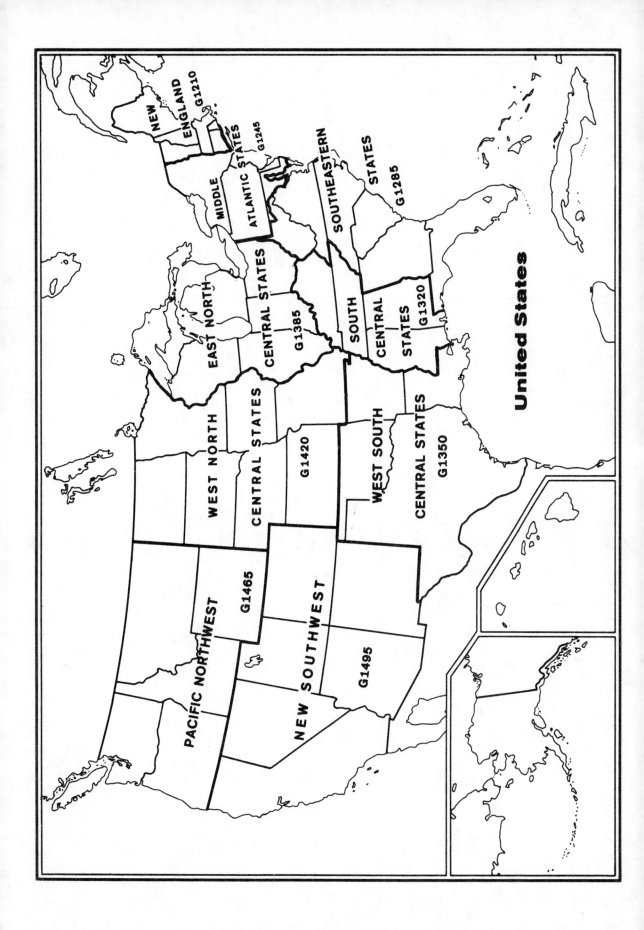

United States

NEW ENGLAND G1210

MIDDLE ATLANTIC STATES G1245

SOUTHEASTERN STATES G1285

EAST NORTH CENTRAL STATES G1385

SOUTH CENTRAL STATES G1320

WEST NORTH CENTRAL STATES G1420

WEST SOUTH CENTRAL STATES G1350

PACIFIC NORTHWEST G1465

NEW SOUTHWEST G1495

G   G

ATLASES

                        By region or country[1]
                          America. Western Hemisphere
                            North America - Continued
1200-1202   United States
1204   Cities and towns collectively
                                  For individual cities and towns, see the state
1205-1207   Northeastern States (Map, p. 15)
                                Eastern United States, 1870 and later
1207   Regions and natural features, etc., A-Z
                                  e. g. .03 Ohio River
1210-1212   New England[2] (Map, p. 16)
1214   Cities and towns collectively
                                  For individual cities and towns, see
                                    the state
1215-1219   Maine
1220-1224   New Hampshire
1225-1229   Vermont
1230-1234   Massachusetts
1235-1239   Rhode Island
1240-1244   Connecticut
1245-1247   Middle Atlantic States. Middle
                                States[2] (Map, p. 16)
                                  Often including Virginia and West Virginia,
                                    sometimes also Ohio and Kentucky
1250-1254   New York
1255-1259   New Jersey
1260-1264   Pennsylvania
1265-1269   Delaware
1270-1274   Maryland
1275-1277   District of Columbia. Washington, D.C.
1277   Regions, natural features, etc., A-Z
                                    e. g. .R6 Rock Creek. Rock Creek Park
1279   Former towns and communities, A-Z
                                    e. g. .G4 Georgetown
1280-1282   Southern States. Confederate States of
                                America (Map, p. 15)
1285-1287   Southeastern States. South Atlantic
                                States[2] (Map, p. 16)
1290-1294   Virginia
1295-1299   West Virginia
1300-1304   North Carolina
1305-1309   South Carolina
1310-1314   Georgia
1315-1319   Florida
1320-1322   South Central States (Map, p. 16)
1325-1327   East South Central States[2]
1330-1334   Kentucky
1335-1339   Tennessee
1340-1344   Alabama
1345-1349   Mississippi
1350-1352   West South Central States. Old
                                  Southwest[2] (Map, p. 16)
1355-1359   Arkansas
1360-1364   Louisiana

---

[1]

For subdivisions, see tables, pp. 206-223

[2]

For county Cutter numbers, see pp. 48-78

ATLASES

<u>By region or country</u>[1]
<u>America. Western Hemisphere</u>
<u>North America</u>
<u>United States</u>
<u>Pacific and Mountain States. Far West</u>
<u>New Southwest</u>[2] – Continued

1515–1519	Utah
1520–1524	Nevada
1525–1529	California
1530–1534	Alaska
1534.2–.24	Hawaii
1535–1537	Caribbean area
1540–1542	<u>Latin America</u> (General)
1545–1549	Mexico
1550–1552	<u>Central America</u>
1555–1559	Guatemala
1560–1564	Belize. British Honduras
1565–1569	Honduras
1570–1574	El Salvador
1575–1579	Nicaragua
1580–1584	Costa Rica
1585–1589	Panama
1590–1594	Canal Zone
1600–1602	<u>West Indies</u>
1605–1609	Cuba
1610–1612	Hispaniola
1615–1619	Haiti
1620–1624	Dominican Republic. Santo Domingo
1625–1629	Jamaica
1630–1634	Puerto Rico
1635–1639	Bahamas. Lucayos
1637	Regions and natural features, islands, A–Z
	Abaco Islands (Great and Little), <u>see</u> G4982.A2
1640–1644	Virgin Islands
	Including atlases of Virgin Islands of the United States, British Virgin Islands
1650–1654	Leeward Islands
1652	Islands, A–Z
	e. g. .S3 Saint Christopher, Nevis, and Anguilla
1660–1664	French West Indies
1662	Islands, A–Z
	e. g. .G8 Guadeloupe
1670–1674	Windward Islands
1672	Islands, A–Z
	e. g. .D6 Dominica
1680–1684	Trinidad and Tobago
1690–1694	Netherlands Antilles. Dutch West Indies
1692	Islands, A–Z
	e. g. .A7 Aruba

---

[1] For subdivisions, <u>see</u> tables, pp. 206–223

[2] For county Cutter numbers, <u>see</u> pp. 117–120

ATLASES

By region or country[1]
   America. Western Hemisphere - Continued

1700–1702	South America
1705–1707	Guianas
1710–1714	Guyana. British Guiana
1715–1719	Surinam. Dutch Guiana
1720–1724	French Guiana
1725–1729	Venezuela
1730–1734	Colombia
1735–1739	Ecuador
1740–1744	Peru
1745–1749	Bolivia
1750–1754	Chile
1755–1759	Argentina
	Falkland Islands, see G2835+
1765–1769	Uruguay
1770–1774	Paraguay
1775–1779	Brazil
1780–1782	Eastern Hemisphere. Eurasia, Africa, etc. (Map, p. 13)
1785–1787	Islamic World. Islamic countries

---

[1]
  For subdivisions, see tables, pp. 206–223

Europe

NORTHERN EUROPE

G2050

WESTERN EUROPE

G1800

CENTRAL EUROPE

G1880

BALKAN
PENINSULA

G1995

SOUTHERN EUROPE

G1955

ATLASES

By region or country[1]
    Eastern Hemisphere. Eurasia, Africa, etc.
        Europe
            Western Europe - Continued
                France
                    By period
1837   15th-16th centuries
1838   17th-18th centuries
1840-1844   1801-1975
    1844.2-.24   1976-
1845-1849   Monaco
                    Benelux countries. Low Countries
                        By period
1850   15th-16th centuries
1851   17th-18th centuries
1855-1857   1801-1975
    1857.2-.22   1976-
1858-1859   Netherlands Union
                            Including atlases of Dutch colonies, depen-
                                dencies, etc. (Collectively)
                            Class individual colonies, dependencies, etc.,
                                according to location, e. g. G1715+,
                                Surinam
1860-1864   Netherlands
1865-1869   Belgium
1870-1874   Luxemburg
1880-1882   Central Europe (Map, p. 21)
1890-1891   Alps
1895-1899   Switzerland
1900-1904   Liechtenstein
1905-1906   German Empire
                            Including atlases of German colonies
                                (Collectively)
                            Class individual colonies, etc., according to
                                location, e. g. G25404, Former German
                                East Africa
                        Germany
                            Including atlases of East and West Germany
                                together
                            By period
1907   Early through 16th century
1908   17th-18th centuries
1910-1912   1801-1975
    1912.2-.22   1976-
1915-1919   East Germany (German Democratic Republic)
1917   Regions and natural features, etc., A-Z
1918   Administrative districts (Bezirke), former states
                            (Länder), etc., A-Z
                            .A5   Anhalt
                                   Berlin, East, see G1919.B4
                            .B7   Brandenburg
                                   Chemnitz (Bezirk), see .K3
                            .C6   Cottbus

---
[1]
    For subdivisions, see tables, pp. 206-223

ATLASES

By region or country[1]
  Eastern Hemisphere. Eurasia, Africa, etc.
    Europe
      Central Europe
        East Germany (German Democratic Republic)

1918
          Administrative districts (Bezirke), former states
            (Länder), etc., A-Z - Continued

.D7	Dresden
.E2	East Prussia (Ostpreussen)
.E7	Erfurt
.F7	Frankfurt
.G4	Gera
.H3	Halle
.K3	Karl-Marx-Stadt (Bezirk). Chemnitz
.L4	Leipzig
.L8	Lübeck
.M3	Magdeburg
.M35	Mecklenburg-Schwerin. Mecklenburg-Vorpommern
.M4	Mecklenburg-Strelitz
.N4	Neubrandenburg
.P5	Pomerania
.P55	Posen
.P6	Potsdam
.P7	Prussia
.R6	Rostock
.S2	Saxony. Königsreich Sachsen
.S25	Saxony (Prussian province). Sachsen-Anhalt
.S3	Schwerin
.S5	Silesia
.S9	Suhl
.T5	Thüringia

1919
          Cities and towns, etc., A-Z

e. g.	.B4	Berlin, East
		Chemnitz (City), see .K3
	.C6	Cottbus
	.H6	Hoyerswerda
	.K3	Karl-Marx-Stadt (City). Chemnitz
	.L4	Leipzig
	.S9	Suhl

1920-1924
        West Germany (Federal Republic of Germany)
1922
         Regions and natural features, etc., A-Z
1923
         States (Länder), former states, etc., A-Z

.B15	Baden
.B2	Baden-Württemberg
.B3	Bavaria
	Berlin, see G1924.B4
	Bremen, see G1924.B7
.B7	Brunswick
	Hamburg, see G1924.H3
.H3	Hanover
.H4	Hesse

---

[1]
  For subdivisions, see tables, pp. 206-223

ATLASES

By region or country[1]
  Eastern Hemisphere. Eurasia. Africa. etc.
    Europe
      Central Europe
        West Germany. Bundesrepublik Deutschland

1923	States (Länder); former states, etc., A–Z – Continued

            .H6   Hohenzollern. Württemberg-Hohenzollern
            .L5   Lippe
            .O4   Oldenburg
            .N6   North Rhine-Westphalia
            .P3   Palatinate (Pfalz)
            .R5   Rhineland-Palatinate. Rhine Province
            .S2   Saarland. Saar
            .S25   Schaumburg-Lippe
            .S3   Lower Saxony (Niedersachsen)
            .S4   Schleswig-Holstein
            .W3   Waldeck
            .W4   Westphalia
            .W8   Württemberg. Württemberg-Baden

1924	Cities and towns, etc., A–Z

        e. g. .B4 Berlin, West
                      Including atlases of East
                         and West Berlin together
                .S9   Stuttgart

1930–1932	**Austria-Hungary**
1935–1939	Austria
1940–1944	Hungary
1945–1949	Czechoslovakia
1950–1954	Poland
1955–1957	**Southern Europe** (Map, p. 21)
1960–1961	**Iberian Peninsula**
1963–1964	Spanish Empire

          Including atlases of Spanish colonies, etc.
            (Collectively)
          Class individual colonies, etc., according
            to location, e. g. G2605+, Spanish Guinea

1965–1969	Spain
1970–1971	Andorra
1973	Portuguese Empire

          Including atlases of Portuguese colonies, etc.
            (Collectively)
          Class individual colonies, etc., according to
            location, e. g. G2550+, Mozambique

1975–1979	Portugal. Lusitania
1980–1981	**Italian Empire. Roman Empire**

          Including atlases of Italian colonies, etc.,
            (Collectively)
          Class individual colonies, etc., according to
            location, e. g. G2515+, Somalia (Italian
            Somaliland)

---

[1]
    For subdivisions, see tables, pp. 206–223

ATLASES

By region or country[1]
    Eastern Hemisphere. Eurasia. Africa. etc.
      Europe
        Southern Europe - Continued
          Italy (Map, p. 152)

	By period
1983	15th-16th centuries
1984	17th-18th centuries
1985-1989	1801-1975
1989.2-.24	1976-
.24	Cities and towns, A-Z
	e. g. .R7 Rome
	.R7:3V3 Vatican
.3-.33	Sicily
.5-.53	Sardinia
1990-1991	San Marino
1992.3-.34	Malta

        Southeastern Europe

1993	General
1994	By subject. Table II[1]
.5	By region, natural feature, etc., A-Z
1995-1997	Balkan Peninsula (Map, p. 21)
2000-2004	Greece
2005-2009	Albania
2010-2014	Yugoslavia
2015-2017	Serbia
2020-2022	Montenegro
2025-2027	Dalmatia
2030-2032	Croatia
2035-2039	Romania
2040-2044	Bulgaria
	Turkey, see G2210+
2050-2052	Scandinavia. Northern Europe (Map, p. 21)
2053-2054	Denmark and colonies
	Including atlases of Danish colonies, etc. (Collectively)
	Class individual colonies, etc., according to location, e. g. G1110+, Greenland
2055-2059	Denmark
2060-2064	Iceland
2065-2069	Norway
2070-2074	Sweden
2075-2079	Finland. Suomi
2080-2082	Eastern Europe
	Includes Poland, Finland, Baltic States, European Russia, Romania, Bulgaria
	Baltic States, see G2120+
	Estonia, see G2125+
	Latvia, see G2130+
	Lithuania, see G2135+

---

[1]
    For subdivisions, see tables, pp. 206-223

By region or country[1]
    Eastern Hemisphere. Eurasia, Africa, etc. - Continued

2110-2114	U.S.S.R. Union of Soviet Socialist Republics. Russia (Map, p. 13)
2115-2118	U.S.S.R. in Europe. Russia in Europe
2118	Political divisions, A-Z
	Except those covered by G2120+
	e. g. .K3 Karelia. Karelo-Finnish S.S.R.
	.M6 Moldavia. Moldavian S.S.R.
2120-2122	Baltic States
2125-2128	Estonia. Estonian S.S.R.
2130-2133	Latvia. Latvian S.S.R.
2135-2138	Lithuania. Lithuanian S.S.R.
2140-2143	Russian Soviet Federated Socialist Republic (R.S.F.S.R.)
2143	European provinces, districts, etc., A-Z
2145-2148	White Russia (Belorussia). Belorussian S.S.R.
2150-2153	Ukraine. Ukrainian S.S.R.
2155-2157	Caucasus
2160-2162	U.S.S.R. in Asia. Russia in Asia
2165-2168	Soviet Central Asia. Russian Central Asia. West Turkestan
2170-2173	Siberia. Northern Asia
2180-2183	Far Eastern region. Far Eastern Republic
2190-2193	Sakhalin

-----
[1] For subdivisions, see tables, pp. 206-223

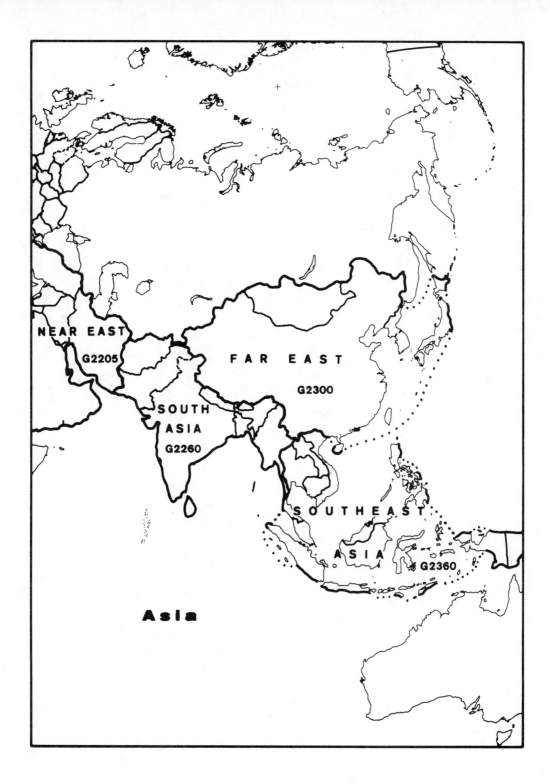

NEAR EAST
G2205

FAR EAST
G2300

SOUTH
ASIA
G2260

SOUTHEAST
ASIA
G2360

Asia

ATLASES

By region or country[1]
        Eastern Hemisphere. Eurasia, Africa, etc. - Continued

2200-2202	Asia
2202	Regions and natural features, etc., A-Z
	e. g. .C4 Central Asia. Turkestan
	Cf. G2165+, Soviet Central Asia
	G2320+, Sinkiang
	.H5 Himalaya Mountains
	Northern Asia, see G2170+
2205-2207	Western Asia. Southwestern Asia. Near East. Middle East. Levant (Map, p. 28)
	Islamic World, see G1785+
2210-2214	Turkey. Ottoman Empire. Asia Minor
	Including Turkey in Europe
2215-2219	Cyprus
2220-2224	Syria
2225-2229	Lebanon
2230-2232	Bible lands
2235-2239	Israel. Palestine
	History
2236.S1	General
.S2	To 70 A.D.
	Cf. G2230+, Bible lands
.S3	70-1453
.S33	70-638
.S4	1454-1800
.S5	1801-1900
.S6	1901-1947
.S65	World War I
.S67	1917-1947
.S7	World War II
.S73	1948-
2240-2244	Jordan
2245-2249	Arabian Peninsula. Arabia
2249.3-.34	Saudi Arabia
.5-.54	Yemen (Yemen Arab Republic)
.55-.59	Yemen (People's Democratic Republic). Southern Yemen. Aden (Colony and Protectorate)
.57	Regions and natural features, etc., A-Z
	e. g. .H3 Hadhramaut
.7-.74	Oman. Muscat and Oman
.75-.79	United Arab Emirates. Trucial States
.8-.84	Qatar
.85-.89	Bahrein
.9-.94	Kuwait
2250-2254	Iraq. Mesopotamia
2255-2259	Iran. Persia
2260-2262	South Asia. South Central Asia (Map, p. 28)
2265-2269	Afghanistan
2270-2274	Pakistan
	Including atlases of West and East Pakistan together
2273	Provinces, etc., A-Z
	e. g. .B3 Baluchistan
2275-2279	Bangladesh. East Pakistan

---

[1] For subdivisions, see tables, pp. 206-223

ATLASES

By region or country[1]
Eastern Hemisphere. Eurasia, Africa, etc.
Asia
South Asia. South Central Asia - Continued

2280-2284	India
2285-2289	Burma
2290-2294	Sri Lanka. Ceylon
2295-2299	Nepal
2299.3-.34	Sikkim
.5-.54	Bhutan
2300-2302	Far East (Map, p. 28)
	History
2301.S1	General
.S2	Early to 1500
.S3	Modern, 1500-
.S4	1500-1800
.S5	19th century
.S6	20th century
.S62	Russo-Japanese War
.S65	World War I
.S7	World War II
2302	Regions and natural features, etc., A-Z
	e. g. .A4 Amur River
	.J3 Japan Sea
2305-2309	China. Chinese Empire
2310-2311	Manchuria
2315-2316	Mongolia
	Class here atlases of Inner Mongolia and Outer Mongolia together. For atlases of Inner Mongolia alone, see G2308.M6. For atlases of Outer Mongolia alone, see G2329.3+
2320-2321	Sinkiang. Chinese Turkestan. East Turkestan. Chinese Central Asia
2325-2326	Tibet
2329.3-.34	Mongolia (Mongolian People's Republic)
2330-2334	South Korea (Republic of Korea)
	Including atlases of Korea as a whole
2334.3-.34	North Korea (Democratic People's Republic)
	Ryukyu Islands, see G2357.R9
2340-2344	Taiwan. Formosa
2353	Japanese Empire
2354	Colonies, dependencies, etc., (Collectively)
	Class individual colonies, dependencies, etc., according to location, e. g. G2330+, South Korea (Former dependency)
2355-2359	Japan
2357	Regions, natural features, islands, etc., A-Z
	e. g. .R9 Ryukyu Islands. Nansei Shoto. Ryukyu Retto
2360-2362	Southeast Asia. Indochina (Map, p. 28)
	Including Vietnam, Cambodia, Laos, Thailand, Malaysia, Philippines, Indonesia and sometimes Burma
	Burma, see G2285+
2365-2366	French Indochina

---

[1]
For subdivisions, see tables, pp. 206-223

ATLASES

By region or country[1]
  Eastern Hemisphere. Eurasia, Africa, etc.
    Asia
      Southeast Asia. Indochina - Continued

2370-2374	Vietnam
2373	Administrative divisions, former states, etc., A-Z
	e. g. .A6 Annam
	.C6 Cochinchina
	.T6 Tonking
2374.3-.34	Cambodia. Khmer Republic
.5-.54	Laos
2375-2379	Thailand. Siam

----

[1] For subdivisions, see tables, pp. 206-223

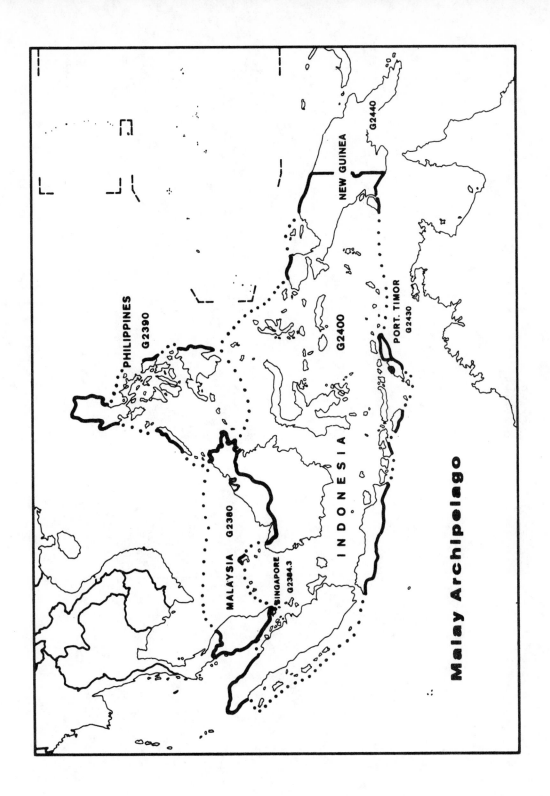

Malay Archipelago

PHILIPPINES G2390

NEW GUINEA G2440

G2400

PORT. TIMOR G2430

INDONESIA

MALAYSIA G2380

SINGAPORE G2384.3

G

G

ATLASES

By region or country[1]
    Eastern Hemisphere. Eurasia, Africa, etc.
      Asia
        Southeast Asia. Indochina - Continued

2380-2384	Malaysia. Malaya
	Including atlases of the Malay Peninsula
2384.3-.34	Singapore (Republic and Colony) (Map, p. 32)
.34	Cities and towns, A-Z
	e. g. .S5 Singapore
2385-2387	Malay Archipelago
2390-2394	Philippines (Map, p. 32)
2400-2402	Indonesia. United States of Indonesia.
	Netherlands Indies. East Indies (Map, p. 32)
2405-2409	Sumatra
2410-2414	Java and Madura
2415-2419	Borneo
	Saba, see G23804
	Sarawak, see G23804
2420-2424	Celebes
2425-2529	Lesser Sunda Islands
2430-2434	Timor (Map, p. 32)
2435-2439	Moluccas. Spice Islands
2440-2444	New Guinea (Map, p. 32)

[1] For subdivisions, see tables, pp. 206-223

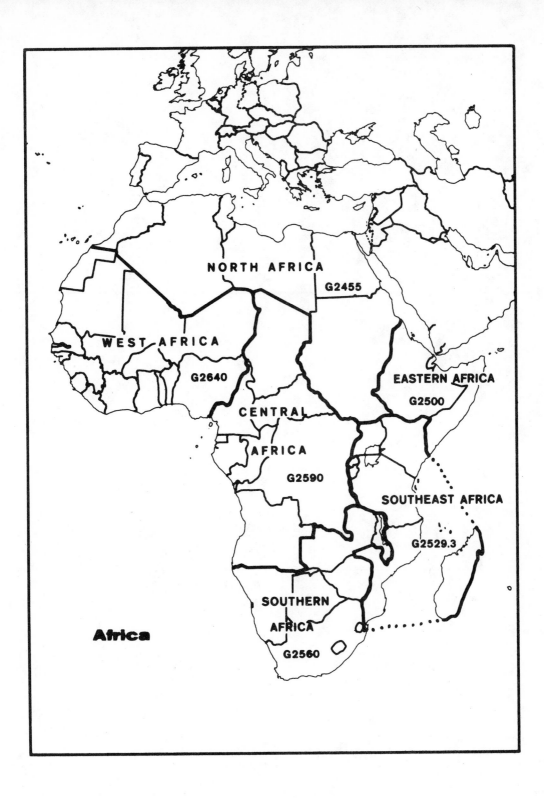

NORTH AFRICA

G2455

WEST AFRICA

G2640

EASTERN AFRICA

G2500

CENTRAL

AFRICA

G2590

SOUTHEAST AFRICA

G2529.3

SOUTHERN

AFRICA

G2560

Africa

ATLASES

By region or country[1]
                    Eastern Hemisphere. Eurasia, Africa, etc. - Continued
2445-2447   Africa
                        Including Sub-Saharan Africa
2447   Regions and natural features, etc., A-Z
                            e. g. .N5 Nile River
                                   .S2 Sahara
2455-2457   North Africa (Map, p. 34)
                        Including the Barbary States and Egypt
2460-2464   Morocco
2465-2469   Algeria
2470-2474   Tunisia. Tunis
2475-2479   Libya
2480-2481   Cyrenaica
2485-2486   Tripolitania. Tripoli
2490-2494   Egypt. United Arab Republic
2495-2499   Sudan. Anglo-Egyptian Sudan
2500-2502   Northeast Africa (Map, p. 34)
2505-2509   Ethiopia. Abyssinia
2510-2511   Eritrea
2515-2519   Somalia. Somaliland
                            Including British Somaliland and Italian
                              Somaliland
2520-2524   French Territory of the Afars and Issas. French
                          Somaliland
     2529.3-.32   Southeast Africa. British East Africa (Map, p. 34)
2530-2534   Kenya. East Africa Protectorate
2535-2539   Uganda
     2539.3-.31   Ruanda-Urundi. Belgian East Africa
        .5-.54   Rwanda
        .7-.74   Burundi
2540-2544   Tanzania. Tanganyika. German East Africa
2545-2546   Zanzibar
2550-2554   Mozambique. Portuguese East Africa
2555-2559   Madagascar. Malagasy Republic
                    East African Islands, see G2857
2560-2562   Southern Africa. British South Africa (Map, p. 34)
2565-2569   Republic of South Africa
2568   Administrative divisions, A-Z
                            e. g. .C3 Cape of Good Hope
2570-2571   Rhodesia
     2574.3-.34   Southern Rhodesia
2575-2579   Zambia. Northern Rhodesia
     2579.3-.34   Lesotho. Basutoland
        .5-.54   Swaziland
        .7-.74   Botswana. Bechuanaland
        .9-.94   Malawi. Nyasaland. Central Africa Protectorate
2580-2584   Southwest Africa (Namibia). German Southwest Africa
2590-2592   Central Africa. Equatorial Africa (Map, p. 34)
2595-2599   Angola. Portuguese West Africa
2600-2604   Zaire. Congo (Democratic Republic). Belgian Congo
2605-2609   Equatorial Guinea. Spanish Guinea
     2609.3-.34   São Tomé e Principe
2610-2612   French Equatorial Africa. French Congo
2615-2619   Gabon
2620-2624   Congo (Brazzaville). Middle Congo
2625-2629   Central African Republic. Ubangi-Shari
2630-2634   Chad (Tchad)

---
[1] For subdivisions, see tables, pp. 206-223

By region or country[1]
　Oceans (General) - Continued

2860-2862	Pacific Ocean (Map, p. 13)
2867	Islands, groups of islands, etc., A-Z
	Class here islands or archipelagoes not classed in or associated with G2870+
2870-2872	Melanesia
	Class here islands or archipelagoes not classed in or associated with G2875+
2875-2879	Solomon Islands
2880-2884	New Hebrides
2885-2889	New Caledonia
2890-2894	Fiji
2900-2902	Micronesia
	Class here islands or archipelagoes not classed in or associated with G2905+
2905-2909	Mariana Islands
2910-2914	Guam
2920-2924	Caroline Islands
2930-2934	Marshall Islands
2970-2972	Polynesia
	Class here islands or archipelagoes not classed in or associated with Samoa Islands
2980-2984	Samoa Islands
	Hawaii, see G1534.2+
3012	East Pacific islands, A-Z
3050-3052	Arctic Ocean (Map, p. 13)
	Class here islands or archipelagoes not classed in or associated with G3055+
	Cf. G1055, Arctic regions
3055-3059	Franz Josef Land
3060-3064	Svalbard. Spitsbergen
3100-3102	Antarctica (Map, p. 13)
3122	Atlases of imaginary, literary, and mythological regions, etc., A-Z
	.A8 Atlantis

---

[1] For subdivisions, see tables, pp. 206-223

GLOBES

3160	Celestial globes
3165-3167	Planetary and lunar globes[1]
3167	Individual planets or moons, A-Z
	e. g. .M3 Mars
	.M6 Moon
	.P5 Phobos
3170-3171	Terrestrial globes[1]
3180-3182	Universe. Solar system[1]
3182	Individual planets, A-Z
	e. g. .M3 Mars

MAPS

For history and description of maps, <u>see</u> GA

3190-3192	Celestial maps[1]
3195-3199	Moon[1]

---

[1] For subdivisions, <u>see</u> tables, pp. 206-223

3200-3202   World[1]
                        Including maps of the known world prior to 1500
                           confined to the Eastern Hemisphere
                        Cf. G9095+, Oceans (General)
3201   By subject
.B71   Terrestrial globe gores
.B72   Individual projections
                       History
.S1   General
.S12   Discovery and exploration
.S2   Ancient and classical history
.S3   Medieval history, 476-1453
.S33   Early medieval history
.S36   11th-15th centuries
.S4   Modern history
.S5   17th-19th centuries
.S6   20th century
.S65   World War I
.S7   World War II
.S73   1945-

---

[1]
  For subdivisions, see tables, pp. 206-223

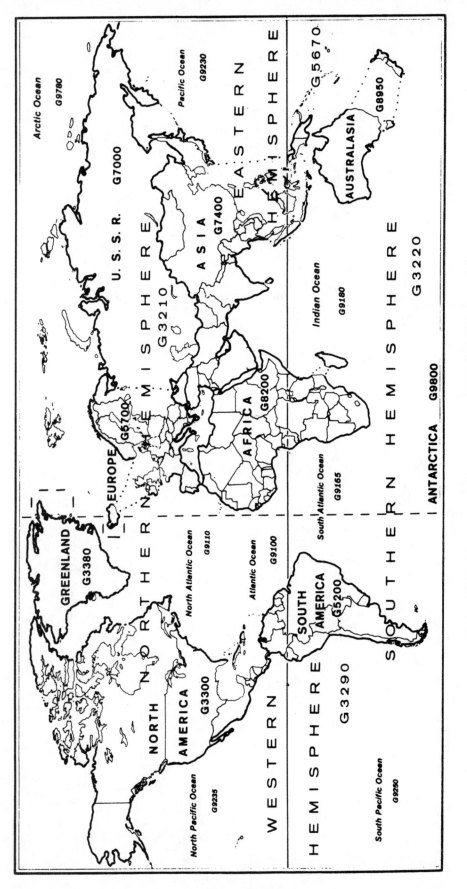

Hemispheres, Continents and Oceans

Arctic Ocean G9780

Pacific Ocean G9230

G5670

AUSTRALASIA G8950

U.S.S.R. G7000

EASTERN HEMISPHERE

ASIA G7400

NORTHERN HEMISPHERE G3210

Indian Ocean G9180

SOUTHERN HEMISPHERE G3220

EUROPE G5700

AFRICA G8200

ANTARCTICA G9800

South Atlantic Ocean G9165

GREENLAND G3380

North Atlantic Ocean G9110

Atlantic Ocean G9100

NORTH AMERICA G3300

SOUTH AMERICA G5200

WESTERN HEMISPHERE G3290

SOUTHERN HEMISPHERE

North Pacific Ocean G9235

South Pacific Ocean G9250

40

	Western Hemisphere, <u>see</u> G3290+
	Eastern Hemisphere, <u>see</u> G5670+
3210-3212	Northern Hemisphere[1] (Map, p. 40)
3220-3222	Southern Hemisphere[1] (Map, p. 40)
3240-3241	Tropics. Torrid Zone[1]
3250-3251	Temperate Zones[1]
3260-3261	Polar regions. Frigid Zones[1]
3270-3272	Arctic regions[1]
	Cf. G9780+, Arctic Ocean
	Antarctica, <u>see</u> G9800+
	<u>By region or country</u>[1]
3290-3292	<u>America. Western Hemisphere</u> (Map, p. 40)
3292	Regions, natural features, etc., A-Z
	e. g. .L3 Latin America
3300-3302	<u>North America</u> (Map, p. 40)
3310-3312	Great Lakes Aggregation

The chain of five lakes and seaway located
within the land area of North America on or
near the Canadian-U.S. border. Includes
and extends through the St. Lawrence Seaway,
but does not include the Gulf of St. Lawrence
Maps of individual physical features associated
with the Great Lakes but located wholly
within the United States or Canada should be
classed according to Table I, p.   , e. g.
G4112.S2, Saginaw Bay; G3462.G39, Georgian
Bay

3312	Regions, natural features, etc., A-Z	
	e. g. .D4	Detroit River
	.E7	Lake Erie
	.H8	Lake Huron
	.M5	Lake Michigan
	.N5	Niagara Falls
	.N52	Niagara River
	.O5	Lake Ontario
	.S43	Lake St. Clair
	.S44	St. Clair River
	.S5	St. Lawrence River
	.S55	St. Marys River
	.S9	Lake Superior

3320-3321	Atlantic coast and continental shelf
3330-3331	Gulf coast and continental shelf
3350-3351	Pacific coast and continental shelf
3380-3384	Greenland (Map, p. 40)
3400-3402	<u>Canada</u>
3402	Regions, natural features, etc., A-Z
	e. g. .S2 Gulf of St. Lawrence
3405-3407	<u>Eastern Canada (1867 and later)</u>
3410-3412	<u>Maritime Provinces</u>
3420-3424	Nova Scotia
3430-3434	New Brunswick
3440-3444	Prince Edward Island
3450-3454	Quebec
3460-3464	Ontario
3462	Regions, natural features, etc., A-Z
	e. g. .G39 Georgian Bay

---

[1]
    For subdivisions, <u>see</u> tables, pp. 206-223

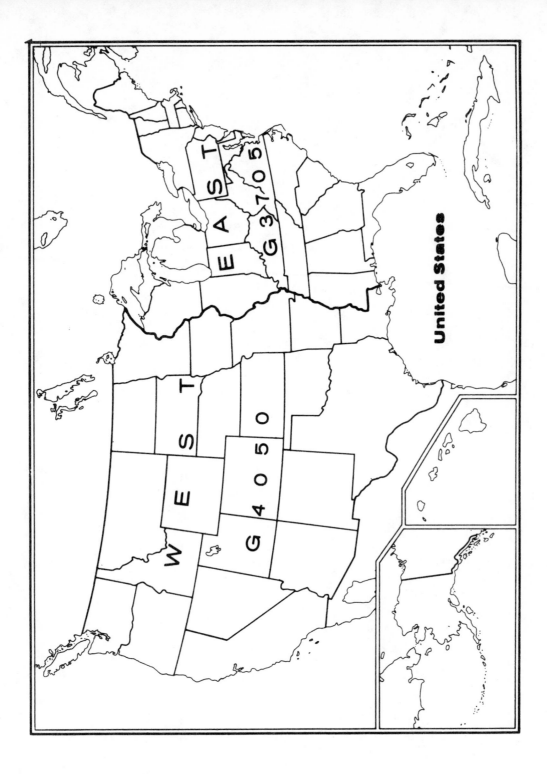

United States

WEST

EAST

G4050

G3705

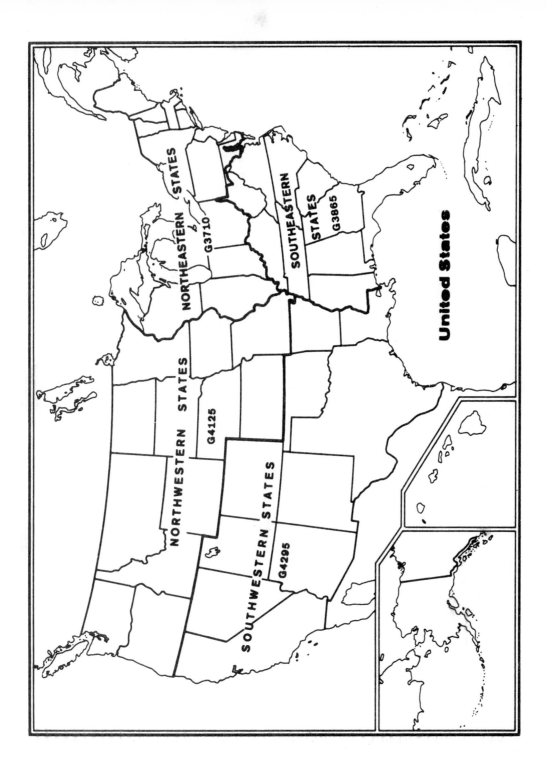

United States

NORTHEASTERN STATES
G3710

SOUTHEASTERN STATES
G3865

NORTHWESTERN STATES
G4125

SOUTHWESTERN STATES
G4295

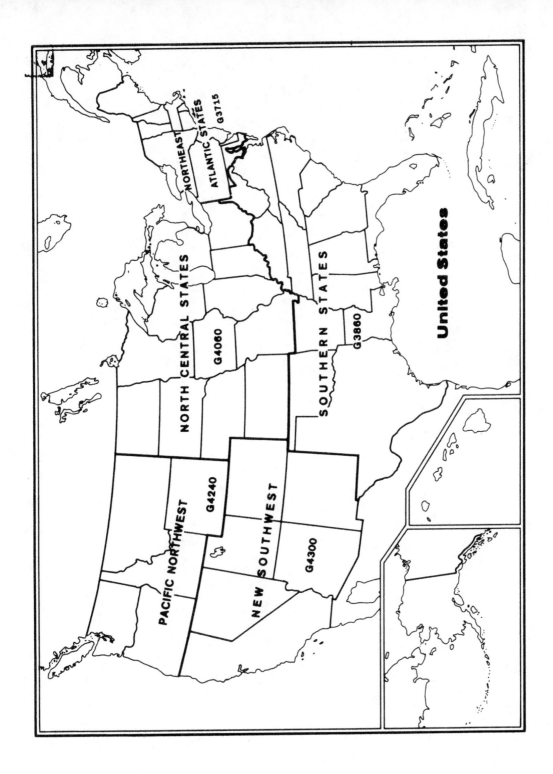

United States

NORTHEAST
ATLANTIC STATES
G3715

NORTH CENTRAL STATES
G4060

SOUTHERN STATES
G3860

PACIFIC NORTHWEST
G4240

NEW SOUTHWEST
G4300

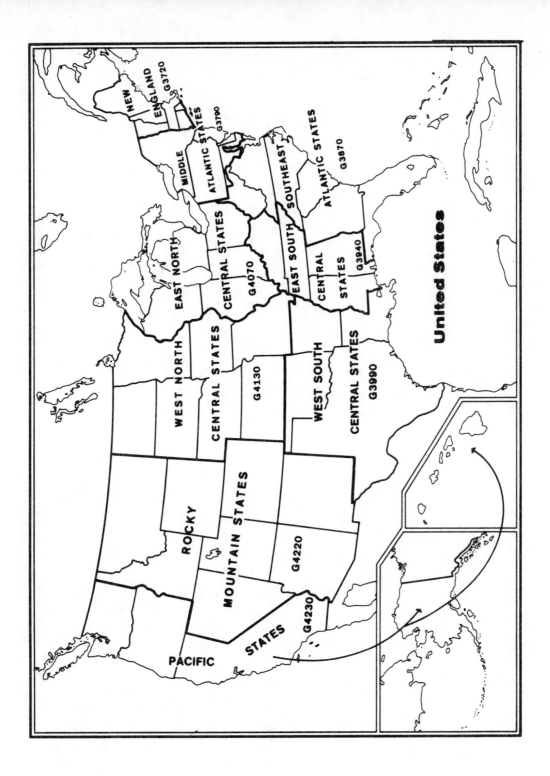

United States

NEW ENGLAND G3720

MIDDLE ATLANTIC STATES G3790

SOUTHEAST ATLANTIC STATES G3870

EAST NORTH CENTRAL STATES G4070

EAST SOUTH CENTRAL STATES G3940

WEST NORTH CENTRAL STATES G4130

WEST SOUTH CENTRAL STATES G3990

ROCKY MOUNTAIN STATES G4220

PACIFIC STATES G4230

46

MAPS

By region or country[1]
America. Western Hemisphere
North America
Canada - Continued

3465-3467	Western Canada
3470-3472	Prairie Provinces
3480-3484	Manitoba
3490-3494	Saskatchewan
3500-3504	Alberta
3510-3514	British Columbia
3512	Regions, natural features, etc., A-Z
	e. g. .V3 Vancouver Island
3520-3524	Yukon
3530-3532	Northwest Territories
3540-3544	Mackenzie District
3550-3554	Keewatin District
3560-3564	Franklin District
3600-3604	Newfoundland
3610-3612	Labrador
3650-3654	Saint Pierre and Miquelon Islands
3690-3691	United States and possessions
	Including maps of United States possessions
	(Collectively)
	Class individual possessions by location,
	e. g. G9415, Guam
3700-3702	United States
	History
3701.S1	General
.S12	Discovery and exploration
	Including exploration of the West
.S2	Colonial period
.S26	French and Indian War, 1755-1763
.S3	Revolution, 1775-1783
.S42	War of 1812
.S44	Mexican War, 1846-1865
.S5	Civil War, 1861-1865
.S55	1865-1900
.S57	Spanish American War, 1898
.S6	1900-1945
.S65	World War I
.S7	World War II
.S73	1945-
3704	Cities and towns (Collectively)
	For individual cities and towns, see the
	state
3705-3707	Eastern United States, 1870 and later (Map, p. 42)
	Area east of the Mississippi River
3707	Regions, natural features, etc., A-Z
	e. g. .A6 Appalachian Mountains
	.05 Ohio River
3709.3-.32	Atlantic States (Map, p. 44)
3709.32	Regions, natural features, etc., A-Z
	e. g. .A6 Appalachian Trail
	.P6 Potomac River

---

[1]

For subdivisions, see tables, pp. 206-223

By region or country[1]
　America.　Western Hemisphere
　　North America
　　　United States
　　　　Eastern United States, 1870 and later - Continued

3710-3712	Northeastern States (Map, p. 43)
3715-3717	Northeast Atlantic States (Map, p. 45)
3720-3722	New England (Map, p. 46)
3730-3734	Maine
3732	Regions, natural features, etc., A-Z
	e. g.　.A3　Acadia National Park
	.M6　Mount Desert Island
	.P4　Penobscot River
3733	Counties, A-Z
	.A5　Androscoggin
	.A6　Aroostook
	.C8　Cumberland
	.F7　Franklin
	.H3　Hancock
	.K4　Kennebec
	.K5　Knox
	.L4　Lincoln
	.O8　Oxford
	.P4　Penobscot
	.P5　Piscataquis
	.S3　Sagadahoc
	.S6　Somerset
	.W3　Waldo
	.W4　Washington
	.Y6　York
3734	Cities, towns, and townships, A-Z
	e. g.　.S589　Skowhegan
	.S59　Skowhegan Township
3740-3744	New Hampshire
3742	Regions, natural features, etc., A-Z
	e. g.　.S65　Squam Lake
	.S67　Squam Mountains
	.W5　White Mountain
	National Park
	.W52　White Mountains
3743	Counties, A-Z
	.B4　Belknap
	.C3　Carroll
	.C5　Cheshire
	.C6　Coos
	.G7　Grafton
	.H4　Hillsboro
	.M4　Merrimack
	.R6　Rockingham
	.S7　Strafford
	.S8　Sullivan
3744	Cities, towns, and townships, A-Z
	e. g.　.E89　Exeter
	.E9　Exeter Township

---

[1] For subdivisions, see tables, pp. 206-223

MAPS

By region or country[1]
America. Western Hemisphere
North America
United States
Eastern United States, 1870 and later
Northeastern States
Northeast Atlantic States
New England - Continued
Vermont

3750-3754
3752   Regions, natural features, etc., A-Z
       e. g. .G7 Green Mountain
                      National Forest

3753   Counties, A-Z
      .A2 Addison
      .B4 Bennington
      .C3 Caledonia
      .C5 Chittenden
      .E7 Essex
      .F7 Franklin
      .G7 Grand Isle
      .L3 Lamoille
      .O6 Orange
      .O7 Orleans
      .R8 Rutland
      .W3 Washington
      .W4 Windham
      .W5 Windsor

3754   Cities, towns, and townships, A-Z
       e. g. .B49 Bennington
              .B5 Bennington Township

3760-3764 Massachusetts
3762   Regions, natural features, etc., A-Z
       e. g. .B4 Berkshire Hills
             .C3 Cape Ann
             .C35 Cape Cod
             .N3 Nantucket Island

3763   Counties, A-Z
      .B3 Barnstable
      .B4 Berkshire
      .B7 Bristol
      .D8 Dukes
      .E7 Essex
      .F7 Franklin
      .H3 Hampden
      .H4 Hampshire
      .M5 Middlesex
            Nantucket, see G3762.N3
      .N6 Norfolk
      .P5 Plymouth
      .S8 Suffolk
      .W6 Worcester

3764   Cities, towns, and townships, A-Z
3770-3774 Rhode Island
3772   Regions, natural features, etc., A-Z
       e. g. .B5 Block Island
             .B55 Block Island Sound

---

[1] For subdivisions, see tables, pp. 206-223

By region or country[1]
America. Western Hemisphere
North America
United States
Eastern United States, 1870 and later
Northeastern States
Northeast Atlantic States
New England
Rhode Island - Continued

3773   Counties, A-Z
.B7 Bristol
.K4 Kent
.N4 Newport
.P7 Providence
.W3 Washington

3774   Cities, towns, and townships, A-Z
e. g. .C59 Coventry
.C6   Coventry Township

3780-3784   Connecticut
3782   Regions, natural features, etc., A-Z
e. g. .M99 Mystic River

3783   Counties, A-Z
.F3 Fairfield
.H3 Hartford
.L5 Litchfield
.M5 Middlesex
.N3 New Haven
.N4 New London
.T6 Tolland
.W5 Windham

3784   Cities, towns, and townships, A-Z
e. g. .S79 Stonington
.S8   Stonington Township

3790-3792   Middle Atlantic States. Middle
States (Map, p. 46)
Often including Virginia, West
Virginia, Ohio, and Kentucky

3792   Regions, natural features, etc., A-Z
e. g. .D44 Delaware River
.S9   Susquehanna River

3800-3804   New York (State)
3802   Regions, natural features, etc., A-Z
e. g. .A2 Adirondack Mountains
.H8 Hudson River
.L6 Long Island
Staten Island, see
G3804.N4:2S8

3803   Counties, A-Z
.A4 Albany
.A5 Allegany
Bronx, see G3804.N4:3B7
.B7 Broome
.C2 Cattaraugus
.C3 Cayuga
.C4 Chautauqua
.C5 Chemung

---

[1]
For subdivisions, see tables, pp. 206-223

By region or country
 America. Western Hemisphere
  North America
   United States
    Eastern United States, 1870 and later
     Northeastern States
      Northeast Atlantic States
       Middle Atlantic States. Middle States
        New York (State)

3803   Counties, A-Z - Continued

   .C6 Chenango
   .C7 Clinton
   .C8 Columbia
   .C9 Cortland
   .D4 Delaware
   .D8 Dutchess
   .E6 Erie
   .E7 Essex
   .F7 Franklin
   .F8 Fulton
   .G4 Genesee
   .G7 Greene
   .H3 Hamilton
   .H4 Herkimer
   .J4 Jefferson
       Kings, see G3804.N4:3B8
   .L4 Lewis
   .L5 Livingston
   .M3 Madison
   .M6 Monroe
   .M7 Montgomery
   .N3 Nassau
       New York, see G3804.N4:2M3
   .N5 Niagara
   .O2 Oneida
   .O3 Onondaga
   .O4 Ontario
   .O5 Orange
   .O6 Orleans
   .O7 Oswego
   .O8 Otsego
   .P8 Putnam
       Queens, see G3804.N4:3Q4
   .R4 Rensselaer
       Richmond, see G3804.N4:2S8
   .R6 Rockland
   .S2 St. Lawrence
   .S3 Saratoga
   .S4 Schenectady
   .S5 Schoharie
   .S55 Schuyler
   .S6 Seneca
   .S7 Steuben
   .S8 Suffolk
   .S9 Sullivan
   .T5 Tioga
   .T6 Tompkins
   .U4 Ulster
   .W2 Warren
   .W3 Washington

MAPS

By region or country[1]
America. Western Hemisphere
North America
United States
Eastern United States, 1870 and later
Northeastern States
Northeast Atlantic States
Middle Atlantic States. Middle
States - Continued

3820-3824	Pennsylvania
3822	Regions, natural features, etc., A-Z
	e. g. .A5 Allegheny River
	.P6 Pocono Mountains
3823	Counties, A-Z

.A2   Adams
.A4   Allegheny
.A6   Armstrong
.B3   Beaver
.B4   Bedford
.B5   Berks
.B6   Blair
.B7   Bradford
.B8   Bucks
.B9   Butler
.C3   Cambria
.C33 Cameron
.C36 Carbon
.C4   Centre
.C5   Chester
.C6   Clarion
.C63 Clearfield
.C66 Clinton
.C7   Columbia
.C8   Crawford
.C9   Cumberland
.D3   Dauphin
.D4   Delaware
.E4   Elk
.E6   Erie
.F3   Fayette
.F6   Forest
.F7   Franklin
.F8   Fulton
.G7   Greene
.H8   Huntingdon
.I5   Indiana
.J4   Jefferson
.J8   Juniata
.L2   Lackawanna
.L3   Lancaster
.L4   Lawrence
.L5   Lebanon
.L6   Lehigh
.L8   Luzerne
.L9   Lycoming
.M2   McKean

---

[1] For subdivisions, see tables, pp. 206-223

MAPS

<u>By region or country</u>[1]
<u>America. Western Hemisphere</u>
 <u>North America</u>
  <u>United States</u>
   <u>Eastern United States, 1870 and later</u>
    <u>Northeastern States</u>
     <u>Northeast Atlantic States</u>
      <u>Middle Atlantic States. Middle States</u>
       <u>Pennsylvania</u>

3823	Counties, A-Z - Continued
	.M4 Mercer
	.M5 Mifflin
	.M6 Monroe
	.M7 Montgomery
	.M8 Montour
	.N6 Northampton
	.N7 Northumberland
	.P3 Perry
	Philadelphia, <u>see</u> G3824.P5
	.P5 Pike
	.P6 Potter
	.S3 Schuylkill
	.S5 Snyder
	.S6 Somerset
	.S7 Sullivan
	.S8 Susquehanna
	.T5 Tioga
	.U5 Union
	.V4 Venango
	.W2 Warren
	.W3 Washington
	.W4 Wayne
	.W5 Westmoreland
	.W9 Wyoming
	.Y6 York
3824	Cities, towns, and urban townships, A-Z
	e. g. .P5 Philadelphia
3830-3834	<u>Delaware</u>
3832	Regions, natural features, etc., A-Z
	e. g. .C5 Christina River
	.D4 Delaware Bay
3833	Counties, A-Z
	.K4 Kent
	.N4 New Castle
	.S8 Sussex
3840-3844	<u>Maryland</u>
3842	Regions, natural features, etc., A-Z
	e. g. .A8 Assateague Island
	.A82 Assateague National Seashore
	.C5 Chesapeake Bay
	.C52 Chester River
	.C8 Cumberland Valley

---

[1] For subdivisions, <u>see</u> tables, pp. 206-223

MAPS

<u>By region or country</u>[1]
  <u>America. Western Hemisphere</u>
    <u>North America</u>
      <u>United States</u>
        <u>Eastern United States, 1870 and later</u>
          <u>Northeastern States</u>
            <u>Northeast Atlantic States</u>
              <u>Middle Atlantic States. Middle States</u>
                Maryland - Continued

3843	Counties, A-Z	
	.A4	Allegany
	.A5	Anne Arundel
	.B3	Baltimore
	.C2	Calvert
	.C3	Caroline
	.C4	Carroll
	.C5	Cecil
	.C6	Charles
	.D6	Dorchester
	.F7	Frederick
	.G3	Garrett
	.H3	Harford
	.H6	Howard
	.K4	Kent
	.M6	Montgomery
	.P7	Prince Georges
	.Q4	Queen Annes
	.S3	St. Marys
	.S6	Somerset
	.T3	Talbot
	.W3	Washington
	.W5	Wicomico
	.W6	Worcester
3850-3854	<u>District of Columbia. Washington, D.C.</u>	
3854	Former towns and communities, A-Z	
	e. g. .G4	Georgetown
3860-3862	<u>Southern States. Confederate States</u>	
	<u>of America</u> (Map, p. 45)	
	Including Gulf States	
3865-3867	<u>Southeastern States</u> (Map, p. 43)	
3870-3872	<u>Southeast Atlantic States</u> (Map, p. 46)	
3872	Regions, natural features, etc., A-Z	
	e. g. .B6	Blue Ridge Mountains
3880-3884	<u>Virginia</u>	
3882	Regions, natural features, etc., A-Z	
	e. g. .H3	Hampton Roads
	.J3	James River
	.J6	John H. Kerr ⌐ ⌐oir
	.S52	Shenandoah Ri⌐
3883	Counties, A-Z	
	.A2	Accomac
	.A3	Albemarle
	.A4	Alleghany
	.A5	Amelia
	.A6	Amherst
	.A7	Appomattox
	.A8	Arlington

---

[1] For subdivisions, <u>see</u> tables, pp. 206-223

MAPS

By region or country
America. Western Hemisphere
North America
United States
Southern States. Confederate States of America
Southeastern States
Southeast Atlantic States
Virginia

3883   Counties, A-Z - Continued
.M5   Middlesex
.M6   Montgomery
Nansemond, see G3884.S9
.N4   Nelson
.N5   New Kent
.N6   Norfolk
.N7   Northampton
.N8   Northumberland
.N9   Nottoway
.O6   Orange
.P2   Page
.P3   Patrick
.P4   Pittsylvania
.P5   Powhatan
.P6   Prince Edward
.P65 Prince George
.P7   Prince William
Princess Anne, see G3884.V8
.P9   Pulaski
.R3   Rappahannock
.R4   Richmond
.R5   Roanoke
.R6   Rockbridge
.R7   Rockingham
.R8   Russell
.S2   Scott
.S3   Shenandoah
.S4   Smyth
.S5   Southampton
.S6   Spotsylvania
.S7   Stafford
.S8   Surry
.S9   Sussex
.T3   Tazewell
.W2   Warren
Warwick, see G3884.N4
.W4   Washington
.W5   Westmoreland
.W6   Wise
.W9   Wythe
.Y6   York

3884   Cities and towns, A-Z
e. g.   Arlington, see G3883.A8
.H2   Hampton
.N4   Newport News
.N6   Norfolk
.S9   Suffolk
.V8   Virginia Beach

MAPS

By region or country[1]
America. Western Hemisphere
North America
United States
Southern States. Confederate States of America
Southeastern States
Southeast Atlantic States - Continued

3890-3894	West Virginia
3892	Regions, natural features, etc., A-Z
	e. g. .K3 Kanawha River
	.M62 Monongahela River
3893	Counties, A-Z

.B3   Barbour
.B4   Berkeley
.B6   Boone
.B7   Braxton
.B8   Brooke
.C2   Cabell
.C3   Calhoun
.C5   Clay
.D6   Doddridge
.F3   Fayette
.G4   Gilmer
.G7   Grant
.G8   Greenbrier
.H2   Hampshire
.H3   Hancock
.H4   Hardy
.H5   Harrison
.J2   Jackson
.J4   Jefferson
.K3   Kanawha
.L4   Lewis
.L5   Lincoln
.L6   Logan
.M2   McDowell
.M3   Marion
.M33 Marshall
.M36 Mason
.M4   Mercer
.M5   Mineral
.M6   Mingo
.M7   Monongalia
.M8   Monroe
.M9   Morgan
.N5   Nicholas
.O3   Ohio
.P4   Pendleton
.P5   Pleasants
.P6   Pocahontas
.P7   Preston
.P8   Putnam
.R3   Raleigh
.R4   Randolph
.R5   Ritchie
.R6   Roane

---

[1]

For subdivisions, see tables, pp. 206-223

MAPS

<u>By region or country</u>[1]
  <u>America. Western Hemisphere</u>
    <u>North America</u>
      <u>United States</u>
        <u>Southern States. Confederate States of America</u>
          <u>Southeastern States</u>
            <u>Southeast Atlantic States</u>
              <u>West Virginia</u>

3893	Counties, A–Z – Continued
	.S8 Summers
	.T3 Taylor
	.T8 Tucker
	.T9 Tyler
	.U7 Upshur
	.W2 Wayne
	.W3 Webster
	.W4 Wetzel
	.W5 Wirt
	.W6 Wood
	.W9 Wyoming
3900–3904	<u>North Carolina</u>
3902	Regions, natural features, etc., A–Z
	e. g. .C2 Cape Hatteras National Seashore
	.G69 Great Smoky Mountains
	.G7 Great Smoky Mountains National Park
	.H35 Cape Hatteras
	.O8 Outer Banks
3903	Counties, A–Z
	.A3 Alamance
	.A4 Alexander
	.A5 Alleghany
	.A6 Anson
	.A7 Ashe
	.A8 Avery
	.B3 Beaufort
	.B4 Bertie
	.B5 Bladen
	.B6 Brunswick
	.B7 Buncombe
	.B8 Burke
	.C2 Cabarrus
	.C23 Caldwell
	.C26 Camden
	.C3 Carteret
	.C33 Caswell
	.C36 Catawb
	.C4 Chatham
	.C43 Cherokee
	..C46 Chowan
	.C5 Clay
	.C55 Cleveland
	.C6 Columbus
	.C7 Craven
	.C8 Cumberland
	.C9 Currituck

---

[1] For subdivisions, <u>see</u> tables, pp. 206–223

MAPS

By region or country
  America. Western Hemisphere
    North America
      United States
        Southern States. Confederate States of America
          Southeastern States
            Southeast Atlantic States
              North Carolina

3903
                Counties, A-Z - Continued

.D3	Dare
.D4	Davidson
.D5	Davie
.D7	Duplin
.D8	Durham
.E2	Edgecombe
.F6	Forsyth
.F7	Franklin
.G3	Gaston
.G4	Gates
.G6	Graham
.G7	Granville
.G8	Greene
.G9	Guilford
.H2	Halifax
.H3	Harnett
.H4	Haywood
.H5	Henderson
.H6	Hertford
.H7	Hoke
.H9	Hyde
.I6	Iredell
.J2	Jackson
.J5	Johnston
.J6	Jones
.L3	Lee
.L4	Lenoir
.L5	Lincoln
.M2	McDowell
.M3	Macon
.M4	Madison
.M5	Martin
.M6	Mecklenburg
.M7	Mitchell
.M8	Montgomery
.M9	Moore
.N3	Nash
.N4	New Hanover
.N6	Northampton
.O5	Onslow
.O6	Orange
.P2	Pamlico
.P3	Pasquotank
.P4	Pender
.P5	Perquimans
.P6	Person
.P7	Pitt
.P8	Polk
.R3	Randolph
.R5	Richmond
.R6	Robeson
.R7	Rockingham

MAPS

By region or country[1]
America. Western Hemisphere
North America
United States
Southern States. Confederate States of America
Southeastern States
Southeast Atlantic States
North Carolina

3903		Counties, A-Z - Continued
	.R8	Rowan
	.R9	Rutherford
	.S2	Sampson
	.S3	Scotland
	.S6	Stanly
	.S7	Stokes
	.S8	Surry
	.S9	Swain
	.T7	Transylvania
	.T9	Tyrrell
	.U5	Union
	.V3	Vance
	.W2	Wake
	.W3	Warren
	.W4	Washington
	.W5	Watauga
	.W6	Wayne
	.W7	Wilkes
	.W8	Wilson
	.Y2	Yadkin
	.Y3	Yancey

South Carolina

3910-3914		South Carolina
3912		Regions, natural features, etc., A-Z
	e. g. .H3	Hartwell Lake
	.M34	Lake Marion
3913		Counties, A-Z
	.A2	Abbeville
	.A3	Aiken
	.A5	Allendale
	.A6	Anderson
	.B2	Bamberg
	.B3	Barnwell
	.B4	Beaufort
	.B5	Berkeley
	.C2	Calhoun
	.C3	Charleston
	.C4	Cherokee
	.C5	Chester
	.C6	Chesterfield
	.C7	Clarendon
	.C8	Colleton
	.D3	Darlington
	.D5	Dillon
	.D6	Dorchester
	.E2	Edgefield
	.F3	Fairfield
	.F5	Florence
	.G4	Georgetown

---

[1] For subdivisions, see tables, pp. 206-223

MAPS

By region or country[1]
America. Western Hemisphere
North America
United States
Southern States. Confederate States of America
Southeastern States
Southeast Atlantic States
South Carolina

	Counties, A-Z - Continued
3913	
.G7	Greenville
.G8	Greenwood
.H3	Hampton
.H6	Horry
.J3	Jasper
.K4	Kershaw
.L2	Lancaster
.L3	Laurens
.L4	Lee
.L5	Lexington
.M2	McCormick
.M3	Marion
.M4	Marlboro
.N4	Newberry
.O2	Oconee
.O6	Orangeburg
.P5	Pickens
.R5	Richland
.S3	Saluda
.S7	Spartanburg
.S8	Sumter
.U5	Union
.W5	Williamsburg
.Y6	York

3920-3924   Georgia

3922   Regions, natural features, etc., A-Z
e. g.   .C46   Chattahoochee River
.O5   Okefenokee Swamp
.S3   Savannah River
.S4   Lake Seminole

3923   Counties, A-Z
.A6   Appling
.A7   Atkinson
.B2   Bacon
.B23   Baker
.B26   Baldwin
.B3   Banks
.B33   Barrow
.B36   Bartow
.B4   Ben Hill
.B45   Berrien
.B5   Bibb
.B55   Bleckley
.B6   Brantley
.B65   Brooks
.B7   Bryan
.B8   Bulloch
.B85   Burke

---

[1] For subdivisions, see tables, pp. 206-223

G   G

MAPS

By region or country[1]
America. Western Hemisphere
North America
United States
Southern States. Confederate States of America
Southeastern States
Southeast Atlantic States
South Carolina

3913   Counties, A-Z - Continued
.G7   Greenville
.G8   Greenwood
.H3   Hampton
.H6   Horry
.J3   Jasper
.K4   Kershaw
.L2   Lancaster
.L3   Laurens
.L4   Lee
.L5   Lexington
.M2   McCormick
.M3   Marion
.M4   Marlboro
.N4   Newberry
.O2   Oconee
.O6   Orangeburg
.P5   Pickens
.R5   Richland
.S3   Saluda
.S7   Spartanburg
.S8   Sumter
.U5   Union
.W5   Williamsburg
.Y6   York

3920-3924   Georgia

3922   Regions, natural features, etc., A-Z
e. g.   .C46   Chattahoochee River
.O5   Okefenokee Swamp
.S3   Savannah River
.S4   Lake Seminole

3923   Counties, A-Z
.A6   Appling
.A7   Atkinson
.B2   Bacon
.B23   Baker
.B26   Baldwin
.B3   Banks
.B33   Barrow
.B36   Bartow
.B4   Ben Hill
.B45   Berrien
.B5   Bibb
.B55   Bleckley
.B6   Brantley
.B65   Brooks
.B7   Bryan
.B8   Bulloch
.B85   Burke

---

[1] For subdivisions, see tables, pp. 206-223

By region or country
America. Western Hemisphere
North America
United States
Southern States. Confederate States of America
Southeastern States
Southeast Atlantic States
Georgia
3923   Counties, A-Z - Continued
          .B9   Butts
          .C2   Calhoun
          .C23   Camden
          .C26   Candler
          .C3   Carroll
          .C35   Catoosa
          .C4   Charlton
          .C45   Chatham
          .C5   Chattahoochee
          .C53   Chattooga
          .C56   Cherokee
          .C6   Clarke
          .C63   Clay
          .C66   Clayton
          .C7   Clinch
          .C73   Cobb
          .C76   Coffee
          .C8   Colquitt
          .C83   Columbia
          .C86   Cook
          .C9   Coweta
          .C93   Crawford
          .C96   Crisp
          .D2   Dade
          .D3   Dawson
          .D4   Decatur
          .D5   De Kalb
          .D6   Dodge
          .D7   Dooly
          .D8   Dougherty
          .D9   Douglas
          .E2   Early
          .E3   Echols
          .E4   Effingham
          .E5   Elbert
          .E6   Emanuel
          .E8   Evans
          .F3   Fannin
          .F4   Fayette
          .F5   Floyd
          .F6   Forsyth
          .F7   Franklin
          .F8   Fulton
          .G3   Gilmer
          .G4   Glascock
          .G5   Glynn
          .G6   Gordon
          .G7   Grady
          .G8   Greene
          .G9   Gwinnett
          .H2   Habersham
          .H25   Hall

By region or country
  America. Western Hemisphere
    North America
      United States
        Southern States. Confederate States of America
          Southeastern States
            Southeast Atlantic States
              Georgia
3923   Counties, A-Z - Continued
                  .H3   Hancock
                  .H4   Haralson
                  .H45   Harris
                  .H5   Hart
                  .H6   Heard
                  .H7   Henry
                  .H8   Houston
                  .I6   Irwin
                  .J2   Jackson
                  .J3   Jasper
                  .J4   Jeff Davis
                  .J5   Jefferson
                  .J6   Jenkins
                  .J7   Johnson
                  .J8   Jones
                  .L2   Lamar
                  .L25   Lanier
                  .L3   Laurens
                  .L4   Lee
                  .L5   Liberty
                  .L6   Lincoln
                  .L7   Long
                  .L8   Lowndes
                  .L9   Lumpkin
                  .M2   McDuffie
                  .M25   McIntosh
                  .M3   Macon
                  .M35   Madison
                  .M4   Marion
                  .M5   Meriwether
                  .M6   Miller
                  .M65   Mitchell
                  .M7   Monroe
                  .M73   Montgomery
                  .M76   Morgan
                  .M8   Murray
                  .M9   Muscogee
                  .N4   Newton
                  .O2   Oconee
                  .O3   Oglethorpe
                  .P2   Paulding
                  .P3   Peach
                  .P4   Pickens
                  .P5   Pierce
                  .P6   Pike
                  .P7   Polk
                  .P8   Pulaski
                  .P9   Putnam
                  .Q5   Quitman
                  .R2   Rabun
                  .R3   Randolph
                  .R5   Richmond

MAPS

By region or country[1]
America. Western Hemisphere
North America
United States
Southern States. Confederate States of America
Southeastern States
Southeast Atlantic States
Georgia

3923
Counties, A-Z - Continued
.R6   Rockdale
.S2   Schley
.S3   Screven
.S4   Seminole
.S6   Spalding
.S7   Stephens
.S8   Stewart
.S9   Sumter
.T2   Talbot
.T25   Taliaferro
.T3   Tattnall
.T35   Taylor
.T4   Telfair
.T45   Terrell
.T5   Thomas
.T55   Tift
.T6   Toombs
.T65   Towns
.T7   Treutlen
.T75   Troup
.T8   Turner
.T9   Twiggs
.U5   Union
.U6   Upson
.W2   Walker
.W25   Walton
.W3   Ware
.W35   Warren
.W4   Washington
.W45   Wayne
.W5   Webster
.W55   Wheeler
.W6   White
.W65   Whitfield
.W7   Wilcox
.W75   Wilkes
.W8   Wilkinson
.W9   Worth

3930-3934   Florida
3932
Regions, natural features, etc., A-Z
e. g. .C25 Cape Canaveral. Cape
Kennedy
.E89   Everglades
.E9   Everglades National Park
.F5   Florida Keys
.T3   Tampa Bay
.W3   Walt Disney World

[1]
For subdivisions, see tables, pp. 206-223

By region or country
America. Western Hemisphere
North America
United States
. Southern States
Southeastern States
Southeast Atlantic States
Florida - Continued

3933   Counties, A-Z
.A4 Alachua
.B2 Baker
.B3 Bay
.B6 Bradford
.B7 Brevard
.B8 Broward
.C3 Calhoun
.C4 Charlotte
.C5 Citrus
.C6 Clay
.C7 Collier
.C8 Columbia
.D3 Dade
.D4 De Soto
.D5 Dixie
.D8 Duval
.E7 Escambia
.F6 Flagler
.F7 Franklin
.G2 Gadsden
.G5 Gilchrist
.G6 Glades
.G8 Gulf
.H2 Hamilton
.H3 Hardee
.H4 Hendry
.H5 Hernando
.H6 Highlands
.H7 Hillsborough
.H8 Holmes
.I5 Indian River
.J3 Jackson
.J4 Jefferson
.L2 Lafayette
.L3 Lake
.L4 Lee
.L5 Leon
.L6 Levy
.L7 Liberty
.M2 Madison
.M3 Manatee
.M4 Marion
.M5 Martin
.M6 Monroe
.N3 Nassau
.O3 Okaloosa
.O4 Okeechobee
.O6 Orange
.O7 Osceola
.P2 Palm Beach
.P3 Pasco

MAPS

By region or country[1]
America. Western Hemisphere
North America
United States
Southern States
Southeastern States
Southeast Atlantic States
Florida

3933		Counties, A-Z - Continued
	.P5	Pinellas
	.P6	Polk
	.P8	Putnam
	.S2	St. Johns
	.S3	St. Lucie
	.S4	Santa Rosa
	.S5	Sarasota
	.S6	Seminole
	.S8	Sumter
	.S9	Suwannee
	.T3	Taylor
	.U5	Union
	.V6	Volusia
	.W3	Wakulla
	.W4	Walton
	.W5	Washington

3935-3937	South Central States (Map, p. 44)	
3940-3942	East South Central States (Map, p. 46)	
3942	Regions, natural features, etc., A-Z	
	e. g. .T4 Tennessee River	
3950-3954	Kentucky	
3952	Regions, natural features, etc., A-Z	
	e. g. .C8 Lake Cumberland	
	.K42 Kentucky River	
3953	Counties, A-Z	
	.A2	Adair
	.A4	Allen
	.A5	Anderson
	.B2	Ballard
	.B3	Barren
	.B35	Bath
	.B4	Bell
	.B5	Boone
	.B55	Bourbon
	.B6	Boyd
	.B65	Boyle
	.B7	Bracken
	.B73	Breathitt
	.B76	Breckinridge
	.B8	Bullitt
	.B9	Butler
	.C2	Caldwell
	.C23	Calloway
	.C26	Campbell
	.C3	Carlisle
	.C33	Carroll
	.C36	Carter

---

[1] For subdivisions, see tables, pp. 206-223

MAPS

By region or country
America. Western Hemisphere
North America
United States
Southern States
South Central States
East South Central States
Kentucky

3953
Counties, A-Z - Continued
.C4   Casey
.C5   Christian
.C6   Clark
.C63   Clay
.C66   Clinton
.C7   Crittenden
.C8   Cumberland
.D3   Daviess
.E2   Edmonson
.E4   Elliott
.E7   Estill
.F3   Fayette
.F5   Fleming
.F6   Floyd
.F7   Franklin
.F8   Fulton
.G3   Gallatin
.G4   Garrard
.G5   Grant
.G6   Graves
.G7   Grayson
.G8   Green
.G9   Greenup
.H2   Hancock
.H3   Hardin
.H35   Harlan
.H4   Harrison
.H5   Hart
.H6   Henderson
.H7   Henry
.H8   Hickman
.H9   Hopkins
.J2   Jackson
.J4   Jefferson
.J5   Jessamine
.J6   Johnson
.K4   Kenton
.K5   Knott
.K6   Knox
.L2   Larue
.L25   Laurel
.L3   Lawrence
.L4   Lee
.L45   Leslie
.L5   Letcher
.L55   Lewis
.L6   Lincoln
.L7   Livingston
.L8   Logan
.L9   Lyon

MAPS

By region or country
America. Western Hemisphere
North America
United States
Southern States
South Central States
East South Central States
Kentucky
Counties, A-Z - Continued

3953

.M2	McCracken
.M23	McCreary
.M26	McLean
.M3	Madison
.M35	Magoffin
.M4	Marion
.M43	Marshall
.M46	Martin
.M5	Mason
.M6	Meade
.M65	Menifee
.M7	Mercer
.M75	Metcalfe
.M8	Monroe
.M83	Montgomery
.M86	Morgan
.M9	Muhlenberg
.N4	Nelson
.N5	Nicholas
.O3	Ohio
.O4	Oldham
.O7	Owen
.O8	Owsley
.P3	Pendleton
.P4	Perry
.P5	Pike
.P6	Powell
.P8	Pulaski
.R5	Robertson
.R6	Rockcastle
.R7	Rowan
.R8	Russell
.S2	Scott
.S5	Shelby
.S6	Simpson
.S7	Spencer
.T3	Taylor
.T6	Todd
.T7	Trigg
.T8	Trimble
.U5	Union
.W2	Warren
.W3	Washington
.W4	Wayne
.W5	Webster
.W6	Whitley
.W7	Wolfe
.W8	Woodford

By region or country[1]
America. Western Hemisphere
North America
United States
Southern States
South Central States
East South Central States - Continued
Tennessee

3960-3964		Regions, natural features, etc., A-Z
3962		e. g. .C85 Cumberland River
		.D3 Dale Hollow Lake
		.J15 J. Percy Priest Reservoir
3963		Counties, A-Z

.A5   Anderson
.B3   Bedford
.B4   Benton
.B5   Bledsoe
.B6   Blount
.B7   Bradley
.C2   Campbell
.C25   Cannon
.C3   Carroll
.C35   Carter
.C4   Cheatham
.C45   Chester
.C5   Claiborne
.C55   Clay
.C6   Cocke
.C65   Coffee
.C7   Crockett
.C8   Cumberland
.D3   Davidson
.D4   Decatur
.D5   De Kalb
.D6   Dickson
.D9   Dyer
.F3   Fayette
.F4   Fentress
.F7   Franklin
.G4   Gibson
.G5   Giles
.G6   Grainger
.G7   Greene
.G8   Grundy
.H2   Hamblen
.H23   Hamilton
.H26   Hancock
.H3   Hardeman
.H35   Hardin
.H4   Hawkins
.H45   Haywood
.H5   Henderson

---

[1]
For subdivisions, see tables, pp. 206-223

By region or country
   America. Western Hemisphere
      North America
         United States
            Southern States
               South Central States
                  East South Central States
                     Tennessee
3963   Counties, A-Z - Continued
                        .H55 Henry
                        .H6   Hickman
                        .H7   Houston
                        .H8   Humphreys
                        .J2   Jackson
                        .J4   Jefferson
                        .J6   Johnson
                        .K6   Knox
                        .L2   Lake
                        .L3   Lauderdale
                        .L4   Lawrence
                        .L5   Lewis
                        .L6   Lincoln
                        .L7   Loudon
                        .M2   McMinn
                        .M25 McNairy
                        .M3   Macon
                        .M35 Madison
                        .M4   Marion
                        .M43 Marshall
                        .M46 Maury
                        .M5   Meigs
                        .M6   Monroe
                        .M7   Montgomery
                        .M8   Moore
                        .M9   Morgan
                        .O2   Obion
                        .O8   Overton
                        .P4   Perry
                        .P5   Pickett
                        .P6   Polk
                        .P8   Putnam
                        .R5   Rhea
                        .R6   Roane
                        .R7   Robertson
                        .R8   Rutherford
                        .S2   Scott
                        .S3   Sequatchie
                        .S4   Sevier
                        .S5   Shelby
                        .S6   Smith
                        .S7   Stewart
                        .S8   Sullivan
                        .S9   Sumner
                        .T5   Tipton
                        .T7   Trousdale
                        .U5   Unicoi
                        .U6   Union
                        .V3   Van Buren
                        .W2   Warren

MAPS

By region or country[1]
America. Western Hemisphere
North America
United States
Southern States
South Central States
East South Central States
Tennessee

3963	Counties, A-Z - Continued	
	.W3	Washington
	.W4	Wayne
	.W5	Weakley
	.W6	White
	.W7	Williamson
	.W8	Wilson
3970-3974	Alabama	
3972	Regions, natural features, etc., A-Z	
	e. g. .M6	Mobile Bay
	.W3	Walter F. George Reservoir
3973	Counties, A-Z	
	.A8	Autauga
	.B2	Baldwin
	.B4	Barbour
	.B5	Bibb
	.B6	Blount
	.B7	Bullock
	.B8	Butler
	.C2	Calhoun
	.C25	Chambers
	.C3	Cherokee
	.C35	Chilton
	.C4	Choctaw
	.C45	Clarke
	.C5	Clay
	.C55	Cleburne
	.C6	Coffee
	.C65	Colbert
	.C7	Conecuh
	.C75	Coosa
	.C8	Covington
	.C85	Crenshaw
	.C9	Cullman
	.D2	Dale
	.D3	Dallas
	.D4	De Kalb
	.E4	Elmore
	.E6	Escambia
	.E7	Etowah
	.F3	Fayette
	.F7	Franklin
	.G4	Geneva
	.G7	Greene
	.H3	Hale
	.H4	Henry
	.H6	Houston

---

[1] For subdivisions, see tables, pp. 206-223

MAPS

By region or country[1]
America. Western Hemisphere
North America
United States
Southern States
South Central States
East South Central States
Alabama

3973		Counties, A-Z - Continued
	.J3	Jackson
	.J4	Jefferson
	.L2	Lamar
	.L3	Lauderdale
	.L4	Lawrence
	.L5	Lee
	.L6	Limestone
	.L7	Lowndes
	.M2	Macon
	.M3	Madison
	.M35	Marengo
	.M4	Marion
	.M5	Marshall
	.M6	Mobile
	.M7	Monroe
	.M8	Montgomery
	.M9	Morgan
	.P4	Perry
	.P5	Pickens
	.P6	Pike
	.R3	Randolph
	.R8	Russell
	.S2	St. Clair
	.S5	Shelby
	.S8	Sumter
	.T3	Talladega
	.T4	Tallapoosa
	.T8	Tuscaloosa
	.W3	Walker
	.W4	Washington
	.W5	Wilcox
	.W6	Winston

3980-3984		Mississippi
3982		Regions, natural features, etc., A-Z
	e. g. .G8	Grenada Lake
	.P4	Pearl River
3983		Counties, A-Z
	.A2	Adams
	.A4	Alcorn
	.A5	Amite
	.A7	Attala
	.B4	Benton
	.B6	Bolivar
	.C2	Calhoun
	.C3	Carroll
	.C4	Chickasaw

----

[1] For subdivisions, see tables, pp. 206-223

MAPS

By region or country
  America. Western Hemisphere
    North America
      United States
        Southern States
          South Central States
            East South Central States
              Mississippi

3983   Counties, A-Z - Continued

                          .C45   Choctaw
                          .C5   Claiborne
                          .C55   Clarke
                          .C6   Clay
                          .C7   Coahoma
                          .C8   Copiah
                          .C9   Covington
                          .D4   De Soto
                          .F6   Forrest
                          .F7   Franklin
                          .G4   George
                          .G6   Greene
                          .G7   Grenada
                          .H2   Hancock
                          .H3   Harrison
                          .H5   Hinds
                          .H6   Holmes
                          .H8   Humphreys
                          .I7   Issaquena
                          .I8   Itawamba
                          .J2   Jackson
                          .J3   Jasper
                          .J4   Jefferson
                          .J5   Jefferson Davis
                          .J6   Jones
                          .K4   Kemper
                          .L2   Lafayette
                          .L25   Lamar
                          .L3   Lauderdale
                          .L35   Lawrence
                          .L4   Leake
                          .L5   Lee
                          .L6   Leflore
                          .L7   Lincoln
                          .L8   Lowndes
                          .M2   Madison
                          .M3   Marion
                          .M4   Marshall
                          .M5   Monroe
                          .M6   Montgomery
                          .N3   Neshoba
                          .N4   Newton
                          .N6   Noxubee
                          .O3   Oktibbeha
                          .P2   Panola
                          .P3   Pearl River
                          .P4   Perry
                          .P5   Pike
                          .P6   Pontotoc
                          .P7   Prentiss
                          .Q5   Quitman

MAPS

By region or country[1]
America. Western Hemisphere
North America
United States
Southern States
South Central States
East South Central States
Mississippi

		Counties, A-Z - Continued
3983	.R3	Rankin
	.S2	Scott
	.S3	Sharkey
	.S4	Simpson
	.S5	Smith
	.S7	Stone
	.S8	Sunflower
	.T3	Tallahatchie
	.T4	Tate
	.T5	Tippah
	.T6	Tishomingo
	.T8	Tunica
	.U5	Union
	.W2	Walthall
	.W3	Warren
	.W4	Washington
	.W5	Wayne
	.W6	Webster
	.W7	Wilkinson
	.W8	Winston
	.Y3	Yalobusha
	.Y4	Yazoo

3990-3992	West South Central States. Old
	Southwest (Map, p.
3992	Regions, natural features, etc., A-Z
	e. g. .R4 Red River
4000-4004	Arkansas
4002	Regions, natural features, etc., A-Z
	e. g. .B9 Bull Shoals Reservoir
	.O9 Ozark Mountains

		Counties, A-Z
4003	.A6	Arkansas
	.A7	Ashley
	.B3	Baxter
	.B4	Benton
	.B6	Boone
	.B7	Bradley
	.C2	Calhoun
	.C25	Carroll
	.C3	Chicot
	.C4	Clark
	.C45	Clay
	.C5	Cleburne
	.C55	Cleveland
	.C6	Columbia
	.C65	Conway
	.C7	Craighead
	.C75	Crawford

---

[1]
For subdivisions, see tables, pp. 206-223

MAPS.

<u>By region or country</u>
  <u>America. Western Hemisphere</u>
    <u>North America</u>
      <u>United States</u>
        <u>Southern States</u>
          <u>South Central States</u>
            <u>West South Central States. Old</u>
              <u>Southwest</u>
              <u>Arkansas</u>

4003
                Counties, A-Z - Continued

.C8	Crittenden
.C9	Cross
.D3	Dallas
.D4	Desha
.D7	Drew
.F3	Faulkner
.F7	Franklin
.F8	Fulton
.G3	Garland
.G6	Grant
.G7	Greene
.H4	Hempstead
.H6	Hot Spring
.H7	Howard
.I7	Independence
.I9	Izard
.J3	Jackson
.J4	Jefferson
.J6	Johnson
.L2	Lafayette
.L3	Lawrence
.L4	Lee
.L5	Lincoln
.L6	Little River
.L7	Logan
.L8	Lonoke
.M2	Madison
.M3	Marion
.M4	Miller
.M5	Mississippi
.M6	Monroe
.M7	Montgomery
.N4	Nevada
.N5	Newton
.O8	Ouachita
.P2	Perry
.P3	Phillips
.P4	Pike
.P5	Poinsett
.P6	Polk
.P7	Pope
.P8	Prairie
.P9	Pulaski
.R3	Randolph
.S2	St. Francis
.S3	Saline
.S4	Scott
.S5	Searcy
.S6	Sebastian
.S7	Sevier

MAPS

By region or country[1]
America. Western Hemisphere
North America
United States
Southern States
South Central States
West South Central States. Old
Southwest
Louisiana

4013		Parishes, A-Z - Continued
	.N3	Natchitoches
		Orleans, see G4014.N5
	.O8	Ouachita
	.P5	Plaquemines
	.P6	Pointe Coupee
	.R3	Rapides
	.R4	Red River
	.R5	Richland
	.S2	Sabine
	.S3	St. Bernard
	.S4	St. Charles
	.S5	St. Helena
	.S6	St. James
	.S65	St. John the Baptist
	.S7	St. Landry
	.S8	St. Martin
	.S85	St. Mary
	.S9	St. Tammany
	.T3	Tangipahoa
	.T4	Tensas
	.T5	Terrebonne
	.U5	Union
	.V4	Vermilion
	.V5	Vernon
	.W3	Washington
	.W4	Webster
	.W5	West Baton Rouge
	.W6	West Carroll
	.W7	West Feliciana
	.W8	Winn
4014		Cities and towns, A-Z
		e. g. .N5 New Orlaans
4020-4024		Oklahoma
4022		Regions, natural features, etc., A-Z
		e. g. .A5 Anadarko Basin
		.T4 Lake Texoma
4023		Counties, A-Z
	.A2	Adair
	.A4	Alfalfa
	.A7	Atoka
	.B3	Beaver
	.B4	Beckham
	.B5	Blaine
	.B7	Bryan
	.C2	Caddo
	.C3	Canadian

---

[1] For subdivisions, see tables, pp. 206-223

MAPS

By region or country
  America. Western Hemisphere
    North America
      United States
        Southern States
          South Central States
            West South Central States. Old
                Southwest
              Oklahoma
4023   Counties, A-Z - Continued
                  .C35   Carter
                  .C4   Cherokee
                  .C45   Choctaw
                  .C5   Cimarron
                  .C55   Cleveland
                  .C6   Coal
                  .C63   Comanche
                  .C66   Cotton
                  .C7   Craig
                  .C8   Creek
                  .C9   Custer
                  .D4   Delaware
                  .D5   Dewey
                  .E4   Ellis
                  .G3   Garfield
                  .G4   Garvin
                  .G6   Grady
                  .G7   Grant
                  .G8   Greer
                  .H2   Harmon
                  .H3   Harper
                  .H4   Haskell
                  .H8   Hughes
                  .J3   Jackson
                  .J4   Jefferson
                  .J6   Johnston
                  .K3   Kay
                  .K4   Kingfisher
                  .K5   Kiowa
                  .L3   Latimer
                  .L4   Le Flore
                  .L5   Lincoln
                  .L6   Logan
                  .L7   Love
                  .M2   McClain
                  .M3   McCurtain
                  .M4   McIntosh
                  .M5   Major
                  .M6   Marshall
                  .M7   Mayes
                  .M8   Murray
                  .M9   Muskogee
                  .N5   Noble
                  .N6   Nowata
                  .O3   Okfuskee
                  .O4   Oklahoma
                  .O5   Okmulgee
                  .O6   Osage
                  .O7   Ottawa

MAPS

By region or country[1]
America. Western Hemisphere
North America
United States
Southern States
South Central States
West South Central States. Old Southwest
Oklahoma

	Counties, A–Z – Continued	
4023	.P3	Pawnee
	.P4	Payne
	.P5	Pittsburg
	.P6	Pontotoc
	.P7	Pottawatomie
	.P8	Pushmataha
	.R5	Roger Mills
	.R6	Rogers
	.S2	Seminole
	.S3	Sequoyah
	.S7	Stephens
	.T4	Texas
	.T5	Tillman
	.T8	Tulsa
	.W2	Wagoner
	.W3	Washington
	.W4	Washita
	.W6	Woods
	.W7	Woodward

Texas

4030–4034	Regions, natural features, etc., A–Z		
4032	e. g.	.G3	Galveston Bay
		.P2	Padre Island
		.T42	Texas Panhandle

	Counties, A–Z	
4033	.A2	Anderson
	.A3	Andrews
	.A4	Angelina
	.A5	Aransas
	.A6	Archer
	.A7	Armstrong
	.A8	Atascosa
	.A9	Austin
	.B2	Bailey
	.B25	Bandera
	.B3	Bastrop
	.B35	Baylor
	.B4	Bee
	.B43	Bell
	.B46	Bexar
	.B5	Blanco
	.B6	Borden
	.B63	Bosque
	.B66	Bowie
	.B7	Brazoria
	.B73	Brazos
	.B76	Brewster
	.B8	Briscoe

---

[1] For subdivisions, see tables, pp. 206–223

By region or country
America. Western Hemisphere
North America
United States
Southern States
South Central States
West South Central States. Old Southwest
Texas
4033   Counties, A-Z - Continued
.B83 Brooks
.B86 Brown
.B9   Burleson
.B95 Burnet
.C2   Caldwell
.C22 Calhoun
.C23 Callahan
.C25 Cameron
.C27 Camp
.C3   Carson
.C33 Cass
.C36 Castro
.C4   Chambers
.C43 Cherokee
.C45 Childress
.C48 Clay
.C5   Cochran
.C52 Coke
.C54 Coleman
.C55 Collin
.C56 Collingsworth
.C58 Colorado
.C6   Comal
.C63 Comanche
.C66 Concho
.C7   Cooke
.C73 Coryell
.C76 Cottle
.C8   Crane
.C83 Crockett
.C86 Crosby
.C9   Culberson
.D2   Dallam
.D22 Dallas
.D27 Dawson
.D3   Deaf Smith
.D4   Delta
.D45 Denton
.D5   De Witt
.D6   Dickens
.D7   Dimmit
.D8   Donley
.D9   Duval
.E2   Eastland
.E3   Ector
.E4   Edwards
.E5   Ellis
.E6   El Paso

MAPS

By region or country
   America. Western Hemisphere
      North America
         United States
            Southern States
               South Central States
                  West South Central States. Old Southwest
                     Texas
4033   Counties, A-Z - Continued
                        .E7   Erath
                        .F2   Falls
                        .F3   Fannin
                        .F35   Fayette
                        .F4   Fisher
                        .F5   Floyd
                        .F6   Foard
                        .F65   Fort Bend
                        .F7   Franklin
                        .F8   Freestone
                        .F9   Frio
                        .G2   Gaines
                        .G25   Galveston
                        .G3   Garza
                        .G4   Gillespie
                        .G5   Glasscock
                        .G6   Goliad
                        .G65   Gonzales
                        .G7   Gray
                        .G75   Grayson
                        .G8   Gregg
                        .G85   Grimes
                        .G9   Guadalupe
                        .H2   Hale
                        .H22   Hall
                        .H25   Hamilton
                        .H27   Hansford
                        .H3   Hardeman
                        .H32   Hardin
                        .H35   Harris
                        .H36   Harrison
                        .H38   Hartley
                        .H4   Haskell
                        .H45   Hays
                        .H5   Hemphill
                        .H55   Henderson
                        .H6   Hidalgo
                        .H65   Hill
                        .H7   Hockley
                        .H75   Hood
                        .H77   Hopkins
                        .H8   Houston
                        .H85   Howard
                        .H9   Hudspeth
                        .H93   Hunt
                        .H96   Hutchinson
                        .I6   Irion
                        .J2   Jack

G

G

MAPS

By region or country
America. Western Hemisphere
North America
United States
Southern States
South Central States
West South Central States. Old Southwest
Texas
Counties, A-Z - Continued

4033

.J25 Jackson
.J3   Jasper
.J4   Jeff Davis
.J5   Jefferson
.J6   Jim Hogg
.J7   Jim Wells
.J8   Johnson
.J9   Jones
.K2   Karnes
.K25 Kaufman
.K3   Kendall
.K35 Kenedy
.K4   Kent
.K45 Kerr
.K5   Kimble
.K6   King
.K7   Kinney
.K8   Kleberg
.K9   Knox
.L2   Lamar
.L25 Lamb
.L3   Lampasas
.L35 La Salle
.L4   Lavaca
.L45 Lee
.L5   Leon
.L55 Liberty
.L6   Limestone
.L65 Lipscomb
.L7   Live Oak
.L75 Llano
.L8   Loving
.L85 Lubbock
.L9   Lynn
.M2   McCulloch
.M23 McLennan
.M25 McMullen
.M27 Madison
.M3   Marion
.M32 Martin
.M34 Mason
.M36 Matagorda
.M38 Maverick
.M4   Medina
.M45 Menard
.M5   Midland
.M55 Milam
.M6   Mills

By region or country
  America. Western Hemisphere
    North America
      United States
        Southern States
          South Central States
            West South Central States. Old Southwest
              Texas
4033   Counties, A-Z - Continued
                .M65 Mitchell
                .M7   Montague
                .M75 Montgomery
                .M8   Moore
                .M85 Morris
                .M9   Motley
                .N2   Nacogdoches
                .N3   Navarro
                .N4   Newton
                .N6   Nolan
                .N8   Nueces
                .O2   Ochiltree
                .O4   Oldham
                .O6   Orange
                .P2   Palo Pinto
                .P3   Panola
                .P4   Parker
                .P5   Parmer
                .P6   Pecos
                .P7   Polk
                .P8   Potter
                .P9   Presidio
                .R2   Rains
                .R25 Randall
                .R3   Reagan
                .R33 Real
                .R36 Red River
                .R4   Reeves
                .R45 Refugio
                .R5   Roberts
                .R6   Robertson
                .R7   Rockwell
                .R8   Runnels
                .R9   Rusk
                .S2   Sabine
                .S22 San Augustine
                .S24 San Jacinto
                .S26 San Patricio
                .S28 San Saba
                .S3   Schleicher
                .S35 Scurry
                .S4   Shackelford
                .S43 Shelby
                .S46 Sherman
                .S5   Smith
                .S6   Somervell
                .S7   Starr

MAPS

<u>By region or country</u>[1]
  <u>America. Western Hemisphere</u>
    <u>North America</u>
      <u>United States</u>
        <u>Southern States</u>
          <u>South Central States</u>
            <u>West South Central States. Old Southwest</u>
              <u>Texas</u>

4033
                Counties, A–Z – Continued

.S75	Stephens
.S8	Sterling
.S85	Stonewall
.S9	Sutton
.S95	Swisher
.T2	Tarrant
.T3	Taylor
.T4	Terrell
.T45	Terry
.T5	Throckmorton
.T55	Titus
.T6	Tom Green
.T7	Travis
.T8	Trinity
.T9	Tyler
.U5	Upshur
.U6	Upton
.U8	Uvalde
.V2	Val Verde
.V3	Van Zandt
.V5	Victoria
.W2	Walker
.W25	Waller
.W3	Ward
.W35	Washington
.W4	Webb
.W5	Wharton
.W55	Wheeler
.W6	Wichita
.W63	Wilbarger
.W65	Willacy
.W67	Williamson
.W7	Wilson
.W75	Winkler
.W8	Wise
.W9	Wood
.Y6	Yoakum
.Y7	Young
.Z2	Zapata
.Z3	Zavala

4040–4042   <u>Central States</u> (Map, p. 44)
4042   Regions, natural features, etc., A–Z
                 e. g. .M5 Mississippi River

---

[1]
  For subdivisions, <u>see</u> tables, pp. 206–223

MAPS

By region or country[1]
America. Western Hemisphere
North America
United States - Continued

4050-4052	The West (Map, p. 42)
	Comprising area west of the Mississippi River
	Cf. G4210+, Pacific and Mountain States
4052	Regions, natural features, etc., A-Z
	e. g. .A7 Arkansas River
	.G75 Great Plains
	.M5 Missouri River
4060-4062	North Central States (Map, p. 45)
4070-4072	East North Central States. Old Northwest (Map, p. 46)
4072	Regions, natural features, etc., A-Z
	e. g. .W3 Wabash River
4080-4084	Ohio
4082	Regions, natural features, etc., A-Z
	e. g. .C8 Cuyahoga River
	.M8 Muskingum River
4083	Counties, A-Z

.A2   Adams
.A5   Allen
.A6   Ashland
.A7   Ashtabula
.A8   Athens
.A9   Auglaize
.B4   Belmont
.B7   Brown
.B8   Butler
.C2   Carroll
.C3   Champaign
.C4   Clark
.C45   Clermont
.C5   Clinton
.C6   Columbiana
.C7   Coshocton
.C8   Crawford
.C9   Cuyahoga
.D2   Darke
.D4   Defiance
.D5   Delaware
.E7   Erie
.F2   Fairfield
.F3   Fayette
.F7   Franklin
.F8   Fulton
.G3   Gallia
.G4   Geauga
.G7   Greene
.G8   Guernsey
.H2   Hamilton
.H25   Hancock
.H3   Hardin

---

[1] For subdivisions, see tables, pp. 206-223

By region or country
    America. Western Hemisphere
        North America
            United States
                .North Central States
                    East North Central States. Old Northwest
                        Ohio
4083   Counties, A-Z - Continued
                            .H4   Harrison
                            .H5   Henry
                            .H6   Highland
                            .H7   Hocking
                            .H8   Holmes
                            .H9   Huron
                            .J2   Jackson
                            .J4   Jefferson
                            .K6   Knox
                            .L2   Lake
                            .L3   Lawrence
                            .L5   Licking
                            .L6   Logan
                            .L7   Lorain
                            .L8   Lucas
                            .M2   Madison
                            .M25   Mahoning
                            .M3   Marion
                            .M4   Medina
                            .M43   Meigs
                            .M46   Mercer
                            .M5   Miami
                            .M6   Monroe
                            .M65   Montgomery
                            .M7   Morgan
                            .M8   Morrow
                            .M9   Muskingum
                            .N6   Noble
                            .O7   Ottawa
                            .P3   Paulding
                            .P4   Perry
                            .P5   Pickaway
                            .P6   Pike
                            .P7   Portage
                            .P8   Preble
                            .P9   Putnam
                            .R5   Richland
                            .R6   Ross
                            .S2   Sandusky
                            .S3   Scioto
                            .S4   Seneca
                            .S5   Shelby
                            .S7   Stark
                            .S8   Summit
                            .T7   Trumbull
                            .T8   Tuscarawas
                            .U5   Union
                            .V3   Van Wert
                            .V5   Vinton

G   G

MAPS

By region or country [1]
America. Western Hemisphere
North America
United States
North Central States
East North Central States. Old Northwest
Ohio

4083	Counties, A–Z – Continued	
	.W2	Warren
	.W3	Washington
	.W4	Wayne
	.W5	Williams
	.W6	Wood
	.W9	Wyandot
4090–4094	Indiana	
4092	Regions, natural features, etc., A–Z	
	e. g. .W5 White River	
4093	Counties, A–Z	
	.A2	Adams
	.A4	Allen
	.B3	Bartholomew
	.B4	Benton
	.B5	Blackford
	.B6	Boone
	.B7	Brown
	.C2	Carroll
	.C3	Cass
	.C4	Clark
	.C5	Clay
	.C6	Clinton
	.C7	Crawford
	.D2	Daviess
	.D3	Dearborn
	.D4	Decatur
	.D5	De Kalb
	.D6	Delaware
	.D8	Dubois
	.E4	Elkhart
	.F3	Fayette
	.F5	Floyd
	.F6	Fountain
	.F7	Franklin
	.F8	Fulton
	.G5	Gibson
	.G6	Grant
	.G7	Greene
	.H2	Hamilton
	.H3	Hancock
	.H4	Harrison
	.H5	Hendricks
	.H6	Henry
	.H7	Howard
	.H8	Huntington
	.J2	Jackson
	.J3	Jasper

[1] For subdivisions, see tables, pp. 206–223

MAPS

<u>By region or country</u>
<u>America. Western Hemisphere</u>
<u>North America</u>
<u>United States</u>
<u>North Central States</u>
<u>East North Central States. Old Northwest</u>
<u>Indiana</u>
4093   Counties, A-Z - Continued
.J4   Jay
.J5   Jefferson
.J6   Jennings
.J7   Johnson
.K5   Knox
.K6   Kosciusko
.L2   Lagrange
.L3   Lake
.L4   La Porte
.L5   Lawrence
.M2   Madison
.M3   Marion
.M4   Marshall
.M5   Martin
.M6   Miami
.M7   Monroe
.M8   Montgomery
.M9   Morgan
.N4   Newton
.N6   Noble
.O3   Ohio
.O6   Orange
.O8   Owen
.P2   Parke
.P3   Perry
.P4   Pike
.P5   Porter
.P6   Posey
.P7   Pulaski
.P8   Putnam
.R3   Randolph
.R5   Ripley
.R8   Rush
.S2   St. Joseph
.S3   Scott
.S4   Shelby
.S5   Spencer
.S6   Starke
.S7   Steuben
.S8   Sullivan
.S9   Switzerland
.T4   Tippecanoe
.T5   Tipton
.U5   Union
.V3   Vanderburgh
.V4   Vermillion
.V5   Vigo
.W2   Wabash
.W3   Warren

<u>By region or country</u>[1]
<u>America. Western Hemisphere</u>
<u>North America</u>
<u>United States</u>
<u>North Central States</u>
<u>East North Central States. Old Northwest</u>
<u>Indiana</u>

4093		Counties, A-Z - Continued
	.W4	Warrick
	.W5	Washington
	.W6	Wayne
	.W7	Wells
	.W8	White
	.W9	Whitley
4100-4104		<u>Illinois</u>
4102		Regions, natural features, etc., A-Z
	e. g. .C5	Chain O'Lakes region
	.F66	Fox River
4103		Counties, A-Z
	.A2	Adams
	.A5	Alexander
	.B5	Bond
	.B6	Boone
	.B7	Brown
	.B8	Bureau
	.C2	Calhoun
	.C25	Carroll
	.C3	Cass
	.C4	Champaign
	.C45	Christian
	.C5	Clark
	.C55	Clay
	.C6	Clinton
	.C65	Coles
	.C7	Cook
	.C8	Crawford
	.C9	Cumberland
	.D4	De Kalb
	.D5	De Witt
	.D6	Douglas
	.D8	Du Page
	.E2	Edgar
	.E3	Edwards
	.E4	Effingham
	.F3	Fayette
	.F6	Ford
	.F7	Franklin
	.F8	Fulton
	.G3	Gallatin
	.G7	Greene
	.G8	Grundy
	.H2	Hamilton
	.H3	Hancock
	.H4	Hardin
	.H5	Henderson
	.H6	Henry

---

[1]
For subdivisions, <u>see</u> tables, pp. 206-223

By region or country
America. Western Hemisphere
North America
United States
North Central States
East North Central States. Old Northwest
Illinois

4103   Counties, A-Z - Continued

.I6	Iroquois
.J2	Jackson
.J3	Jasper
.J4	Jefferson
.J5	Jersey
.J6	Jo Daviess
.J7	Johnson
.K2	Kane
.K3	Kankakee
.K4	Kendall
.K6	Knox
.L2	Lake
.L3	La Salle
.L4	Lawrence
.L5	Lee
.L6	Livingston
.L7	Logan
.M2	McDonough
.M23	McHenry
.M26	McLean
.M3	Macon
.M35	Macoupin
.M4	Madison
.M43	Marion
.M46	Marshall
.M5	Mason
.M55	Massac
.M6	Menard
.M65	Mercer
.M7	Monroe
.M75	Montgomery
.M8	Morgan
.M9	Moultrie
.O3	Ogle
.P3	Peoria
.P4	Perry
.P5	Piatt
.P6	Pike
.P7	Pope
.P8	Pulaski
.P9	Putnam
.R3	Randolph
.R5	Richland
.R6	Rock Island
.S2	St. Clair
.S3	Saline
.S4	Sangamon
.S5	Schuyler

.MAPS

By region or country[1]
America. Western Hemisphere
North America
United States
North Central States
East North Central States. Old Northwest
Illinois

4103	Counties, A-Z - Continued	
	.S6	Scott
	.S7	Shelby
	.S8	Stark
	.S9	Stephenson
	.T3	Tazewell
	.U5	Union
	.V4	Vermillion
	.W2	Wabash
	.W3	Warren
	.W35	Washington
	.W4	Wayne
	.W5	White
	.W55	Whiteside
	.W6	Will
	.W7	Williamson
	.W8	Winnebago
	.W9	Woodford

Michigan

4110-4114	Michigan		
4112	Regions, natural features, etc., A-Z		
	e. g.	.B4	Beaver Islands
		.I8	Isle Royale
		.M2	MacKinac Island
		.S2	Saginaw Bay
		.U6	Upper Peninsula
4113	Counties, A-Z		
	.A3	Alcona	
	.A4	Alger	
	.A5	Allegan	
	.A6	Alpena	
	.A7	Antrim	
	.A8	Arenac	
	.B2	Baraga	
	.B3	Barry	
	.B4	Bay	
	.B5	Benzie	
	.B6	Berrien	
	.B7	Branch	
	.C2	Calhoun	
	.C3	Cass	
	.C4	Charlevoix	
	.C5	Cheboygan	
	.C6	Chippewa	
	.C7	Clare	
	.C8	Clinton	
	.C9	Crawford	
	.D4	Delta	
	.D5	Dickinson	

---

[1] For subdivisions, see tables, pp. 206-223

88

G

MAPS

By region or country

America. Western Hemisphere

North America

United States

North Central States

East North Central States. Old Northwest

Michigan

4113   Counties, A-Z - Continued
.E2 Eaton
.E4 Emmet
.G4 Genesee
.G5 Gladwin
.G6 Gogebic
.G7 Grand Traverse
.G8 Gratiot
.H5 Hillsdale
.H6 Houghton
.H8 Huron
.I4 Ingham
.I5 Ionia
.I6 Iosco
.I7 Iron
.I8 Isabella
.J2 Jackson
.K2 Kalamazoo
.K3 Kalkaska
.K4 Kent
.K5 Kewcenaw
.L2 Lake
.L3 Lapeer
.L4 Leelanau
.L5 Lenawee
.L6 Livingston
.L8 Luce
.M2 Mackinac
.M25 Macomb
.M3 Manistee
.M33 Marquette
.M36 Mason
.M4 Mecosta
.M45 Menominee
.M5 Midland
.M55 Missaukee
.M6 Monroe
.M7 Montcalm
.M8 Montmorency
.M9 Muskegon
.N4 Newaygo·
.O2 Oakland
.O3 Oceana
.O4 Ogemaw
.O5 Ontonagon
.O6 Osceola
.O7 Oscoda
.O8 Otsego
.O9 Ottawa

MAPS

<u>By region or country</u>[1]
   <u>America. Western Hemisphere</u>
     <u>North America</u>
       <u>United States</u>
         <u>North Central States</u>
           <u>East North Central States. Old Northwest</u>
             <u>Michigan</u>

4113		Counties, A-Z - Continued
	.P7	Presque Isle
	.R6	Roscommon
	.S2	Saginaw
	.S3	St. Clair
	.S4	St. Joseph
	.S5	Sanilac
	.S6	Schoolcraft
	.S7	Shiawassee
	.T8	Tuscola
	.V3	Van Buren
	.W2	Washtenaw
	.W3	Wayne
	.W4	Wexford
4114		Cities and towns, A-Z

       e. g. .E4 East Lansing
               .E4:2M4 Michigan State
                           University

4120-4124		<u>Wisconsin</u>
4122		Regions, natural features, etc., A-Z

       e. g. .A65 Apostle Islands
              .C3   Castle Rock flowage
              .G7   Green Bay
              .W6   Wolf River

4123		Counties, A-Z
	.A2	Adams
	.A8	Ashland
	.B3	Barron
	.B4	Bayfield
	.B7	Brown
	.B8	Buffalo
	.B9	Burnett
	.C3	Calumet
	.C4	Chippewa
	.C5	Clark
	.C6	Columbia
	.C7	Crawford
	.D3	Dane
	.D5	Dodge
	.D6	Door
	.D7	Douglas
	.D8	Dunn
	.E2	Eau Claire
	.F5	Florence
	.F6	Fond du Lac
	.F7	Forest
	.G6	Grant
	.G7	Green

---

[1]
  For subdivisions, <u>see</u> tables, pp. 206-223

By region or country
America. Western Hemisphere
North America
United States
North Central States
East North Central States. Old Northwest
Wisconsin

4123   Counties, A-Z - Continued
.G8   Green Lake
.I5   Iowa
.I6   Iron
.J2   Jackson
.J4   Jefferson
.J8   Juneau
.K4   Kenosha
.K5   Kewaunee
.L2   La Crosse
.L3   Lafayette
.L4   Langlade
.L5   Lincoln
.M2   Manitowoc
.M3   Marathon
.M4   Marinette
.M5   Marquette
.M54   Menominee
.M6   Milwaukee
.M7   Monroe
.O2   Oconto
.O5   Oneida
.O8   Outagamie
.O9   Ozaukee
.P4   Pepin
.P5   Pierce
.P6   Polk
.P7   Portage
.P8   Price
.R2   Racine
.R5   Richland
.R6   Rock
.R8   Rusk
.S2   St. Croix
.S3   Sauk
.S4   Sawyer
.S5   Shawano
.S6   Sheboygan
.T3   Taylor
.T7   Trempealeau
.V4   Vernon
.V5   Vilas
.W2   Walworth
.W3   Washburn
.W4   Washington
.W5   Waukesha
.W6   Waupaca
.W7   Waushara
.W8   Winnebago
.W9   Wood

By region or country[1]
America. Western Hemisphere
North America
United States - Continued

4125-4127	Northwestern States (Map, p. 43)
	The area between the Great Lakes and the Pacific Ocean
4127	Regions, natural features, etc., A-Z
	e. g. .O7 Oregon Trail
	.W5 Williston Basin
4130-4132	West North Central States (Map, p. 46)
	The area between the Great Lakes and the Rocky Mountains
4140-4144	Minnesota
4142	Regions, natural features, etc., A-Z
	e. g. .C92 Crow Wing River
	.M66 Lake Minnetonka
	.M67 Minnesota River
	.W4 White Earth State Forest
4143	Counties, A-Z
	.A3 Aitkin
	.A5 Anoka
	.B2 Becker
	.B3 Beltrami
	.B4 Benton
	.B5 Big Stone
	.B6 Blue Earth
	.B7 Brown
	.C2 Carlton
	.C25 Carver
	.C3 Cass
	.C4 Chippewa
	.C45 Chisago
	.C5 Clay
	.C55 Clearwater
	.C6 Cook
	.C7 Cottonwood
	.C8 Crow Wing
	.D3 Dakota
	.D5 Dodge
	.D6 Douglas
	.F3 Faribault
	.F5 Fillmore
	.F7 Freeborn
	.G6 Goodhue
	.G7 Grant
	.H4 Hennepin
	.H6 Houston
	.H8 Hubbard
	.I7 Isanti
	.I8 Itasca
	.J2 Jackson
	.K3 Kanabec
	.K4 Kandiyohi
	.K5 Kittson
	.K6 Koochiching

---
[1]

For subdivisions, see tables, pp. 206-223

MAPS

By region or country
  America. Western Hemisphere
    North America
      United States
        Northwestern States
          West North Central States
            Minnesota
              Counties, A-Z - Continued

4143

                .L2   Lac qui Parle
                .L3   Lake
                .L4   Lake of the Woods
                .L5   Le Sueur
                .L6   Lincoln
                .L9   Lyon
                .M2   McLeod
                .M3   Mahnomen
                .M35   Marshall
                .M4   Martin
                .M45   Meeker
                .M5   Mille Lacs
                .M6   Morrison
                .M7   Mower
                .M8   Murray
                .N5   Nicollet
                .N6   Nobles
                .N7   Norman
                .O4   Olmsted
                .O6   Otter Tail
                .P3   Pennington
                .P4   Pine
                .P5   Pipestone
                .P6   Polk
                .P7   Pope
                .R2   Ramsey
                .R3   Red Lake
                .R4   Redwood
                .R5   Renville
                .R6   Rice
                .R7   Rock
                .R8   Roseau
                .S2   St. Louis
                .S3   Scott
                .S4   Sherburne
                .S5   Sibley
                .S6   Stearns
                .S7   Steele
                .S8   Stevens
                .S9   Swift
                .T6   Todd
                .T7   Traverse
                .W2   Wabasha
                .W3   Wadena
                .W4   Waseca
                .W5   Washington
                .W6   Watonwan
                .W7   Wilkin
                .W8   Winona
                .W9   Wright
                .Y4   Yellow Medicine

MAPS

<u>By region or country</u>[1]
  <u>America. Western Hemisphere</u>
    <u>North America</u>
      <u>United States</u>
        <u>Northwestern States</u>
          <u>West North Central States</u> - Continued

4150-4154	Iowa
4152	Regions, natural features, etc., A-Z
	e. g. .B5 Black Hawk Creek
	.E36 East Okoboji Lake
	.W45 West Okoboji Lake
4153	Counties, A-Z

     .A2   Adair
     .A3   Adams
     .A5   Allamakee
     .A6   Appanoose
     .A8   Audubon
     .B3   Benton
     .B4   Black Hawk
     .B5   Boone
     .B6   Bremer
     .B7   Buchanan
     .B8   Buena Vista
     .B9   Butler
     .C2   Calhoun
     .C3   Carroll
     .C35 Cass
     .C4   Cedar
     .C45 Cerro Gordo
     .C5   Cherokee
     .C55 Chickasaw
     .C6   Clarke
     .C65 Clay
     .C7   Clayton
     .08   Clinton
     .C9   Crawford
     .D2   Dallas
     .D3   Davis
     .D4   Decatur
     .D5   Delaware
     .D6   Des Moines
     .D7   Dickinson
     .D8   Dubuque
     .E5   Emmet
     .F2   Fayette
     .F5   Floyd
     .F7   Franklin
     .F8   Fremont
     .G7   Greene
     .G8   Grundy
     .G9   Guthrie
     .H2   Hamilton
     .H3   Hancock
     .H4   Hardin
     .H5   Harrison
     .H6   Henry
     .H7   Howard

---

[1] For subdivisions, <u>see</u> tables, pp. 206-223

MAPS

By region or country
America. Western Hemisphere
North America
United States
Northwestern States
West North Central States
Iowa

4153

Counties, A–Z – Continued

.H8	Humboldt
.I2	Ida
.I6	Iowa
.J2	Jackson
.J3	Jasper
.J4	Jefferson
.J5	Johnson
.J6	Jones
.K4	Keokuk
.K6	Kossuth
.L4	Lee
.L5	Linn
.L6	Louisa
.L8	Lucas
.L9	Lyon
.M2	Madison
.M25	Mahaska
.M3	Marion
.M35	Marshall
.M4	Mills
.M5	Mitchell
.M6	Monona
.M7	Monroe
.M8	Montgomery
.M9	Muscatine
.O2	O'Brien
.O7	Osceola
.P2	Page
.P3	Palo Alto
.P4	Plymouth
.P5	Pocahontas
.P6	Polk
.P7	Pottawattamie
.P8	Poweshiek
.R5	Ringgold
.S2	Sac
.S3	Scott
.S5	Shelby
.S6	Sioux
.S8	Story
.T2	Tama
.T3	Taylor
.U5	Union
.V3	Van Buren
.W2	Wapello
.W25	Warren
.W3	Washington
.W35	Wayne
.W4	Webster
.W5	Winnebago
.W6	Winneshiek
.W7	Woodbury
.W8	Worth
.W9	Wright

MAPS

<u>By region or country</u>[1]
  <u>America. Western Hemisphere</u>
    <u>North America</u>
      <u>United States</u>
        <u>Northwestern States</u>
          <u>West North Central States</u> - Continued

4160-4164	<u>Missouri</u>
4162	Regions, natural features, etc., A-Z

            e. g. .L35 Lake of the Ozarks
                    .M3   Mark Twain National
                                Forest
                    .T15 Table Rock Lake

4163   Counties, A-Z

.A2	Adair
.A5	Andrew
.A7	Atchison
.A8	Audrain
.B2	Barry
.B3	Barton
.B4	Bates
.B5	Benton
.B6	Bollinger
.B7	Boone
.B8	Buchanan
.B9	Butler
.C2	Caldwell
.C23	Callaway
.C26	Camden
.C3	Cape Girardeau
.C33	Carroll
.C36	Carter
.C4	Cass
.C45	Cedar
.C5	Chariton
.C55	Christian
.C6	Clark
.C63	Clay
.C7	Clinton
.C75	Cole
.C8	Cooper
.C9	Crawford
.D2	Dade
.D3	Dallas
.D4	Daviess
.D5	De Kalb
.D6	Dent
.D7	Douglas
.D8	Dunklin
.F7	Franklin
.G3	Gasconade
.G4	Gentry
.G7	Greene
.G8	Grundy
.H3	Harrison
.H4	Henry
.H5	Hickory
.H6	Holt

---

[1]
  For subdivisions, <u>see</u> tables, pp. 206-223

By region or country
America. Western Hemisphere
North America
United States
Northwestern States
West North Central States
Missouri

4163

Counties, A-Z - Continued

.H7	Howard
.H8	Howell
.I6	Iron
.J2	Jackson
.J3	Jasper
.J4	Jefferson
.J6	Johnson
.K6	Knox
.L2	Laclede
.L3	Lafayette
.L4	Lawrence
.L5	Lewis
.L6	Lincoln
.L7	Linn
.L8	Livingston
.M2	McDonald
.M23	Macon
.M26	Madison
.M3	Maries
.M35	Marion
.M4	Mercer
.M5	Miller
.M55	Mississippi
.M6	Moniteau
.M7	Monroe
.M8	Montgomery
.M9	Morgan
.N4	New Madrid
.N5	Newton
.N6	Nodaway
.O6	Oregon
.O7	Osage
.O8	Ozark
.P3	Pemiscot
.P4	Perry
.P45	Pettis
.P5	Phelps
.P55	Pike
.P6	Platte
.P65	Polk
.P7	Pulaski
.P8	Putnam
.R2	Ralls
.R3	Randolph
.R4	Ray
.R5	Reynolds
.R6	Ripley
.S2	St. Charles
.S25	St. Clair
.S3	St. Francois
.S35	St. Louis
.S4	Ste. Genevieve
.S5	Saline

MAPS

By region or country[1]
America. Western Hemisphere
North America
United States
Northwestern States
West North Central States
Missouri

4163	Counties, A-Z - Continued	
	.S55	Schuyler
	.S6	Scotland
	.S65	Scott
	.S7	Shannon
	.S75	Shelby
	.S8	Stoddard
	.S85	Stone
	.S9	Sullivan
	.T3	Taney
	.T4	Texas
	.V4	Vernon
	.W2	Warren
	.W3	Washington
	.W4	Wayne
	.W5	Webster
	.W6	Worth
	.W7	Wright

4170-4174   North Dakota
4172   Regions, natural features, etc., A-Z
                 e. g. .S5 Sheyenne National Grass-
                                 land
                     .T8 Turtle Mountains

4173	Counties, A-Z	
	.A2	Adams
	.B3	Barnes
	.B4	Benson
	.B5	Billings
	.B6	Bottineau
	.B7	Bowman
	.B8	Burke
	.B9	Burleigh
	.C3	Cass
	.C4	Cavalier
	.D5	Dickey
	.D6	Divide
	.D8	Dunn
	.E2	Eddy
	.E5	Emmons
	.F6	Foster
	.G5	Golden Valley
	.G6	Grand Forks
	.G7	Grant
	.G8	Griggs
	.H4	Hettinger
	.K5	Kidder
	.L3	La Moure
	.L6	Logan

----

[1] For subdivisions, see tables, pp. 206-223

MAPS

By region or country[1]
America. Western Hemisphere
North America
United States
Northwestern States
West North Central States
North Dakota

4173	Counties, A-Z - Continued
	.M2 McHenry
	.M3 McIntosh
	.M4 McKenzie
	.M5 McLean
	.M6 Mercer
	.M7 Morton
	.M8 Mountrail
	.N4 Nelson
	.O4 Oliver
	.P4 Pembina
	.P5 Pierce
	.R2 Ramsey
	.R3 Ransom
	.R4 Renville
	.R5 Richland
	.R6 Rolette
	.S2 Sargent
	.S3 Sheridan
	.S4 Sioux
	.S5 Slope
	.S6 Stark
	.S7 Steele
	.S8 Stutsman
	.T6 Towner
	.T7 Traill
	.W2 Walsh
	.W3 Ward
	.W4 Wells
	.W5 Williams

4180-4184	South Dakota
4182	Regions, natural features, etc., A-Z
	e. g. .B3 Bad Lands
	.B32 Badlands National Monument
	.B5 Black Hills
	.P5 Pineridge Indian Reservation

4183	Counties, A-Z
	.A6 Armstrong
	.A8 Aurora
	.B2 Beadle
	.B3 Bennett
	.B4 Bon Homme
	.B5 Brookings
	.B6 Brown
	.B7 Brule
	.B8 Buffalo
	.B9 Butte

---

[1] For subdivisions, see tables, pp. 206-223

MAPS

<u>By region or country</u>
<u>America. Western Hemisphere</u>
<u>North America</u>
<u>United States</u>
<u>Northwestern States</u>
<u>West North Central States</u>
<u>South Dakota</u>

4183   Counties, A-Z - Continued

.C2	Campbell
.C3	Charles Mix
.C4	Clark
.C5	Clay
.C6	Codington
.C7	Corson
.C8	Custer
.D2	Davison
.D3	Day
.D4	Deuel
.D5	Dewey
.D6	Douglas
.E2	Edmunds
.F3	Fall River
.F4	Faulk
.G6	Grant
.G7	Gregory
.H2	Haakon
.H3	Hamlin
.H4	Hand
.H5	Hanson
.H6	Harding
.H7	Hughes
.H8	Hutchinson
.H9	Hyde
.J2	Jackson
.J4	Jerauld
.J6	Jones
.K5	Kingsbury
.L2	Lake
.L3	Lawrence
.L5	Lincoln
.L9	Lyman
.M2	McCook
.M3	McPherson
.M4	Marshall
.M5	Meade
.M6	Mellette
.M7	Miner
.M8	Minnehaha
.M9	Moody
.P3	Pennington
.P4	Perkins
.P6	Potter
.R6	Roberts
.S2	Sanborn
.S5	Shannon
.S7	Spink
.S8	Stanley
.S9	Sully
.T6	Todd
.T7	Tripp
.T8	Turner

MAPS

By region or country[1]
  America. Western Hemisphere
    North America
      United States
        Northwestern States
          West North Central States
            South Dakota

4183	Counties, A-Z - Continued
	.U5 Union
	.W2 Walworth
	.W3 Washabaugh
	.W4 Washington
	.Y3 Yankton
	.Z5 Ziebach
4190-4194	Nebraska
4192	Regions, natural features, etc., A-Z
	e. g. .E45 Elkhorn River
4193	Counties, A-Z
	.A2 Adams
	.A5 Antelope
	.A6 Arthur
	.B3 Banner
	.B4 Blaine
	.B5 Boone
	.B6 Box Butte
	.B65 Boyd
	.B7 Brown
	.B8 Buffalo
	.B85 Burt
	.B9 Butler
	.C2 Cass
	.C3 Cedar
	.C4 Chase
	.C45 Cherry
	.C5 Cheyenne
	.C6 Clay
	.C7 Colfax
	.C8 Cuming
	.C9 Custer
	.D2 Dakota
	.D3 Dawes
	.D4 Dawson
	.D5 Deuel
	.D6 Dixon
	.D7 Dodge
	.D8 Douglas
	.D9 Dundy
	.F4 Fillmore
	.F6 Franklin
	.F7 Frontier
	.F8 Furnas
	.G2 Gage
	.G3 Garden
	.G4 Garfield
	.G6 Gosper
	.G7 Grant

---

[1]
For subdivisions, see tables, pp. 206-223

MAPS

By region or country
America. Western Hemisphere
North America
United States
Northwestern States
West North Central States
Nebraska

4193   Counties, A-Z - Continued
.G8   Greeley
.H2   Hall
.H3   Hamilton
.H4   Harlan
.H5   Hayes
.H6   Hitchcock
.H7   Holt
.H8   Hooker
.H9   Howard
.J4   Jefferson
.J6   Johnson
.K3   Kearney
.K4   Keith
.K5   Keya Paha
.K6   Kimball
.K7   Knox
.L3   Lancaster
.L4   Lincoln
.L5   Logan
.L6   Loup
.M2   McPherson
.M3   Madison
.M4   Merrick
.M6   Morrill
.N3   Nance
.N4   Nemaha
.N8   Nuckolls
.O7   Otoe
.P3   Pawnee
.P4   Perkins
.P5   Phelps
.P6   Pierce
.P7   Platte
.P8   Polk
.R4   Red Willow
.R5   Richardson
.R6   Rock
.S2   Saline
.S3   Sarpy
.S35   Saunders
.S4   Scotts Bluf
.S5   Seward
.S6   Sheridan
.S7   Sherman
.S8   Sioux
.S9   Stanton
.T4   Thayer
.T5   Thomas
.T6   Thurston
.V3   Valley
.W2   Washington
.W3   Wayne
.W4   Webster

MAPS

<u>By region or country</u>[1]
<u>America. Western Hemisphere</u>
<u>North America</u>
<u>United States</u>
<u>Northwestern States</u>
<u>West North Central States</u>
<u>Nebraska</u>

4193	Counties, A-Z - Continued
	.W5 Wheeler
	.Y6 York
4200-4204	<u>Kansas</u>
4202	Regions, natural features, etc., A-Z
	e. g. .C55 Cimarron National Grass-land
	.K3 Kansas River
4203	Counties, A-Z

                .A4   Allen
                .A5   Anderson
                .A6   Atchison
                .B2   Barber
                .B3   Barton
                .B6   Bourbon
                .B7   Brown
                .B8   Butler
                .C2   Chase
                .C3   Chautauqua
                .C4   Cherokee
                .C45   Cheyenne
                .C5   Clark
                .C6   Clay
                .C65   Cloud
                .C7   Coffey
                .C75   Comanche
                .C8   Cowley
                .C9   Crawford
                .D4   Decatur
                .D5   Dickinson
                .D6   Doniphan
                .D7   Douglas
                .E2   Edwards
                .E3   Elk
                .E4   Ellis
                .E5   Ellsworth
                .F4   Finney
                .F6   Ford
                .F7   Franklin
                .G2   Geary
                .G3   Gove
                .G4   Graham
                .G5   Grant
                .G6   Gray
                .G7   Greeley
                .G8   Greenwood
                .H2   Hamilton
                .H3   Harper
                .H4   Harvey

---

[1] For subdivisions, <u>see</u> tables, pp. 206-223

MAPS

By region or country
America.   Western Hemisphere
North America
United States
Northwestern States
West North Central States
Kansas
4203   Counties, A-Z - Continued
.H5   Haskell
.H6   Hodgeman
.J2   Jackson
.J4   Jefferson
.J5   Jewell
.J6   Johnson
.K3   Kearny
.K4   Kingman
.K5   Kiowa
.L2   Labette
.L3   Lane
.L4   Leavenworth
.L5   Lincoln
.L6   Linn
.L7   Logan
.L9   Lyon
.M2   McPherson
.M3   Marion
.M35   Marshall
.M4   Meade
.M5   Miami
.M6   Mitchell
.M7   Montgomery
.M8   Morris
.M9   Morton
.N3   Nemaha
.N4   Neosho
.N5   Ness
.N6   Norton
.O6   Osage
.O7   Osborne
.O8   Ottawa
.P3   Pawnee
.P5   Phillips
.P6   Pottawatomie
.P7   Pratt
.R2   Rawlins
.R3   Reno
.R4   Republic
.R5   Rice
.R6   Riley
.R7   Rooks
.R8   Rush
.R9   Russell
.S2   Saline
.S3   Scott
.S4   Sedgwick
.S45   Seward
.S5   Shawnee
.S55   Sheridan
.S6   Sherman
.S65   Smith
.S7   Stafford

G

By region or country[1]
America. Western Hemisphere
North America
United States
Northwestern States
West North Central States
Kansas

4203		Counties, A-Z - Continued
	.S75	Stanton
	.S8	Stevens
	.S9	Sumner
	.T5	Thomas
	.T7	Trego
	.W2	Wabaunsee
	.W3	Wallace
	.W4	Washington
	.W5	Wichita
	.W6	Wilson
	.W7	Woodson
	.W9	Wyandotte

4210-4214   Pacific and Mountain States. Far West (Map, p. 44)

4220-4222   Rocky Mountain States (Map, p. 46)
4222   Regions, natural features, etc., A-Z
                        e. g. .R6 Rocky Mountain region

4230-4232   Pacific States (Map, p. 46)
                  Alaska, California, Hawaii, Oregon, and Washington
4232   Regions, natural features, etc., A-Z
                        e. g. .C3 Cascade Range
                                   .P3 Pacific Crest Trail

4240-4242   Pacific Northwest (Map, p. 45)
                  The old Oregon country, comprising the present states of Oregon, Washington, and Idaho, parts of Montana and Wyoming, and the province of British Columbia
4242   Regions, natural features, etc., A-Z
                        e. g. .C62 Columbia River
                                   .S6   Snake River

4250-4254   Montana
4252   Regions, natural features, etc., A-Z
                        e. g. .B5 Bitterroot River
                                   .G5 Glacier National Park
                                   .Y3 Yellowstone River

4253		Counties, A-Z
	.B4	Beaverhead
	.B5	Big Horn
	.B6	Blaine
	.B7	Broadwater
	.C2	Carbon
	.C3	Carter
	.C4	Cascade
	.C5	Chouteau
	.C8	Custer
	.D3	Daniels
	.D4	Dawson

---

[1] For subdivisions, see tables, pp. 206-223

G

G

MAPS

By region or country
America. Western Hemisphere
North America
United States
Pacific and Mountain States. "Far West"
Pacific Northwest
Montana
Counties, A-Z - Continued

4253

.D5 Deer Lodge
.F3 Fallon
.F4 Fergus
.F5 Flathead
.G3 Gallatin
.G4 Garfield
.G5 Glacier
.G6 Golden Valley
.G7 Granite
.H4 Hill
.J4 Jefferson
.J8 Judith Basin
.L3 Lake
.L4 Lewis and Clark
.L5 Liberty
.L6 Lincoln
.M2 McCone
.M3 Madison
.M4 Meagher
.M5 Mineral
.M6 Missoula
.M8 Musselshell
.P3 Park
.P4 Petroleum
.P5 Phillips
.P6 Pondera
.P7 Powder River
.P8 Powell
.P9 Prairie
.R3 Ravalli
.R5 Richland
.R6 Roosevelt
.R7 Rosebud
.S3 Sanders
.S4 Sheridan
.S5 Silver Bow
.S7 Stillwater
.S8 Sweet Grass
.T4 Teton
.T6 Toole
.T7 Treasure
.V3 Valley
.W4 Wheatland
.W5 Wibaux
.Y4 Yellowstone

110

MAPS

<u>By region or country</u>[1]
   <u>America. Western Hemisphere</u>
     <u>North America</u>
       <u>United States</u>
         <u>Pacific and Mountain States. "Far West"</u>
           <u>Pacific Northwest</u> - Continued

4260-4264	<u>Wyoming</u>
4262	Regions, natural features, etc., A-Z

               e. g. .B48 Big Horn Mountains
                      .G7   Grand Teton National
                               Park
                      .Y4   Yellowstone National
                                 Park

4263   Counties, A-Z

      .A4 Albany
      .B5 Big Horn
      .C3 Campbell
      .C4 Carbon
      .C6 Converse
      .C7 Crook
      .F7 Fremont
      .G6 Goshen
      .H6 Hot Springs
      .J6 Johnson
      .L3 Laramie
      .L5 Lincoln
      .N3 Natrona
      .N5 Niobrara
      .P3 Park
      .P5 Platte
      .S5 Sheridan
      .S8 Sublette
      .S9 Sweetwater
      .T4 Teton
      .U5 Uinta
      .W3 Washakie
      .W4 Weston

4270-4274	<u>Idaho</u>
4272	Regions, natural features, etc., A-Z

               e. g. .C6   Coeur d'Alene Lake
                      .C7   Craters of the Moon
                                National Monument
                      .S32 Salmon River

4273   Counties, A-Z

      .A3   Ada
      .A4   Adams
      .B2   Bannock
      .B3   Bear Lake
      .B4   Benewah
      .B5   Bingham
      .B55 Blaine
      .B6   Boise
      .B7   Bonner
      .B75 Bonneville
      .B8   Boundary
      .B9   Butte

---

[1]
For subdivisions, <u>see</u> tables, pp. 206-223

By region or country[1]
America. Western Hemisphere
North America
United States
Pacific and Mountain States. "Far West"
Pacific Northwest
Idaho

4273   Counties, A-Z - Continued

- .C2 Camas
- .C3 Canyon
- .C4 Caribou
- .C5 Cassia
- .C6 Clark
- .C7 Clearwater
- .C9 Custer
- .E4 Elmore
- .F6 Franklin
- .F7 Fremont
- .G4 Gem
- .G6 Gooding
- .I2 Idaho
- .J4 Jefferson
- .J5 Jerome
- .K6 Kootenai
- .L2 Latah
- .L3 Lemhi
- .L4 Lewis
- .L5 Lincoln
- .M3 Madison
- .M5 Minidoka
- .N4 Nez Perce
- .O5 Oneida
- .O8 Owyhee
- .P3 Payette
- .P6 Power
- .S5 Shoshone
- .T4 Teton
- .T8 Twin Falls
- .V3 Valley
- .W3 Washington

4280-4284   Washington (State)

4282   Regions, natural features, etc., A-Z

e. g. .F5 Fidalgo Island
- .O4 Olympic Peninsula
- .P8 Puget Sound
- .R2 Mount Rainier

4283   Counties, A-Z

- .A2 Adams
- .A7 Asotin
- .B4 Benton
- .C3 Chelan
- .C4 Clallam
- .C5 Clark
- .C6 Columbia
- .C7 Cowlitz
- .D6 Douglas

---

[1] For subdivisions, see tables, pp. 206-223

MAPS

<u>By region or country</u>[1]
  <u>America. Western Hemisphere</u>
    <u>North America</u>
      <u>United States</u>
        <u>Pacific and Mountain States. "Far West"</u>
          <u>Pacific Northwest</u>
            <u>Washington (State)</u>

4283		Counties, A-Z - Continued
	.F4	Ferry
	.F7	Franklin
	.G3	Garfield
	.G7	Grant
	.G8	Grays Harbor
	.I7	Island
	.J4	Jefferson
	.K3	King
	.K4	Kitsap
	.K5	Kittitas
	.K6	Klickitat
	.L4	Lewis
	.L5	Lincoln
	.M3	Mason
	.O3	Okanogan
	.P2	Pacific
	.P4	Pend Oreille
	.P5	Pierce
	.S2	San Juan
	.S4	Skagit
	.S5	Skamania
	.S6	Snohomish
	.S7	Spokane
	.S8	Stevens
	.T5	Thurston
	.W2	Wahkiakum
	.W3	Walla Walla
	.W5	Whatcom
	.W6	Whitman
	.Y3	Yakima
4290-4294		Oregon
4292		Regions, natural features, etc., A-Z
	e. g. .C6	Coos Bay
	.R7	Rogue River
	.W5	Willamette River
4293		Counties, A-Z
	.B3	Baker
	.B4	Benton
	.C4	Clackamas
	.C5	Clatsop
	.C6	Columbia
	.C7	Coos
	.C8	Crook
	.C9	Curry
	.D4	Deschutes
	.D6	Douglas

---

[1]
  For subdivisions, <u>see</u> tables, pp. 206-223

By region or country[1]
America. Western Hemisphere
North America
United States
Pacific and Mountain States. "Far West"
Pacific Northwest
Oregon
4293   Counties, A-Z - Continued
.G5 Gilliam
.G7 Grant
.H3 Harney
.H6 Hood River
.J2 Jackson
.J4 Jefferson
.J6 Josephine
.K5 Klamath
.L3 Lake
.L4 Lane
.L5 Lincoln
.L6 Linn
.M3 Malheur
.M4 Marion
.M6 Morrow
.M8 Multnomah
.P6 Polk
.S5 Sherman
.T5 Tillamook
.U5 Umatilla
.U6 Union
.W2 Wallowa
.W3 Wasco
.W4 Washington
.W5 Wheeler
.Y3 Yamhill
4295-4297   Southwestern States (Map, p. 43)
Including West South Central States and
New Southwest
4297   Regions, natural features, etc., A-Z
e. g. .R5 Rio Grande
4300-4302   New Southwest (Map, p. 45)
Roughly corresponds with the old Spanish
province of New Mexico
4302   Regions, natural features, etc., A-Z
e. g. .C6 Colorado River
4310-4314   Colorado
4312   Regions, natural features, etc., A-Z
e. g. .P5 Pikes Peak
.R6 Rocky Mountain National
Park
4313   Counties, A-Z
.A2 Adams
.A4 Alamosa
.A6 Arapahoe
.A7 Archuleta
.B2 Baca
.B4 Bent
.B6 Boulder
.C2 Chaffee

----

[1]
For subdivisions, see tables, pp. 206-223

MAPS

By region or country
 America. Western Hemisphere
  North America
   United States
    Southwestern States
     New Southwest
      Colorado

4313   Counties, A-Z – Continued

.C3 Cheyenne
.C4 Clear Creek
.C5 Conejos
.C6 Costilla
.C7 Crowley
.C8 Custer
.D3 Delta
    Denver, see G4314.D4
.D5 Dolores
.D6 Douglas
.E2 Eagle
.E4 Elbert
.E5 El Paso
.F7 Fremont
.G3 Garfield
.G5 Gilpin
.G7 Grand
.G8 Gunnison
.H5 Hinsdale
.H8 Huerfano
.J3 Jackson
.J4 Jefferson
.K4 Kiowa
.K5 Kit Carson
.L2 Lake
.L3 La Plata
.L4 Larimer
.L5 Las Animas
.L6 Lincoln
.L7 Logan
.M3 Mesa
.M4 Mineral
.M5 Moffat
.M6 Montezuma
.M7 Montrose
.M8 Morgan
.O7 Otero
.O8 Ouray
.P3 Park
.P4 Phillips
.P5 Pitkin
.P7 Prowers
.P8 Pueblo
.R4 Rio Blanco
.R5 Rio Grande
.R6 Routt

MAPS

By region or country[1]
America. Western Hemisphere
North America
United States
Southwestern States
New Southwest
Colorado

4313	Counties, A-Z - Continued
	.S2 Saguache
	.S3 San Juan
	.S4 San Miguel
	.S5 Sedgwick
	.S8 Summit
	.T4 Teller
	.W3 Washington
	.W4 Weld
	.Y8 Yuma
4314	Cities and towns, A-Z
	e. g. .D4 Denver
4320-4324	New Mexico
4322	Regions, natural features, etc., A-Z
	e. g. .C3 Carlsbad Caverns
	National Park
	.P4 Pecos River
4323	Counties, A-Z
	.B4 Bernalillo
	.C3 Catron
	.C5 Chaves
	.C6 Colfax
	.C8 Curry
	.D4 De Baca
	.D6 Dona Ana
	.E2 Eddy
	.G7 Grant
	.G8 Guadalupe
	.H3 Harding
	.H5 Hidalgo
	.L4 Lea
	.L5 Lincoln
	.L6 Los Alamos
	.L8 Luna
	.M2 McKinley
	.M6 Mora
	.O7 Otero
	.Q3 Quay
	.R5 Rio Arriba
	.R6 Roosevelt
	.S2 San Juan
	.S3 San Miguel
	.S4 Sandoval
	.S5 Santa Fe
	.S6 Sierra
	.S7 Socorro
	.T3 Taos

---

[1] For subdivisions, see tables, pp. 206-223

By region or country[1]
America. Western Hemisphere
North America
United States
Southwestern States
New Southwest
New Mexico

4323		Counties, A-Z - Continued
	.T6	Torrance
	.U5	Union
	.V3	Valencia
4330-4334		Arizona
4332		Regions, natural features, etc., A-Z
	e. g. .G7	Grand Canyon National Park
	.S3	Salt River
	.S9	Superstition Mountains
4333		Counties, A-Z
	.A6	Apache
	.C5	Cochise
	.C6	Coconino
	.G5	Gila
	.G7	Graham
	.G8	Greenlee
	.M3	Maricopa
	.M6	Mohave
	.N3	Navajo
	.P4	Pima
	.P5	Pinal
	.S3	Santa Cruz
	.Y3	Yavapai
	.Y8	Yuma
4340-4344		Utah
4342		Regions, natural features, etc., A-Z
	e. g. .G5	Glen Canyon National Recreation Area
	.G7	Great Salt Lake
	.P6	Lake Powell
4343		Counties, A-Z
	.B4	Beaver
	.B6	Box Elder
	.C2	Cache
	.C3	Carbon
	.D3	Daggett
	.D4	Davis
	.D8	Duchesne
	.E5	Emery
	.G3	Garfield
	.G7	Grand
	.I6	Iron
	.J8	Juab
	.K3	Kane
	.M5	Millard
	.M6	Morgan
	.P5	Piute

---

[1]
For subdivisions, see tables, pp. 206-223

MAPS

By region or country[1]
America. Western Hemisphere
North America
United States
Southwestern States
New Southwest
Utah

4343		Counties, A-Z – Continued
	.R5	Rich
	.S2	Salt Lake
	.S3	San Juan
	.S4	Sanpete
	.S5	Sevier
	.S8	Summit
	.T6	Tooele
	.U3	Uintah
	.U7	Utah
	.W2	Wasatch
	.W3	Washington
	.W4	Wayne
	.W5	Weber

4350-4354 Nevada

4352		Regions, natural features, etc., A-Z
	e. g.	.C3	Carson River
		.H79	Hoover Dam
		.M3	Lake Mead
4353		Counties, A-Z	
	.C5	Churchill	
	.C6	Clark	
	.D6	Douglas	
	.E4	Elko	
	.E7	Esmeralda	
	.E8	Eureka	
	.H8	Humboldt	
	.L3	Lander	
	.L5	Lincoln	
	.M5	Mineral	
	.N9	Nye	
		Ormsby, see G4354.C4	
	.P4	Pershing	
	.S8	Storey	
	.W3	Washoe	
	.W5	White Pine	
4354		Cities and towns, A-Z	
	e. g.	.C4	Carson City

4360-4364 California

4362		Regions, natural features, etc., A-Z
	e. g.	.D4	Death Valley
		.M7	Monterey Bay
		.M78	Monterey Peninsula
		.S22	San Francisco Bay
		.S57	Sierra Nevada Mountains
		.T15	Lake Tahoe
		.Y6	Yosemite National Park

---

[1]
For subdivisions, see tables, pp. 206-223

MAPS

By region or country
America. Western Hemisphere
North America
United States
Southwestern States
New Southwest
California - Continued

4363   Counties, A-Z

.A3	Alameda
.A4	Alpine
.A5	Amador
.B8	Butte
.C3	Calaveras
.C5	Colusa
.C6	Contra Costa
.D4	Del Norte
.E4	El Dorado
.F7	Fresno
.G5	Glenn
.H8	Humboldt
.I5	Imperial
.I6	Inyo
.K4	Kern
.K5	Kings
.L2	Lake
.L3	Lassen
.L6	Los Angeles
.M1	Madera
.M2	Marin
.M3	Mariposa
.M4	Mendocino
.M5	Merced
.M6	Modoc
.M7	Mono
.M8	Monterey
.N3	Napa
.N4	Nevada
.O7	Orange
.P5	Placer
.P6	Plumas
.R5	Riverside
.S2	Sacramento
.S22	San Benito
.S23	San Bernardino
.S24	San Diego
	San Francisco, see G4364.S5
.S26	San Joaquin
.S27	San Luis Obispo
.S28	San Mateo
.S3	Santa Barbara
.S4	Santa Clara
.S5	Santa Cruz
.S6	Shasta
.S63	Sierra
.S66	Siskiyou
.S7	Solano
.S75	Sonoma
.S8	Stanislaus
.S9	Sutter

MAPS

<u>By region or country</u>[1]
<u>America. Western Hemisphere</u>
<u>North America</u>
<u>United States</u>
<u>Southwestern States</u>
<u>New Southwest</u>
<u>California</u>

4363   Counties, A-Z - Continued
 .T4 Tehama
 .T7 Trinity
 .T8 Tulare
 .T9 Tuolumne
 .V4 Ventura
 .Y6 Yolo
 .Y8 Yuba

4364   Cities and towns, A-Z
 e. g. .S5 San Francisco

4370-4374   <u>Alaska</u>
4372   Regions, islands, natural features, etc., A-Z
 e. g. .A4 Aleutian Islands
  .K76 Kodiak Island
  .M3 Matanuska Valley

4373   Boroughs, census divisions, etc., A-Z
 .A4 Aleutian Islands Division
 .A5 Anchorage Division
 .A6 Angoon Division
 .B3 Barrow-North Slope Division
 .B4 Bethel Division
 .B7 Bristol Bay Borough Division. Bristol
  Bay Borough
 .B75 Bristol Bay Division
 .C6 Cordova-McCarthy Division
 .F3 Fairbanks Division
 .F35 Fairbanks North Star Borough
 .G5 Greater Anchorage Area Borough
  Greater Juneau Borough, <u>see</u> .J8
  Great Sitka Borough, <u>see</u> .S5
 .H3 Haines Borough
 .H35 Haines Division
 .J8 Juneau Division
 .K4 Kenai-Cook Inlet Division
 .K45 Kenai Peninsula Borough
 .K5 Ketchikan Division
  Ketchikan Gateway Borough, <u>see</u> .K5
 .K6 Kobuk Division
 .K65 Kodiak Division
 .K68 Kodiak Island Borough
 .K8 Kuskokwim Division
 .M3 Matanuska-Susitna Divisi   Matanuska-Susitna Borough
 .N6 Nome Division
 .N65 North Slope Borough
 .O8 Outer Ketchikan Division
 .P7 Prince of Wales Division
 .S4 Seward Division
 .S5 Sitka Division
 .S55 Skagway-Yakutat Division

---

[1]
For subdivisions, <u>see</u> tables, pp. 206-223

MAPS

By region or country[1]
America. Western Hemisphere
North America
United States
Alaska

4373	Boroughs, census divisions, etc., A–Z – Continued
	.S6 Southeast Fairbanks Division
	.U6 Upper Yukon Division
	.V3 Valdez-Chitina-Whittier Division
	.W3 Wade Hampton Division
	.W7 Wrangell-Petersburg Division
	.Y8 Yukon-Koyukuk Division
4380–4384	Hawaii. Sandwich Islands
4382	Regions, natural features, islands, etc., A–Z
	e. g. .H3 Hawaii (Island)
	.K3 Kahoolawe
	.K4 Kauai (Island). Kaieiewaho
	.L3 Lanai
	.M3 Maui (Island)
	.M6 Molokai
	.N5 Niihau
	.O2 Oahu
4383	Counties, A–Z
	Hawaii, see G4382.H3
	Honolulu (County), see G4382.O2
	Kalawao, see G4383.M3:2K3
	.K38 Kauai
	Including Kauai (Island) and Niihau
	.M3 Maui
	Includes Kahoolawe, Lanai, Maui (Island) and Molokai
	.M3:2K3 Kalawao
4390–4392	Caribbean area
4392	Regions, natural features, islands, etc., A–Z
	e. g. .C3 Caribbean Sea
	Swan Islands, see G4832.S9
	Latin America, see G3292.L3
4410–4414	Mexico
4414	Cities and towns, A–Z
	e. g. .M6 Mexico City
4420–4422	Northern States
4430–4433	Tamaulipas
4440–4443	Nuevo León
4450–4453	Coahuila
4460–4463	Chihuahua
4470–4473	Sonora
4475–4477	Baja California (Region)
44477	Regions, natural features, etc., A–Z
	e. g. .G8 Guadelupe Island
4480–4483	Baja California (Norte)
4485–4488	Baja California Sur

---

[1] For subdivisions, see tables, pp. 206–223

MAPS

By region or country[1]
America. Western Hemisphere
North America
Mexico
Northern States - Continued

4490-4493	Sinaloa
4500-4503	Durango
4510-4513	Zacatecas
4520-4523	San Luis Potosí
4530-4532	Central States
4540-4543	Veracruz
4550-4553	Puebla
4560-4563	Tlaxcala
4570-4573	Hidalgo
4580-4583	Mexico (State)
4590-4593	Mexico (Federal District)
4600-4603	Morelos
4610-4613	Michoacán
4620-4623	Querétaro
4630-4633	Guanajuato
4640-4643	Jalisco
4650-4653	Aguascalientes
4660-4663	Nayarit
4670-4673	Colima
4680-4682	Southern States
4682	Regions, natural features, etc., A-Z
	e. g. .T4 Isthmus of Tehuantepec
4690-4693	Guerrero
4700-4703	Oaxaca
4720-4723	Chiapas
4730-4733	Tabasco
4740-4743	Campeche
4750-4753	Yucatán
4760-4763	Quintana Roo
4800-4802	Central America
4810-4814	Guatemala
4820-4824	Belize. British Honduras
4830-4834	Honduras
4832	Regions, natural features, islands, etc., A-Z
	e. g. .S9 Swan Islands (Great and Little)
4840-4844	El Salvador
4850-4854	Nicaragua
4860-4864	Costa Rica
4870-4874	Panama
4880-4884	Canal Zone
4900-4902	West Indies
4902	Regions, natural features, islands, etc., A-Z
	Class here maps of West Indian islands and archipelagoes not classed in or associated with G4910
	Swan Islands, see G4832.S9
4910-4912	Greater Antilles
4920-4924	Cuba
4930-4932	Hispaniola
4940-4944	Haiti
4950-4954	Dominican Republic. Santo Domingo

---

[1] For subdivisions, see tables, pp. 206-223

MAPS

<u>By region or country</u>[1]
   <u>America. Western Hemisphere</u>
     <u>North America</u>
      <u>West Indies</u>
       <u>Greater Antilles</u> - Continued

4960-4964	Jamaica
4965-4969	Cayman Islands
4967	Regions, natural features, islands, etc., A-Z

          e. g. .C3 Cayman Brac
                 .G7 Grand Cayman
                 .L5 Little Cayman

4970-4974	Puerto Rico
4980-4984	<u>Bahamas. Lucayos</u>
4982	Regions, natural features, islands, etc., A-Z

          e. g. .A2 Abaco Islands (Great and Little)
                 .A3 Acklins Island
                 .A5 Andros Island
                     Atwood Cay, <u>see</u> .S2
                 .B4 Berry Islands
                 .B5 Bimini Islands
                 .C3 Cat Island
                 .C4 Cay Lobos
                 .C7 Crooked Island
                 .E4 Eleuthera Island
                 .E9 Exuma Islands (Great and Little)
                 .G7 Grand Bahama Island
                     Great Abaco Island, <u>see</u> .A2
                     Great Exuma Island, <u>see</u> .E9
                     Great Inagua Island, <u>see</u> .I5
                 .G72 Great Isaac Cay
                 .G8 Gun Cay
                 .H3 Harbour Island
                 .I5 Inagua Islands (Great and Little)
                     Little Abaco Island, <u>see</u> .A2
                     Little Exuma Island, <u>see</u> .E9
                     Little Inagua Island, <u>see</u> .I5
                 .L58 Long Cay
                 .L6 Long Island
                 .M3 Mayaguana Island
                 .N4 New Providence Island
                 .P5 Plana Cays
                 .R3 Ragged Island
                 .R8 Rum Cay
                 .S2 Samana Cay. Atwood Cay
                 .S3 San Salvador Island. Watlings Island
                 .S6 Spanish Wells Island
                     Watlings Island, <u>see</u> .S3

---

[1] For subdivisions, <u>see</u> tables, pp. 206-223

MAPS

By region or country[1]
America. Western Hemisphere
North America
West Indies
Greater Antilles - Continued

4985-4989	Turks and Caicos Islands
4987	Regions, natural features, islands, etc., A-Z

    e. g. .C3 Caicos Islands
          .C6 Cockburn Harbour
          .G7 Grand Turk Island
          .P7 Providence Island
          .T8 Turk Islands

5000-5002	Lesser Antilles. Caribbees
5005-5007	Virgin Islands (General)
5010-5014	Virgin Islands of the United States
5012	Regions, natural features, islands, etc., A-Z

    e. g. .S2 Saint Croix Island
          .S3 Saint John Island
          .S4 Saint Thomas Island

5020-5024	British Virgin Islands
5022	Regions, natural features, islands, etc., A-Z

    e. g. .A5 Anegada Island
          .J6 Jost Van Dyke Island
          .N6 Norman Island
          .P4 Peter Island
          .S2 Salt Island
          .T6 Tortola Island
          .V5 Virgin Gorda Island

5030-5032	Leeward Islands
5032	Regions, natural features, islands, etc., A-Z

    e. g. .S2 Saba Island
          .S3 Saint Eustatius Island
             Saint Martin Island, see G5072.S25

5040-5044	Saint Christopher (Island). Saint Kitts Including maps of St. Christopher-Nevis, St. Christopher, Nevis, and Anguilla
5042	Regions, natural features, islands, etc., A-Z

    e. g.   Anguilla, see G5045+
          .N4 Nevis
          .S6 Sombrero Island

5045-5049	Anguilla
5050-5054	Antigua (Island and independent State)
5052	Regions, natural features, islands, etc., A-Z

    e. g. .B3 Barbuda
          .R4 Redonda

5055-5059	Montserrat

---

[1] For subdivisions, see tables, pp. 206-223

MAPS

America. Western Hemisphere
        North America
            West Indies - Continued

5060-5061		French West Indies
5070-5074		Guadeloupe
5072		Regions, natural features, islands, etc., A-Z
	e. g. .B3	Basse-Terre Island
	.G7	Grande-Terre Island
	.L3	La Désirade
	.L5	Les Saintes
	.M3	Marie-Galante
	.P4	Petite Terre Islands
	.S2	Saint-Barthélemy Island
	.S25	Saint Martin. Sint Maarten

> Class here maps of the island as a whole as well as maps covering only the northern portion administered by Guadeloupe or the southern portion administered by Netherlands Antilles

5080-5084		Martinique
5090-5092		Windward Islands
5100-5104		Dominica
5110-5114		Saint Lucia
5120-5124		Saint Vincent (Island and independent State)
5122		Regions, natural features, islands, etc., A-Z
	e. g. .B4	Bequia Island
	.C3	Cannouan Island
	.M8	Mustique Island
	.N6	Northern Grenadines

> For maps of the Grenadines as a group, see G5132.G7

	.U5	Union Island
5130-5134		Grenada (Island and independent State)
5132		Regions, natural features, islands, etc., A-Z
	e. g. .C3	Carriacou Island. Hillsborough Island
	.G7	Grenadine Islands (General)

> Hillsborough Island, see .C3
>
> Little Martinique Island, see .P4

	.P4	Petite Martinique Island
	.R6	Ronde Island
	.S6	Southern Grenadines
5140-5144		Barbados

---

[1] For subdivisions, see tables, pp. 206-223

MAPS

<pre>
                        By region or country¹
                          America. Western Hemisphere
                            North America
                              West Indies
                                Windward Islands - Continued
    5145-5149   Trinidad and Tobago
    5150-5152   Trinidad
    5160-5162   Tobago
    5165-5167   Netherlands Antilles. Dutch West Indies
        5167   Regions, natural features, islands,
                                      etc., A-Z
                                      Saba Island, see G5032.S2
                                      Saint Eustatius Island, see G5032.S3
                                      Saint Martin Island (Southern),
                                        see G5072.S25
    5170-5174   Aruba
    5175-5179   Bonaire
    5180-5184   Curaçao
    5200-5202   South America (Map, p. 40)
        5202   Regions, natural features, etc., A-Z
                                    e. g. .R5 Rio de la Plata Basin
    5220-5221   Atlantic coast and continental shelf
    5230-5231   Pacific coast and continental shelf
    5240-5242   Guianas
    5250-5254   Guyana. British Guiana
    5260-5264   Surinam. Dutch Guiana
    5270-5274   French Guiana
    5280-5284   Venezuela
    5290-5294   Colombia
    5300-5304   Ecuador
        5302   Regions, natural features, etc., A-Z
                                      e. g. .G3 Galapagos Islands
                                             .O6 Oriente
    5310-5314   Peru
    5320-5324   Bolivia
    5330-5334   Chile
        5332   Regions, natural features, etc., A-Z
                                      Easter Islands, see G9665+
    5350-5354   Argentina
        5352   Regions, natural features, etc., A-Z
                                      Islas Malvinas, see G9175+
                                      Rio de la Plata Basin, see G5202.R5
    5370-5374   Uruguay
    5380-5384   Paraguay
    5400-5404   Brazil
        5404   Cities and towns, A-Z
                                      e. g. .R3 Recife. Pernambuco
                                             .S7 São Paulo
                                                    Including "Municipio
                                                      Capital"
    5410-5412   North Brazil. Amazon Basin
    5420-5423   Rondônia. Guaporé
    5430-5433   Acre
    5440-5443   Amazonas
</pre>

---

¹
    For subdivisions, see tables, pp. 206-223

MAPS

By region or country[1]
  America. Western Hemisphere
    South America
      Brazil
        North Brazil. Amazon Basin - Continued

5460-5463	Roraima. Rio Branco
5470-5473	Pará
5490-5493	Amapá
5500-5502	Northeast Brazil
5505-5508	Maranhão
5510-5513	Piauí (Piauhy)
5515-5518	Ceará
5520-5523	Rio Grande do Norte
5525-5528	Paraíba
5530-5533	Pernambuco
5540-5543	Alagôas
5545-5548	Fernando de Noronha
5550-5552	East Brazil. Southeastern States
5555-5558	Sergipe
5560-5563	Bahia
5570-5573	Minas Gerais
5580-5583	Espírito Santo
5590-5593	Rio de Janeiro (State)
5595-5598	Guanabara
	Until April 1960 known as Distrito Federal
5600-5602	South Brazil
5605-5608	São Paulo
5610-5613	Paraná
5615-5618	Santa Catarina
5620-5623	Rio Grande do Sul
5630-5632	Central West Brazil
5640-5643	Mato Grosso
5660-5663	Goías
5665-5668	Distrito Federal (1960-)
5670-5672	Eastern Hemisphere. Eurasia, Africa, etc. (Map, p. 40)
	For maps of the known world prior to 1500, which are confined to the Eastern Hemisphere, see G3200
5672	Regions, natural features, etc., A-Z
	e. g. .M4 Mediterranean region
5680-5682	Islamic World
	Including maps of Arab countries together, Islamic Empire, etc.
5685-5687	Asia and Africa
5687	Regions, natural features, etc., A-Z
	e. g. .R3 Red Sea
5690-5692	Eurasia
5692	Regions, natural features, etc., A-Z
	e. g. .B5 Black Sea
	.C3 Caspian Sea
	Ural Mountains, see G7002.U72
5695-5696	Europe and Africa

---

[1]
    For subdivisions, see tables, pp. 206-223

Europe

SCANDINAVIA

G6910

WESTERN EUROPE

G5720

CENTRAL EUROPE

G6030

BALKAN

PENINSULA

G6800

SOUTHERN EUROPE

G6530

Europe

BENELUX
G5990

BRITISH ISLES   G5740

EASTERN EUROPE

G6965

IBERIAN PENINSULA

G6540

By region or country[1]
  Eastern Hemisphere. Eurasia, Africa, etc. - Continued

5700-5702	Europe
5702	Regions, natural features, etc., A-Z

    e. g.   Alps, see G6035+
       .B3 Baltic Sea
       .N6 North Sea
       .P9 Pyrenees
       .R5 Rhine River
       .R53 Riviera

5720-5722	Western Europe (Map, p. 128)
5730-5731	British Empire. Commonwealth of Nations

      Including maps of British colonies,
       dependencies, etc. (Collectively)
      Class individual colonies, dependencies,
       etc. according to location, e. g.
      G9120+, Bermuda

5740-5742	British Isles. Great Britain (Map, p. 129)
	History
5741.S1	General
.S2	To 1066
.S3	Medieval period, 1066-1485
.S33	Norman period, 1066-1154
.S35	Plantagenets, 1154-1399
.S37	15th century
.S4	Modern period, 1485-
.S45	16th century: Tudors, 1485-1603
.S5	17th century: Stuarts, 1603-1714
.S53	Commonwealth and protectorate, 1660-1688
.S54	18th century
.S55	19th century
.S6	20th century
.S65	World War I
.S7	World War II
5750-5754	England

      Including maps of England and Wales ated
      together

5753		Counties, A-Z
	.A9	Avon
	.B3	Bedfordshire
	.B4	Berkshire
	.B8	Buckinghamshire
	.C3	Cambridgeshire (Pre-1965; Post-1974)
	.C35	Cambridgeshire and Isle of Ely
		(1965-1974)
	.C5	Cheshire
	.C55	Cleveland
	.C6	Cornwall
	.C8	Cumberland
	.C9	Cumbria
	.D3	Derbyshire
	.D4	Devonshire
	.D6	Dorsetshire

---

[1]
 For subdivisions, see tables, pp. 206-223

MAPS

<u>By region or country</u>
  <u>Eastern Hemisphere. Eurasia, Africa, etc.</u>
    <u>Europe</u>
      <u>Western Europe</u>
        <u>British Isles. Great Britain</u>
          <u>England</u>

5753   <u>Counties, A-Z</u> - Continued
              .D8   Durham
              .E3   East Sussex
              .E7   Essex
              .G6   Gloucestershire
                      For Greater London (Metropolitan
                        county), <u>see</u> G5754.L7
                      For Greater Manchester (Metropolitan
                        county), <u>see</u> G5754.M3
              .H3   Hampshire
              .H37 Hereford and Worcester
              .H4   Herefordshire
              .H5   Hertfordshire
              .H7   Humberside
              .H8   Huntingdonshire
              .K4   Kent
              .L3   Lancashire
              .L4   Leicestershire
              .L5   Lincolnshire
                  .L5:3H6 Parts of Holland
                  .L5:3K4 Parts of Kesteven
                  .L5:3L5 Parts of Lindsey
                London, Greater (Metropolitan county),
                    <u>see</u> G5754.L7
                Manchester, Greater (Metropolitan
                    county), <u>see</u> G5754.M3
              .M4   Merseyside
              .M5   Middlesex
              .N4   Norfolk
              .N45 North Yorkshire
              .N5   Northamptonshire
              .N6   Northumberland
              .N7   Nottinghamshire
              .O8   Oxfordshire
              .R8   Rutlandshire
              .S4   Salop. Shropshire
              .S5   Somersetshire
              .S55 South Yorkshire
              .S6   Staffordshire
              .S7   Suffolk
              .S8   Surrey
              .S9   Sussex
              .T9   Tyne and Wear
              .W3   Warwickshire
              .W33 West Midlands
              .W35 West Sussex
              .W37 West Yorkshire
              .W4   Westmorland
              .W5   Wiltshire
              .W6   Worcestershire
              .Y6   Yorkshire
                  .Y6:3E3 East Riding
                  .Y6:3N6 North Riding
                  .Y6:3W4 West Riding

MAPS

<u>By region or country</u>[1]
   <u>Eastern Hemisphere. Eurasia, Africa, etc.</u>
      <u>Europe</u>
         <u>Western Europe</u>
            <u>British Isles. Great Britain</u>
               <u>England</u> - Continued

Class		Caption
5754		Cities and towns, A–Z
	e. g. .L7	London
	.M3	Manchester
5760–5764		<u>Wales</u>
5763		Counties, A–Z
	.A5	Anglesey
	.B7	Brecknockshire
	.C2	Caernarvonshire
	.C3	Cardiganshire
	.C6	Carmarthenshire
	.C7	Clwyd
	.D4	Denbighshire
	.D8	Dyfed
	.F5	Flintshire
	.G5	Glamorganshire
	.G8	Gwent
	.G9	Gwynedd
	.M4	Merionethshire
	.M5	Mid Glamorgan
	.M55	Monmouthshire
	.M6	Montgomeryshire
	.P4	Pembrokeshire
	.P6	Powys
	.R3	Radnorshire
	.S6	South Glamorgan
	.W4	West Glamorgan
5770–5774		<u>Scotland</u>
		History
5771.S1		General
.S2		To 1057
.S3		1057–1603
.S34		War of Independence, 1285–1371
.S36		Stuarts to the Union, 1371–1707
.S4		17th century
.S45		Revolution of 1688
.S5		18th century
.S52		Jacobite Rebellion, 1715
.S53		Jacobite Rebellion, 1745–1746
.S55		19th century
.S6		20th century
.S65		World War I
.S7		World War II
5772		Regions, natural features, etc., A–Z
	e. g. .H4	Hebrides Islands
	.O6	Orkney Islands
	.O8	Outer Hebrides Islands
	.S5	Shetland Islands

----

[1] For subdivisions, <u>see</u> tables, pp. 206–223

By region or country[1]
  Eastern Hemisphere. Eurasia, Africa, etc.
    Europe
      Western Europe
        British Isles. Great Britain
          Scotland - Continued
5773   Counties, A-Z
            .A2   Aberdeenshire
            .A5   Angus. Forfarshire
            .A6   Argyllshire
            .A9   Ayrshire
            .B3   Banffshire
            .B4   Berwickshire
            .B6   Borders
            .B8   Buteshire
            .C3   Caithness
            .C4   Central
            .C5   Clackmannanshire
            .D7   Dumfries and Galloway
            .D8   Dumfriesshire
            .D9   Dunbartonshire
            .E3   East Lothian
            .F5   Fifeshire
                  Forfarshire, see .A5
            .F6   Forth
            .G6   Grampian
            .H5   Highlands
            .I5   Inverness-shire
            .K4   Kincardineshire
            .K5   Kinross-shire
            .K6   Kirkcudbrightshire
            .L3   Lanarkshire
            .L6   Lothian
            .M5   Midlothian
            .M6   Morayshire
            .N3   Nairnshire
                  Orkney, see G5772.O6
            .P3   Peeblesshire
            .P4   Perthshire
            .R4   Renfrewshire
            .R6   Ross and Cromarty
            .R7   Roxburghshire
            .S4   Selkirkshire
                  Shetland, see G5772.S5
            .S7   Stirlingshire
            .S75 Strathclyde
            .S8   Sutherland
            .T3   Tayside
            .W4   West Lothian
                  Western Isles, see G5772.O8
            .W5   Wigtownshire

By region or country[1]
  Eastern Hemisphere. Eurasia, Africa, etc.
    Europe
      Western Europe
        British Isles. Great Britain - Continued

5780-5784   Eire. Irish Free State
            Including maps of the island of Ireland
            treated as a whole
5783   Counties and provinces, A-Z
    .C3 Carlow
    .C4 Cavan
    .C5 Clare
    .C6 Connacht (Province)
    .C7 Cork
    .D5 Donegal
    .D8 Dublin
    .G3 Galway
    .K4 Kerry
    .K5 Kildare
    .K6 Kilkenny
       King's, see .O2
    .L2 Laoighis. Leix. Queen's
    .L3 Leinster (Province)
    .L4 Leitrim
       Leix, see .L2
    .L5 Limerick
    .L7 Longford
    .L8 Louth
    .M3 Mayo
    .M4 Meath
    .M6 Monaghan
    .M8 Munster (Province)
    .O2 Offaly. King's
       Queen's, see .L2
    .R6 Roscommon
    .S5 Sligo
    .T5 Tipperary
    .U4 Ulster (Province)
        Cf. G5790+, Northern Ireland
    .W3 Waterford
    .W4 Westmeath
    .W5 Wexford
    .W6 Wicklow
5784   Cities and towns, A-Z
      e. g. .C6 Cork
            .D7 Dublin

5790-5794   Northern Ireland
5793   Counties, etc., A-Z
    .A5 Antrim
    .A6 Armagh
    .D6 Down
    .F4 Fermanagh
    .L6 Londonderry
    .T9 Tyrone
5794   Cities and towns, A-Z
      e. g. .B4 Belfast
            .L6 Londonderry

---

[1]
  For subdivisions, see tables, pp. 206-223

MAPS

By region or country[1]
   Eastern Hemisphere. Eurasia, Africa, etc.
      Europe
         Western Europe
           British Isles. Great Britain - Continued

5800-5804	Isle of Man
5810-5814	Channel Islands
5820-5821	French Empire. French Union

               Including maps of French colonies,
                  dependencies, etc., (Collectively)
               Class individual colonies, dependencies,
                  etc., according to location, e. g.
                  G8680+, French Equatorial Africa

5830-5834	France
5832	Regions, natural features, etc., A-Z

                e. g. .M6   Mont Blanc
                     .P35 Région Parisienne
                            A governmental region
                            comprising the departments
                            of Essonne, Hauts-de-Seine,
                            Seine-St.-Denis, Val-de=
                            Marne, Val d'Oise, Yvelines,
                            plus Paris

     5833   Provinces, departments, etc., A-Z

                 .A2   Ain
                 .A25 Aisne
                 .A3   Allier (Department). Bourbonnais
                       (Province)
                 .A35 Alpes-Maritimes
                 .A37 Alsace
                 .A4   Alsace-Lorraine
                       For Lorraine, see .L65
                    Angoumois, see .C4
                 .A45 Anjou
                 .A5   Ardèche
                 .A55 Ardennes
                 .A6   Ariège (Department). Foix (Comté)
                    Artois, see .P3
                 .A7   Aube
                 .A75 Aude
                 .A8   Aunis
                 .A85 Auvergne
                 .A9   Aveyron
                 .B2   Bas-Rhin
                 .B3   Basses-Alpes
                 .B4   Basses Pyrénées (Department). Béarn
                       (Province)
                    Béarn, see .B4
                 .B5   Territoire de Belfort
                 .B55 Berry
                 .B6   Bouches-du-Rhône
                    Bourbonnais, see .A3
                    Bourgogne, see .B8
                 .B7   Brittany. Bretagne
                 .B8   Burgundy. Bourgogne

---

[1] For subdivisions, see tables, pp. 206-223

<u>By region or country</u>
  <u>Eastern Hemisphere. Eurasia, Africa, etc.</u>
    <u>Europe</u>
      <u>Western Europe</u>
        <u>France</u>

5833
           Provinces, departments, etc., A-Z - Continued

.C2	Calvados
.C25	Cantal
.C3	Cévennes
.C35	Champagne
.C4	Charente (Department). Angoumois (Province)
	Charente-Inférieure, <u>see</u> .C5
.C5	Charente-Maritime
.C6	Cher
	Comtat, Comtat Venaissin, <u>see</u> .V3
.C7	Corrèze
	Corse, <u>see</u> G5970+
.C8	Côte d'Or
.C85	Côtes-du-Nord
.C9	Creuse (Department). Marche (Province)
.D3	Dauphiné
.D4	Deux-Sèvres
.D5	Dordogne
.D6	Doubs
.D7	Drôme
.E6	Essonne
.E7	Eure
.E8	Eure-et-Loire
.F5	Finistère
	Flanders, French, <u>see</u> .N6
	Foix, <u>see</u> .A6
.F7	Franche-Comté
	French Flanders, <u>see</u> .N6
.G2	Gard
.G3	Gascony
.G4	Gers
.G5	Gironde
.G8	Guyenne
.H2	Haut-Rhin
.H3	Haute-Garonne
.H35	Haute-Loire
.H4	Haute-Marne
.H45	Haute-Saône
.H5	Haute-Savoie
.H55	Haute-Vienne
.H6	Hautes-Alpes
.H7	Hautes-Pyréntées
.H75	Hauts-de-Seine
.H8	Hérault
.I3	Île-de-France
.I4	Ille-et-Vilaine
.I5	Indre
.I6	Indre-et-Loire (Department). Touraine (Province)
.I8	Isère
.J8	Jura

MAPS

By region or country
  Eastern Hemisphere. Eurasia. Africa. etc.
    Europe
      Western Europe
        France
5833   Provinces, departments, etc., A-Z - Continued
          .L2   Landes
          .L3   Languedoc
          .L35 Limousin
          .L4   Loir-et-Cher
          .L45 Loire
          .L5   Loire Atlantique
          .L6   Loiret
          .L65 Lorraine
          .L7   Lot
          .L75 Lot-et-Garonne
          .L8   Lozère
          .L9   Lyonnais
          .M2   Maine
          .M25 Maine-et-Loire
          .M3   Manche
                Marche, see .C9
          .M35 Marne
          .M4   Mayenne
          .M5   Meurthe-et-Moselle
          .M6   Meuse
          .M7   Morbihan
          .M8   Moselle
          .N5   Nièvre (Department). Nivernais
                  (Province)
                Nivernais, see .N5
          .N6   Nord (Department). French Flanders
                  (Province)
          .N7   Normandy
          .O5   Oise
          .O6   Orléanais
          .O7   Orne
                Paris, see G5834.P3
                Paris region, see G5832.P35
          .P3   Pas-de-Calais (Department). Artois
                  (Province)
          .P4   Périgord
          .P5   Picardy
          .P6   Poitou
          .P7   Provence
          .P8   Puy-de-Dôme
          .P85 Pyrénées-Atlantiques
          .P9   Pyrénées-Orientales (Department).
                  Roussillon (Province)
                Région Parisienne, see G5832.P35
          .R5   Rhône
                Roussillon, see .P9
          .S2   Saintonge
          .S3   Saône-et-Loire
          .S35 Sarthe
          .S4   Savoie

By region or country[1]
  Eastern Hemisphere. Eurasia, Africa, etc.
    Europe
      Western Europe
        France

5833	Provinces, departments, etc., A-Z - Continued
	.S45 Savoy (Countship and Duchy)
	Cf. G5833.H5, Haute-Savoie (Department)
	G5833.S4, Savoie (Department)
	.S5 Seine
	.S55 Seine-et-Marne
	.S57 Seine-et-Oise
	.S6 Seine-Inférieure
	.S65 Seine-Maritime
	.S7 Seine-Saint-Denis
	.S8 Somme
	.T3 Tarn
	.T4 Tarn-et-Garonne
	Touraine, see .I6
	.V2 Val-de-Marne
	.V25 Val d'Oise
	.V27 Var
	.V3 Vaucluse (Department). Comtat
	Venaissin (Comtat). Venaissin
	(Province)
	Venaissin, see .V3
	.V4 Vendée
	.V5 Vienne
	.V6 Vosges
	.Y6 Yonne
	.Y9 Yvelines
5834	Cities and towns, A-Z
	e. g. .P3 Paris
5970-5973	Corsica (Corse)
5980-5984	Monaco
5990-5992	Benelux countries. Low countries (Map, p. 129)
5995-5996	Netherlands Union
	Including maps of Dutch colonies, dependencies,
	etc. (Collectively)
	Class individual colonies, dependencies, etc.,
	according to location, e. g. G5165+,
	Netherlands Antilles
6000-6004	Netherlands
6002	Regions, natural features, etc., A-Z
	e. g. .G66 Gooi
	.I5 IJsselmeer
6003	Provinces, A-Z
	.D7 Drenthe
	.F7 Friesland
	.G4 Gelderland
	.G7 Groningen
	.H5 Holland (Province)
	.L5 Limburg
	.N6 Noordbrabant
	.N7 Noordholland

---

[1]
   For subdivisions, see tables, pp. 206-223

By region or country[1]
  Eastern Hemisphere. Eurasia, Africa, etc.
    Europe
      Western Europe
        Benelux countries. Low countries
          Netherlands

6003
            Provinces, A-Z - Continued
            .O8 Overijssel
               South Holland, see .Z8
            .U8 Utrecht
            .Z4 Zeeland
            .Z8 Zuidholland

6010-6014   Belgium
6013   Provinces, A-Z
            .A6 Antwerp
            .B7 Brabant
               East Flanders, see .O8
            .F5 Flanders
            .H3 Hainaut
            .L4 Liége
            .L5 Limburg
            .L8 Luxemburg
            .N3 Namur
            .O8 Oost-Vlaanderen
               Vlaanderen, see .F5
            .W4 West-Vlaanderen

6020-6024   Luxemburg
6023   Provinces, A-Z
            .D5 Diekirch
            .G7 Grevenmacher
            .L9 Luxemburg

6030-6032   Central Europe (Map, p. 128)
6032   Regions, natural features, etc., A-Z
          e. g.   Alps, see G6035+
           .C6 Lake Constance. Bodensee
           .D3 Danube River
           .E6 Elbe River
              Erzgebirge, see G6092.E7
           .M6 Moselle River

6035-6036   Alps
        Class here maps of the Alps as a whole.
        For regions and natural features within
        the Alps, see the country or region in
        which they are located, according to
        the provisions of Table I
          e. g. G5832.M6 Mont Blanc
             G6042.E5 Engadine
             G6422.B28 Bavarian Alps

6040-6044   Switzerland
6042   Regions, natural features, etc., A-Z
        e. g. .E5 Engadine

---

[1] For subdivisions, see tables, pp. 206-223

By region or country[1]
  Eastern Hemisphere. Eurasia, Africa, etc.
    Europe
      Central Europe
        Switzerland - Continued

6043	Cantons, A-Z	
	.A2	Aargau
	.A6	Appenzell
	.A7	Appenzell Ausserrhoden
	.A8	Appenzell Innerrhoden
	.B3	Basel
	.B4	Bern
	.F7	Fribourg
	.G4	Geneva
	.G5	Glarus
	.G7	Grisons (Graubünden)
	.L8	Lucerne
	.N4	Neuchâtel (Neuenburg)
	.S2	Saint Gall
	.S3	Schaffhausen
	.S4	Schwyz
	.S6	Solothurn (Soleure)
	.T4	Thurgau
	.T5	Ticino (Tessin)
	.U5	Unterwalden
	.U6	Unterwalden nid dem Wald
	.U7	Unterwalden ob dem Wald
	.U8	Uri
	.V2	Valais (Wallis)
	.V3	Vaud (Waadt)
	.Z7	Zürich
	.Z8	Zug

6050-6054   Liechtenstein
6070-6071   German Empire
        Including maps of German colonies
          dependencies, etc. (Collectively)
        Class individual colonies according to
          location, e. g. G8620+, Southwest Africa.
          German Southwest Africa
6080-6081   Germany
        Including maps of East and West Germany
          together, Prussia as a whole, and the
          Holy Roman Empire
        For East Prussia, see G6523.05
        For Pomerania, see G6522.P58
        For Posen, see G6523.P6
        For Silesia, see G6523.S5
        For West Prussia, see G6522.P8
6090-6094   East Germany (German Democratic Republic)
6092   Regions, natural features, etc., A-Z
        e. g. .E7 Erzgebirge
             Harz Mountain region, see
               G6322.H33
          .L8 Lusatia
          .M8 Mulde River

---

[1] For subdivisions, see tables, pp. 206-223

<pre>
                  By region or country¹
                      Eastern Hemisphere. Eurasia, Africa, etc.
                          Europe
                              Central Europe
                                  Germany
                                      East Germany (German Democratic Republic) –
                                          Continued
     (6093)   Administrative districts (Bezirke),
                                              former states (Länder), etc., see G6105+
     6094   Cities and towns, A–Z
                                                e. g. .B3 East Berlin
                                                                For maps of Berlin as
                                                                    a whole, see G6299.B3
                                                       .D7 Dresden
                                                       .G4 Gera
     6105–6108   Cottbus
     6115–6118   Dresden
        6117   Regions, natural features, etc., A–Z
                                                e. g. .D7 Dresden Heath
                                                            Elbsandsteingebirge, see
                                                              .S3
                                                       .S3 Saxon Switzerland
                                                       .Z5 Zittau Mountains
                                            East Berlin (Bezirk), see G6094.B3
     6125–6128   Erfurt
        6128   Landkreise, etc., A–Z
                                                e. g. .A6 Apolda
                                                       .A7 Arnstadt
                                                       .S3 Saxe-Coburg-Gotha
                                                            Cf. G6423.C6, Coburg
                                                       .S4 Saxe-Weimar-Eisenach
                                                       .S5 Schwarzburg-Sonderhausen
     6135–6138   Frankfurt
     6145–6148   Gera
        6148   Landkreise, etc., A–Z
                                                e. g. .R4 Reuss (Elder line)
                                                       .R5 Reuss (Younger line)
                                                       .S4 Schwarzburg-Rudolstadt
     6150–6151   Brandenburg
     6155–6158   Halle
     6165–6168   Karl-Marx-Stadt (Bezirk). Chemnitz
     6175–6178   Leipzig
        6178   Landkreise, etc., A–Z
                                                e. g. .S3 Saxe-Altenburg
     6185–6188   Madgeburg
     6195–6196   Mecklenburg. Mecklenburg-Vorpommern
                                                Including Mecklenburg-Schwerin and
                                                  Mecklenburg-Strelitz
     6205–6208   Neubrandenberg
     6215–6218   Potsdam
</pre>

---

¹
   For subdivisions, see tables, pp. 206–223

By region or country[1]
   Eastern Hemisphere. Eurasia, Africa, etc.
    Europe
     Central Europe
      Germany
       East Germany (German Democratic Republic) –
        Continued

6225-6228	Rostock
6227	Regions, natural features, etc., A-Z
	e. g. .D3 Darss Peninsula
	.R8 Rügen Island
6228	Landkreise, etc., A-Z
	e. g. .G6 Greifswald
	Rügen (Kreis), see G6227.R8
6230-6231	Saxony-Anhalt
	Including Anhalt and Saxony (Prussian province)
6240-6241	Saxony
6260-6263	Schwerin
6280-6283	Suhl
6283	Landkreise, etc., A-Z
	e. g. .N4 Neuhaus
	.S2 Saxe-Meiningen
6290-6291	Thuringia
6295-6299	West Germany (Federal Republic of Germany)
6297	Regions, natural features, etc., A-Z
	e. g. .F7 Franconia (Duchy)
	.S8 Swabia (Duchy)
(6298)	Administrative districts (Länder, Regierungsbezirke, Landkreise, etc.), see G6310+
6299	Cities and towns, A-Z
	e. g. .B3 West Berlin
	Including maps of Berlin as a whole
	.B3:3C5 Charlottenburg
	.B3:3M3 Markisches Viertel
	.B3:3N4 Neukölln
	.B3:3R4 Reinickendorf
	.B3:3T4 Tempelhof
	.B7 Bremen (City and Land)
	.H3 Hamburg (City and Land)
	.H5 Heidelberg (City and Landkreis)
	.H8614 Homburg vor der Höhe
	.L9 Lüneburg (City and Province)
	.M8 Munich
	.M8:206 Olympiapark

[1] For subdivisions, see tables, pp. 206-223

By region or country[1]
   Eastern Hemisphere. Eurasia, Africa, etc.
      Europe
         Central Europe
            Germany
               West Germany (Federal Republic of Germany) –

	Continued
6310-6313	Schleswig-Holstein
6312	Regions, natural features, etc., A-Z
	e. g. .F6 Föhr Island
	.H4 Helgoland
	.H6 Holsteinische Schweiz
	.K5 Kiel Fjord
	.N6 North Friesland
	.T7 Trave River
	Hamburg (Land), see G6299.H3
6320-6323	Lower Saxony (Niedersachsen). Hanover
6322	Regions, natural features, etc., A-Z
	e. g. .H3 Naturpark Harz
	.H33 Harz Mountain region
	.W3 Wangerooge
6323	Administrative districts (Regierungsbezirke, Landkreise, etc.), A-Z
	e. g. .A7 Aurich (Kreis)
	.A8 Aurich (Regierungsbezirk). East Friesland
	.B69 Brunswick (Kreis)
	.B7 Brunswick (Verwaltungsbezirk). Brunswick (Land) Lüneburg (Province), see G6299.L9
	.O5 Oldenburg (Landkreis)
	.O6 Oldenburg (Verwaltungsbezirk). Oldenburg (Land)
	.S3 Schaumburg-Lippe
	.V4 Verden
	Bremen (Land), see G6299.B7
6360-6363	North Rhine-Westphalia. Westphalia
6362	Regions, natural features, etc., A-Z
	e. g. .N6 Naturpark Nordeifel
	.R59 Naturpark Rothaargebirge
	.R6 Rothaargebirge (Mountains)
	.R8 Ruhr River
	.S2 Sauerland
6363	Administrative districts (Regierungsbezirke, Landkreise, etc.), A-Z
	e. g. .D4 Detmold (Landkreis)
	.D42 Detmold (Regierungsbezirk)
	.L4 Lemgo
	.M78 Münster (Landkreis)
	.M8 Münster (Regierungsbezirk)
	.W5 Wiedenbrück (Landkreis)

---

[1] For subdivisions, see tables, pp. 206-223

By region or country[1]
    Eastern Hemisphere.   Eurasia, Africa, etc.
        Europe
            Central Europe
                Germany
                    West Germany (Federal Republic of Germany) -

			Continued
6370-6373			Hesse
			Including Hesse-Darmstadt and Hesse-Nassau
6372			Regions, natural features, etc., A-Z
	e. g.	.D5	Naturpark Diemelsee
		.H34	Naturpark Habichtswald
		.H4	Naturpark Hessischer Spessart
		.H6	Naturpark Hoher Vogelsberg
6373			Administrative districts (Regierungsbezirke, Landkreise, etc.), A-Z
	e. g.	.B4	Bergstrasse
		.D29	Darmstadt (Landkreis)
		.D3	Darmstadt (Regierungsbezirk)
			Hesse Homburg, see G6299.H8614
		.H42	Hesse-Kassel. Kurhessen
		.H6	Hofgeismar
			Kurhessen, see .H42
		.L3	Lauterbach. Starkenburg (Province)
			Nassau (Duchy), see .W5
			Rheinhessen, see G6393.R5
		.U6	Upper Hesse
		.W3	Waldeck (Landkreis). Waldeck (Principality)
		.W5	Wiesbaden (Regierungsbezirk). Nassau
6390-6393			Rhineland-Palatinate. Rhine Province
6392			Regions, natural features, etc., A-Z
	e. g.	.E5	Eifel
		.P3	Palatinate. Lower Palatinate Including maps of Lower and Upper Palatinate together. For maps of Upper Palatinate alone, see G6423.03
6393			Administrative districts (Regierungsbezirke, Landkreise, etc.), A-Z
	e. g.	.K3	Kaiserslautern (Landkreis)
		.K7	Kreuznach (Kreis)
		.R5	Rheinhessen
6395-6398			Saarland (Saar)

---

[1]
  For subdivisions, see tables, pp. 206-223

By region or country[1]
　Eastern Hemisphere. Eurasia, Africa, etc.
　　Europe
　　　Central Europe
　　　　Germany
　　　　　West Germany (Federal Republic of Germany) –
　　　　　　Continued

6420-6423	Bavaria
6422	Regions, natural features, etc., A-Z

　　　　　　　　　e. g. .B28 Bavarian Alps
　　　　　　　　　　　　.B3   Bavarian Forest
　　　　　　　　　　　　.C5   Chiem See
　　　　　　　　　　　　.W4   Werdenfelser Land

6423	Administrative districts (Regierungsbezirke, Landkreise, etc.), A-Z

　　　　　　　　　e. g. .A5   Ansbach
　　　　　　　　　　　　.C6   Coburg
　　　　　　　　　　　　　　　Cf. G6128.S3,
　　　　　　　　　　　　　　　　　　Saxe-Coburg-Gotha
　　　　　　　　　　　　.D3   Dachau
　　　　　　　　　　　　　　　Franconia, see G6297.F7
　　　　　　　　　　　　.L66 Lower Bavaria (Nierderbayern)
　　　　　　　　　　　　.L68 Lower Franconia (Unterfranken)
　　　　　　　　　　　　.M5   Middle Franconia
　　　　　　　　　　　　　　　(Mittelfranken)
　　　　　　　　　　　　.O2   Oberpfalz (Regierungsbezirk).
　　　　　　　　　　　　　　　Upper Palatinate (Duchy)
　　　　　　　　　　　　　　　For maps of Lower and
　　　　　　　　　　　　　　　　Upper Palatinate
　　　　　　　　　　　　　　　　together, see G6392.P3
　　　　　　　　　　　　.S38 Schwaben (Regierungsbezirk)
　　　　　　　　　　　　.U6   Upper Bavaria (Oberbayern)
　　　　　　　　　　　　.U7   Upper Franconia (Oberfranken)

6425-6428	Baden-Württemberg

　　　　　　　　Including Baden, Württemberg-Baden,
　　　　　　　　　Württemberg-Hohenzollern, Hohenzollern,
　　　　　　　　　Württemberg

6427	Regions, natural features, etc., A-Z

　　　　　　　　e. g. .B5 Black Forest (Schwarzwald)

6428	Administrative districts (Regierungsbezirke, Landkreise, etc.), A-Z

　　　　　　　　　e. g.   Heidelberg (Landkreis), see
　　　　　　　　　　　　　　　G6299.H5
　　　　　　　　　　　　.K6   Konstanz (Landkreis)
　　　　　　　　　　　　.S8   Südbaden (Regierungsbezirk)
　　　　　　　　　　　　.T7   Tübingen (Landkreis)

6480-6482	Austria-Hungary
6490-6494	Austria
6493	Bundesländer, A-Z

　　　　　　　　.A8 Lower Austria (Niederösterreich)
　　　　　　　　.A9 Upper Austria (Oberösterreich)
　　　　　　　　.B8 Burgenland
　　　　　　　　.C3 Carinthia (Kärnten)
　　　　　　　　.S3 Salzburg

---

[1] For subdivisions, see tables, pp. 206-223

MAPS

By region or country[1]
Eastern Hemisphere. Eurasia, Africa, etc.
Europe
Central Europe
Austria Hungary
Austria

6493	Bundesländer, A-Z - Continued
	.S8 Styria (Steiermark)
	.S8:3B7 Bruck an der Mur
	.S8:3D4 Deutschlandsberg
	.T6 Tirol
	Vienna, see G6494.V4
	.V6 Vorarlberg
6494	Cities and towns, A-Z
	e. g. .V4 Vienna
6500-6504	Hungary
6502	Regions, natural features, etc., A-Z
	e. g. .B35 Balaton Lake
6503	Counties (Megye), A-Z
	.B2 Bács-Kiskun
	.B3 Baranya
	.B4 Békés
	.B6 Borsod-Abaúj-Zemplén
	.C7 Csongrád
	.F4 Fejér
	.G9 Győr-Sopron
	.H3 Hajdú-Bihar
	.H4 Heves
	.K6 Komárom
	.N6 Nógrád
	.P4 Pest
	.S5 Somogy
	.S7 Szabolcs-Szatmár
	.S9 Szolnok
	.T6 Tolna
	.V3 Vas
	.V4 Veszprém
	.Z3 Zala
6510-6514	Czechoslovakia. Czech Socialist Republic and Slovak Socialist Republic
	History
6511.S1	General
.S2	Early and medieval through 1526
.S3	16th-18th centuries
.S4	1789-1815
.S5	1815-1918
.S65	World War I
.S67	1918-1945
.S7	World War II
.S8	1945-
6512	Regions, natural features, etc., A-Z
	e. g. Erzgebirge (Krušné Hory), see G6092.E7
	.S8 Sudetenland

---

[1]

For subdivisions, see tables, pp. 206-223

MAPS

By region or country[1]
 Eastern Hemisphere. Eurasia, Africa, etc.
  Europe
   Central Europe
    Austria-Hungary
     Czechoslovakia. Czech Socialist Republic and
      Slovak Socialist Republic - Continued

6513		Provinces, etc., A-Z
	e. g.	.B6 Bohemia
		Including Kingdom of Bohemia
		.J5 Jihočeský
		.J6 Jihomoravský
		.M6 Moravia
		.S3 Severočesky
		.S4 Severomoravský
		.S5 Silesia
		Cf. G6523.S5, Silesia
		(Polish voivodeship)
		.S6 Slovakia
		.S7 Středočeský
		.S8 Středoslovenský
		.V8 Východočeský
		.V9 Východoslovenský
		.Z3 Západočeský
		.Z4 Západoslovenský

6520-6524	Poland
	History
6521.S1	General
.S2	Early to 1573
.S3	1573-1795
.S4	1795-1830
.S5	1830-1918
.S65	World War I
.S67	1918-1945
.S7	World War II
.S73	1945-
6522	Regions, natural features, etc., A-Z
	e. g. .B3 Baltic Sea region
	.M35 Mazury region
	.P58 Pomerania
	.P8 West Prussia
6523	Voivodeships, etc., A-Z
	.B5 Białystok
	Breslau, see .W7
	.B8 Bydgoszcz
	Danzig, see .G4
	.G4 Gdańsk
	.K3 Katowice
	.K5 Kielce
	.K6 Koszalin
	.K7 Krakow
	.L6 Łódź
	.L8 Lublin
	.O5 Olsztyn. East Prussia

---

[1]
    For subdivisions, see tables, pp. 206-223

By region or country[1]
  Eastern Hemisphere. Eurasia, Africa, etc.
    Europe
      Central Europe
        Poland
6523   Voivodeships, etc., A–Z – Continued
                .06 Opole
                .P6 Posen
                .R9 Rzeszów
                .S5 Silesia
                       Cf. G6513.S5, Silesia (Czech province)
                     Stalinogrod, see .K3
                .S9 Szczecin
                .W3 Warsaw
                .W7 Wrocław
                .Z5 Zielona Góra
6530–6532   Southern Europe (Map, p. 128)
                Cf. G5672.M4 Mediterranean region
6540–6541   Iberian Peninsula (Map, p. 129)
6550–6551   Spanish Empire
                 Including maps of Spanish colonies, etc.
                   (Collectively)
                 Class individual colonies, etc., according
                   to location, e. g. G8232.S7, Spanish
                   Morocco
6560–6564   Spain
6562   Regions, natural features, etc., A–Z
                   e. g. .A5   Andalusia
                          .B25 Balearic Islands
                          .B3   Basque Provinces (Provincias
                                  Vascongadas)
                                Canary Islands, see G9150
                          .C3   Cantabrian Mountains
                          .C35 New Castile
                          .C37 Old Castile
                          .E7   Estremadura
                          .M3   La Mancha
6563   Provinces and kingdoms, A–Z
                   .A2 Álava
                   .A3 Albacete
                   .A4 Alicante
                   .A5 Almería
                   .A6 Aragón (Kingdom)
                        Asturias, see .O8
                   .A8 Ávila
                   .B2 Badajoz
                        Baleares, see G6562.B25
                   .B4 Barcelona
                   .B8 Burgos
                   .C3 Cáceres
                   .C4 Cádiz
                   .C5 Castellón (Castellón de la Plana)
                   .C55 Castile (Kingdom)
                          New Castile, see G6562.C35
                          Old Castile, see G6562.C37

----

[1] For subdivisions, see tables, pp. 206–223

By region or country
   Eastern Hemisphere. Eurasia, Africa, etc.
     Europe
       Southern Europe
        Iberian Peninsula
         Spain

6563
          Provinces and kingdoms, A-Z - Continued

.C56	Catalonia (Kingdom)
.C6	Ciudad Real
.C7	Córdoba
.C8	La Coruña
.C9	Cuenca
.G3	Galicia (Kingdom)
.G4	Gerona
.G7	Granada (Kingdom)
.G75	Granada (Province)
.G8	Guadalajara
.G9	Guipúzcoa
.H8	Huelva
.H9	Huesca
.J3	Jaén
	La Coruña, see .C8
	Las Palmas, see G9153.L3
.L4	León (Kingdom)
.L45	León (Province)
.L5	Lérida
.L6	Logroño
.L8	Lugo
.M2	Madrid
.M3	Málaga
.M8	Murcia (Kingdom)
.M85	Murcia (Province)
.N3	Navarra (Kingdom)
.N35	Navarra (Province)
	New Castile, see G6562.C35
	Old Castile, see G6562.C37
.O7	Orense
.O8	Oviedo (Asturias)
.P2	Palencia
	Palmas, Las, see G9150+
.P6	Pontevedra
.S2	Salamanca
	Santa Cruz de Tenerife, see G9153.S2
.S3	Santander
.S4	Saragossa (Zaragoza)
.S5	Segovia
.S6	Sevilla
.S7	Soria
.T3	Tarragona
.T4	Teruel
.T6	Toledo
.V2	Valencia (Kingdom)
.V25	Valencia (Province)
.V3	Valladolid
.V5	Vizcaya
.Z2	Zamora
	Zaragoza, see .S4

By region or country[1]
    Eastern Hemisphere. Eurasia, Africa, etc.
      Europe
        Southern Europe
          Iberian Peninsula - Continued

6660-6664	Andorra
6670-6672	Gibraltar
6680-6681	Portuguese Empire

              Including maps of Portuguese colonies,
                etc. (Collectively). Class individual
                colonies according to location, e. g.
                G8640+, Angola

6690-6694   Portugal. Lusitania
    6692   Regions, natural features, etc., A-Z
              e. g.   Azores, see G9130+
                    .E8 Serra da Estrella
                        Madeira Islands, see G9140+
    6693   Provinces, districts, etc., A-Z
              e. g. .A4 Alentejo
                    .A7 Algarve
                        Angra do Heroísmo, see
                          G9133.A5
                    .A9 Aveiro
                    .B3 Beira
                            Including Beira Atla,
                              Beira Baixa, and
                              Beira Litoral
                    .B4 Beja
                    .B7 Braga
                    .B8 Bragança
                    .C3 Castelo Branco
                    .C6 Coimbra
                    .D6 Douro Litoral
                    .E5 Entre-Minho-e-Douro.
                          Entre-Douro-e-Minho
                    .E8 Estremadura
                    .E9 Évora
                    .F3 Faro
                        Funchal, see G9140+
                    .G8 Guarda
                        Horta, see G9133.H6
                    .L4 Leiria
                    .L5 Lisbon (District)
                        Minho, see .E5
                    .O6 Oporto. Pôrto
                        Ponta Delgada, see G9133.P6
                    .P6 Portalegre
                        Pôrto, see .O6
                        Ribatejo, see .S3
                    .S3 Santarém. Ribatejo
                    .S4 Setúbal
                    .V4 Viana do Castelo
                    .V5 Vila Real
                    .V6 Viseu

---
[1] For subdivisions, see tables, pp. 206-223

MAPS

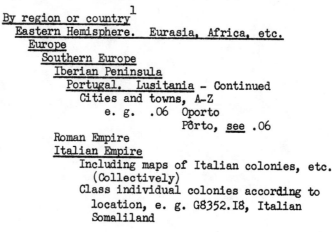

By region or country[1]
    Eastern Hemisphere. Eurasia, Africa, etc.
      Europe
        Southern Europe
          Iberian Peninsula
            Portugal. Lusitania - Continued

6694	Cities and towns, A-Z
	e. g. .06 Oporto
	Pôrto, see .06
6700-6701	Roman Empire
6705-6706	Italian Empire

            Including maps of Italian colonies, etc.
              (Collectively)
            Class individual colonies according to
              location, e. g. G8352.I8, Italian
              Somaliland

---

[1] For subdivisions, see tables, pp. 206-223

Italy

Administrative Divisions

Regione boundary
Province boundary
⊗ National capital
• Province capital

Provinces are named after their respective capitals.

0   25   50   75 Miles
0 25 50 75 Kilometers

TRENTINO
Bolzano
ALTO Trento
ADIGE
FRIULI-
VENEZIA
GIULIA
Udine
Belluno
Gorizia
Pordenone
Sondrio
Treviso
VALLE
D'AOSTA
Aosta
Varese
Como
Bergamo
Vicenza
VENETO
Trieste
Turin
(Torino)
Milan
(Milano)
Brescia
Verona
Padova
Venice
(Venezia)
Novara
LOMBARDIA
Vercelli
Pavia
Cremona
Mantova
Rovigo
Asti
Piacenza
Parma
Reggio
Nell' Emilia
Modena
Ferrara
PIEMONTE
Alessandria
Bologna
Cuneo
LIGURIA
Genoa
(Genova)
Savona
EMILIA ROMAGNA
Ravenna
Imperia
La Spezia
Massa
Pistoia
Lucca
Forli
SAN MARINO
Pesaro
MONACO
Pisa
Florence
(Firenze)
Arezzo
Ancona
Leghorn
(Livorno)
TOSCANA
MARCHE
Macerata
Siena
Perugia
Ascoli
Piceno
ISOLA
D'ELBA
(Livorno)
Grosseto
UMBRIA
Terni
Teramo
Pescara
Viterbo
Rieti
'Aquila
Chieti
LAZIO
ABRUZZI
ROME ⊗
(ROMA)
Frosinone
MOLISE
Campobasso
Foggia
Latina
CAMPANIA
Caserta
Benevento
Bari
Naples
(Napoli)
Avellino
PUGLIA
Brindisi
Salerno
Potenza
Matera
BASILICATA
Taranto
Lecce
Sassari
Nuoro
SARDEGNA
Cagliari
Cosenza
CALABRIA
ISOLE EOLIE
(Messina)
Catanzaro
Trapani
Palermo
Messina
Reggio di Calabria
SICILIA
Enna
Catania
Caltanissetta
Agrigento
Syracuse
(Siracusa)
Ragusa
ISOLA DI PANTELLERIA
(Trapani)

MAPS

<u>By region or country</u>[1]
  <u>Eastern Hemisphere. Eurasia. Africa. etc.</u>
    <u>Europe</u>
      <u>Southern Europe</u> - Continued

```
6710-6714                  Italy (Map, p. 152)
   6713                      Regioni, etc., A-Z
                              .A3  Abruzzi
                                     .A3:3C5  Chieti
                                     .A3:3L3  L'Aquila
                                     .A3:3P4  Pescara
                                     .A3:3T4  Teramo
                              .A4  Abruzzi e Molise
                                   Aosta, see .V3
                              .B3  Basilicata (Regione)
                                     .B3:3B3  Basilicata (Province)
                                     .B3:3M3  Matera
                                     .B3:3P6  Potenza
                              .C3  Calabria
                                     .C3:3C3  Catanzaro
                                     .C3:3C6  Cosenza
                                     .C3:3R4  Reggio di Calabria
                              .C4  Campania
                                     .C4:3A8  Avellino
                                     .C4:3B4  Benevento
                                     .C4:3C3  Caserta
                                     .C4:3N3  Napoli
                                     .C4:3S3  Salerno
                              .E5  Emilia-Romagna
                                     .E5:3B6  Bologna
                                     .E5:3F4  Ferrara
                                     .E5:3F6  Forli
                                     .E5:3M6  Modena
                                     .E5:3P3  Parma
                                     .E5:3P5  Piacenza
                                     .E5:3R4  Reggio nell'Emilia
                              .F7  Friuli-Venezia Giulia
                                     .F7:3C3  Carnaro.  Fiume
                                              Friuli, see .F7:3U4
                                     .F7:3G6  Gorizia
                                     .F7:3I8  Istria.  Pola
                                     .F7:3P6  Pordenone
                                     .F7:3T7  Trieste
                                     .F7:3U4  Udine.  Friuli
                              .L3  Lazio
                                     .L3:3F7  Frosinone
                                     .L3:3L3  Latina.  Littoria
                                     .L3:3R5  Rieti
                                     .L3:3R6  Roma
                                              Vatican, see G6714.R7:3V3
                                     .L3:3V5  Viterbo
```

---

[1]
  For subdivisions, <u>see</u> tables, pp. 206-223

MAPS

By region or country
  Eastern Hemisphere. Eurasia, Africa, etc.
    Europe
      Southern Europe
        Italy

6713   Regioni, etc., A-Z - Continued

           .L5 Liguria
               .L5:3G4 Genova
               .L5:3I5 Imperia
               .L5:3S3 Savona
               .L5:3S6 Spezia (La Spezia)
           .L6 Lombardia
               .L6:3B4 Bergamo
               .L6:3B7 Brescia
               .L6:3C6 Como
               .L6:3C7 Cremona
               .L6:3M3 Mantova
               .L6:3M5 Milano
               .L6:3P3 Pavia
               .L6:3S6 Sondrio
               .L6:3V3 Varese
         .M3 Marche
               .M3:3A5 Ancona
               .M3:3A8 Ascoli Piceno
               .M3:3M3 Macerata
               .M3:3P4 Pesaro
         .M6 Molise
               .M6:3C3 Campobasso
               .M6:3I8 Isernia
         .P3 Papal States
         .P5 Piemonte
               .P5:3A5 Alessandria
               .P5:3A8 Asti
               .P5:3C9 Cuneo
               .P5:3N6 Novara
               .P5:3T6 Torino
               .P5:3V4 Vercelli
         .P8 Puglia
               .P8:3B3 Bari
               .P8:3F6 Foggia
                      Ionio, see .P8:3T3
               .P8:3L4 Lecce
               .P8:3T3 Taranto. Ionio
         Sardinia, see G6770+
         Sicilia, see G6760+
         .T6 Toscana
                      Apuania, see .T6:3M3
               .T6:3A7 Arezzo
               .T6:3F5 Firenze (Florence)
               .T6:3G7 Grosseto
               .T6:3L5 Livorno
               .T6:3L8 Lucca
               .T6:3M3 Massa-Carrara (Massa). Apuania
               .T6:3P5 Pisa
               .T6:3P6 Pistoia
               .T6:3S5 Siena

MAPS

By region or country[1]
Eastern Hemisphere. Eurasia. Africa. etc.
Europe
Southern Europe
Italy

6713
Regioni, etc., A-Z – Continued
.T7 Trentino-Alto Adige
.T7:3B6 Bolzano
.T7:3T7 Trento
.T7:3V4 Venezia Tridentina
.U5 Umbria
.U5:3P4 Perugia
.U5:3T4 Terni
.V3 Valle d'Aosta
.V3:3A6 Aosta
.V4 Veneto. Venezia Euganea
.V4:3B4 Belluno
.V4:3P3 Padova
.V4:3R6 Rovigo
.V4:3T7 Treviso
.V4:3V3 Venetian Republic
.V4:3V4 Venezia (Venice)
.V4:3V5 Verona
.V4:3V6 Vicenza
.V5 Venezia Giulia

6714
Cities and towns, A-Z
e. g. .R7 Rome
.R7:3V3 Vatican

6760-6763
Sicily

6762
Regions, natural features, and adjacent
islands, A-Z
e. g. .E8 Etna
.P3 Pantelleria

6763
Provinces, etc., A-Z
.A3 Agrigento
.C3 Caltanissetta
.C4 Catania
.E5 Enna
.M4 Messina
.P3 Palermo
.R3 Ragusa
.S9 Syracuse
.T7 Trapani

6770-6773
Sardinia

6773
Provinces, etc., A-Z
.C3 Cagliari
.N8 Nuoro
.S2 Sassari

---

[1]
For subdivisions, see tables, pp. 206-223

MAPS

By region or country[1]
   Eastern Hemisphere. Eurasia, Africa, etc.
     Europe
       Southern Europe - Continued

6780–6784	San Marino
6790–6794	Malta
6792	Regions, natural features, individual islands, etc., A–Z
	e. g. .G6 Gozo
6800–6802	Balkan Peninsula. Southeastern Europe (Map, p. 128)
6802	Regions, natural features, etc., A–Z

          e. g. .M2 Macedonia (General)
               Cf. G6812.M3, Macedonia (Greek region)
               G6845+, Macedonia (Federated Republic)
        .T5 Thrace (General)
               Cf. G6812.T5, Thrace (Greek region)
               G7430+, Turkey in Europe (Eastern Thrace)

6810–6814	Greece
6812	Regions, natural features, dhiamérismata, etc., A–Z

     e. g. .A4 Aegean Islands (General)
         .C7 Crete
         .D5 Dodecanese Islands
            Cf. G6813.D5, Dodecanese (Nome)
         .E6 Epirus
         .I6 Ionian Islands (General)
         .M3 Macedonia
         .P4 Peloponnesos
         .S8 Steréa Ellás (Central Greece and Euboea)
         .T4 Thessaly
         .T5 Thrace
          Zákinthos, see G6813.Z3

6813	Provinces (Nomoi), etc., A–Z

    .A4 Aitolía kai Akarnanía
    .A5 Akhaïa
    .A6 Argolis
    .A65 Arkadhía
    .A7 Árta
    .A8 Attica
    .A9 Áyion Óros
    .B6 Boetia
    .C4 Cephalonia
    .C6 Corfu
    .C9 Cyclades
    .D5 Dodecanese (Nome)
       Cf. G6812.D5, Dodecanese Islands
    .D7 Drama

---

[1] For subdivisions, see tables, pp. 206-223

MAPS

By region or country
    Eastern Hemisphere. Eurasia, Africa, etc.
        Europe
            Balkan Peninsula. Southeastern Europe
                Greece
6813   Provinces (Nomoi), etc., A-Z - Continued
                    .E7   Euboea
                    .E75   Evritanía
                    .E8   Évros
                            Evvoia, see .E7
                    .F5   Flórina
                            Fokís, see .P45
                    .F8   Fthiótis
                    .G7   Grevená
                    .I4   Ilía
                    .I5   Imathía
                    .I6   Ioánnina
                    .I7   Iráklion
                    .K2   Kardhítsa
                    .K3   Kastoría
                    .K4   Kavála
                            Kefallinia, see .C4
                            Kérkira, see .C6
                    .K5   Khalkidikí
                    .K53   Khanía
                    .K56   Khíos
                            Kikládhes, see .C9
                    .K6   Kilkís
                            Komotiní, see .R6
                    .K7   Korinthía
                    .K8   Kozáni
                    .L2   Lakonía
                    .L25   Lárisa
                    .L3   Lasíthi
                    .L4   Lésvos
                    .L5   Levkás
                    .M3   Magnisía
                    .M4   Messenía
                            Mount Athos, see .A9
                    .P4   Pélla
                    .P45   Phocis
                    .P5   Piería
                    .P6   Piraieus
                    .P7   Préveza
                    .R4   Rethimnon
                    .R6   Rodhópi. Komotini
                    .S2   Sámos
                    .S3   Sérrai
                    .T4   Thesprotía
                    .T5   Thessalonike
                    .T6   Tríkala
                            Voiotía, see .B6
                    .X3   Xánthi
                    .Z3   Zákinthos

MAPS

By region or country[1]
    Eastern Hemisphere. Eurasia. Africa, etc.
       Europe
         Balkan Peninsula. Southeastern Europe - Continued

6830–6834	Albania
6840–6844	Yugoslavia
6842	Regions, natural features, etc., A–Z
	e. g. .D3 Dalmatia
	.S3 Sava River
	Administrative areas, see G6845+
6844	Cities and towns, A–Z
	e. g. .B5 Belgrad
	.L5 Ljubljana
	.S2 Sarajevo
	.Z3 Zagreb
6845–6848	Macedonia (Federated Republic)
6850–6853	Serbia
6853	Administrative areas, provinces, etc., A–Z
	e. g. .K6 Kosovo i Metohija (Autonomous
	Province)
	.V6 Voivodina (Autonomous Province)
6855–6858	Montenegro (Crna Gora)
6860–6863	Bosnia and Herzegovina
6870–6873	Croatia (Hrvatska)
6875–6878	Slovenia
6877	Regions, natural features, etc., A–Z
	e. g. .J8 Julian Alps
6880–6884	Romania
6882	Regions, natural features, etc., A–Z
	e. g. .B3 Banta
	.D6 Dobrogea
6883	Provinces, etc., A–Z
	e. g. .A5 Alba
	.A6 Arad
	.A7 Argeş
	.B3 Bacău
	.B5 Bihor
	.B55 Bistriţa-Năsăud
	.B6 Botoşani
	.B65 Brăila
	.B7 Braşov
	.B8 Bucureşti
	.B85 Buzău
	.C3 Caraş-Severin
	.C5 Cluj
	.C6 Constanţa
	.C65 Covasna
	.D5 Dîmboviţa
	.D6 Dolj
	.G3 Galaţi

---

[1]
  For subdivisions, see tables, pp. 206–223

MAPS

<u>By region or country</u>[1]
    <u>Eastern Hemisphere. Eurasia. Africa. etc.</u>
      <u>Europe</u>
        <u>Balkan Peninsula. Southeastern Europe</u>
          <u>Romania</u>

6883	Provinces, etc., A–Z – Continued		
	e. g.	.G6	Gorj
		.H3	Harghita
		.H8	Hunedoara
		.I2	Ialomiţa
		.I25	Iaşi
		.I5	Ilfov
		.M3	Maramureş
		.M4	Mehedinti
		.M8	Mures
		.N4	Neamt
		.O5	Olt
		.P7	Prahova
		.S2	Sălaj
		.S25	Satu Mare
		.S5	Sibiu
		.S8	Suceava
		.T4	Teleorman
		.T5	Timiş
		.T8	Tulcea
		.V3	Vaslui
		.V7	Vrancea

          <u>Bulgaria</u>

6890-6894			
6893	Provinces, etc., A–Z		
	e. g.	.B5	Blagoevgrad
		.B8	Burgas
			Dimitrovo, <u>see</u> .P4
		.G3	Gabrovo
		.K5	Khaskovo
		.K8	Kurdzhali
		.K9	Kyustendil
		.L6	Lovech
		.M5	Mikhaylovgrad
		.P3	Pazardzhik
		.P4	Pernik. Dimitrovo
		.P5	Pleven
		.P6	Plovdiv
		.R3	Razgrad
		.R8	Ruse
		.S3	Shumen
		.S4	Silistra
		.S5	Sliven
		.S6	Smolyan
		.S7	Sofia (Province)
		.S8	Stara Zagora
		.T6	Tolbukhin

---

[1] For subdivisions, <u>see</u> tables, pp. 206-223

MAPS

By region or country[1]
　　Eastern Hemisphere. Eurasia, Africa, etc.
　　　Europe
　　　　Balkan Peninsula. Southeastern Europe
　　　　　Bulgaria

6893	Provinces, etc., A-Z - Continued
	.T7 Turgovishte
	Turnovo, <u>see</u> .V4
	.V3 Varna (Province)
	.V4 Veliko Turnovo
	Formerly Turnovo
	.V5 Vidin
	.V7 Vratsa
	.Y3 Yambol
6894	Cities and towns, A-Z
	e. g. .P6 Plovdiv
	.S6 Sofia
	.V2 Varna

6910-6912	<u>Scandinavia. Northern Europe</u> (Map, p. 128)
6912	Regions, natural features, etc., A-Z
	e. g. .L3 Lapland
	Cf. G6963.L3, Lappi (Department
	of Finland)

6915-6916	Denmark and colonies
	Including maps of Danish colonies (Collectively)
	Class individual colonies, etc., according to
	location, e. g. G3380+, Greenland

6920-6924	<u>Denmark</u>
6922	Regions, natural features, A-Z
	e. g. .B6 Bornholm
	.F3 Falster
	.F9 Fyen
	.J8 Jutland
	Laaland, <u>see</u> .L6
	.L3 Langeland
	.L5 Lim Fjord
	.L6 Lolland
	.M6 Møen
	.S3 Samsø
	.S5 Sjaelland (Zealand)
	Zealand, <u>see</u> .S5
6923	Counties (Amter), etc., A-Z
	.A2 Åbenrå. Aabenraa-Sønderborg
	Cf. G6923.S5, Sønderborg
	.A3 Ålborg
	.A4 Århus
	.A8 Assens
	Bornholm, <u>see</u> G6922.B6
	.C6 Copenhagen
	Faerø, <u>see</u> G6925+

---

[1] For subdivisions, <u>see</u> tables, pp. 206-223

MAPS

<u>By region or country</u>[1]
  <u>Eastern Hemisphere. Eurasia. Africa. etc.</u>
    <u>Europe</u>
      <u>Scandinavia. Northern Europe</u>
        <u>Denmark</u>

6923		Counties (Amter), etc., A-Z - Continued
	.F7	Frederiksborg
	.F9	Fyns
		Cf. G6922.F9, Fyen (Island)
	.H3	Haderslev
	.H5	Hjørring
	.H6	Holbaek
	.M3	Maribo
	.N6	Nordjylland
	.O2	Odense
	.P7	Praestø
	.R3	Randers
	.R4	Ribe
	.R5	Ringkøbing
	.R6	Roskilde
	.S4	Skanderborg
	.S5	Sonderborg
		Cf. G6923.A2, Åbenrå
	.S55	Sonderjylland
	.S6	Sorø
	.S8	Storstrøm
	.S9	Svendborg
	.T5	Thisted
	.T6	Tønder
	.V4	Vejle
	.V45	Vestjylland
	.V5	Viborg

        Faeroe Islands
6925-6929
        Greenland, <u>see</u> G3380+
6930-6934   <u>Iceland</u>
  6932   Regions, natural features, etc., A-Z
               e. g.   .S5 Skaftafell Glacier
  6933   Provinces (Sýsler), kjördaemi, etc., A-Z

	.A6	Arnessýsla
	.A8	Austur Barðastranarsýsla
	.A82	Austur Skaftafellssýsla
	.A9	Austurlandskjördaemi (East District)
	.B6	Borgarfjarðarsýsla
	.D3	Dalasýsla
	.E9	Eyjafjarðarsýsla
	.G8	Gullbringusýsla
	.H5	Hnappadalsýsla
	.K5	Kjósarsýsla
	.M5	Miðvasturlandskjördaemi (West District)
	.M9	Mýrasýsla
	.N6	Norður Isafjarðarsýsla
	.N615	Norður Mulasýsla

---

[1]
    For subdivisions, <u>see</u> tables, pp. 206-223

MAPS

By region or country[1]
   Eastern Hemisphere. Eurasia, Africa, etc.
     Europe
      Scandinavia. Northern Europe
       Iceland

6933
        Provinces (Sýsler), kjördaemi, etc., A-Z - Continued
         .N62 Norður Þingeyjarsýsla
         .N7   Norðurlandskjördaemi eystra (Northland East District)
         .N715 Norðurlandskjördaemi vestra (Northland West District)
         .R3   Rangarvallasýsla
         .R4   Reykjaneskjördaemi (Reykjanes area District)
         .S5   Skagafjarðarsýsla
         .S6   Snaefellsnessýsla
         .S7   Strandasýsla
         .S8   Suður Múlasýsla
         .S815 Suður Þingeyjarsýsla
         .S9   Suðurlandskjördaemi (South District)
         .V3   Vestfjarðakjördaemi (Western Peninsula District)
         .V4   Vestur Barðastrandarsýsla
         .V415 Vestur Húnavatnssýsla
         .V42 Vestur Isafjarðarsýsla
         .V43 Vestur Skaftafellssýsla

6934
       Cities and towns, A-Z
        Class urban municipalities with their respective cities
        e. g. .R4 Reykjavík

6940-6944 Norway
6942
     Regions, natural features, etc., A-Z
      e. g. .H3 Hardanger Vidda
6943
     Counties (Fylker), etc., A-Z
      .A4 Akershus
      .A8 Aust-Agder
      Bergen, see G6944.B4
      .B8 Buskerud
      .F5 Finnmark
      .H4 Hedmark
      .H6 Hordaland
      .M6 Møre og Romsdal
      .N5 Nord-Trøndelag
      .N6 Nordland
      .O3 Østfold. Smaalenene
      .O6 Opland. Kristian
      Oslo, see G6944.O9
      .R6 Rogaland
      .S6 Sør-Trøndelag
      .S7 Sogn og Fjordane
      .T4 Telemark
      .T7 Troms
      Trøndelag, see .N5, .S6
      .V4 Vest-Agder
      .V5 Vestfold

---

[1] For subdivisions, see tables, pp. 206-223

MAPS

By region or country[1]
  Eastern Hemisphere. Eurasia. Africa. etc.
    Europe
      Scandinavia. Northern Europe
        Norway - Continued

6944   Cities and towns, A-Z
                e. g. .B4 Bergen
                      .O9 Oslo

6950-6954   Sweden
6952   Regions, natural features, etc., A-Z
                e. g. .G6 Gotland (Island)
                      .V3 Västergötland

6953   Provinces (Länni), etc., A-Z
                .A3 Älvsborg
                .B5 Blekinge
                .G3 Gävleborg
                .G6 Gothenburg and Bohus
                .G7 Gotland
                      Cf. G6952.G6, Gotland (Island)
                .H3 Halland
                .J3 Jämtland
                .J6 Jönköping
                .K3 Kalmar
                .K6 Kopparberg
                .K7 Kristianstad
                .K8 Kronoberg
                .M3 Malmöhus
                .N6 Norrbotten
                .O7 Örebro
                .O8 Östergötland
                .S5 Skaraborg
                .S6 Södermanland
                .S8 Stockholm (Län)
                      Cf. G6954.S7, Stockholm (City)
                .U6 Uppsala
                .V2 Värmland
                .V3 Västerbotten
                .V4 Västernorrland
                .V5 Västmanland

6954   Cities and towns, etc., A-Z
                e. g. .S7 Stockholm

6960-6964   Finland. Suomi
6962   Regions, natural features, etc., A-Z
                e. g. .A2 Åland Islands

6963   Departments, etc., A-Z
                  Ahvenanmaa, see G6962.A2
                .H3 Häme (Tavastland)
                .K4 Keski-Suomi. Mellersta Finland
                .K8 Kuopio
                .K9 Kymi
                .L3 Lappi
                .M5 Mikkeli (Sankt Michel)

---

[1]   For subdivisions, see tables, pp. 206-223

MAPS

By region or country[1]
    Eastern Hemisphere. Eurasia, Africa, etc.
        Europe
            Scandinavia. Northern Europe
                Finland. Suomi
6963   Departments, etc., A-Z - Continued
                            .09 Oulu (Uleåborg)
                            .P6 Pohjois-Karjala (Norra Karelen)
                            .T9 Turku-Pori (Åbo-Björneborg)
                            .U9 Uusimaa (Nyland)
                            .V2 Vaasa
6965-6966   Eastern Europe (Map, p. 129)
                    Including Poland, Finland, Baltic States,
                        European Russia, Romania, Bulgaria, Soviet
                        zone of influence, 1946-
                    Baltic States, see G7020-
                        Estonia, see G7030+
                        Latvia, see G7040+
                        Lithuania, see G7050+
                    Finland, see G6960+
                    Poland, see G6520+
7000-7004   Union of Soviet Socialist Republics
                (U.S.S.R.). Russia (Map, p. 40)
                History
7001.S1   General
    .S2   Early through 1613
    .S3   17th century
    .S4   18th century
    .S5   1801-1917
    .S54   Crimean War
    .S57   Rebellion, 1905-1907
    .S65   World War I
    .S67   1917-1921
    .S68   1921-1945
    .S7   World War II
    .S72   1945-
7002   Regions, natural features, etc., A-Z
                    e. g.   .U72 Ural Mountains
7004   Cities and towns, A-Z
                    e. g.   .L4 Leningrad
                            Petrograd, see .L4
                            Saint Petersburg, see .L4
7010-7012   U.S.S.R. in Europe. Russia in Europe
7020-7022   Baltic States
7030-7033   Estonia. Estonian S.S.R.
7040-7043   Latvia. Latvian S.S.R.
7050-7053   Lithuania. Lithuanian S.S.R.

---

[1]
    For subdivisions, see tables, pp. 206-223

MAPS

By region or country[1]
  Eastern Hemisphere. Eurasia. Africa. etc.
    Union of Soviet Socialist Republics (U.S.S.R.). Russia
      U.S.S.R. in Europe. Russia in Europe - Continued

7060–7063	Russian Soviet Federated Socialist Republic (R.S.F.S.R.)
	Asian provinces, districts, etc., see G7220+
7063	European provinces, districts, etc., A–Z
	e. g. .K45 Karelia. Karelian A.S.S.R.
	Karelo–Finnish S.S.R.
	.M8 Murmansk (Province)
	Karelia, see G7063.K45
7090–7093	Belorussia (White Russia). Belorussian S.S.R.
7100–7103	Ukraine. Ukrainian S.S.R.
7110–7113	Moldavia. Moldavian S.S.R.
7120–7122	Caucasia
7130–7133	Georgia. Georgian S.S.R.
7140–7143	Azerbaijan. Azerbaijan S.S.R.
7150–7153	Armenia. Armenian S.S.R.
7200–7202	U.S.S.R. in Asia. Russia in Asia
7210–7212	Soviet Central Asia. Russian Central Asia. West Turkestan
7220–7223	Kazakhstan. Kazakh S.S.R.
7230–7233	Uzbekistan. Uzbek S.S.R.
7240–7243	Turkmenistan. Turkmen S.S.R.
7250–7253	Kirgizia. Kirgiz S.S.R.
7260–7263	Tadzhikistan. Tadzhik S.S.R.
7270–7273	Siberia. Northern Asia
7273	Administrative divisions, A–Z
	e. g. .T8 Tannu Tuva
7300–7303	Buryat A.S.S.R. Buryat–Mongol A.S.S.R.
7310–7313	Yakutia. Yakutsk A.S.S.R.
7320–7323	Far Eastern region (Far Eastern Republic). Dal'nevostochnyy Kray
7323	Provinces, districts, etc., A–Z
	e. g. .M3 Maritime Province
7330–7333	Sakhalin
7340–7342	Kuril Islands (Chishima Retto)

---

[1] For subdivisions, see tables, pp. 206–223

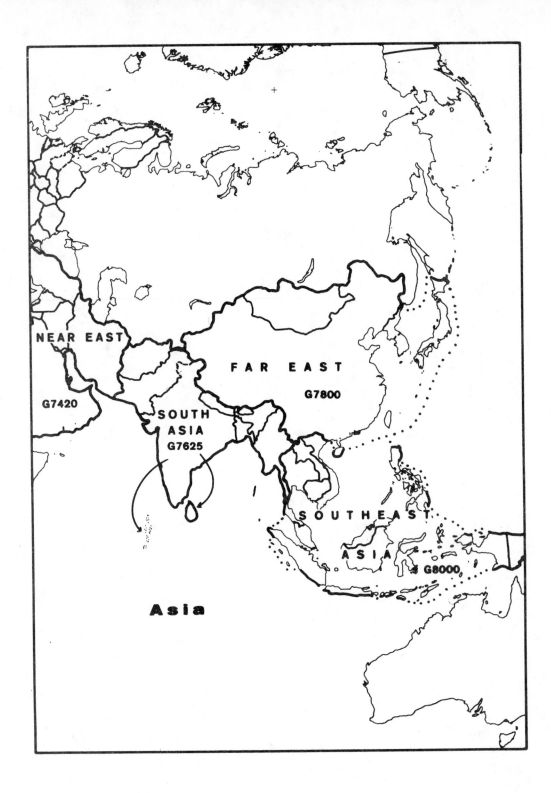

NEAR EAST

G7420

FAR EAST

G7800

SOUTH
ASIA
G7625

SOUTHEAST

ASIA

G8000

Asia

166

By region or country[1]
Eastern Hemisphere. Eurasia, Africa, etc. - Continued

7400-7402	Asia (Map, p. 40)
7402	Regions, natural features, etc., A-Z
	e. g. .H5 Himalaya Mountains
	Northern Asia, see G7270+
7405-7406	Central Asia. Inner Asia. Turkestan
	Including Sinkiang and Soviet Central Asia
	together, and often including Mongolia,
	Tibet, Jammu and Kashmir, and Northern
	Afghanistan
7420-7422	Near East. Middle East. Levant (Map, p. 166)
	Often including Egypt and Sudan, and sometimes
	Libya, Ethiopia, Afghanistan, and Pakistan
	Islamic Empire, see G5680+
7430-7434	Turkey. Ottoman Empire. Asia Minor
	Including Turkey in Europe (Eastern Thrace)
	Cf. G6802.T5, Thrace (General)
	G6812.T5, Thrace (Greek region)
7450-7454	Cyprus
7460-7464	Syria
7470-7474	Lebanon
7480-7481	Bible lands
7481.2	Old Testament
	Including maps of special aspects of the
	Old Testament, e. g. Exodus, the Kingdom
	of David and Solomon, etc.
.3	New Testament
	Including maps of special aspects of the
	New Testament, e. g. the life of Jesus,
	Paul's journeys, etc.
7500-7504	Israel. Palestine
	History
7501.S1	General
.S2	To 70 A.D.
	Cf. G7480+, Bible lands
.S3	70-1453
.S4	1454-1800
.S5	1801-1899
.S6	1900-1947
.S65	World War I
.S7	World War II
.S73	1948-
7502	Regions, natural features, etc., A-Z
	Sinaitic Peninsula, see G8302.S5
7510-7514	Jordan
7520-7522	Arabian Peninsula. Arabia
7530-7534	Saudi Arabia
7540-7544	Yemen (Yemen Arab Republic)
7550-7554	Yemen (People's Democratic Republic). Southern
	Yemen. Aden
7560-7564	Oman. Muscat and Oman

---

[1] For subdivisions, see tables, pp. 206-223

By region or country[1]
   Eastern Hemisphere. Eurasia, Africa, etc.
    Asia
     Near East. Middle East. Levant
      Arabian Peninsula. Arabia - Continued

7570-7574	United Arab Emirates. Trucial States
7573	Sheikdoms, etc., A-Z
	e. g. .A2 Abu Dhabi
	.A4 Ajman
	.D8 Dubai
	.F8 Fujairah
	.R3 Ras al Khaimah
	.S5 Sharjah
	.U4 Umm al Qaiwain
7580-7584	Qatar
7590-7594	Bahrein
7600-7604	Kuwait
7610-7614	Iraq. Mesopotamia
7620-7624	Iran. Persia
	History
7621.S1	General
.S2	Ancient, to 226 A.D.
.S23	Median Empire, 640-558 B.C.
.S25	Persian Empire, 558-330 B.C.
.S27	Parthian Empire, 246 B.C.-226 A.D.
.S3	Modern, 226-
.S34	Sassanian Empire, 226-651
.S37	Arab and Mongol rule, 651-1500
.S4	Safawids and Afghans, 1500-1736
.S5	Kajar dynasty, 1794-1925
.S6	Pahlavi dynasty, 1925-
7623	Provinces, governorships, etc., A-Z
	.A8 Azarbaijan-e Gharbi (Western Azerbaijan)
	.A85 Azarbaijan-e Sharqi (Eastern Azerbaijan)
	.B2 Bakhtiari va Chahar Mahall
	.B3 Baluchestan va Sistan
	.B6 Boyer Ahmadi-ye Sardsir va Kohkiluyeh
	.F3 Fars
	.G5 Gilan
	Including Zanjan
	.H3 Hamadan
	.I5 Ilan va Poshtkuh
	.I8 Isfahan
	Including Yazd
	.J3 Jazayer va Banader-e Khalij-e
	Fars va Darya-ye Oman
	.K3 Kerman
	.K35 Kermanshahan
	.K4 Khorasan
	.K45 Khuzestan
	.K8 Kurdestan
	.M3 Mazandaran
	.S4 Semnan
	.T4 Teheran (Province)
	Yazd, <u>see</u> .I8
	Zanjan, <u>see</u> .G5

---

[1]
For subdivisions, <u>see</u> tables, pp. 206-223

MAPS

By region or country[1]
    Eastern Hemisphere. Eurasia, Africa, etc.
      Asia - Continued

7625-7627	South Asia (Map, p. 166)
7630-7634	Afghanistan
7640-7644	Pakistan

           Including maps of West and East Pakistan
             together

7643   Provinces, etc.
          .A9 Azad Kashmir
          .B3 Baluchistān
              e. g. .B3:3K3 Kalāt
                    .B3:3K4 Karāchi
                    .B3:3Q4 Quetta
         East Pakistan, see G7645+
         Islamabad (Capital Territory), see G7644.I8
          .N6 North-west Frontier Province
              e. g. .N6:3D4 Dera Ismāīl Khān
                    .N6:3M3 Malākand
                    .N6:3P4 Peshāwar
          .P8 Punjab
              e. g. .P8:3B3 Bahāwalpur
                    .P8:3L3 Lahore
                    .P8:3M8 Multān
                    .P8:3R3 Rāwalpindi
                    .P8:3S3 Sargodha
          .S5 Sind
              e. g. .S5:3H9 Hyderābād
                    .S5:3K5 Khairpur

7644   Cities and towns, A-Z
              e. g. .I8 Islamabad

7645-7649   Bangladesh. East Pakistan
7648   Provinces, etc.
          .C5 Chittagong
          .D3 Dacca
          .K5 Khulna
          .R3 Rājshāhi

7650-7654   India
7652   Regions, natural features, etc., A-Z
              e. g. .A4   Amindivi Islands
                    .A5   Andaman Islands
                    .K3   Karnala Bird Sanctuary
                    .L25 Laccadive Islands
                    .M5   Minicoy Island
                    .N5   Nicobar Islands
                    .P46 Periyār Sanctuary

7653   States, territories, etc., A-Z
          .A5 Andaman and Nicobar Islands
              Cf. G7652.A5, Andaman Islands
                G7652.N5, Nicobar Islands
          .A6 Andhra Pradesh
          .A8 Assam
          .B5 Bihar
          .B6 Bombay
          .C5 Chandigarh
          .D3 Dadra and Nagar Haveli

---

[1] For subdivisions, see tables, pp. 206-223

MAPS

By region or country[1]
    Eastern Hemisphere. Eurasia, Africa, etc.
        Asia
            South Asia
                India

7653		States, territories, etc., A-Z - Continued
	.D4	Delhi
	.G6	Goa, Daman, and Diu
	.G8	Gujarat
	.H3	Haryana
	.H5	Himachal Pradesh
	.H9	Hyderabad
	.J3	Jammu and Kashmir
	.K3	Karnataka. Mysore
	.K4	Kerala
	.L3	Lakshadweep. Laccadive, Minicoy, and
		Amindivi Islands
		Cf. G7652.A4, Amindivi Islands
		G7652.L25, Laccadive Islands
		G7652.M5, Minicoy Island
	.M2	Madhya Pradesh
	.M3	Maharashtra
	.M35	Manipur
	.M4	Meghalaya
		Mysore, see .K3
	.N3	Nagaland
	.O7	Orissa
	.P6	Pondicherry
		Including Karikal, Yanan, and Mahe
	.P8	Punjab
	.R3	Rajasthan
	.R33	Rajputana
	.S5	Sikkim
	.T3	Tamil Nadu. Madras
	.T6	Tripura
	.U8	Uttar Pradesh
	.W4	West Bengal
7720-7724		Burma
7750-7754		Sri Lanka. Ceylon
7760-7764		Nepal
7763		Zones, districts, etc., A-Z
	e. g. .B2	Bāgmati
	.B8	Bheri
	.D6	Dhaulāgiri
	.G3	Gandaki
	.J3	Janakpur
	.K5	Karnali
	.K9	Kosi
	.L8	Lumbini
	.M13	Mahakali
	.M4	Mechi
	.N3	Nārāyani
	.R3	Rāpti
	.S15	Sagarmatha
	.S4	Seti
		Sikkim, see G7653.S5
7780-7784		Bhutan

---

[1] For subdivisions, see tables, pp. 206-223

By region or country[1]
 Eastern Hemisphere. Eurasia, Africa, etc.
  <u>Asia</u> - Continued

7800-7802	<u>Far East</u> (Map, p. 166)
7810-7812	Chinese Empire
	Including maps of Chinese dependencies, etc. (Collectively)
	Class individual dependencies, etc. according to location, e. g. G7830+, Manchuria
7820-7824	<u>China. People's Republic of China</u>
7822	Regions, natural features, etc., A-Z
	e. g. .H9 Hwang-ho. Yellow River
	.Y3 Yantze River
7823	Provinces, etc., A-Z

     .A5 Anhwei (Nganhui)
     .A6 Antung
     .C4 Chabar
     .C5 Chekiang (Tche-Kiang)
         Ch'ing-hai, <u>see</u> .T8
         Fengtien, <u>see</u> .L4
     .F8 Fukien
     .H3 Heilungchiang
     .H35 Hokiang
     .H4 Honan
     .H5 Hopei
         Hsik'ang, <u>see</u> .S6
     .H7 Hunan
     .H8 Hsingan. Khingan
     .H9 Hupei
     .J4 Jehol. Zhekhe
     .K3 Kansu
         Khingan, <u>see</u> .H8
     .K4 Kiangsi
     .K5 Kiangsu
     .K6 Kirin
         Koko Nor, <u>see</u> .T8
     .K7 Kwangsi (Autonomous region)
     .K8 Kwangtung
     .K9 Kweichow
     .L4 Liaoning. Fengtien. Shengking
     .L5 Liaopei
         Nganhui, Nganhwei, <u>see</u> .A5
     .N5 Ninghsia (Autonomous region)
     .N8 Nunkiang
     .S3 Shansi
     .S4 Shantung
         Shengking, <u>see</u> .L4
     .S5 Shensi
     .S6 Sikang (Hsik'ang)
         Sinkiang (Autonomous region). <u>see</u> G7880+
     .S8 Suiyuan
     .S85 Sungkiang
     .S9 Szechwan
         Tche-Kiang, <u>see</u> .C5
     .T8 Tsinghai (Ch'ing-hai). Koko Nor
     .Y8 Yunnan
         Zhekhe, <u>see</u> .J4

By region or country[1]
  Eastern Hemisphere. Eurasia, Africa, etc.
    Asia
      Far East
        China. People's Republic of China - Continued

7824	Cities and towns, A-Z
	e. g. .L4 Lhasa
	.M9 Mukden
	.P4 Peiping
7830-7831	Manchuria
7850-7852	Inner Mongolia (Autonomous region)
	Kwangsi (Autonomous region), see G7823.K7
	Ninghsia (Autonomous region), see G7823.N5
	Tannu Tuva, see G7273.T8
7880-7882	Sinkiang (Autonomous region). Chinese Turkestan. East Turkestan
7890-7892	Tibet (Autonomous region)
7895-7899	<u>Mongolia (Mongolian People's Republic). Outer Mongolia</u>
	Including maps of Inner and Outer Mongolia together
7897	Regions, natural features, etc., A-Z
	e. g. .G6 Gobi Desert
	.G62 Gobi Altai Mountains
7900-7904	South Korea (Republic of Korea). Chosen
	Including maps of Korea as a whole
7902	Regions, natural features, islands, etc., A-Z
	e. g. .H3 Han River
7905-7909	North Korea (Democratic People's Republic)
7907	Regions, natural features, islands, etc., A-Z
	e. g. .T33 Tae-dong River
	Ryukyu Islands, see G7962.R9
7910-7914	Taiwan. Formosa
7912	Regions, natural features, islands, etc., A-Z
	e. g. .C5 Chungyang Shań-mo
	.P4 Pescadores (Boko-retto, Hoko-gunto, Pêng-hu Islands)
7940-7944	<u>Hongkong (Crown colony)</u>
7942	Regions, natural features, islands, etc., A-Z
	e. g. .H6 Hongkong (Island)
	.L3 Lan Tao Island
	.N4 New Territories
7944	Cities and towns, A-Z
	e. g. .K6 Kowloon
	.V5 Victoria
7945-7947	Macao (Colony and city)
7950-7951	Japanese Empire
	Including maps of Japanese colonies, dependencies, etc. (Collectively)
	Class individual colonies, dependencies, etc., according to location, e. g. G7335+, Karafuto

----

[1] For subdivisions, see tables, pp. 206-223

By region or country[1]
  Eastern Hemisphere. Eurasia, Africa, etc.
    Asia
     Far East - Continued

7960-7964   Japan
7962   Regions, natural features, islands, archipelagoes, etc., A-Z

e. g. .B6 Bonin Islands
    .C4 Chūbu region
    .C47 Chūgoku region
    .H5 Hokkaidō
    .H6 Honshū
    .I8 Iwo Jima
    .K3 Kantō region
    .K54 Kinki region
    .K9 Kyūshū
    .M5 Miyako Jima
    .O6 Okinawa Island
    .R9 Ryukyu Islands. Nansei Shotō. Ryukyu Retto
    .S5 Shikoku
    .T6 Tōhoku region
    .V6 Volcano Islands. Kazan Retto

7963   Prefectures (Ken) etc., A-Z
.A4 Aichi
.A5 Akita
.A6 Aomori
.C4 Chiba
.E4 Ehime
.F84 Fukui
.F86 Fukuoka
.F88 Fukushima
.G5 Gifu
.G8 Gumma
.H5 Hiroshima
Hokkaidō, see G7962.H5
.H8 Hyōgo
.I2 Ibaraki
.I6 Ishikawa
.I8 Iwate
.K3 Kagawa
.K34 Kagoshima
.K36 Kanagawa
.K6 Kōchi
.K8 Kumamoto
.K85 Kyōto
.M4 Mie
.M56 Miyagi
.M58 Miyazaki
.N3 Nagano
.N34 Nagasaki
.N4 Nara
.N5 Niigata

[1]
  For subdivisions, see tables, pp. 206-223

MAPS

By region or country[1]
   Eastern Hemisphere. Eurasia, Africa, etc.
     Asia
      Far East
       Japan

7963   Prefectures (Ken) etc., A-Z - Continued
           .05 Ōita
           .06 Okayama
           .065 Okinawa
           .08 Ōsaka
           .S2 Saga
           .S25 Saitama
           .S4 Shiga
           .S44 Shimane
           .S5 Shizuoka
           .T5 Tochigi
           .T54 Tokushima
           .T6 Tōkyō
           .T64 Tottori
           .T67 Toyama
           .W34 Wakayama
           .Y3 Yamagata
           .Y34 Yamaguchi
           .Y36 Yamanashi

8000-8002   Southeast Asia. Indochina (Map, p. 166)
         Sometimes including Burma
        Burma, see G7720+
8005-8006   French Indochina
8010-8014   Cambodia. Khmer Republic
    8012   Regions, natural features, etc., A-Z
          e. g. .T6 Tônlé Sap
8015-8019   Laos
    8017   Regions, natural features, etc., A-Z
          e. g. .J3 Plain of Jars
                .T5 Theun River
8020-8024   Vietnam
         Including maps of Vietnam as a whole, as well
           as maps of North or South Vietnam separately
    8022   Regions, natural features, islands, etc., A-Z
          e. g. .C6 Côn Son Islands
                .M4 Mekong Delta
8025-8029   Thailand. Siam
    8027   Regions, natural features, etc., A-Z
          e. g. .K7 Isthmus of Kra. Khokhok Kra

---

[1]
  For subdivisions, see tables, pp. 206-223

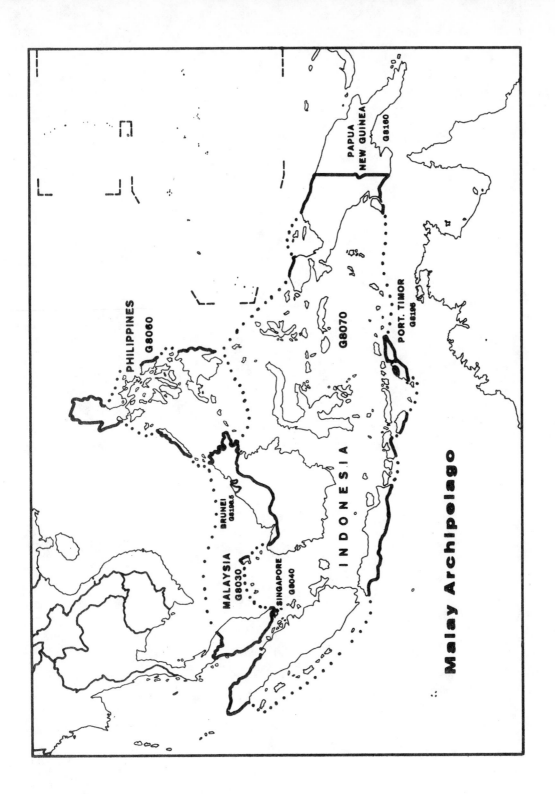

PHILIPPINES
G8060

MALAYSIA
G8030

BRUNEI
G8104.5

SINGAPORE
G8040

INDONESIA

G8070

PORT. TIMOR
G8195

PAPUA
NEW GUINEA
G8150

Malay Archipelago

175

By region or country[1]
  Eastern Hemisphere. Eurasia, Africa, etc.
    Asia
      Southeast Asia. Indochina - Continued
8030-8034   Malaysia. Malaya
          Including maps of the Malay Peninsula
8032   Regions, natural features, etc., A-Z
          e. g. .E5 Endau River
                .J4 Jelai River
                .R3 Rajang River
8033   States, A-Z
          .J6 Johore
          .K3 Kedah (Quedah). Langkasuka
          .K4 Kelantan
               Langkasuka, see .K3
          .M3 Malacca
          .N4 Negri Sembilan
          .P2 Pahang
          .P3 Penang
          .P4 Perak
          .P5 Perlis
          .S3 Sabah. British North Borneo. North
                  Borneo
          .S35 Sarawak
          .S4 Selangor
          .T7 Trengganu
8040-8044   Singapore (Republic, Colony, and Island).
          Straits Settlements, 1826-1946 (Map., p. 175)
8044   Cities and towns, A-Z
          e. g. .S5 Singapore (City)
8050-8052   Malay Archipelago
8060-8064   Philippines (Map, p. 175)
8062   Islands, archipelagoes, regions, natural
            features, etc., A-Z
          e. g. .B2 Babuyan Islands
               .B3 Batan Islands. Bashi Islands
                  Bisayas, see .V5
               .B6 Bohol
               .C3 Calamian Islands
               .C4 Cebu (Sugbu)
                  Central Philippines, see .V5
               .J6 Jolo Group
               .J7 Jolo Island
               .L4 Leyte
               .L8 Luzon
               .M3 Manila Bay
               .M35 Marinduque
               .M4 Masbate
               .M5 Mindanao
               .M6 Mindoro
               .M9 Musa Bay
               .N4 Negros
               .P3 Palawan. Paragua
               .P4 Panay
               .P45 Panguil Bay
               .S3 Samar
                  Sugbu, see .C4
               .S8 Sulu Archipelago
               .V5 Visayan Islands (Bisayas)

---

[1] For subdivisions, see tables, pp. 206-223

MAPS

By region or country[1]
  Eastern Hemisphere. Eurasia, Africa, etc.
    Asia
      Southeast Asia. Indochina - Continued

8070-8074   Indonesia. United States of Indonesia. Netherlands
          Indies. East Indies (Map, p. 175)
8072   Regions, natural features, etc., A-Z
            For individual islands and archipelagoes,
              see G8080+
            e. g. .J3 Java Sea
                  .M3 Malacca Strait
8073   Provinces, etc., A-Z
            e. g. .I7 Irian Jaya. Irian Barat
                  .N8 Nusa Tenggara
8074   Cities and towns, A-Z
            e. g. .B3 Bandung
                  .D3 Djakarta

8080-8082   Sumatra
8082   Regions, natural features, adjacent islands,
          etc., A-Z
            e. g. .A8 Asahar River

8090-8092   Java. Djawa
8092   Regions, natural features, adjacent islands,
          etc., A-Z
            e. g. .M2 Madura

8100-8102   Borneo. Kalimantan
         For British North Borneo, see G8033.S3;
           Brunei, see G8145+; North Borneo, see
           G8033.S3; Sarawak, see G8033.S35
8102   Regions, natural features, adjacent islands,
          etc., A-Z
            e. g. .M3 Mahakam River

8110-8112   Celebes. Sulawesi
8112   Regions, natural features, adjacent islands,
          etc., A-Z
            e. g. .B6 Boetoeng. Butung. Buton

8115-8117   Lesser Sunda Islands
8117   Regions, natural features, adjacent islands,
          etc., A-Z
            e. g. .B3 Bali (Island)

8130-8132   Moluccas. Spice Islands
8132   Regions, natural features, adjacent islands,
          archipelagoes, etc., A-Z
            e. g. .A5 Ambelau
                  .A6 Amboina
                  .A7 Aru Islands
                  .B2 Babar Islands
                  .B3 Bachian (Batjan)
                  .B4 Banda Islands
                  .B6 Boeroe (Buru)
                  .C4 Ceram. Serang
                  .G3 Gagy
                  .G4 Gebe
                  .H3 Halmahera. Gilolo (Djailolo,
                        Jilolo)

----

[1] For subdivisions, see tables, pp. 206-223

By region or country[1]
　Eastern Hemisphere.　Eurasia, Africa, etc.
　　Asia
　　　Southeast Asia.　Indochina
　　　　Indonesia.　United States of Indonesia.　Netherlands
　　　　　Indies.　East Indies
　　　　　Moluccas.　Spice Islands

8132	Regions, natural features, adjacent islands, archipelagoes, etc., A-Z - Continued

　　　　　　　　e. g.　.K3　Kai (Kei) Islands
　　　　　　　　　　　.L4　Leti
　　　　　　　　　　　.M5　Moa
　　　　　　　　　　　.M6　Morotai
　　　　　　　　　　　.O2　Obi Islands
　　　　　　　　　　　.S3　Selaroe
　　　　　　　　　　　　　Serang, see .C4
　　　　　　　　　　　.S4　Sermata
　　　　　　　　　　　.S6　Soela (Xulla) Islands
　　　　　　　　　　　.T2　Taliaboe
　　　　　　　　　　　.T3　Tanimbar Islands.　Timor Laut
　　　　　　　　　　　.T4　Ternate
　　　　　　　　　　　.T5　Tidore
　　　　　　　　　　　.W4　Wetar
　　　　　　　　　　　　　Xulla Islands, see .S6

8140-8142	New Guinea
8142	Regions, natural features, etc., A-Z

　　　　　　Class here regions and natural features located
　　　　　　　within Irian Barat or common to Irian Barat
　　　　　　　and Papua New Guinea
　　　　　　e. g.　.B3　Baliem River
　　　　　　　　　.F5　Fly River
　　　　　　　　　.P8　Purari River
　　　　Irian Jaya.　Irian Barat.　Netherlands New
　　　　　Guinea, see G8073.I7

8160-8164	Papua New Guinea (Map, p. 175)

　　　　　　Including maps of Territory of Papua (formerly
　　　　　　　British New Guinea) and Trust Territory of
　　　　　　　New Guinea (formerly German New Guinea)

8162	Islands, regions, natural features, etc., A-Z

　　　　　　Class here maps of individual islands or
　　　　　　　island groups not classed in or associated
　　　　　　　with G8180+
　　　　　　e. g.　　　Bougainville, see G9282.B6
　　　　　　　　　　Buka, see G9282.B8
　　　　　　　　　　Green Islands, see G9282.G7
　　　　　　　　.K5　Kiwai Island

8180-8182	Bismarck Archipelago
8182	Islands, archipelagoes, regions, natural features, etc., A-Z

　　　　　　e. g.　.A2　Admiralty Islands
　　　　　　　　　.M3　Manus Island
　　　　　　　　　.N4　New Britain
　　　　　　　　　.N5　New Ireland

_____

[1]
　For subdivisions, see tables, pp. 206-223

MAPS

By region or country[1]
 Eastern Hemisphere. Eurasia, Africa, etc.
  Asia
   Southeast Asia. Indochina
    New Guinea
     Papua New Guinea - Continued

8185-8187	Louisiade Archipelago
8187	Islands, archipelagoes, regions, natural features, etc., A-Z
	e. g. .M5 Misima. Saint Aignan
	.R6 Rossel
	.T3 Tagula
8190-8192	D'Entrecasteaux Islands
8192	Islands, archipelagoes, regions, natural features, etc., A-Z
	e. g. .D6 Dobu. Goulvain
	.F4 Fergusson. Kaluwawa
	.G6 Goodenough. Morata
	.N6 Normanby. Duau
8195-8197	Timor
	Western Timor, see G8073.N8
8198.2-.24	Portuguese Timor (Map, p. 175)
.5-.54	Brunei (Map, p. 175)

---

[1] For subdivisions, see tables, pp. 206-223

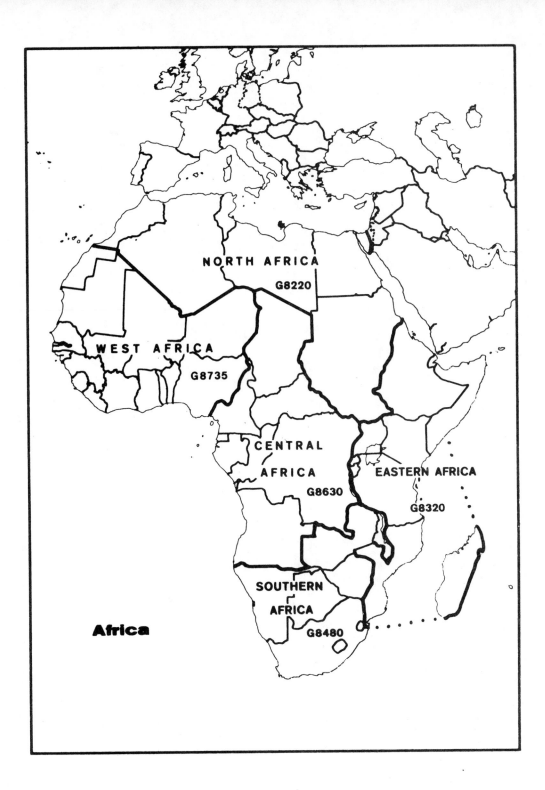

NORTH AFRICA
G8220

WEST AFRICA
G8735

CENTRAL
AFRICA
G8630

EASTERN AFRICA
G8320

SOUTHERN
AFRICA
G8480

Africa

By region or country[1]
Eastern Hemisphere. Eurasia, Africa, etc. - Continued

8200-8202	Africa (Map, p. 40)
	Including Sub-Saharan Africa
8202	Regions, natural features, etc., A-Z
	e. g. .C5 Lake Chad
	.N5 Nile River
	.N9 Lake Nyasa (Lake Malawi)
	.S2 Sahara
	.T3 Lake Tanganyika
	.Z3 Zambesi River
8220-8222	North Africa (Map, p. 180)
	Including Barbary States and Northeast Africa
8222	Regions, natural features, etc., A-Z
	e. g. .A8 Atlas Mountains
8230-8234	Morocco
	Including French Morocco
	For maps of Spanish Morocco, see G8232.S7
8232	Regions, natural features, etc., A-Z
	e. g. .I3 Ifni
	.S7 Spanish Morocco
	For maps of Zona Sur del Protectorado de Marruecos (Southern Protectorate of Morocco), see G8233.T3
8233	Provinces, A-Z
	e. g. .T2 Tangier
	Including the International Zone
	.T3 Tarfaya
	Including Zona Sur del Protectorado de Marruecos (Southern Protectorate of Morocco)
8240-8244	Algeria
8250-8254	Tunisia. Tunis
8260-8264	Libya
8262	Regions, natural features, etc., A-Z
	e. g. .C9 Cyrenaica
	.T7 Tripolitania. Tripoli
8300-8304	Egypt. United Arab Republic
8302	Regions, natural features, etc., A-Z
	e. g. Nile River, see G8202.N5
	.S5 Sinaitic Peninsula (Sinai)
	.S9 Suez Isthmus and Canal
8310-8314	Sudan. Anglo-Egyptian Sudan
8320-8322	Eastern Africa (Map, p. 180)
8330-8334	Ethiopia. Abyssinia
8333	Provinces, A-Z
	e. g. .E7 Eritrea
8350-8354	Somalia. Somaliland
8352	Regions, natural features, etc., A-Z
	e. g. .B7 British Somaliland
	French Somaliland, see G8360+
	.I8 Italian Somaliland
8360-8364	French Territory of the Afars and Issas. French Somaliland

---

[1]
For subdivisions, see tables, pp. 206-223

G

G

MAPS

By region or country[1]
　Eastern Hemisphere.　Eurasia, Africa, etc.
　　Africa
　　　Eastern Africa - Continued

8400-8402	Southeast Africa. British East Africa
8402	Regions, natural features, etc., A-Z
	e. g.　.V5　Lake Victoria
8410-8414	Kenya. East Africa Protectorate
8412	Regions, natural features, etc., A-Z
	e. g.　.K4　Mount Kenya
	.R8　Lake Rudolf
8413	Provinces, A-Z
	.C4　Central
	.C6　Coast
	.E3　Eastern
	.N3　Nairobi Area
	.N6　North-Eastern
	.N9　Nyanza
	.R5　Rift Valley
	.W4　Western
8420-8424	Uganda
8425-8426	Ruanda-Urundi. Belgian East Africa
8430-8434	Rwanda
8435-8439	Burundi
8440-8444	Tanzania. Tanganyika. German East Africa
8442	Regions, natural features, islands, etc., A-Z
	e. g.　.K5　Kilimanjaro
	.P4　Pemba
	Lake Tanganyika, see G8202.T3
	.Z3　Zanzibar
8450-8454	Mozambique. Portuguese East Africa
8460-8464	Madagascar. Malagasy Republic
8480-8482	Southern Africa. British South Africa (Map, p. 180)
8482	Regions, natural features, etc., A-Z
	e. g.　.K3　Kalahari Desert
	Zambesi River, see G8202.Z3
8500-8504	Republic of South Africa
8502	Regions, natural features, etc., A-Z
	e. g.　.D7　Drakensberg Mountains
	Marion Island, see G9182.M29
	.O7　Orange River
	Prince Edward Island, see G9182.P7
	.V3　Vaal River
(8503)	Administrative areas, see G8510+
8504	Cities and towns, A-Z
	e. g.　.C3　Cape Town
	.D8　Durban
	.J6　Johannesburg
	.P7　Pretoria
8510-8513	Cape of Good Hope. Cape Province
8513	Administrative areas, etc., A-Z
	Walvis Bay, see G8623.W3
8520-8523	Orange Free State

---

[1] For subdivisions, see tables, pp. 206-223

182

MAPS

By region or country[1]
    Eastern Hemisphere. Eurasia, Africa, etc.
      Africa
        Southern Africa. British South Africa
          Republic of South-Africa - Continued

8530-8533   Natal
8532   Regions, natural features, etc., A-Z
             e. g. .Z8 Zululand
8540-8543   Transvaal
8542   Regions, natural features, etc., A-Z
             e. g. .W5 Witwatersrand
8550-8551   Rhodesia
           Including the Federation of Rhodesia and
              Nyasaland
           For maps limited to Nyasaland, see G8610+
8560-8564   Southern Rhodesia
8562   Regions, natural features, etc., A-Z
             e. g. .K3 Lake Kariba
                  .V5 Victoria Falls
                  Zambesi River, see G8202.Z3
8570-8574   Zambia. Northern Rhodesia
8580-8584   Lesotho. Basutoland
8590-8594   Swaziland
8600-8604   Botswana. Bechuanaland
8610-8614   Malawi. Nyasaland. Central Africa Protectorate
           For maps of the Federation of Rhodesia and
               Nyasaland, see G8550+
8620-8624   Southwest Africa (Namibia). German Southwest Africa
8622   Regions, natural features, etc., A-Z
             e. g. .N3 Namib Desert
8623   Administrative areas, A-Z
             e. g. .W3 Walvis Bay
8630-8632   Central Africa. Equatorial Africa (Maps, p. 180)
8632   Regions, natural features, etc., A-Z
            e. g. .C6 Congo River (Zaire River)
8640-8644   Angola. Portuguese West Africa
8650-8654   Zaire. Congo (Democratic Republic). Belgian Congo
8652   Regions, natural features, etc., A-Z
           Congo River, see G8632.C6
           Lake Tanganyika, see G8202.T3
8653   Provinces, A-Z
            .B2   Bandundu
            .B3   Bas-Zaïre. Kongo-Central
            .E7   Équateur
            .H3   Haut-Zaïre. Orientale
            .K22 Kasai-Occidental
            .K24 Kasai-Oriental
               Katanga, see .S5
            .K4   Kinshasa (Federal District). Leopoldville
               (Federal District)
            .K5   Kivu
               Kongo-Central, see .B3
               Leopoldville (Federal District), see .K4
               Orientale, see .H3
            .S5   Shaba. Katanga

---

[1] For subdivisions, see tables, pp. 206-223

MAPS

By region or country[1]
  Eastern Hemisphere. Eurasia, Africa, etc.
    Africa
      Central Africa. Equatorial Afriaa
        Zaire. Congo (Democratic Republic). Belgian
          Congo - Continued

8654	Cities and towns, A-Z
	e. g. .K7 Kinshasa. Leopoldville
	.K8 Kisangani. Stanleyville
	.L6 Lubumbashi. Elisabethville
8660-8664	Equatorial Guinea. Spanish Guinea
8662	Regions, natural features, islands, etc., A-Z
	e. g. .A5 Annobon (Pagalu)
	.C6 Corisco
	.F4 Fernando Po (Macias Nguema Biyogo)
8663	Provinces, A-Z
	Fernando Po, see G8662.F4
	.R5 Rio Muni. Continental Guinea
8675-8679	São Tomé e Príncipe
8677	Regions, natural features, islands, etc., A-Z
	e. g. .P7 Príncipe
	.S3 São Tomé
8680-8682	French Equatorial Africa. French Congo
8690-8694	Gabon
8700-8704	Congo (Brazzaville). Middle Congo
8710-8714	Central African Republic. Ubangi-Shari
8720-8724	Chad (Tchad)
8722	Regions, natural features, etc., A-Z
	Lake Chad, see G8202.C5
8724	Cities and towns, A-Z
	e. g. .N4 N'Djamena. Fort-Lamy
8730-8734	Cameroon. French Cameroons. German
	Cameroons (Kamerun)
	For maps of British Cameroons, see G8842.C3
8732	Regions, natural features, etc., A-Z
	e. g. .E3 East Cameroon
	.W4 West Cameroon
	Including Southern Cameroons
8733	Provinces, A-Z
	.C4 Centre-Sud
	.E8 Est
	.L5 Littoral
	.N6 Nord
	.N7 Nord-Ouest
	.O9 Ouest
	.S9 Sud-Ouest
8735-8737	West Africa (Map, p. 180)
	Including the West Coast and Northwest Africa
8737	Regions, natural features, etc., A-Z
	e. g. .N5 Niger River

---

[1] For subdivisions, see tables, pp. 206-223

MAPS

By region or country[1]

Eastern Hemisphere. Eurasia, Africa, etc.
Africa
West Africa - Continued

8740-8742	French West Africa
8742	Regions, natural features, etc., A-Z
	e. g. .S4 Sénégal River
8750-8754	Dahomey
8760-8764	Togo. French Togoland. Togoland
	For maps of British Togoland (Trans-Volta Togoland), see G8853.V6
8770-8774	Niger
8780-8784	Ivory Coast
8790-8794	Guinea. French Guinea
8800-8804	Mali. French Sudan
8805-8809	Upper Volta
8810-8814	Senegal
8812	Regions, natural features, etc., A-Z
	e. g. .C3 Cape Verde
8820-8824	Mauritania
8830-8832	British West Africa
8840-8844	Nigeria
8842	Regions, natural features, etc., A-Z
	e. g. .C3 British Cameroons
8843	States, A-Z
	.B4 Benue-Plateau
	Central-Eastern, see .E3
	.E3 East-Central. Central-Eastern
	.K3 Kano
	.K8 Kwara
	.L3 Lagos
	.M5 Mid-Western
	.N5 North-Central
	.N6 North-Eastern
	.N7 North-Western
	.R5 Rivers
	.S6 South-Eastern
	.W4 Western
8850-8854	Ghana. Gold Coast
8853	Administrative regions, A-Z
	.A2 Accra (Capital District)
	.A8 Ashanti
	.B7 Brong-Ahafo
	.C4 Central
	.E3 Eastern
	.N6 Northern
	.U6 Upper
	.V6 Volta
	Including maps of British Togoland (Trans-Volta Togoland)
	.W4 Western
8860-8864	Sierra Leone
8870-8874	Gambia
8874	Cities and towns, A-Z
	e. g. .B3 Banjul. Bathurst
8880-8884	Liberia
8890-8894	Guinea-Bissau. Portuguese Guinea

[1] For subdivisions, see tables, pp. 206-223

185

MAPS

<pre>
                    By region or country[1]
                      Eastern Hemisphere. Eurasia, Africa, etc.
                        Africa
                          West Africa- Continued
8900-8904   Spanish Sahara
                              Including Spanish West Africa as a whole
                              For maps limited to Ifni, see G8232.I3; for
                                Zona Sur del Protectorado de Marruecos
                                (Southern Protectorate of Morocco), see
                                G8233.T3
8903   Administrative areas, A-Z
                              .R5 Rio de Oro
                              .S3 Saguia El Hamra (Sekia El Hamra)
8950-8952   Australasia (Map, p. 40)
                          Cf. G9250+, South Pacific
8960-8964   Australia
                          History
8961.S1   General
    .S12   Discovery and exploration
    .S2   To 1788
    .S3   1788-1900
    .S4   1901-1945
    .S7   World War II
    .S73   1945-
8964   Cities and towns, A-Z
                            e. g. .A2 Adelaide
                                   .C3 Canberra
8970-8973   New South Wales
8980-8983   Australian Capital Territory
                          For Canberra, see G8964.C3
8990-8993   Victoria
9000-9003   Queensland
9010-9013   South Australia
9020-9023   Western Australia
9040-9043   Northern Territory
9060-9063   Tasmania
9080-9084   New Zealand
9082   Regions, natural features, islands, etc., A-Z
                            e. g.   Kermadec Islands, see G9590+
                                   .N6 North Island
                                   .S6 South Island
9095-9096   Oceans (General)
                      Class an island or group of islands not
                        provided with classification numbers
                        and situated close to a continent,
                        larger island, or group of islands with
                        the neighboring land area
9100-9102   Atlantic Ocean (Map, p. 40)
9110-9112   North Atlantic (Map, p. 40)
9112   Regions, bays, etc., A-Z
                          e. g. .E5   English Channel
                                 .G65 Grand Banks of Newfoundland
                                 .N6   North Sea
9120-9124   Bermuda
9122   Regions, natural features, islands, etc., A-Z
                          e. g. .N6 Nonsuch Island
                                 .S3 Saint Georges (Island)
</pre>

---

[1] For subdivisions, see tables, pp. 206-223

By region or country[1]
Oceans (General)
Atlantic Ocean
North Atlantic
Bermuda - Continued

9123   Counties, A-Z
    .D4 Devonshire
    .H3 Hamilton
    .P3 Paget
    .P4 Pembroke
    .S3 Saint Georges
    .S4 Sandys
    .S5 Smiths
    .S6 Southampton
    .W3 Warwick

9130-9134   Azores
9132   Regions, natural features, islands, etc., A-Z
    e. g. .C6 Corvo
       .F3 Faial
       .F5 Flores
       .G7 Graciosa
       .P5 Pico
       .S2 Santa Maria
       .S3 São Jorge
       .S4 São Miguel
       .T4 Terceira

9133   Districts, etc., A-Z
    e. g. .A5 Angra do Heroismo
       .H6 Horta
       .P6 Ponta Delgada

9140-9144   Madeira Islands. Funchal (District of Portugal)
9142   Regions, natural features, archipelagoes,
    islands, etc., A-Z
    e. g. .D4 Desertas
       .M2 Madeira
       .P6 Porto Santo
       .S3 Salvages

9150-9154   Canary Islands
    Including two provinces of Spain: Las
    Palmas (Las Palmas de Gran Canaria) and
    Santa Cruz de Tenerife
9152   Regions, natural features, islands, etc., A-Z
    e. g. .A2 Alegranza
        Ferro, see .H5
       .F8 Fuerteventura
       .G6 Gomera
       .G7 Graciosa
       .G8 Gran Canaria
       .H5 Hierro (Ferro)
       .L2 Lanzarote
       .L3 La Palma (Palma). San Miguel
         de la Palma
       .L6 Lobos
       .M6 Montaña Clara
        Palma, see .L3
       .R6 Roca del Este
       .R7 Roca del Oueste
       .T4 Tenerife

---

[1] For subdivisions, see tables, pp. 206-223

MAPS

<u>By region or country</u>[1]
<u>Oceans (General)</u>
<u>Atlantic Ocean</u>
<u>North Atlantic</u>
<u>Canary Islands</u> - Continued

9153   Provinces, etc., A-Z
                 .L3   Las Palmas
                 .S2   Santa Cruz de Tenerife

9160-9164   <u>Cape Verde Islands</u>
9162   Regions, natural features, archipelagoes,
              islands, etc., A-Z
            e. g.   .B6   Boa Vista
                 .B7   Branco
                 .B8   Brava
                 .F6   Fogo
                 .G7   Grande
                 .M3   Maio
                 .R3   Razo.   Rodonda
                 .R6   Rombo Islands.   Secos Islands
                 .S2   Sal
                 .S3   Santa Luzia
                       Santiago, <u>see</u> .S6
                 .S4   Santo Antão
                 .S5   São Nicolau
                 .S6   São Tiago.   Santiago
                 .S7   São Vicente

9165-9167   <u>South Atlantic</u>
9167   Regions, natural features, archipelagoes, islands,
            etc., A-Z
            Class here maps of South Atlantic islands and
              archipelagoes not classed in or associated
              with G9170+
           e. g.   .B6   Bouvet Island
                     Islas Malvinas, <u>see</u> G9175+
                 .S6   South Orkney Islands
                     Administered by the British
                       Antarctic Territory; for maps
                       of the territory as a whole,
                       <u>see</u> G9803.B7
                 .S65   South Shetland Islands
                     Administered by the British
                       Antarctic Territory; for maps
                       of the territory as a whole,
                       <u>see</u> G9803.B7

9170-9174   <u>Saint Helena (Colony)</u>
9172   Regions, natural features, archipelagoes,
              islands, etc., A-Z
           e. g.   .A7   Ascension
                 .G6   Gough Island
                 .I5   Inaccessible Island
                 .N3   Nightingale Island
                 .S2   Saint Helena (Island)
                 .T7   Tristan da Cunha Group
                 .T72   Tristan Island

---

[1]
    For subdivisions, <u>see</u> tables, pp. 206-223

By region or country[1]
Oceans (General)
Atlantic Ocean
South Atlantic - Continued
Falkland Islands (Colony)

9175-9179
9177   Regions, natural features, archipelagoes,
islands, dependencies, etc., A-Z
e. g. .E2 East Falkland
.S6 South Georgia
.S65 South Sandwich Islands
.W4 West Falkland

9180-9182   Indian Ocean (Map, p. 40)
9182   Regions, natural features, archipelagoes,
islands, etc., A-Z
Class here maps of Indian Ocean islands
and archipelagoes not classed in or
associated with G9185+
e. g. .A5 Amsterdam Island
Administered by the territory
of French Southern and
Antarctic Lands; for maps of
the territory as a whole, see
G9803.F7
.A8 Ashmore Reef
Including maps of the Territory
of Ashmore and Cartier Island
.C3 Cartier Island
.C5 Crozet Islands
Administered by the territory
of French Southern and
Antarctic Lands; for maps of
the territory as a whole, see
G9803.F7
.H4 Heard Island
Including maps of the Territory of
Heard and McDonald Islands
.K4 Kerguelen Islands
Administered by the territory
of French Southern and
Antarctic Lands; for maps of
the territory as a whole, see
G9803.F7
Laccadive Islands, see G7652.L25
.M28 McDonald Islands
.M29 Marion Island
.M3 Mascarene Islands
Cf. G9185+, Mauritius
G9190+, Réunion
.P7 Prince Edward Island
.S2 Saint Paul Island
Administered by the territory of
French Southern and Antarctic
Lands; for maps of the territory
as a whole, see G9803.F7
.S5 Shag Island

---

[1] For subdivisions, see tables, pp. 206-223

By region or country[1]
Oceans (General)
Indian Ocean - Continued

9185-9189   Mauritius
                        Cf. G9182.M3, Mascarene Islands
       9187   Regions, natural features, archipelagoes,
                        islands, dependencies, etc., A-Z
                          e. g. .A3 Agalega Islands
                                 .C3 Cargados Carajos Shoals
                                 .R6 Rodriguez Island

9190-9194   Réunion. Isle de Bourbon
                        Cf. G9182.M3, Mascarene Islands
       9192   Regions, natural features, archipelagoes,
                        islands, dependencies, etc., A-Z
                          e. g. .B3 Bassas de India (Reefs)
                                 .E9 Europa
                                 .G55 Glorieuses (Islands)
                                 .J8 Juan de Nova
                                 .T7 Tromelin

9195-9199   British Indian Ocean Territory
       9197   Regions, natural features, archipelagoes,
                        islands, etc., A-Z
                          e. g. .A57 Aldabra Islands
                                 .A8 Assumption Island
                                 .C5 Chagos Archipelago
                                 .D4 Desroches Island
                                 .D5 Diego Garcia Island
                                 .F3 Farquhar Group

9200-9204   Seychelles
       9202   Regions, natural features, archipelagoes,
                        islands, dependencies, etc., A-Z
                          e. g.   Aldabra Islands, see G9197.A57
                                 .A58 Alphonse Island
                                 .A6 Amirante Isles
                                      Assumption Island, see G9197.A8
                                 .B5 Bijoutier Island
                                 .C4 Cerf Island
                                 .C58 Coetivy Island
                                 .C6 Cosmoledo Group
                                 .C8 Curieuse Island
                                      Desroches Island, see G9197.D4
                                 .F4 Félicité Island
                                 .L3 La Digue Island
                                 .M3 Mahé Island
                                 .N6 North Island
                                 .P58 Platte Island
                                 .P7 Praslin Island
                                 .P72 Providence Island
                                 .S2 Saint François Island
                                 .S22 Saint Pierre Island
                                 .S5 Silhouette Island

---

[1]
   For subdivisions, see tables, pp. 206-223

By region or country[1]
Oceans (General)
Indian Ocean - Continued
Cocos Islands. Keeling Islands

9205-9209
9207   Regions, natural features, archipelagoes,
             islands, etc., A-Z
                 e. g. .D5 Direction Island
                        .H6 Home Island. New Selma Island
                        .H62 Horsburgh Island
                             New Selma Island, see .H6
                        .N6 North Keeling Island
                        .S6 South Island
                        .W4 West Island

9210-9214   Comoro Islands
9212   Regions, natural features, archipelagoes,
             islands, etc., A-Z
                 e. g. .A5 Anjouan
                        .G7 Grande Comore
                        .M3 Majotte
                        .M6 Moheli

9215-9219   Maldives
9217   Regions, atolls, archipelagoes, islands, etc., A-Z
                 e. g. .A3 Addu
                        .A7 Ari
                        .F3 Fadiffolu
                        .F4 Felidu
                        .H3 Haddummati
                        .H6 Horsburgh
                        .I35 Ihavandiffulu
                        .K6 Kolumadulu
                        .M3 Makunudu. Malcom Atoll
                        .M32 Male
                        .M5 Miladummadulu
                        .M8 Mulaku
                        .N6 North Malosmadulu Atoll
                        .N62 North Nilandu Atoll
                        .S6 South Male Atoll
                        .S62 South Malosmadulu Atoll
                        .S623 South Nilandu Atoll
                        .S89 Suvadiva
                        .T5 Tiladummati

9230-9232   Pacific Ocean (Map, p. 40)
9235-9237   North Pacific (Map, p. 40)
9237   Regions, atolls, archipelagoes, islands, etc., A-Z
                 e. g. B4   Bering Sea
                             Bonin Islands, see G7962.B6
                        .J6 Johnston Atoll
                        .M5 Midway Islands
                             Volcano Islands, see G7962.B6
                        .W3 Wake Island

---

[1] For subdivisions, see tables, pp. 206-223

<u>By region or country</u>[1]
　　　<u>Oceans (General)</u>
　　　　<u>Pacific Ocean</u> - Continued
9250-9251　　　　<u>South Pacific. Oceania</u> (Map, p. 40)
　　　　　　Cf. G8950+, Australasia
9260-9262　　　　<u>Melanesia</u>
9262　　　　　Regions, natural features, archipelagoes,
　　　　　　islands, etc., A-Z
　　　　　　　Class here maps of Melanesian islands
　　　　　　　and archipelagoes not classed in or
　　　　　　　associated with G9275+
　　　　　　　e. g.　　Bismarck Archipelago, <u>see</u> G8180+
　　　　　　　　　　Louisiade Archipelago, <u>see</u> G8185+
　　　　　　　.N6　Norfolk Island
9275-9277　　　<u>British Solomon Islands Protectorate</u>
9280-9284　　　　<u>Solomon Islands</u>
9282　　　　　Regions, natural features, archipelagoes,
　　　　　　islands, etc., A-Z
　　　　　　　e. g.　.A6　Arundel. Ndokulu
　　　　　　　　　　Bauro, <u>see</u> .S2
　　　　　　　　.B6　Bougainville
　　　　　　　　.B7　Bougainville Strait
　　　　　　　　　　Bugotu, <u>see</u> .S3
　　　　　　　　.B8　Buka
　　　　　　　　　　Cape Marsh Islands, <u>see</u> .R8
　　　　　　　　.C5　Choiseul
　　　　　　　　.F5　Florida
　　　　　　　　.G3　Ganongga
　　　　　　　　.G5　Gizo (Keso)
　　　　　　　　.G7　Green Islands
　　　　　　　　.G8　Guadalcanal
　　　　　　　　　　Isabel Island, <u>see</u> .S3
　　　　　　　　　　Keso, <u>see</u> .G5
　　　　　　　　.K7　Kolombangara
　　　　　　　　　　Makira, <u>see</u> .S2
　　　　　　　　.M2　Malaita
　　　　　　　　.M5　Marovo
　　　　　　　　.M6　Mono
　　　　　　　　　　Montgomery, <u>see</u> .T4
　　　　　　　　　　Ndokulu, <u>see</u> .A6
　　　　　　　　.N4　New Georgia Group
　　　　　　　　　　Parara, <u>see</u> .W3
　　　　　　　　.P3　Pavuvu Island
　　　　　　　　.R4　Rendova. Uweli
　　　　　　　　.R5　Rennell
　　　　　　　　.R8　Russell Islands. Cape
　　　　　　　　　　Marsh Islands
　　　　　　　　.S2　San Cristóbal. Bauro.
　　　　　　　　　　Makira
　　　　　　　　.S3　Santa Isabel. Isabel
　　　　　　　　　　Island. Bugotu
　　　　　　　　.S4　Savo
　　　　　　　　.S5　Shortland
　　　　　　　　.T4　Tetipari. Montgomery
　　　　　　　　.T7　Treasury Islands
　　　　　　　　.T8　Tulagi

---

[1] For subdivisions, <u>see</u> tables, pp. 206-223

By region or country[1]
Oceans (General)
Pacific Ocean
South Pacific. Oceania
Melanesia
British Solomon Islands Protectorate
Solomon Islands

9282   Regions, natural features, archipelagoes,
                    islands, etc., A-Z - Continued
                        e. g.   .U4 Ulawa
                                     Uweli, see .R4
                                .V3 Vangunu
                                .V4 Vella Lavella
                                .W3 Wanawana. Parara

9290-9294   Santa Cruz Islands. Queen Charlotte Islands
9292   Regions, natural features, archipelagoes,
                    islands, etc., A-Z
                        e. g.   La Pérouse Islands, see .V3
                                .N4 Ndeni. Santa Cruz Island
                                     Santa Cruz Island, see .N4
                                .T5 Tinakula. Tamami. Volcano
                                .V3 Vanikoro Islands. La
                                         Pérouse Islands
                                     Volcano, see .T5

9295-9297   New Hebrides. Anglo-French Condominium of
                   the New Hebrides
9300-9304   New Hebrides Islands
9302   Regions, natural features, archipelagoes,
                    islands, etc., A-Z
                        e. g.   .A4 Ambrim
                                .A5 Aneityum
                                     Api, see .E5
                                     Aragharagh, see .P4
                                     Aurora, see .M2
                                .E3 Efate (Vate)
                                .E5 Epi (Api). Tasiko
                                .E6 Eromanga
                                     Espíritu Santo, see .S3
                                .M2 Maewo. Aurora
                                .M3 Malékoula
                                     Marina, see .S3
                                .P4 Pentecost. Aragharagh.
                                         Whitsuntide
                                .S3 Santo. Espíritu Santo.
                                         Marina
                                .T3 Tanna
                                     Tasiko, see .E5
                                .T6 Torres Islands
                                     Vate, see .E3
                                     Whitsuntide, see .P4

9310-9314   Banks Islands
9312   Regions, natural features, archipelagoes,
                    islands, etc., A-Z
                        e. g.   Gaua, see .S3
                                     Gog, see .S3
                                .S3 Santa Maria. Gaua. Gog
                                .V3 Vaunua Lava

---
[1]
For subdivisions, see tables, pp. 206-223

By region or country[1]
Oceans (General)
Pacific Ocean
South Pacific. Oceania
Melanesia - Continued

9340-9344	New Caledonia (Island or territory)
9342	Regions, natural features, archipelagoes, islands, dependencies, etc., A-Z

      e. g. .B4 Belep Islands
                     Chesterfield Archipelago, see
                        G9370+
           .H79 Hunter Island
           .H8 Huon Island
           .I8 Isle of Pines. Kunie
                 Loyalty Islands, see G9350+
           .M3 Matthew Island
           .S3 Sable Island
           .W3 Walpole Island

9350-9354	Loyalty Islands
9352	Regions, natural features, archipelagoes, islands, etc., A-Z

      e. g.   Chabrol, see .L5
                  Halgan, see .U8
           .L5 Lifou. Chabrol
           .M3 Maré
           .U8 Uvéa. Halgan

9370-9374	Chesterfield Archipelago

Futuna Islands, see G9525+
Wallis Islands, see G9520+

9380-9384	Fiji
9382	Regions, natural features, archipelagoes, islands, dependencies, etc., A-Z

      e. g. .K3 Kandavu
           .K6 Koro
           .L3 Lau Group
           .N5 Ngau
           .O9 Ovalau
           .R6 Rotuma
           .T3 Taveuni
           .V3 Vanua Levu
           .V5 Viti Levu
           .Y3 Yasawa Group

---

[1] For subdivisions, see tables, pp. 206-223

By region or country[1]
Oceans (General)
Pacific Ocean
South Pacific. Oceania - Continued

9400-9402	Micronesia
9402	Regions, natural features, archipelagoes, islands, etc., A-Z
	Class here maps of Micronesian islands or archipelagoes not classed in or associated with G9405+
9405-9406	Trust Territory of the Pacific Islands
	Including the Caroline, Marshall, and Mariana Islands, except Guam
	Class here maps of the Trust Territory as a whole
9410-9414	Mariana Islands. Ladrone Islands
9412	Regions, natural features, archipelagoes, islands, etc., A-Z

e. g. .A34 Agrihan
.A35 Aguijan
.A4   Alamagan
.A5   Anatahan
.A8   Asuncion
Guam, see G9415+
.G8   Guguan
.M3   Maug Islands
.M4   Farallon de Medinilla
.P3   Pagan
.P32 Farallon de Pajaros
.R6   Rota
.S3   Saipan
.S32 Sarigan
.T5   Tinian

9415-9419	Guam
9420-9424	Caroline Islands
9422	Regions, natural features, atolls, islands, etc., A-Z

Class here maps of islands or atolls
in the Carolines not classed in or
associated with G9425+

e. g.   Armstrong, see .K8
.E2   Eauripik Atoll
Endabi Shoto, see .P8
Enderby, see .P8
Experiment, see .K8
.F3   Fais
.F32 Faraulep Atoll
.G3   Gaferut
Hall Islands, see G9435+
.H4   Helen Island
Hope, see .K8
.I35 Ifalik Atoll
Kata, see .P8
.K3   Kapingamarangi Atoll

---

[1] For subdivisions, see tables, pp. 206-223

By region or country[1]
 Oceans (General)
  Pacific Ocean
   South Pacific. Oceania
    Micronesia
     Trust Territory of the Pacific Islands
      Caroline Islands

9422
       Regions, natural features, atolls,
        islands, etc., A-Z - Continued
         e. g.   .K8   Kusaie. Armstrong.
                        Experiment. Hope.
                        Quollen. Strong. Teyoa.
                        Ualang
                       Losap Islands, see G9445+
                       Luguen, see .P8
                       Mortlock Islands, see
                        G9450+
              .M4   Merir
              .N3   Namonuito Atoll
              .N48 Ngatik Atoll
              .N5   Ngulu Atoll
              .N8   Nukuoro Atoll
              .O7   Oroluk Atoll
                    Palau Islands, see G9425+
              .P5   Pingelap Atoll
                    Poloat, see .P8
              .P6   Ponape
              .P79 Pulap Atoll
              .P795 Pulo Anna
              .P8   Puluwat Atoll (Poloat).
                        Endabi Shoto. Enderby.
                        Kata. Luguen
                    Quollen, see .K8
              .S3   Satawal
              .S5   Senyavin Islands
              .S6   Sonsorol Islands
                    Strong, see .K8
                    Teyoa, see .K8
              .T6   Tobi
                    Truk Islands, see G9440+
                    Ualang, see .K8
              .U4   Ulithi Atoll
              .W4   West Fayu Atoll
              .W6   Woleai Atoll
                    Yap, see G9430+
      Palau Islands. Pelew Islands
9425-9427
9427
       Regions, natural features, archipelagoes,
        islands, etc., A-Z
         e. g.   .A5   Angaur
              .A7   Arakabesan
              .A9   Auluptagel
              .B3   Babelthuap
              .K3   Kayangel Islands
              .K6   Koror
              .M3   Malakal
              .P4   Peleliu
              .U7   Urukthapel

---

[1] For subdivisions, see tables, pp. 206-223

By region or country[1]
Oceans (General)
Pacific Ocean
South Pacific. Oceania
Micronesia
Trust Territory of the Pacific Islands
Caroline Islands - Continued

9430-9432	Yap
9432	Regions, natural features, archipelagoes islands, etc., A-Z
	e. g. .G3 Gagil-Tomil
	.M3 Map
	.R82 Rumung
9435-9437	Hall Islands. Horu Shoto
9437	Regions, atolls, archipelagoes, islands, etc., A-Z
	e. g. .M8 Murilo
	.N6 Nomwin
9440-9442	Truk Islands. Hogoleu Islands. Mototokko Shoto
9442	Regions, atolls, archipelagoes, islands, etc., A-Z
	e. g. .D8 Dublon
	.F4 Fefan
	.K8 Kuop
	.M63 Moen
	.T6 Tol
	.U3 Udot
9445-9447	Losap Atoll
9450-9452	Mortlock Islands. Nomoi Islands
9452	Regions, atolls, archipelagoes, islands, etc., A-Z
	e. g. .E8 Etal
	.L8 Lukunor
	.S2 Satawan
9460-9464	Marshall Islands
9465-9467	Ralik Chain
9467	Regions, atolls, archipelagoes, islands, etc., A-Z
	e. g. .A35 Ailinginae
	.A36 Ailinglapalap
	.B5 Bikini
	.E2 Ebon
	.E5 Eniwetok
	.J3 Jaluit
	.K6 Kili
	.K85 Kwajalein (Island and atoll)
	.L3 Lae
	.N3 Namorik
	.N32 Namu
	.R6 Rongelap
	.R62 Rongerik
	.U38 Ujae
	.U39 Ujelang
	.W6 Wotho

---

[1]
For subdivisions, see tables, pp. 206-223

By region or country[1]
Oceans (General)
Pacific Ocean
South Pacific. Oceania
Micronesia
Trust Territory of the Pacific Islands
Marshall Islands - Continued

9470-9472   Ratak Chain
9472   Regions, atolls, archipelagoes, islands,
etc., A-Z
e. g.   .A35   Ailuk
.A7   Arno
.A9   Aur
.B5   Bikar
.E7   Erikub
.K6   Knox
.L5   Likiep
.M3   Majuro
.M32   Maloelap
.M5   Mili
.T3   Taka
.T32   Taongi
.U8   Utirik
.W6   Wotje

9475-9476   Gilbert and Ellice Islands Colony
Including the Gilbert Islands, Ellice
Islands, Ocean Island, and islands
claimed by the United Kingdom in the
Phoenix and Line Islands
Class here maps of the entire colony
For maps of component islands, regions,
etc., see G9480+, G9485+, G9510+,
G9530+, and G9540+

9480-9484   Gilbert Islands. Kingsmill Islands
9482   Regions, atolls, archipelagoes,
islands, etc., A-Z
e. g.   .A2   Abaiang
.A22   Abemama
.A7   Aranuka
.A72   Arorae
.B3   Beru
.B33   Betio
.K8   Kuria
.M3   Maiana
.M32   Makin
.M33   Marakei
.N5   Nikunau
.N6   **Nonouti**
.O5   Onotoa
.T3   Tabiteuea
.T32   Tamana
.T35   Tarawa

---

[1]
For subdivisions, see tables, pp. 206-223

By region or country[1]
Oceans (General)
Pacific Ocean
South Pacific. Oceania
Micronesia - Continued

9485-9489	Ocean Island. Banaba
	Administered by Gilbert and Ellice Islands Colony; for maps of the colony as a whole, see G9475+
9490-9494	Nauru. Navodo. Pleasant
9500-9502	Polynesia. Western Polynesia
9502	Regions, atolls, archipelagoes, islands, etc., A-Z
	Class here maps of Western Polynesian islands not classed in or associated with G9510+
	e. g. .B3 Baker Island
	.H6 Howland Island
9510-9514	Ellice Islands. Lagoon Islands
	Administered by Gilbert and Ellice Islands Colony; for mape of the colony as a whole, see G9475+
9512	Regions, atolls, archipelagoes, islands, etc., A-Z
	e. g. .F8 Funafuti (Island and atoll)
	.N3 Nanomea
	.N32 Nanumanga
	.N5 Niutao
	.N8 Nui
	.N82 Nukufetau
	.N823 Nukulailai
	.N825 Nurakita
	.V3 Vaitupu
9515-9517	Territory of Wallis and Futuna
9520-9524	Wallis Islands
9522	Regions, natural features, archipelagoes, islands, etc., A-Z
	e. g. .U9 Uvéa
9525-9529	Futuna Islands. Hoorn Islands
9527	Regions, natural features, archipelagoes, islands, etc., A-Z
	e. g. .A6 Alofi
9530-9534	Line Islands. Equatorial Islands
	Christmas, Fanning, Washington, Caroline, Flint, Malden, and Vostock Islands are administered by Gilbert and Ellice Islands Colony; for maps of the colony as a whole, see G9475+
9532	Regions, natural features, atolls, archipelagoes, islands, etc., A-Z
	e. g. .C3 Caroline (Island and atoll)
	.C5 Christmas (Island and atoll)
	.F3 Fanning (Island and atoll)
	.F55 Flint Island
	.J3 Jarvis Island
	.K5 Kingman Reef
	.M3 Malden Island

---

[1] For subdivisions, see tables, pp. 206-223

MAPS

<u>By region or country</u>[1]
<u>Oceans (General)</u>
<u>Pacific Ocean</u>
<u>South Pacific. Oceania</u>
<u>Polynesia. Western Polynesia</u>
<u>Line Islands. Equatorial Islands</u>

9532	Regions, natural features, atolls, archipelagoes, islands, etc., A-Z - Continued

    e. g. .P3 Palmyra Atoll
         .S8 Starbuck Island
         .V6 Vostok Island
         .W3 Washington Island

9540-9544	<u>Phoenix Islands</u>

  Birnie, Gardner, Hull, McKean, Phoenix and Sydney Islands are administered by Gilbert and Ellice Islands Colony; for maps of the colony as a whole, <u>see</u> G9475+

9542	Regions, atolls, archipelagoes, islands, etc., A-Z

    e. g. .B5 Birnie (Island and atoll)
         .C3 Canton (Island and atoll)
         .E5 Enderbury (Island and atoll)
         .G3 Gardner (Island and atoll)
         .H8 Hull (Island and atoll)
         .M3 McKean (Island and atoll)
         .P5 Phoenix (Island and atoll)
         .S9 Sydney (Island and atoll)

9550-9554	<u>Tokelau Islands. Union Islands</u>
9552	Regions, atolls, archipelagoes, islands, etc., A-Z

    e. g. .A8 Atafu
         .F3 Fakaofu
         .N8 Nukunono

9555-9557	<u>Samoa Islands. Navigators Islands</u>
9560-9564	American Samoa
9562	Regions, atolls, archipelagoes, islands, etc., A-Z

    e. g. .A9 Aunuu
         .M3 Manua Islands
         .R6 Rose Island
         .S9 Swains (Island and atoll)
         .T8 Tutuila

9565-9569	Western Samoa
9567	Regions, atolls, archipelagoes, islands, etc., A-Z

    e. g. .A6 Apolima
         .M3 Manono
         .S3 Savai'i
         .U6 Upolu

---

[1] For subdivisions, <u>see</u> tables, pp. 206-223

By region or country[1]
  Oceans (General)
    Pacific Ocean
      South Pacific. Oceania
        Polynesia. Western Polynesia – Continued

9570-9574   Tonga. Friendly Islands
9572   Regions, natural features, archipelagoes,
           islands, etc., A-Z
            e. g. .H3 Haapai Group
                .N5 Niaufoo
                .N52 Niuatoputapu
                .O8 Otu Tolu Group
                .T3 Tafahi
                .T6 Tongatapu (Island)
                .T62 Tongatapu Group
                .V29 Vavau (Island)
                .V3 Vavau Group

9580-9584   Niue. Savage Island
9590-9594   Kermadec Islands
9592   Regions, natural features, archipelagoes,
          islands, etc., A-Z
           e. g. .S8 Sunday. Raoul

9600-9604   Cook Islands
9602   Regions, atolls, archipelagoes, islands,
          etc., A-Z
           e. g. .A3 Aitutaki (Whytootake)
                Anchorage, see .S9
            .A7 Atiu (Vatiu, Wateeo)
                Avarau, see .P3
                Danger Atoll, see .P8
                Hervey Islands, see .M4
                Humphrey Island, see .M3
            .M2 Mangaia
            .M3 Manihiki. Humphrey Islands
            .M4 Manuae Atoll. Hervey Islands
            .M5 Mauke. Parry
            .M6 Mitiaro
            .N3 Nassau Island
            .P3 Palmerston. Avarau
                Parry, see .M5
            .P4 Penryhn. Tongareva
            .P8 Pukapuka. Danger Atoll
            .R3 Rakahanga. Reirson Island
            .R6 Rarotonga
            .S9 Suwarrow (Suvorov). Anchorage
            .T3 Takutea
                Tongareva, see .P4
                Vatiu, see .A7
                Wateeo, see .A7
                Whytootake, see .A3

[1] For subdivisions, see tables, pp. 206-223

By region or country[1]
Oceans (General)
Pacific Ocean
South Pacific. Oceania
Polynesia. Western Polynesia - Continued

9610-9612	French Oceania (Territory of French Polynesia)
9612	Regions, atolls, archipelagoes, islands, etc., A-Z

Class here maps of miscellaneous French
Polynesian islands not classed in or
associated with G9620+
Clipperton, see G9762.C5

9620-9624	Marquesas Islands
9622	Regions, natural features, atolls, archipelagoes, islands, etc., A-Z

    e. g.   Adams, see .U3
Chanal, see .H3
Dominica, see .H5
.E3 Eiao (Hiaou, Hiau).
    Knox. Masse
.F3 Fatu Hiva. Magdalena
.F32 Fatu Huku. Hood
.H3 Hatutu (Fattu-uhu).
    Chanal. Hancock.
    Langdon
Hiaou, see .E3
Hiau, see .E3
.H5 Hiva Oa. Dominica
Hood, see .F32
Hua Pou, see .U3
Knox, see .E3
Langdon, see .H3
Magdalena, see .F3
Marchand, see .N8
Massachusetts, see .U2
Masse, see .E3
.M6 Motane
Motu Iti, see G9642.M7
.N8 Nuku Hiva. Marchand
Ouahouka, see .U2
Ouapou, see .U3
Santa Christina, see .T3
.T3 Tahuata. Santa Christina
.U2 Ua Huka (Ouahouka). Washington. Massachusetts
.U3 Ua Pu (Hua Pou, Ouapou). Adams
Washington, see .U2

---

[1] For subdivisions, see tables, pp. 206-223

<u>By region or country</u>[1]
<u>Oceans (General)</u>
<u>Pacific Ocean</u>
<u>South Pacific. Oceania</u>
<u>Polynesia. Western Polynesia</u>
<u>French Oceania (Territory of</u>
<u>Polynesia)</u> - Continued

9630-9634   <u>Tuamoto Archipelago (Îles Tuamoto et Gambier,</u>
<u>Paumotu Islands). Low Archipelago</u>

9632   Regions, atolls, archipelagoes, islands,
etc., A-Z

e. g.   .A5   Anaa. Chain
Aurora, <u>see</u> .M3
Bow, <u>see</u> .H3
Chain, <u>see</u> .A5
Clermont-Tonnerre, <u>see</u> .R4
Deans, <u>see</u> .R3
.D8   Duke of Gloucester Islands
.F3   Fakarava. Wittgenstein
.G3   Gambier Islands. Mangareva
Group
.H3   Hao. Bow. Harp
.H35   Haraiki
.H5   Hikueru
.M29   Magareva
.M3   Makatéa Aurora
Mangareva Group, <u>see</u> .G3
Nairsa, <u>see</u> .R3
.R3   Rangiroa (Rahiroa). Deans.
Nairsa. Vliegen
.R4   Réao. Clermont-Tonnerre
Vliegen, <u>see</u> .R3
Wittgenstein, <u>see</u> .F3

9640-9644   <u>Society Islands</u>
9642   Regions, atolls, archipelagoes, islands,
etc., A-Z

e. g.   .B6   Bora Bora (Pora Pora)
Eimeo, <u>see</u> .M6
.H8   Huahiné
.L4   Leeward Islands (Isles sous le Vent)
Makatéa, <u>see</u> G9632.M3
.M3   Maupiti (Maurua)
.M4   Mehetia
.M6   Mooréa. Eimeo
.M65   Mopelia
.M66   Mopihaa
.M7   Motu Iti. Tubai
Otaha, <u>see</u> .T2
Otaheite, <u>see</u> .T3
Pora Pora, <u>see</u> .B6
.R3   Raiatéa. Ulietea
.T2   Tahaa (Otaha)
.T3   **Tahiti** (Otaheite)
Tubai, <u>see</u> .M7
Ulietea, <u>see</u> .R3
.W5   Windward Group (Îles du Vent)

---

[1]
For subdivisions, <u>see</u> tables, pp. 206-223

By region or country[1]
  Oceans (General)
    Pacific Ocean
      South Pacific. Oceania
        Polynesia. Western Polynesia
          French Oceania (Territory of French Polynesia) - Con.
9650-9654   Austral Islands. Tubuai Islands
9652   Regions, natural features, archipelagoes,
                       islands, etc., A-Z
                         e. g.   Oheteroa, <u>see</u> .R8
                                      Oparo, <u>see</u> .R3
                                  .R2 Raevavae. Vavitao
                                  .R3 Rapa. Oparo
                                  .R5 Rimatara
                                  .R8 Rurutu. Oheteroa
                                  .T8 Tubuai
                                      Vavitao, <u>see</u> .R2
9660-9664   Pitcairn (Island and colony)
9662   Regions, atolls, archipelagoes, islands,
                       etc., A-Z
                         e. g. .D8 Ducie
                                .H4 Henderson. Elizabeth
                                .O2 Oeno
9665-9669   Easter Island
                   Hawaiian Islands, <u>see</u> G4380+
9760-9762   East Pacific
                   Class maps of islands relatively close to the
                     American continents with the country or
                     subdivision of the country to which they
                     belong
9762   Regions, archipelagoes, islands, etc., A-Z
                     e. g. .C5 Clipperton
                                 Galapagos Islands, <u>see</u> G5302.G3
                                 Guadalupe, <u>see</u> G4482.G8
9780-9782   <u>Arctic Ocean</u> (Map, p. 40)
                 Cf. G3270+, Arctic regions
9782   Regions, natural features, archipelagoes,
                   islands, etc., A-Z
                   Class here maps of Arctic islands and archi-
                     pelagoes not classed in or associated with
                     G9785+
                   e. g. .J3 Jan Mayen Island
9785-9789   Franz Josef Land. Fridtjof Nansen Land
9790-9794   Svalbard. Spitsbergen

---

[1] For subdivisions, <u>see</u> tables, pp. 206-223

G

By region or country[1] - Continued

9800-9804   Antarctica (Map, p. 40)
9803   Territories, administrative districts, etc., A-Z
       e. g.   .B7   British Antarctic Territory

Class here maps of the territory
as a whole and the continental
areas, including the South
Shetland Islands, the South Orkney
Islands, and the British sector of
Antarctica (including Graham Land
peninsula), treated collectively
For maps of component islands, see
G9167.S6, and G9167.S65
.F7   French Southern and Antarctic Lands
Class here maps of the territory as
a whole and the continental area,
including the Kerguelen Islands,
Crozet Islands, Saint Paul Island,
Amsterdam Island, and Terre Adélie
on the Antarctic continent, treated
collectively
For maps of component islands, see
G9182.A5, G9182.C5, G9182.K4,
and G9182.S2

UNLOCALIZED MAPS

9900   Theoretical maps
Class here maps whose primary intent is the
illustration or definition of terms and
concepts and maps designed to illustrate
methods of map making. Class maps of a de-
terminable geographic area with the area
9930   Maps of imaginary places
9980   Maps of unidentified places

---

[1] For subdivisions, see tables, pp. 206-223

SPECIAL INSTRUCTIONS AND TABLES
OF SUBDIVISIONS FOR ATLASES
AND MAPS

I

CALL NUMBER CONSTRUCTION

Call numbers for area atlases consist of three parts;
call numbers for area maps, three or four parts.
For example:

(1) Major area atlas
        G1251 New York State (area number)
          .A5 American Automobile Association
               (Cutter number for the authority
               responsible for the atlas)
         1974 Date of atlas publication

(2) Sub-area atlas
        G1253 New York State counties (area number)
        .M6M7 Monroe County and Monroe County Good Roads
               Committee (sub-area Cutter number plus
               Cutter number for authority responsible
               for the atlas)
         1974 Date of atlas publication

(3) Major area map
        G3800 New York State (area number)
         1974 Date of map situation[1]
          .C7 Cram (George F.) Company (Cutter number
               for authority responsible for the map)

(4) Sub-area map
        G3803 New York State counties (area number)
          .M6 Monroe County (sub-area Cutter number)
         1974 Date of map situation[1]
          .M6 Monroe County Good Roads Committee (Cutter
               number for the authority responsible for
               the map)

---

[1]
     The date in a map call number is always the date of situation, except
when a history (S+) Cutter has been used, in which case the date in the
call number is that of publication

SPECIAL INSTRUCTIONS

I

CALL NUMBER CONSTRUCTION - Continued

Sets of maps are usually cataloged with an open entry.
In the call number, the date is replaced by the denominator of the "representative fraction" scale, minus the
last three digits. To distinguish the scale indicator
from a date in the call number of a general or closed
entry map, a small "s" precedes the scale indicator.
For sets of maps with scales larger than 1:1,000
(e. g. 1:200; 1:950; etc.) the denominator of the
fraction is treated as a decimal and is preceded by
a zero. Sets file after (or separate from) the
general or closed entry maps of the same area which
are arranged by date,

e. g. (1) G3800 New York State (area number)
            s25   Scale number (denominator of
                     scale, 1:25,000, minus last
                     three digits signalled by "s")
            .U5   United States Army Map Service
                     (Cutter number for authority
                     responsible for the maps)

       (2) G5834 France (major area number)
            .P3   Paris (sub-area Cutter number)
            s05   Scale number (denominator of
                     scale, 1:500, treated as a
                     decimal signalled by "s" for
                     scale and zero for decimal)
            .F7   France. Institut géographique
                     national (Cutter number for
                     the authority responsible for
                     the maps)

II

FILING ARRANGEMENT FOR MAP CLASSIFICATION
     NUMBERS (excluding author Cutter)

Example:

serial map	G3804.N4 year	New York City
single map	G3804.N4 1974	New York City
set map with definite scale	G3804.N4 s20	New York City
set map with varying scales	G3804.N4 svar	New York City
single map showing subject	G3804.N4P2 1974	New York City road map
set map showing subject	G3804.N4P2 svar	New York City road map
region within a city	G3804.N4:2J6 1974	John F. Kennedy Interna- tional Airport
region within a city showing subject	GJ804.N4:2J6A3 1974	aerial view of John F. Kennedy International Airport
administrative division of a city	G3804.N4:3Q4 1974	Queens
administrative division of a city showing subject	G3804.N4:3Q4P1 1974	transportation map of Queens

SPECIAL INSTRUCTIONS

III

AREA SUBDIVISIONS

Each sequence of two or more numbers assigned
to a geographic area is subdivided in accordance
with the following plan:

(1) 0 or 5 General
                e. g. G1250 New York State (general atlas
                                      number)
                        G3800 New York State (general map
                                      number)

(2) 1 or 6 By subject
              Subarranged by Table IV, pp.
              e. g. G1251 New York State (atlas subject-
                                      area number)
                 .P3   Railroads
                    G3801 New York State (map subject-area
                                      number)
                 .P3   Railroads

(3) 2 or 7 By region, natural feature, etc., when
              not assigned individual numbers, A-Z[1]
              e. g. G1252 New York State (atlas regional
                                      number)
                 .A2   Adirondack Mountains
                    G3802 New York State (map regional
                                      number)
                 .A2   Adirondack Mountains
              Physical features which cross political bounda-
              ries are classified by the following rules:
              A feature in 2 administrative divisions is
              classified with the division containing
              the greater portion of the feature
              e. g. G3822 Pennsylvania
                 .A5   Allegheny River (located
                                      mostly in Pennsylvania
                                      but also in New York)[2]
              A feature in 2 administrative divisions,
              each containing equal parts of the feature,
              is classified with the first alphabetically
              e. g. G3832 Delaware
                 .D4   Delaware Bay (located
                                      equally in Delaware
                                      and New Jersey)
              A feature in 3 or more administrative divi-
              sions is classified with the next larger
              geographical region which includes the
              entire feature
              e. g. G3707   Eastern United States
                 .A6   Appalachian Mountains
                                      (located in numerous
                                      states)

---

[1]   In rare instances a former administrative division may be treated
as a region, e. g. West Prussia, G6522.P8

[2]   A river and valley are classified together

SPECIAL INSTRUCTIONS

III

AREA SUBDIVISIONS

(3) 2 or 7 By region, natural feature, etc., when not
             assigned individual numbers, A-Z[1] - Continued
             An island without distinctive number is treated
                as a regional division of the area of which
                it is a geographical part. This treatment is
                also preferred if the island is a political
                unit
                  e. g. G3762 Regions, A-Z (Massachusetts)
                          .N3   Nantucket Island
                                   Not G3763.N3, Nantucket
                                   County

(4) 3 or 8 By major political division (Counties, states,
             provinces, etc.) when not assigned individual
             numbers, A-Z
                Administrative divisions are arranged alphabetically
                   using Cutter numbers for each political division
                  e. g. G1253 New York State (atlas county
                                   number)
                          .W3   Washington County
                         G3803 New York State (map county
                                   number)
                          .W3   .Washington County
                Smaller political divisions within any major
                   political division may be classified with
                   the use of a colon (:) followed by the
                   number 3, indicating that the subdivision
                   is an administrative one, and a Cutter for
                   the subordinate division
                  e. g. G5753   England (map county number)
                          .L5:3H6 Lincolnshire, Parts of
                                     Holland
                         G3823   Pennsylvania (map county
                                     number)
                          .F3:3P4 Fayette Co., Perry Township

---

[1]
    In rare instances a former administrative division may be treated
as a region, e. g. West Prussia, G6522.P8

SPECIAL INSTRUCTIONS

III

AREA SUBDIVISIONS

(5) 4 or 9 By city or town, A-Z
    .A1 Cities (Collective)
           e. g. G1819.A1, Atlas of cities of England
    Cities and towns of most countries are grouped
    under the country, not under the political sub-
    division in which they are located. Exceptions
    to this rule follow:
        (1) United States cities and towns are
            classified under each state. New
            England towns (i. e. townships) and
            other townships which are urban or
            suburban in character, are classified
            with the cities of the state
        (2) Canadian cities and towns are classified
            under each province
    e. g. G1254 New York State (atlas city and
               town number)
        .R6   Rochester
       G3804 New York State (map city and
               town number)
        .R6   Rochester

Regions and political divisions within a city or
    town may be classified with the use of a colon
    (:) followed by the number 2 or 3, indicating
    whether the subdivision is (2) geographic or
    (3) political, and a Cutter for the subdivision
    e. g. G4364   California (map city and town
                  number)
       .L8:2G7   Los Angeles, Griffith Park
               (classified as a region)
       G4114   Michigan (map city and town
               number)
       .E4:2M4   East Lansing, Michigan State
               University (classified as
               a region)
       G3804   New York State (map city and
               town number)
       .N4:3Q4   New York City, Queens
               (classified as a political
               division of the city)

G

TABLES OF SUBJECT SUBDIVISIONS
FOR ATLASES AND MAPS

IV

SUBJECT SUBDIVISIONS

Subject subdivisions are used in classifying atlases and maps with special subject interest. There are seventeen major subject groups, designated by capital letters, followed by numbers representing subtopics. These numbers are not Cutter numbers and have no alphabetical significance.

Call numbers for atlases consist of three parts; call numbers for maps, four parts;

e. g. (1) Major area subject atlas
G1251 New York State (subject–area number)
.P2A5 Roads and American Automobile Association (subject letter–number plus Cutter number for the authority responsible for the atlas)
1974 Date of publication

(2) Sub-area subject atlas
G1253 New York counties (area number)
.M6P2M7 Monroe County road atlas and Monroe County Good Roads Committee (sub-area Cutter number plus Cutter number for the authority responsible for the atlas)
1974 Date of publication

(3) Major area subject map
G3801 New York State (subject–area number)
.P2 Roads (subject letter–number)
Year Serial
.A5 American Automobile Association (Cutter number for the authority responsible for the map)

(4) Sub-area subject map
G3803 New York counties (area number)
.M6P2 Monroe County and Roads (sub-area Cutter number plus subject letter–number)
1974 Date of map
.M6 Monroe County Good Roads Committee (Cutter number for the authority responsible for the map)

TABLES OF SUBJECT SUBDIVISIONS

Summary of Form and Subject Subdivisions

A Special category maps and atlases
B Mathematical geography
C Physical sciences
D Biogeography
E Human and cultural geography. Anthropogeography.
    Human ecology
F Political geography
G Economic geography
H Mines and mineral resources
J Agriculture
K Forests and forestry
L Aquatic biological resources
M Manufacturing and processing. Service industries
N Technology. Engineering. Public works
P Transportation and communication
Q Commerce and trade. Finance
R Military and naval geography
S Historical geography

Table of Form and Subject Subdivisions

Class with any subject subdivision works which
encompass two or more of its listed subtopics
or any subtopic(s) not listed

Works on individual social, geographic, or
socio-geographic features such as canals,
dams, forests, university campuses, historic
trails, etc., are classed as geographic
features, e. g., G4352.H79, Hoover Dam.
Works showing the distribution of a certain
type of feature are classed with the
subject, e. g., G4301.N2, Dams in the New
Southwest

IV
SUBJECT SUBDIVISIONS

A   <u>Special Category</u> <u>Maps</u> <u>and</u> <u>Atlases</u>
            Class here works which cannot be
            placed in any subject group
            but, because of special format
            or treatment, are to be separated
            from general maps and atlases

.A1   Outline and base maps. Cities (Collective).
            Suburbs and city regions
               e. g. G3701.A1   Outline maps of the United States
                      G3704.A1   Cities and towns of the United
                                    States
                      G3804.N4A1 Suburbs, or area around New
                                    York City
.A15   Business district, center, or downtown of cities
.A2   Index maps
               Class here topographic map indexes only;
                  class indexes of special subject maps
                  with the subject, e. g. indexes to
                  geological maps are classed in .C5,
                  Geology
.A3   Aerial views. Bird's-eye views
.A35   Panoramas
.A4   Photomaps. Orthophotomaps. Pictomaps
.A45   Anaglyphs and stereographs
.A5   Pictorial maps
.A6   Cartoon maps
.A63   Cartograms
.A67   Mental maps
.A7   Maps for the blind
.A8   Special geographical names
               Class here works on place names of special
                  historical, national, or religious
                  significance, e. g. Christmas, Santa
                  Claus, etc.
.A85   Biographical maps. Maps showing travels of
            individuals
               Class maps showing special groups of people
                  under the subject, e. g. actors are
                  classified in .E645
.A9   Special format
               Class here postcards, business cards, placemats,
                  games, mechanical devices, slides, transparencies,
                  metal, stone, stationery, stick charts, fans,
                  powder horns, clay tablets, cloth maps, glass,
                  etc.

B   <u>Mathematical Geography</u>
            Class here works on aspects of cartography,
               surveying, and mapping

.B1   Astronomical observatories and observations
.B2   Movements of the earth
               Including international date line, time zones
.B3   Geodetic surveys
               Including triangulation networks, prime
                  meridians, base-measuring

IV

SUBJECT SUBDIVISIONS

B   Mathematical geography - Continued

.B5   Surveying. Extent of areas surveyed or mapped
.B52   Aerial photography. Status. Progress
.B7   Cartography
.B71   Globe gores
        Class here pictures of globes or any
          two-dimensional representation of a globe
.B72   Projections
        Class here maps whose purpose it is to illustrate
          a particular projection
.B8   Comparative area maps. Comparison diagrams
        Class here works showing area comparisons by
          superimposition, distortion, etc., and
          composite drawings comparing mountain
          heights, river lengths, etc.

C   Physical Sciences
        Class here works on the distribution of
          natural phenomena of the earth, the
          atmosphere, and subsurface features

.C1   General
.C18   Relief models. Raised relief globes
.C2   Physiography. Geomorphology
        Including relief features and bathymetry
.C21   Natural geographic regions. Geophysical divisions
.C23   Caves. Underground grottoes
.C28   Ground characteristics. Surface quality. Terrain
        studies. Slope
.C3   Hydrology. Hydrogeology
        Cf. .N44, Water utilities
.C31   Hydrographic surveys. Status. Progress
.C315   Drainage basins. Catchment areas
.C32   Floods
        Cf. .N22, Flood control
.C34   Ground water. Water table
.C35   Water composition and quality
.C36   Mineral waters
        For spas, etc., see .E635
.C38   Glaciers. - Glaciology
        Cf. .C74, Icebergs
.C5   Geology
.C51   Geological surveys. Status. Progress
.C55   Dynamic and structural geology. Tectonics.
        Earthquakes (Seismology). Vulcanology
.C57   Stratigraphy and paleontology. Historical geology
.C7   Oceanography
        For characteristics and morphology of the ocean
          bottom, see .C2; distribution of aquatic life,
          see .D1; economic aspects of aquatic life, see .L
.C72   Temperature of ocean water
.C73   Salinity and density of ocean water
.C74   Icebergs
.C75   Ocean currents
.C76   Ocean tides

SUBJECT SUBDIVISIONS

C   Physical Sciences - Continued

  .C8   Meteorology and climatology. Climate
                 classification systems
  .C813   Climate regions
                   Class here works on climate zones,
                     distribution of arid regions, deserts,
                     permafrost areas, tundra, etc.
  .C815   Weather forecasting
  .C82   Atmospheric temperature
  .C83   Insolation and radiation
  .C84   Structure and mechanics of atmosphere.
                 Atmospheric circulation. Wind systems
                   Cf. .N852, Air pollution. Smog
  .C842   Atmospheric pressure. Surface winds
  .C86   Storms
  .C87   Atmospheric electricity
  .C88   Atmospheric moisture and precipitation
  .C882   Condensation and evaporation. Dew.
                   Fog. Frost. Cloud cover
  .C883   Rain
  .C884   Snow. Snowmelt
  .C885   Hail
  .C886   Droughts
  .C887   Artificial precipitation. Rainmaking
  .C9   Geophysics
  .C92   Radioactivity
                   For atmospheric pollution caused by
                     radioactive fallout explosions, see .N852
  .C93   Terrestrial magnetism
  .C95   Gravity

D   Biogeography
             Class here works on the distribution of plant
               and animal life, exclusive of man and his
               economic activities

  .D1   General
               Cf. .L, Aquatic biological resources
  .D2   Plant geography. Botany. Vegetation
  .D4   Animal geography. Zoogeography
               Including birds, insects, fish, etc.
               For sport fishing and hunting, see .E63
  .D5   Wildlife conservation and reserves. Wildlife refuges
               Cf. .G3, Conservation (General)

SUBJECT SUBDIVISIONS

E   Human and Cultural Geography. Anthropogeography.
         Human Ecology
               Class here works that are concerned with man
               as a physical and social being

.E1   General
               Including ethnology, tribes, ethnic groups, etc.
.E15   Archaeological sites. Cities and towns which
           are ruined, extinct, etc.
.E2   Population
.E24   Vital statistics. Population increase and
           decrease. Birth control
.E25   Statistical areas. Census tracts
.E27   Movements of population (Voluntary)
               Class here works on emigration, immigration,
                 nomadism, tribal migration, transhumance,
                 etc.
.E272   Regulation. Quotas
.E29   Demographic aspects of disasters
               For technical aspects, see special fields,
                 e. g. .C55, Earthquakes; .C32, Floods;
                 .E59, Famine; etc.
.E3   Languages. Ethnolinguistics
.E4   Religions
.E42   Christianity
.E423   Ecclesiastical organizations, sects, denominations,
             administrative areas, etc.
.E424   Missions
.E43   Judaism
.E44   Islam
.E45   Hinduism
.E452   Brahmanism
.E47   Buddhism
.E5   Medical geography
.E51   Diseases
.E52   Medical professions
.E55   Public health
.E58   Hospitals. Clinics. Dispensaries
.E59   Nutrition. Malnutrition. Famine
               Cf. .E29, Disasters
.E6   Social and cultural geography. Civilizations
.E62   Customs and folklore
.E622   Social customs (Social and ethnic aspects).
             Eating and drinking habits. Clothing
               For technical and industrial aspects, see .M
.E6225   Genealogy. Families
.E623   Heraldry
.E624   Social organizations
.E625   Social problems
               Class here works on problems arising from the
                 interplay of social forces, e. g. crime,
                 narcotics traffic, slavery, race relations,
                 school integration efforts, efforts at
                 revamping educational systems, confrontations,
                 demonstrations, etc.
.E627   Folklore. Mythology

SUBJECT SUBDIVISIONS

E   <u>Human</u> <u>and</u> <u>Cultural</u> Geography. <u>Anthropogeography</u>.
                <u>Human</u> <u>Ecology</u>
                    Social and cultural geography. Civilizations - Cont.
.E63   Recreation. Sports
                    Including recreational trails and specific
                        recreational activities, e. g. hiking,
                        camping, hunting, fishing, etc.
                    Class individual trails as geographic
                        features; for historic trails, <u>see</u> .P25
.E635   Tourist maps. Tourist trade
.E64   Intellectual and aesthetic life. The arts
.E642   Crafts. Special interests. Hobbies
.E644   Architecture
.E645   Theaters. Drama. Motion pictures
.E646   Music
.E648   Painting and sculpture
.E65   Literature
.E655   Museums
.E67   Libraries
                    Class here works on the location and distribution
                        of libraries, those outlining library area
                        classification schemes, etc.
.E68   Education
.E7   Material culture
.E73   Housing. Shelter
                    Cf. .E644, Architecture
.E74   Income. Income tax
.E75   Treasure trove
                    Cf. .P57, Wreck charts
.E9   Slavery

F   <u>Political</u> <u>Geography</u>
                    Class here works on boundaries, administrative
                        and political divisions, sovereignty, spheres
                        of influence, and national aspirations

.F1   General
.F2   International boundaries
.F3   Sovereignty
                    Class here works on occupation zones, occupied
                        territories, territorial waters, etc.
.F33   Colonial possessions
.F35   Territorial expansion
.F37   Flags. Military colors
.F5   International relations
                    Class here works on treaty enforcements, inter-
                        national cooperation (League of Nations, United
                        Nations, Atlantic Pact, Marshall Plan, etc.)
.F55   Diplomatic and consular service
                    Class here works on location of embassies,
                        legations, consulates, etc.
.F7   Administrative and political divisions
                    Class here works on political subdivisions, minor
                        civil divisions of a political jurisdiction,
                        congressional districts, and election districts
                    For courts and judicial divisions, <u>see</u> .F85

IV

SUBJECT SUBDIVISIONS

F   Political Geography - Continued

  .F8   Government
  .F81   Forms of government
              Class here works on the distribution of
                 governing systems within a given area
  .F82   Departments, agencies, bureaus, commissions
            (together with their administrative areas)
  .F85   Laws and law enforcement
              Class here works on the location of courts,
                 judicial divisions, penal institutions,
                 legal societies, etc.
  .F86   Concentration camps. Detention centers, etc.
  .F9   Political campaigns. Election results. Votes in
         legislature. Political results

G   Economic Geography
            For works on the economic geography of the
               specialized fields of mines and minerals,
               agriculture, forests and forestry, fisheries,
               manufactures and processing, technology,
               engineering, public works, transportation
               and communication, and commerce and trade,
               see subdivisions .H through .Q

  .G1   General. Economic conditions
  .G15   Economic planning
             Cf. .G45, Planning
  .G16   Economic cycles. Business cycles
  .G17   Economic assistance (Domestic)
             For international economic assistance, see .F5
  .G2   Economic regions. Economic spheres of influence
  .G3   Natural resources. Conservation (General)
             Cf. .D5, Wildlife conservation and reserves
                 .J4, Soil conservation
                 .K3, Forest conservation
  .G4   Land. Land use. Land capabilities and classification
  .G44   Zoning
  .G45   Planning
             Cf. .G15, Economic planning
  .G455   Urban renewal
  .G46   Cadastral maps. Land ownership. Real property
  .G465   Land grants
  .G47   Real property tax. Tax assessment
             For income tax, see .E74
  .G475   Insurance. Fire protection
             Class here works showing data specifically
               useful in determining fire and other property
               rates, etc.
  .G5   Public lands
  .G52   Parks and monuments
             Class here works on cultural and historic
               monuments, parks, zoos, etc.; individual
               parks are classified as regions
             Cf. .D5, Wildlife conservation and reserves
                 .K1, Forests
  .G54   Cemeteries

SUBJECT SUBDIVISIONS

G   Economic Geography - Continued

.G6   Ethnic reservations
.G7   Business and professional organizations
.G8   Labor
                Class here works on the distribution of
                    the labor force or individual skills,
                    labor relations, employment, strikes,
                    unions, etc.

H   Mines and Mineral Resources
                Including mineral rights and leases
                For "Rock hound guides," see .E63

.H1   General
.H2   Metallic group
.H5   Nonmetallic group
                Including works on hydrocarbons (General), e. g.
                    coal and petroleum
.H8   Petroleum and natural gas
.H9   Coal. Lignite. Peat

J   Agriculture

.J1   General. Agricultural regions
.J15   Agricultural economics. Economic aspects
               of agriculture
.J2   Systems of agriculture. Agricultural methods.
             Farming techniques
.J3   Soils. Soil classification. Soil
             capability and utilization
.J4   Soil conservation. Reclamation. Irrigation.
             Erosion
                Cf. .C3, Hydrology
                    .G3, Conservation (General)
                    .N22, Flood control
.J48   Fertilizers
.J5   Animal husbandry. Livestock
.J6   Crops
.J61   Cereals
.J67   Forage crops. Legumes
.J7   Vegetables
.J73   Fruits. Nuts
.J77   Sugar and starch
                Class here works on the distribution of
                    crops specifically cultivated for the
                    production of sugar and starch
.J8   Industrial agricultural products
.J82   Cordage and textile fibers
                Including cotton, flax, hemp, etc.
.J84   Rubber, gum, and resin plants
.J86   Oil bearing plants

IV

SUBJECT SUBDIVISIONS

J   <u>Agriculture</u> – Continued

   .J9   Other plants
   .J912   Beverage plants
               Including coffee, tea, etc.
   .J92   Medicinal plants
   .J93   Spices. Condiments
   .J94   Tobacco
   .J95   Floriculture. Nurseries

K   <u>Forests</u> <u>and</u> <u>Forestry</u>

   .K1   General
   .K2   Distribution of forest areas and forest types
               Class individual forests as regions
   .K3   Conservation. Reforestation. Afforestation
               Cf. .G3, Conservation (General)
   .K4   Silviculture. Tree farms
   .K5   Agents of forest destruction. Forest fires
   .K6   Lumbering. Exploitation
               Cf. .M4, Wood processing and manufacture

L   <u>Aquatic</u> <u>Biological</u> <u>Resources</u>
               Class here works on the economic aspects of
               aquatic life, including aquatic vegetation,
               aquaculture, and pelagic mammals

   .L1   General
               Cf. .D, Plant and animal distribution
               For hunting or fishing as a recreational
               activity, <u>see</u> .E63
   .L2   Fishing and fisheries. Fish hatcheries. Sea
               animal products
   .L4   Aquatic vegetation. Aquaculture
   .L5   Pelagic mammals. Sealing. Whaling

M   <u>Manufacutring</u> <u>and</u> <u>Processing</u>. <u>Service</u> <u>Industries</u>

   .M1   General
   .M2   Mineral processing and manufacture
   .M3   Chemical processing and manufacture
   .M4   Wood processing and manufacture
   .M5   Paper processing and manufacture
   .M6   Fiber, textile, and hide processing and manufacture
   .M8   Food and beverage processing and manufacture
   .M9   Transport equipment manufacture
   .M95   Service industries

SUBJECT SUBDIVISIONS

N   Technology. Engineering. Public works

  .N1   General
                Including inventions
  .N18   Engineering
  .N2   Hydraulic engineering. Dams
                  Class individual dams as geographic features
  .N22   Flood control
  .N23   Civil engineering. Building and construction.
                  Building materials
  .N3   Power
  .N32   Steam. Geothermal steam sources. Thermoelectric
                  power generation
  .N33   Water power. Hydroelectric power generation
  .N34   Wind power. Aeroelectric power generation
  .N35   Nuclear power. Magnetohydrodynamics
                  Cf. .C92, Radioactivity
  .N36   Solar power
  .N39   Utilities
  .N4   Electric utilities. Service areas. Power lines
  .N42   Gas utilities
  .N44   Water utilities. Water storage, distribution,
                  and purification plants
                    Cf. .C3, Hydrology
  .N46   Sewerage. Waste disposal
  .N85   Pollution and pollution control
  .N852   Air pollution
  .N854   Pollution of land
                    Including soil pollution, despoliation of
                      the land by billboards and by the
                      accumulation of refuse such as abandoned
                      motor vehicles, etc.
  .N856   Water pollution
  .N858   Noise pollution

P   Transportation and Communication

  .P1   General
  .P15   Distances
  .P19   Trafficability. Traffic feasibility surveys
  .P2   Roads
  .P21   Traffic surveys
  .P22   Bus routes. Truck routes
  .P24   Bridges and tunnels
  .P25   Trails (Historic)
                    Class individual trails as geographic features
                    For scenic and recreational trails, see .E63
  .P3   Railroads
  .P33   Urban and interurban railroads
                    Including elevated railroads, street railways,
                      trams, subways, etc.
  .P4   Pipe lines

SUBJECT SUBDIVISIONS

P   Transportation and Communication - Continued

   .P5   Water transportation. Nautical charts. Pilot charts
                  Class individual canals, lakes, etc. as geographic
                     features
   .P53   Inland waterways
                     Class here works on navigable lakes, rivers,
                        canals, and protected inshore channels
   .P54   Ocean routes. Shipping lines. Load line charts
   .P55   Ports and port facilities
   .P57   Wreck charts
                  Cf. .E75, Treasure trove
   .P58   Electronic navigation charts
                  Class here Consol, Decca, Loran, and other
                     hyperbolic navigation charts
                  For regular chart series with electronic lattice
                     overprints, see .P5 and .P6
   .P6   Air transportation. Aeronautical charts
   .P61   Airports, landing fields, etc.
   .P62   Air routes
   .P7   Space transportation
   .P75   Satellite tracks, etc.
   .P78   Other transportation systems
                  Including conveyor belts, cable ways
   .P8   Postal service. Postal zones. Zip codes
   .P9   Communications
   .P92   Telegraph
   .P93   Submarine cables
   .P94   Telephone. Area codes
   .P95   Radio
   .P96   Television
   .P97   Dissemination of information. The press. Printing.
                  Propaganda. Public opinion

Q   Commerce and Trade. Finance

   .Q1   General
   .Q2   Business statistics
   .Q3   Movement of commodities
                  Class here works on trade routes, caravan routes,
                     etc.
                  Cf. .Q5, Tariffs and other trade barriers
                  For maps and atlases which emphasize the carrier
                     and show specific routes, see .P
   .Q4   Marketing
   .Q42   Trade centers and trading areas
   .Q44   Shopping centers. Shopping malls
   .Q46   Retail sales outlets
   .Q48   Fairs, exhibitions, etc.
                     Class individual fairs and exhibitions as
                        regions, e. g. New York Worlds Fair, and
                        Transpo '72
   .Q5   Tariffs and other trade barriers
   .Q8   Finance
                  Class here works on coins and currencies, foreign
                     exchange credit, special types of financial
                     institutions, individual financial firms, etc.

IV

SUBJECT SUBDIVISIONS

R   <u>Military</u> <u>and</u> <u>Naval</u> <u>Geography</u>
               Class here works on the administration and
                 general operation of peacetime military
                 and naval forces
               For maps and atlases that portray historical
                 events of a military nature, <u>see</u> .S

.R1	General
.R2	Military and naval districts and establishments. Troop disposition
.R22	Air Force
.R24	Army
.R26	Coast Guard
.R28	Navy
.R282	Marine Corps
.R3	Military operations. Strategy and tactics. War games
.R4	Defenses. Fortifications
.R5	Logistics
	Class here works on military support systems, munitions, lines of communication, etc.
.R6	Civil defense

S   <u>Historical</u> <u>Geography</u>
               Class here maps and atlases that portray specific
                 historical events, including disposition of
                 troops, battle lines, or a series of events
               A map or atlas, either contemporary or reconstructed,
                 which gives only general geographical information
                 about an area at the time of a given event or
                 series of events is treated without subject
                 subdivision.
               A chronological subdivision for each area, based
                 on its own history, is to be preferred to any
                 universal arrangement except that the following
                 Cutter numbers are to remain constant throughout
                 the schedule:

.S1	General
.S12	Discovery and exploration
.S65	World War I
.S7	World War II

             For examples of such arrangements, <u>see</u> G3201.S1+,
               World history, and G3701.S1+, United States
               history

MATHEMATICAL GEOGRAPHY
CARTOGRAPHY

Cf. QB275+, Geodesy
QB631+, Astronomical geography

MATHEMATICAL GEOGRAPHY

1	Periodicals. Societies. Serials
	Collected works (nonserial)
2	Several authors
.5	Individual authors
	<u>Study and teaching. Research</u>
.7	General works
	By region or country
.8	United States
.9	Other regions or countries, A-Z
3	History
	Cf. GA201+, Cartography
	GA260+, Globes
4	Handbooks, tables, etc.
	<u>General works, treatises, and textbooks</u>
5	Early through 1500
6	16th century. Cosmographies
7	17th-18th centuries
	1801-1974
9	Comprehensive works
12	Compends
	Cf. GA260+, History, description and construction
	of globes
13	1975-
23	General special (Special aspects of the subject as a whole)
	Including calculation of geographical areas
	<u>Surveys (General)</u>
	Cf. QB301+, Geodetic surveys
	QE61+, Geological surveys
	TA590+, Topographical surveying (Engineering)
	VK588+, Hydrographic surveys
	History, organization, methods, etc.
51	General works
	Individual regions or countries, <u>see</u> GA55+
53	General special
55	International surveys
56	Several countries
	Not limited to one continent
57	America
59	United States
61	By state, A-W
63	Other American countries, A-Z
65	Europe
66	By country, A-Z
70	Asia
71	By country, A-Z
75	Africa
76	By country, A-Z

CARTOGRAPHY

Mathematical geography
    Surveys (General) – Continued
80   Australia and Pacific islands
85   Australia
86   By state or territory, A–Z
.5   New Zealand
87   Pacific islands, A–Z

CARTOGRAPHY

Class here works on map making and works about maps (General)
For works on the construction, use, and reading of maps in a
special field, see B–Z, e. g. QC878, Construction of weather
maps; UG470, Military mapping; S494.5.C3, Agricultural cartography, etc. For maps themselves, see G3200+

Cf. GN476.5, Primitive cartography

101   Periodicals. Societies. Serials
.2   Congresses
       Collected works (nonserial)
.5   Several authors
.7   Individual authors
102   Dictionaries. Encyclopedias
.2   Terminology. Abbreviations. Notation
         Cf. GA155, Map symbols
.25   Directories
.3   Philosophy. Relation to other topics. Methodology
.4   Special methods, A–Z
         .E4 Electronic data processing
.5–.7   Study and teaching. Research
         Subdivided like GA2.7–.9
       General works, treatises, and advanced textbooks
         Including thematic cartography (General)
103   Early through 1800
105   1801–1974
.3   1975–
       Elementary textbooks, see GA130
.5   Popular works
.6   Juvenile works
108   Addresses, essays, lectures
.5   Handbooks, tables, etc.
.7   General special (Special aspects of the subject as a whole)
109   Aerial cartography
        Cf. TA593, Aerial surveying
          TL587, Aeronautical charts
.5   Cadastral mapping
.8   Statistical mapping
       Projection
110   General works
115   Special types (not A–Z)
         Including orthomorphic, equal area, perspective, as
          well as individual methods, e. g. Mercator's,
          Lambert's, etc.
116   Grids
       Latitude and longitude, see QB224.5+

CARTOGRAPHY

118	Map scales
125	Topographic drawing
	Cf. TA616, Surveying
130	Elementary map drawing and reading
	Including juvenile textbooks
135	Maps for the visually handicapped
138	Block diagrams
140	Relief maps
145	Modeling
150	Map printing, engraving, etc.
.5	Equipment, machinery, supplies
.7	Reproduction, photocopying, etc.
151	Map reading (General)
	For military map reading, see UG470
	Cf. G107.5+, Geographic terms
	GA102.2, Cartographic terms
	GA130, Elementary map drawing and reading
155	Conventional signs and symbols
190	Museums. Exhibitions
	Subdivided by author
	Collections of maps, globes, etc. Map libraries
	Cf. GA361, Collections of marine charts
	Z692.M3, Handling of maps in libraries
	Z695.6, Cataloging of maps
192	Periodicals. Societies. Serials
193	By region or country, A-Z
195	Individual public collections. By place, A-Z
	e. g. .W64 Wolfenbüttel. Herzog-August-Bibliothek
197	Individual private collections. By collector, A-Z
.3	Collector's manuals. History of collecting
	Cartographers
.5	Cartography as a profession
198	Biography (General)
	Including biography (General) of globe makers
	For biography of globe makers by country, see GA281+
	For biography of cartographers by country, see
	GA407; GA473; GA483; etc.
	History
201	General
203	General special
	Including cartographical sources, value of maps in
	boundary disputes, popes as geographers
	By period
	Ancient
	Cf. G83+, History of geography
205	General
	Special
207	Chinese
209	Egyptian
211	Indian
213	Greek and Roman
221	Medieval
231	16th century (1450-1600)
236	17th-18th centuries
241	19th century
246	20th century

CARTOGRAPHY

History – Continued
By country, <u>see</u> GA401+
<u>Globe making. Globes</u>
For globes themselves, <u>see</u> G3170+
Cf. GA192+, Collections of globes
GA198, 281+, Biography of globe makers

260	General works
263	General special
265	Manuals for the use of globes
	<u>By period</u>
267	Before 16th century
271	16th century
273	17th century
275	18th century
277	19th century
278	20th century
	<u>By country</u>

Under each:

	I	II	
	Successive	1 no.	
	Cutter nos.		
	.x	.A1–4	General works
			Including collective biography
	.x2	.A5–Z7	Individual biography
	.x3	.Z8	Special globes. By date or approximate date
			Subarranged by globe maker and author

e. g. .I7–9   Italy
   .I7   General works
   .I8   Individual biography, A–Z
   .I9   Special globes

281	United States (II)
282	Canada (II)
283	Other American countries, A–Z (I)
284	Europe, A–Z (I)
285	Asia, A–Z (I)
286	Africa, A–Z (I)
287	Australia (II)
.5	New Zealand (II)
288	Pacific islands, A–Z (I)

<u>World maps, general atlases, etc.</u>
Class here works on the history and description of atlases and maps. For the atlases and maps themselves, <u>see</u> G1001+

300	General works
	Early Oriental
301	Identified. By date[1]
302	Not identified
	Date and cartographer unknown
	Subarranged by author of history or description

---

[1] Subarranged (1) by cartographer or title, (2) by author or editor

CARTOGRAPHY

<u>World maps, general atlases, etc.</u> - Continued
    Ancient and medieval to 1400

303	By date[1]
	Undated
304.A1-Z4	By cartographer or title of map[2]
.Z51-99	Anonymous maps arranged by approximate date[2]

        .Z5 Before 1000
        .Z6 11th century
        .Z7 12th century
        .Z8 13th century
        .Z9 14th century

    15th century

307	By date[1]
	Undated
308.A1-Z4	By cartographer or title of map[2]
.Z51-99	Anonymous maps arranged by approximate date[2]

        .Z5 Before 1425
        .Z6 1425-1450
        .Z7 1450-1475
        .Z8 1475-1500
        .Z9 1400-1500

    16th century

311	By date[1]
312	Undated
	Divided like GA308

    17th century

315	By date[1]
316	Undated
	Divided like GA308

    18th century

317	By date
318	Undated
	Divided like GA308

    19th century

319	By date[1]
320	Undated
	Divided like GA308
.5	Series of maps by special publishers, A-Z

        e. g. .S7 Society for the Diffusion of Useful
                        Knowledge

    20th century

321	By date[1]
322	Undated
	Subdivided like GA308
323	International Map Committee
325	Series of maps by special publishers, A-Z

---

[1] Subarranged (1) by cartographer or title, (2) by author or editor

[2] Subarranged by author or editor

CARTOGRAPHY

	Maps. By region or country
	Class here works on the history of map production in particular regions or countries and works on the history and description of maps of special regions or countries
341	Eastern Hemisphere
	Western Hemisphere, see GA401+
345	Northern Hemisphere
347	Southern Hemisphere
	Polar regions
351	General works
355	Arctic regions
357	Antarctic regions. Antarctica
	Oceans. Seas. Marine cartography
359	General works
361	Collections of nautical charts
	For collections issued by individual countries, see GA401+
	Arctic Ocean
364	General works
365	Special parts, A-Z
	Atlantic Ocean
368	General works
	North Atlantic
369	General works
370	North Sea
371	Baltic Sea
372	English Channel. St. George's Channel
373	Bay of Biscay
374	Strait of Gibraltar
	Mediterranean Sea
375	General works
376	Special parts, A-Z
378	Black Sea
380	South Atlantic
381	Caribbean Sea and Gulf of Mexico
	Pacific Ocean
383	General works
	North Pacific
384	General works
385	Bering Sea. Sea of Okhotsk
386	Japan Sea
387	Yellow Sea
388	China Sea
390	South Pacific
	Indian Ocean
392	General works
394	Red Sea
395	Persian Gulf
396	Arabian Sea
397	Bay of Bengal

CARTOGRAPHY

	Maps. By region or country - Continued
401	America. Western Hemisphere
	North and South America together or North America alone
402	Individual maps. By date or approximate date[1]
	United States
405	General works. General history of cartography in the United States
.5	General special
406	Official works. Documents
	Biography of cartographers
	Cf. GA281, Biography of globe makers
407.A1A-Z	Collective
.A2-Z	Individual, A-Z
408	Individual maps. By date or approximate date[1]
	Including maps of regions: New England, Northwest, etc.
	Individual states
409	Alabama
410	Alaska
411	Arizona
412	Arkansas
413	California
414	Colorado
415	Connecticut
416	Delaware
417	District of Columbia
418	Florida
419	Georgia
.5	Hawaii
420	Idaho
421	Illinois
422	Indian Territory
423	Indiana
424	Iowa
425	Kansas
426	Kentucky
427	Louisiana
428	Maine
429	Maryland
430	Massachusetts
431	Michigan
432	Minnesota
433	Mississippi
434	Missouri
435	Montana
436	Nebraska
437	Nevada
438	New Hampshire
439	New Jersey

------

[1] Subarranged (1) by cartographer or title, (2) by author or editor

CARTOGRAPHY

Maps. By region or country
  United States
   Individual states - Continued

440	New Mexico
441	New York
442	North Carolina
443	North Dakota
444	Ohio
445	Oklahoma
446	Oregon
447	Pennsylvania
448	Rhode Island
449	South Carolina
450	South Dakota
451	Tennessee
452	Texas
453	Utah
454	Vermont
455	Virginia
456	Washington
457	West Virginia
458	Wisconsin
459	Wyoming
460	Individual cities and towns, A-Z

  Other regions or countries
   Under each country:
    1 General works. General history of cartography
    2 Official works. Documents
    3 Collective biography
     By period, see subdivisions, 3.1-3.7
    History. By period
     Under each:
      .A1A-Z History. Collective biography
      .A3-Z Individual biography, A-Z
        Cf. GA282+, Biography of
          globe makers
     .1 Early to 500
     .3 Medieval (500 to 1500)
     .5 16th century
     .6 17th-18th centuries
     .7 19th-20th centuries
    4 Individual maps. By date or approximate date[1]
    5 Local, A-Z

471-475	Canada. British North America
481-485	Mexico

  Central America

491	General works
501-505	Belize. British Honduras
511-515	Costa Rica
521-525	Guatemala
531-535	Honduras

---

[1]
  Subarranged (2) by cartographer or title, (2) by author or editor

CARTOGRAPHY

Maps. By region or country
  Other regions or countries [1]
    Central America - Continued

541-545	Nicaragua
546-550	Panama
551-555	Salvador

    West Indies

561	General works
571-575	Bahamas
581-585	Cuba
591-595	Haiti
601-605	Jamaica
611-615	Puerto Rico
621	Other islands, A-Z
631-635	Bermudas

    South America

641	General works
651-655	Argentina
661-665	Bolivia
671-675	Brazil
681-685	Chile
691-695	Colombia
701-705	Ecuador
	Guianas
711	General works
716-720	Guyana
721-725	Surinam
726-730	French Guiana
741-745	Paraguay
751-755	Peru
761-765	Uruguay
771-775	Venezuela

    Europe

781	General works
787	Alps
	Not confined to one country

      Great Britain. England (General)

791-794	General works
795	England (Local), A-Z
801-805	Northern Ireland
811-815	Scotland
821-825	Wales
826-829	Ireland
831-834	Austria
	Including Austria-Hungary
841-845	Czechoslovakia
851-855	Hungary
861-865	France
871-875	Germany
	Including West Germany
876-880	East Germany

---

[1]

  For subarrangement, see table p. 231

CARTOGRAPHY

Maps. By region or country[1]
Other regions or countries[1]
Europe - Continued

881-885	Greece
891-895	Italy
	Low Countries. Benelux
901	General works
911-915	Belgium
921-925	Netherlands (Holland)
931-935	Russia
941-945	Poland
	Scandinavia
951	General works
961-965	Denmark
971-975	Iceland
981-985	Norway
991-995	Sweden
1001-1004	Spain and Portugal. Spain (General)
1005	Spain (Local), A-Z
1011-1015	Portugal
1021-1025	Switzerland
	Balkan States
1031	General works
1036-1040	Albania
1041-1045	Bulgaria
1061-1065	Romania
1071-1075	Yugoslavia
1077	Other European regions or countries, A-Z
	Asia
1081	General works
1091-1095	Afghanistan
1101-1105	Arabia
1121-1125	China
1131-1135	India
1136-1140	Pakistan
	Indochina
1141	General works
1151-1155	Vietnam. Annam
1161-1165	Cambodia
1191-1195	Thailand. Siam
1201-1205	Malaysia
1211	East Indies
1221-1225	Indonesia
1231-1235	Philippine Islands
1241-1245	Japan
1251-1255	Korea
1261-1265	Iran. Persia
	Russia in Asia
1271	General works
1281-1285	Central Asia
1291-1295	Siberia
1297	Other Asian regions or countries, A-Z

---

[1]
For subarrangement, see table, p. 231

CARTOGRAPHY

Maps. By region or country
Other regions or countries[1]
Asia - Continued

1301-1305	Turkey
	Armenia, see GA935.A7
1321-1325	Israel. Palestine
1331-1335	Syria
1340	Other Asian countries, A-Z
	Africa
1341	General works
1346	North Africa
	Including Northeast Africa
1348-1352	Morocco
1358-1362	Algeria
1368-1372	Tunisia
1378-1382	Libya
1388-1392	Egypt
1398-1402	Sudan
1408-1412	Canary Islands
1414	Other regions or countries, A-Z
1418	Sudan region and the Sahara
	East Africa
1428	General works
1434-1438	Ethiopia
1439-1443	Afars and Issas
1444-1448	Somalia
1454-1458	Kenya
1464-1468	Uganda
1474-1478	Rwanda
1484-1488	Burundi
1494-1498	Tanzania
1499	Other regions or countries, A-Z
	Central Africa
1500	General works
1508-1512	Central African Republic
1518-1522	Gabon
1528-1532	Congo (Brazzaville)
1538-1542	Zaire
1543	Other regions or countries, A-Z
	West Africa
1550	General works
1558-1562	Mauritania
1568-1572	Senegal
1578-1582	Liberia
1588-1592	Nigeria
1598-1602	Cameroon
1603	Other regions or countries, A-Z

---

[1]
    For subarrangement, see table, p. 231

CARTOGRAPHY

<u>Maps. By region or country</u>
    <u>Other regions or countries</u>[1]
      <u>Africa</u> – Continued
        <u>Southern Africa</u>

1604	General works
1608–1612	Zambia
1618–1622	Malawi
1628–1632	Mozambique
1638–1642	Southwest Africa
1648–1652	Rhodesia
1658–1662	South Africa
1668–1672	Madagascar
1673	Other regions or countries, A–Z
1681–1685	Australia
1765–1769	New Zealand
	<u>Pacific islands</u>
1771	General works
1776	Marshall Islands

---

[1] For subarrangement, <u>see</u> table, p. 231

PHYSICAL GEOGRAPHY

<pre>
               Cf. GC, Oceanography
                   QC851+, Meteorology. Climatology
                   QE, Geology
                   QH, Natural History
                   QK, Botany
                   QL, Zoology
                   S590+, Soils

               Periodicals, see G1
               Societies, see G2+
        3   Congresses
               Collected works (nonserial)
        5   Several authors
        9   Individual authors
       10   Dictionaries. Encyclopedias
       11   History
               Philosophy. Relation to other topics. Methodology
       21   General works
        .5   Special methods, A-Z
                      .M33 Mathematics
                      .R43 Remote sensing
                      .S55 Simulation methods
                      .S7   Statistical methods
               Study and teaching. Research
       23   General works
       24   Problems, exercises, examinations
       25   Fieldwork
        .5   Laboratory manuals
                  By region or country
       26   United States
        .2   Other regions or countries, A-Z
       27   Museums. Exhibitions
                  Subdivided by author
               General works, treatises, and advanced textbooks
       51   Early through 1800
       53   1801-1974
       54.5   1975-
       55   Elementary textbooks
        .5   Outlines, syllabi
        .6   Pictorial works
       58   Juvenile works
       59   Popular works
        .5   Addresses, essays, lectures
        .6   Handbooks, tables, etc.
       60   General special (Special aspects of the subject as a whole)
               By region or country¹
      111   America
      115   North America
                     United States
      121   General works
      124   By region, A-Z
                        e. g. .N4 New England
      126   By state, A-W
</pre>

---

¹
    Regions, islands, or countries, with two numbers: (1) General works;
(2) By region, country, island, province, or state, A-Z

	By region or country[1]
	America
	North America – Continued
131–132	Canada
133–134	Mexico
136–139	Central America
142–143	West Indies. Caribbean area
	South America
144	General works
151	Argentina
153	Bolivia
155	Brazil
156	Chile
157	Colombia
158	Ecuador
	Guianas
159	General works
160	Guyana (British Guiana)
161	Surinam (Dutch Guiana)
162	French Guiana
163	Paraguay
165	Peru
167	Uruguay
169	Venezuela
170–170.2	South Atlantic islands
	Europe
171	General works
	By region or country
174	Northern Europe
178	Mediterranean Basin
	Great Britain. England
181	General works
184	England. By region or county, A–Z
186–189	Northern Ireland
191–194	Scotland
196–199	Wales
200–200.2	Ireland (Éire)
201–204	Austria
205–205.2	Bulgaria
.4–.5	Czechoslovakia
.7–.8	Finland
206–209	France
211–214	Germany
	Including West Germany
215–215.2	East Germany
216–219	Greece
220–220.2	Hungary
221–224	Italy
	Low countries
225	General works
226–229	Belgium
231–234	Netherlands
235	Luxemburg

---

[1] Regions, islands, or countries with two numbers: (1) General works; (2) By region, country, island, province, or state, A–Z

PHYSICAL GEOGRAPHY

<table>
<tr><td></td><td>By region or country[1]</td></tr>
<tr><td></td><td>Europe - Continued</td></tr>
<tr><td>235.4-.5</td><td>Poland</td></tr>
<tr><td>.7-.8</td><td>Romania</td></tr>
<tr><td>236-239</td><td>Russia</td></tr>
<tr><td></td><td>Scandinavia</td></tr>
<tr><td>240</td><td>General works</td></tr>
<tr><td>241-244</td><td>Denmark</td></tr>
<tr><td>246-249</td><td>Norway</td></tr>
<tr><td>251-254</td><td>Sweden</td></tr>
<tr><td>256-259</td><td>Spain</td></tr>
<tr><td>261-264</td><td>Portugal</td></tr>
<tr><td>266-269</td><td>Switzerland</td></tr>
<tr><td>275-275.2</td><td>Yugoslavia</td></tr>
<tr><td>276</td><td>Other regions or countries, A-Z</td></tr>
<tr><td></td><td>e. g. .A35 Alps</td></tr>
<tr><td></td><td>Asia</td></tr>
<tr><td>280</td><td>General works</td></tr>
<tr><td></td><td>By region or country</td></tr>
<tr><td></td><td>Near East. Middle East</td></tr>
<tr><td>281</td><td>General works</td></tr>
<tr><td>283</td><td>Syria</td></tr>
<tr><td>284</td><td>Israel</td></tr>
<tr><td>285</td><td>Saudi Arabia. Arabian Peninsula</td></tr>
<tr><td>286</td><td>Iraq</td></tr>
<tr><td>287</td><td>Jordan</td></tr>
<tr><td>288</td><td>Iran</td></tr>
<tr><td>289</td><td>Lebanon</td></tr>
<tr><td>.2</td><td>Turkey</td></tr>
<tr><td>.4</td><td>Other regions or countries, A-Z</td></tr>
<tr><td>290</td><td>Central Asia</td></tr>
<tr><td>293</td><td>Himalaya Mountains</td></tr>
<tr><td></td><td>Southern Asia. Southeastern Asia</td></tr>
<tr><td>295</td><td>General works</td></tr>
<tr><td>297</td><td>Afghanistan</td></tr>
<tr><td>299</td><td>Pakistan</td></tr>
<tr><td>301-302</td><td>India</td></tr>
<tr><td>303</td><td>Sri Lanka</td></tr>
<tr><td>304</td><td>Burma</td></tr>
<tr><td>305</td><td>Vietnam</td></tr>
<tr><td>306</td><td>Thailand</td></tr>
<tr><td>308-309</td><td>Malaysia</td></tr>
<tr><td>311-312</td><td>Indonesia</td></tr>
<tr><td>313</td><td>Philippine Islands</td></tr>
<tr><td>314</td><td>Other regions or countries, A-Z</td></tr>
<tr><td></td><td>Eastern Asia. Far East</td></tr>
<tr><td>315</td><td>General works</td></tr>
<tr><td></td><td>China</td></tr>
<tr><td>316</td><td>General works</td></tr>
<tr><td>317</td><td>Tibet</td></tr>
<tr><td></td><td>For Himalaya Mountains, see GB293</td></tr>
<tr><td>318</td><td>Other regions or provinces, A-Z</td></tr>
<tr><td></td><td>e. g. .S5 Sinkiang. East Turkestan</td></tr>
<tr><td>.5</td><td>Taiwan</td></tr>
<tr><td>319</td><td>Korea</td></tr>
</table>

---

[1]
   Regions, islands, or countries with two numbers: (1) General works;
(2) By region, country, island, province, or state, A-Z

	By region or country[1]
	Eastern Asia. Far East – Continued
322	Japan
	Northern Asia. Siberia. Russia in Asia
325	General works
326	Soviet Central Asia
327	Other regions or republics, A–Z
328	Islands of the Pacific, A–Z
	Africa
330	General works
331	North Africa
.5	Algeria
332	Egypt
334	Libya
336	Morocco
337	Tunisia
338	Sahara
349	Sub-Saharan Africa
	Central Africa
350	General works
351	Congo (Brazzaville)
352	Zaire. Congo (Democratic Republic)
	West Africa
355	General works
356	Nigeria
359	Other regions or countries, A–Z
	e. g. .A5 Angola
	.L5 Liberia
	.S6 Spanish Sahara. Rio de Oro
	Southern Africa
360	General works
362	Mozambique
363	South Africa
365	Other regions or countries, A–Z
	e. g. .S55 Southern Rhodesia
	.S6 Southwest Africa
	.Z3 Zambia
	Eastern Africa. East Africa
370	General works
375	By region or country, A–Z
	e. g. .E8 Ethiopia
	.K4 Kenya
	.T3 Tanzania
	.U3 Uganda
378	Islands, A–Z
	e. g. .C3 Canary Islands
	.M3 Madagascar
381–384	Australia
385–386	New Zealand
	Pacific islands
391	General works
394	By island or group of islands, A–Z
395	Arctic regions
397	Antarctic regions

---

[1]
    Regions, islands, or countries with two numbers: (1) General works;
(2) By region, country, island, province, or state, A–Z

PHYSICAL GEOGRAPHY

By region or country - Continued

398	Arid regions
	Cf. GB611+, Geomorphology
	GB841, Hydrology
.5	Cold regions
	Cf. GB641+, Geomorphology
	GB2401+, Ice. Glaciers. Ice sheets. Sea ice
.7	Tropics
	Cf. GB446, Geomorphology

Geomorphology. Landforms. Terrain

Cf. QE500+, Dynamic and structural geology

400	Periodicals. Societies. Serials
.2	Congresses
.3	Dictionaries. Encyclopedias
.4	Methodology
.42	Special methods, A-Z
	.A35 Aerial photography in geomorphology
	.A8 Astronautics in geomorphology
	.E4 Electronic data processing
	.M3 Mapping
	.M33 Mathematical models
	.M34 Mathematics
	.S7 Statistical methods
.5	Study and teaching. Research
	By region or country
.6	United States
.65	Other regions or countries, A-Z
.7	History

General works, treatises, and advanced textbooks

401	1801-1974
.5	1975-
402	Elementary textbooks
403	Pictorial works
405	Addresses, essays, lectures
406	General special

By region or country

	America
425	General works
	North America
427	General works
	United States
.5	General works
428	By region or state, A-Z
.5	Other regions or countries, A-Z
	Central America
429	General works
430	By region or country, A-Z
	South America
431	General works
432	By region or country, A-Z
434	South Atlantic islands, A-Z
	Europe
435	General works
436	By region or country, A-Z
	Asia
437	General works
438	By region or country, A-Z

PHYSICAL GEOGRAPHY

Geomorphology. Landforms. Terrain
    By region or country - Continued
        Africa
439   General works
440   By region or country, A-Z
441   Australia
442   New Zealand
444   Arctic regions
445   Antarctic regions
446   Tropics
447 Climatic geomorphology
448 Slopes
    Coasts
        Including beaches, coast changes, and shorelines
        Cf. -F, History and description of individual
                countries
            GC, Oceanography
            QE39, Submarine geology
            TC330+, Shore protection
450   Periodicals. Societies. Serials
   .2   Congresses
   .4   Dictionaries. Encyclopedias
   .6   Terminology. Abbreviations. Notations
   .8   Instruments and apparatus
        General works, treatises, and textbooks
451   1801-1974
   .2   1975-
452   Pictorial works
   .2   Handbooks, tables, etc.
454   By special coastal landform, A-Z
            For landforms of special regions, see GB455+
        .B3   Beach cusps
        .F5   Fiords
        .R5   Ripple marks
        .S3   Sand
        .S66   Spits
        .W3   Washover fans
    By region
        Cf. GB460, Coasts, shorelines, etc. By continent
                or country
        Arctic Ocean
455   General works
   .2   Alaska
   .3   Canada
   .4   Greenland
   .6   Norway
   .7   Finland
   .8   Russia. Siberia
456   Antarctic regions
    Atlantic Ocean
457   General works
            Western Atlantic, see GB459+

Geomorphology. Landforms. Terrain
  Coasts
    By region
      Atlantic Ocean - Continued
        Northeastern Atlantic Ocean

457	General works
.12	Iceland. Faroe Islands

North Sea. Skagerrak

.2	General works

British Isles. England
  Including coasts on the Atlantic Ocean
    and Irish Sea

.21	General works
.22	Scotland
.24	Hebrides
.25	Wales
.26	Isle of Man
.27	Northern Ireland
.28	Channel Islands
.285	Ireland (Éire)
.3	Norway
.4	Denmark
.5	Germany
.53	Netherlands
.54	Belgium

Baltic Sea. Cattegat

.545	General works
.55	Denmark
.56	Bornholm
.57	Other islands of the Baltic, A-Z
.58	Germany
.59	Poland
.6	Russia. Baltic States
.62	Finland
.63	Sweden
.64	English Channel

    For Channel Islands, <u>see</u> GB457.28

.66	France
.68	Bay of Biscay
.69	Spain
.695	Portugal

Mediterranean Sea

.71	General works
.72	Spain
.73	France
.74	Italy
.75	Balkan Peninsula
.755	Black Sea. Sea of Azov
.76	Turkey. Near East
.78	North Africa
.79	Islands of the Mediterranean, A-Z
.8	African coast
.82	Eastern Atlantic Islands, A-Z

    e. g. .C3 Cape Verde Islands
         .M3 Madeira Islands

Geomorphology. Landforms. Terrain
  Coasts
    By region - Continued
      Indian Ocean

457.825	General works
.83	African coast
.84	Islands, A-Z
.85	Red Sea. Gulf of Aden
.86	Persian Gulf. Gulf of Oman
.87	Arabian Sea
.88	Bay of Bengal

      Pacific Ocean

458	General works

        Northwestern Pacific Ocean

.1	General works
.15	Gulf of Siam
.2	China Sea
.25	Yellow Sea
.3	Japan Sea
.33	Sea of Okhotsk. Western Bering Sea
.35	North Pacific islands, A-Z

        South Pacific

.4	General works
.5	Australia
.55	New Zealand
	South Pacific islands, A-Z
.6	General works
.62	By island or group of islands, A-Z

        Eastern Pacific Ocean

.67	General works
.7	Alaska. Eastern Bering Sea
	British Columbia
.73	General works
.75	Vancouver Island
.8	United States
.85	Mexico
.87	Central America
.9	South America

      Western Atlantic Ocean

459	General works
.15	South America
.17	Caribbean Sea
.2	West Indies, A-Z
	Gulf of Mexico
.25	General works
.3	Florida Keys
	United States
.4	General works
.5	Inland waters, A-Z
.6	Nova Scotia. New Brunswick. Quebec
.7	Newfoundland and Labrador

PHYSICAL GEOGRAPHY

Geomorphology. Landforms. Terrain
    Coasts - Continued
      By continent or country
          Class here only works dealing with the coast or
             coasts of a continent or country which border
             more than one of the water areas in GB455+.
             For works dealing with a coast bordering on
             only one of these water areas, see GB455-459.7

460.A1	America
.A2	North America
.A25	Central America
.A3	South America
.A4	Europe
.A5	Asia
.A6	Africa
	Australia, see GB458.5
	Antarctica, see GB456
.A7-Z	By country, A-Z

    Reefs
      Cf. QE565+, Geology

461	General works
	America
463	General works
	United States
464	General works
465	By state, A-W
466	By reef, A-Z
468	Other countries (Table I, decimally)[1]
471-478	Islands

      Subdivided like GB461-468
      Cf. G500, Voyages and travels
  Earth movements, subsidences, etc., see QE598+
  Hypsometry. Tables of heights, see QC895
  Leveling, see TA606+
  Mountains. Orography
      Cf. GV199.8+, Mountaineering
         QE522+, Volcanoes
         QE621, Mountain building

500	Periodicals. Societies. Serials
.5	Dictionaries. Encyclopedias
	General works
501	1801-1974
.2	1975-
511	Popular works
512	Juvenile works
515	Mountain passes
	By region or country
	America
521	General works
	United States
525	General works
.5	By region, state, or mountain range, A-Z
530	Other countries, A-Z
531	By region or mountain range, A-Z (except United States)

---

[1]
  For Table I, see pp. 380-381

PHYSICAL GEOGRAPHY

Geomorphology. Landforms. Terrain
   Mountains. Orography
     By region or country - Continued
       Europe

541	General works
542	By country, A-Z
543	By region or mountain range, A-Z

          e. g.   Alps
              .A4   General works
              .A5   Special, A-Z
                    e. g. .A5J8 Jungfrau

       Asia

544	General works
545	By country, A-Z
546	By region or mountain range, A-Z

       Africa

547	General works
548	By country, A-Z
549	By region or mountain range, A-Z
551	Australia
552	New Zealand
553	Pacific islands
554	Arctic regions
555	Antarctic regions

      Other natural landforms
       Under each (unless otherwise provided for):
        (1) General works
        (2) General special
        (3) America
        (4) United States
        (5)   By state, A-W
        (6)   Special, A-Z
        (8) Other countries (Table I, decimally)[1]

561-568	Floodplains, river channels, valleys, watersheds
571-578	Peneplains, piedmonts, plains, plateaus, steppes, tundras
581-588	Glacial landforms
591-598	Alluvial fans, deltas, terraces

      Karst landforms

599	Periodicals. Societies. Serials
.2	Congresses
600	General works

       By region or country
        United States

.2	General works
.3	By region or state, A-Z
.4	Other regions or countries, A-Z
.5	Juvenile works
.6	Addresses, essays, lectures

      Caves. Speleology
       Cf. GN783+, Prehistoric archaeology

601.A1A-Z	Periodicals. Societies. Serials
.A4A-Z	History
.A6-Z	General works
.2	Juvenile works

---
[1] For Table I, see pp. 380-381

PHYSICAL GEOGRAPHY

<u>Geomorphology. Landforms. Terrain</u>
  <u>Other natural landforms</u>
    <u>Karst landforms</u>
      <u>Caves. Speleology</u> - Continued

601.3	Popular works
.4	Pictorial works
	Biography
.58	Collective
.6	Individual, A-Z
.8	Marine caves
	<u>Cave exploration. Spelunking</u>
602.A1A-Z	Periodicals. Societies. Serials
.A3-Z	General works
.5	Cave diving
	<u>By region or country</u>
	America
603	General works
	United States
604	General works
605	By region or state, A-Z
606	By cave, A-Z
608	Other (Table I, decimally)[1]
609	Polje. Interior valleys
.2	Sinkholes
611-618	Deserts. Arid regions
621-628	Moors, marshes, peatbogs, bogs, heaths, swamps
631-638	Dunes
641-648	Frozen ground. Cold regions
649	Other, A-Z
.D8	Duricrusts
.E3	Earth pyramids
.L3	Lava tubes
.S3	Sand waves

---

[1]
   For Table I, <u>see</u> pp. 380-381

PHYSICAL GEOGRAPHY

HYDROLOGY. WATER

Cf. HD1691+, Water rights
QC920; QC924.5+, Water in meterology
QE581, Aqueous erosion
S494.5.W3, Water in agriculture
TC, Hydraulic engineering
TD201+, Water supply

651	Periodicals. Societies. Serials
652	Congresses
	Collected works (nonserial)
653	Several authors
.2	Individual authors
655	Dictionaries. Encyclopedias
.5	Terminology. Abbreviations. Notation
	Methodology
656	General works
.2	Special methods, A-Z
	.A37 Aerial photography in hydrology
	.A9 Automation
	.C63 Computer programs
	.E42 Electromechanical analogies
	.E43 Electronic data processing
	.H9 Hydrologic models
	.M33 Mathematical models
	.R3 Radar in hydrology
	.R34 Radioisotopes in hydrology
	.S7 Statistical methods
	Communication of information
657	General works
.2	Information services
	Study and teaching. Research
658	General works
.3	Problems, exercises, examinations
.4	Fieldwork
.5	Laboratory manuals
	By region or country
.7	United States
.8	Other regions or countries, A-Z
659	Instruments and apparatus
	Museums. Exhibitions
.4	General works
.5	By region or country, A-Z
	Under each country:
	.x General works
	.x2 Special. By city, A-Z
.6	History
	General works, treatises, and advanced textbooks
.9	Early through 1800
661	1801-1974
.2	1975-
662	Outlines, syllabi
.3	Juvenile works

PHYSICAL GEOGRAPHY

	Hydrology. Water - Continued
662.4	Addresses, essays, lectures
.5	Handbooks, tables, etc.
665	General special
671	Popular works
	By region or country[1]
	Class here works on general hydrology. For groundwater and special types of bodies of water, see GB1001+
	Cf. GC, Oceanography
	VK, Hydrography and navigation
	North America
	United States
701	General works
705	By region or state, A-Z
	For Hawaii, see GB832
707-708	Canada
711-712	Mexico
714-715	Central America
717	West Indies
718-719	South America
	Europe
720	General works
721-722	Great Britain
	e. g. GB722.S3, Scotland
725-725.2	Austria
726-726.2	Bulgaria
727-727.2	Czechoslovakia
727.4-.5	Finland
728-729	France
731-732	Germany
	Including West Germany
733.5-.6	East Germany
734-735	Greece
736-736.2	Hungary
737-738	Italy
	Low countries
739	General works
740-741	Belgium
743-744	Netherlands
745-745.2	Poland
745.4-.5	Romania
746-747	Russia
	Scandinavia
748.5	General works
749-750	Denmark
752-753	Norway
755-756	Sweden
758-759	Spain
761-762	Portugal
767-768	Switzerland
771-771.2	Yugoslavia

---

[1]
    Regions, islands, or countries, with two numbers: (1) General works;
(2) By region, country, island, province, or state, A-Z

Hydrology. Water
By region or country[1]
Europe - Continued

772	Other European regions or countries, A-Z

Under each country:
.x   General works
.x2 Local, A-Z
e. g.   .C7-72 Crete
.L8-82 Luxemburg

Asia

773	General works

Eastern Asia. Far East

.2	General works
.4	Burma
.6	Cambodia
.8	Sri Lanka
774-775	China
776	Taiwan
777-778	India
779-779.2	Indonesia
781-782	Japan
783	Korea
784	Malaysia
785	Pakistan
786-786.2	Philippine Islands
787-788	Russia in Asia. Siberia
790	Thailand

Near East. Middle East

791	General works
792	Iran
.5	Iraq
793	Israel
.5	Jordan
794	Lebanon
.5	Saudi Arabia. Arabian Peninsula
795	Syria
.5	Turkey
796	Other regions or countries, A-Z

Africa

| 800 | General works |

North Africa

.2	General works
.4	Algeria
801	Egypt
.5	Libya
802	Morocco
.5	Tunisia
803	Sahara
.5	Other regions or countries, A-Z

Eastern Africa

804	General works
.5	Ethiopia
805	Kenya
.5	Somalia
806	Sudan
.5	Tanzania
807	Uganda

---

[1] Regions, islands, or countries, with two numbers: (1) General works;
(2) By region, country, island, province, or state, A-Z

PHYSICAL GEOGRAPHY

Hydrology. Water
By region or country[1]
Africa - Continued
Central Africa

808	General works
.5	Zaire
809	Other regions or countries, A-Z
	West Africa
812	General works
.5	Ghana
813	Niger
.5	Nigeria
814	Senegal
.5	Upper Volta
815	Other regions or countries, A-Z
	Southern Africa
817	General works
.5	Malawi
818	Mozambique
.5	South Africa
819	Southwest Africa
.5	Zambia
820	Other regions or countries, A-Z
821-822	Australia
823	New Zealand
	Pacific islands
831	General works
832	Hawaii
833	Other islands or groups of islands, A-Z
835	Arctic regions
839	Antarctic regions
841	Arid regions
845	Hydrological forecasting
848	Hydrologic cycle
850	Water transport phenomena
855	Natural water chemistry
	Cf. GC98, Chemical oceanography
	GC101+, Properties of sea water
	QD142, Water analysis
	QH90+, Hydrobiology
	By region or country
857	United States
.2	By region or state, A-Z
.3	Other regions or countries, A-Z

---

[1]   Regions, islands, or countries, with two numbers: (1) General works;
(2) By region, country, island, province, or state, A-Z

GB   GB

PHYSICAL GEOGRAPHY

Hydrology. Water - Continued

980-2998   Ground and surface waters

Each topic assigned a span of numbers is
to be subarranged as follows:

1	Periodicals. Societies. Serials
.2	Congresses
.4	Dictionaries. Encyclopedias
.5	Terminology. Abbreviations. Notations

Methodology

.7	General works
.72	Special methods, A-Z

.A37	Aerial photography
.A38	Aeronautics
.A83	Astronautics
.A9	Automation
.C55	Classification
.E42	Electromechanical analogies
.E45	Electronic data processing
.M32	Mapping
.M35	Mathematical models
.R34	Radioisotopes
.R42	Remote sensing
.S7	Statistical methods

Communication of information

.8	General works
.82	Information services

Study and teaching. Research

2	General works
.2	Problems, exercises, examinations
.3	Fieldwork
.4	Laboratory manuals
	By region or country
.5	United States
.6	Other regions or countries, A-Z

General works

.8	Early through 1800
3	1801-1974
.2	1975-
.6	Pictorial works
.7	Popular works
.8	Juvenile works
4	Addresses, essays, lectures
.2	Handbooks, tables, etc.
5	General special
	By region or country
	America
11	General works
	North America
12	General works
	United States
15	General works
	East. Atlantic coast
16	General works
.3	New England
.5	Appalachian region
.7	Lake region
17	Mississippi Valley

		Hydrology. Water
980-2998		Ground and surface waters
		By region or country
		America
		North America
		United States - Continued
	18	South. Gulf States
		West
	19	General works
	20	Northwest
	21	Pacific Coast
	22	Southwest
	25	By state, A-W
	27	By spring, river, etc., A-Z
	29-198	Other regions or countries (Table II, nos. 29-198)[1]
		Watersheds. Runoff. Drainage
980		General works
		By region or country
		United States
990		General works
991		By region or state, A-Z
992		Other regions or countries, A-Z
1001-1197.5		Groundwater. Hydrogeology
		Cf. QE640+, Stratigraphy
1197.6		Groundwater exploration
.7		Groundwater flow
		Cf. TC176, Underground flow
		Saltwater encroachment. Salinity
.8		General works
		By region or country
		United States
.82		General works
.83		By region or state, A-Z
.84		Other regions or countries, A-Z
		Springs. Hot springs
		Cf. RA791+, Health resorts, spas, etc.
		TN923+, Mineral waters
1198		General works
		By region or country
		United States
.2		General works
.3		By region or state, A-Z
.4		Other regions or countries, A-Z
		Geysers
.5		General works
		By region or country
		United States
.6		General works
.7		By region or state, A-Z
.8		Other regions or countries, A-Z
		Aquifers
1199		General works
		By region or country
		United States
.2		General works
.3		By region or state, A-Z
.4		Other regions or countries, A-Z

[1]
For Table II, <u>see</u> pp. 380-381

PHYSICAL GEOGRAPHY

Hydrology. Water
  Ground and surface waters
    Groundwater. Hydrogeology - Continued
      Geothermal resources

	Cf. TK1041, Production of electric energy from heat
1199.5	General works
	By region or country
	United States
.6	General works
.7	By region or state, A-Z
.8	Other regions or countries, A-Z
1201-1398	Rivers. Stream measurements
	For technique of stream measuring, see TC175
	Cf. GB561+, Floodplains, river channels, valleys, watersheds, etc.
1217	Great Lakes watershed
	Ice on rivers
1398.2	General works
	By region or country
	United States
.3	General works
.4	By region or state, A-Z
.5	Other regions or countries, A-Z
	River temperatures
.6	General works
	By region or country
	United States
.7	General works
.8	By region or state, A-Z
.9	Other regions or countries, A-Z
	Floods
	Cf. TC530+, Flood control
1399	General works
.2	Flood forecasting
	By region or country
	United States
.3	General works
.4	By region or state, A-Z
.5	Other regions or countries, A-Z
1401-1598	Waterfalls
1601-1798	Lakes. Limnology
	For freshwater biology of lakes, see QH98
	Subdivide the Great Lakes as follows:
	GB1627.G8 General works
	Lake Ontario
	.G81 General works
	.G82 By region, A-Z
	Other lakes
	Subdivided like .G81-82
	e. g. GB1627.G84S2 Sandusky Bay (Lake Erie)
	.G83-84 Lake Erie
	.G85-86 Lake Huron
	.G87-88 Lake Michigan
	.G89-895 Lake Superior
	Ice on lakes
1798.2	General works
	By region or country
	United States
.3	General works
.4	By region or state, A-Z
.5	Other regions or countries, A-Z

Hydrology. Water
  Ground and surface waters
    Lakes. Limnology - Continued
      Lake temperatures

1798.6	General works
	By region or country
	United States
.7	General works
.8	By region or state, A-Z
.9	Other regions or countries, A-Z
1801-1998	Ponds
	For freshwater biology, see QH98
2201-2398	Lagoons
	For freshwater biology, see QH98
2401-2598	Ice. Glaciers. Ice sheets. Sea ice

                    Cf. GB581+, Glacial landforms
                        GB1398.2, Ice on rivers
                        GB1798.2, Ice on lakes
                        QE575+, Glacial erosion
                        QE697, Pleistocene. Glacial epoch
                        TA714, Avalanche control
                        VK1299, Icebergs and navigation

| 2601-2798| Snow. Snow surveys |

                    Cf. TA714, Snow mechanics. Avalanche control

| 2801-2998| Hydrometeorology |

                    Cf. QC851+, Meteorology. Climatology
  Natural disasters
        Cf. GB1399+, Floods
            GC221+, Tidal waves
            GC225+, Storm surges
            GF85, Hazardous environments (Human ecology)
            HV8080.D5, Disaster operations (Police works)
            QC929.A8, Avalanches
            QC941+, Storms
            QE521+, Volcanoes and earthquakes
            QE598+, Earth movements
            SD421, Forest fires
            TF539, Damage to railroads
        For works which discuss natural disasters in general
            as historic events, see D24; for specific dis-
            asters treated as historic events in individual
            countries, see the country, D - F

5000	Periodicals. Societies. Serials
5001	Congresses
	Study and teaching. Research
5005	General works
	By region or country
5007	United States
5008	Other regions or countries, A-Z
	By region or country
5010	United States
5011	Other regions or countries (Table I, decimally)[1]
5014	General works
5018	Popular works
5019	Juvenile works
5020	Addresses, essays, lectures
5030	Natural disaster warning systems

------

[1]
    For Table I, see pp. 380-381

OCEANOGRAPHY

Cf. GB651+, Hydrology
    QC801+, Geophysics
    QE39, Submarine geology
    QE350.2+, Geology of the Atlantic
      and Pacific Oceans
    QH91+, Marine biology
    QK103, 108+, Marine flora
    QL121+, Marine fauna

1	Periodicals. Societies. Serials
2	Congresses
	Collected works (nonserial)
6	Several authors
7	Individual authors
9	Dictionaries. Encyclopedias
.2	Terminology. Abbreviations. Notation
10	Directories
	Philosophy. Relation to other topics. Methodology
.2	General works
.4	Special methods, A-Z
.A3	Aeronautics
.A8	Astronautics
.E4	Electronic data processing
.M33	Mapping
.M36	Mathematical models
.N8	Nuclear energy
.P5	Photography
.R3	Radioactive tracers
.R4	Remote sensing
.S5	Simulation methods
.S7	Statistical methods
	General works, treatises, and advanced textbooks
.9	Early works through 1800
11	1801-1974
.2	1975-
16	Elementary textbooks
20	Outlines, syllabi
21	Popular works
.5	Juvenile works
24	Handbooks, tables, etc.
26	Addresses, essays, lectures
28	General special (Special aspects of the subject as a whole)
	History
29	General works
.2	By region or country, A-Z
	Biography
30.A1A-Z	Collective
.A2-Z	Individual
.5	Oceanography as a profession
	Study and teaching
	For research, see GC57+
31	General works
.2	Audiovisual aids
.3	Problems, exercises, examinations
.4	Observations
.5	Laboratory manuals
	By region or country
.6	United States
.7	Other regions or countries, A-Z

	Museums. Exhibitions
35	General works
.2	By region or country, A-Z
	Under each country:
	.x General works
	.x2 Special. By city, A-Z
	Communication of oceanographic information
37	General works
.5	Information services
38	Exchange of oceanographic information
41	Instruments and apparatus
	For special instruments, etc., see GC78, 155, 177, 235, 306, etc.
	For hydrographic instruments and methods of observation in navigation, see VK593.5+
	Oceanographic research
	Cf. VM453, Oceanographic research ships
	For results of oceanographic research, see the topic studied, e. g. GC301-, Tides
57	General works
	By region or country
58	United States
59	Other regions or countries (Table I, decimally)[1]
	Oceanographic expeditions
63.A1A-Z	Collective
.A2-Z	By name of expedition, or name of ship
	Underwater exploration
	Cf. CC, Archaeology
	G521+, Treasure trove
	GB602.5, Cave diving
	GV840.S78, Skin diving
	QH90+, Marine biology
	TR800, Submarine photography
	VM975+, Diving (Marine engineering)
65	General works
66	Manned underwater stations
67	Oceanographic submersibles
	Deep-sea soundings
	For soundings in special regions, see GC84+
75	General works
78	Special instruments, A-Z
	Cf. VK584.S6, Sounding apparatus in navigation
	Submarine topography
	Cf. QE39, Submarine geology
83	General works
.2	Local, A-Z
	Continental margins
84	General works
.2	Local, A-Z
	Continental shelves
85	General works
.2	Local, A-Z
	Continental slopes
86	General works
.2	Local, A-Z

---

[1]
    For Table I, see pp. 380-381

<u>Submarine topography</u> - Continued
Ocean bottom. Ocean basin
87   General works
  .2   Local, A-Z
  .6   Special ocean bottom features, A-Z
              .S4 Seamounts
89   Sea level
<u>Estuarine oceanography</u>
          For oceanography of special estuaries, <u>see</u> GC401+
96   Periodicals. Societies. Serials
97   General works
          Estuarine sediments
  .7   General works
  .8   Local, A-Z
<u>Seawater</u>
          For seawater in special regions, <u>see</u> GC401+
100   Congresses
          General works
  .8   Early through 1800
101   1801-1974
  .2   1975-
103   Addresses, essays, lectures
<u>Chemical oceanography</u>
          For chemical oceanography in special regions,
              <u>see</u> GC401+
109   Periodicals. Societies. Serials
110   Congresses
          General works
111   1801-1974
  .2   1975-
113   Addresses, essays, lectures
116   General special
117   Special elements and groups of elements, A-Z
              .N5 Nitrogen
          <u>Salinity</u>
120   Congresses
            General works
121   1801-1974
  .2   1975-
122   Methodology
            Distribution of salinity
123   General works
125   Surface
127   Deep sea
130   Local, A-Z
141   Absorbed gases
149   Radioactivity
<u>Physical oceanography</u>
          For physical oceanography (General) in special
              regions, <u>see</u> GC401+
150   Periodicals. Societies. Serials
  .2   Congresses
          General works
  .4   1801-1974
  .5   1975-
  .7   Addresses, essays, lectures
          Density
151   General works
155   Methodology. Hydrometers

OCEANOGRAPHY

	<u>Physical oceanography</u> - Continued
	<u>Temperature</u>
160	Congresses
	General works
161	1801-1974
.2	1975-
166	General special
.5	Charts, diagrams
167	Local, A-Z
	Distribution of temperatures
171	General works
173	Surface
175	Deep sea
177	Methodology
	<u>Optical oceanography</u>
.6	Congresses
	General works
178	1801-1974
.2	1975-
179	Addresses, essays, lectures
180	General special
181	Underwater light
	<u>Ocean-atmosphere interaction</u>
	General works
190	1801-1974
.2	1975-
.3	Addresses, essays, lectures
.5	Methodology
	<u>Dynamics of the ocean</u>
	Cf. QA911+, Hydrodynamics
	For dynamics of the ocean (General) in special
	regions, <u>see</u> GC401+
200	Congresses
	General works
201	1801-1974
.2	1975-
202	Addresses, essays, lectures
203	General special
	<u>Waves</u>
	Cf. QA927, Mathematical theory
	QC157, Mechanics
205	Periodicals. Societies. Serials
206	Congresses
	General works
211	1801-1974
.2	1975-
.6	Juvenile works
213	Addresses, essays, lectures
	Methodology
.5	General works
.7	Special methods, A-Z
	.M3 Mathematical models
214	Local, A-Z
215	Waves in inland waters
	Seiches
217	General works
218	Local, A-Z
	<u>Tsunamis. Tidal waves</u>
219	Congresses

OCEANOGRAPHY

<u>Dynamics of the ocean</u>
  <u>Waves</u>
    <u>Tsunamis. Tidal waves</u> - Continued

220	Study and teaching. Research
	By region or country
.3	United States
.4	Other regions or countries, A-Z
	General works
221	1801-1974
.2	1975-
.7	Addresses, essays, lectures
.8	Handbooks, tables, etc.
222	Local, A-Z
223	Warning systems
	Storm surges
225	General works
226	Local, A-Z
	Ocean circulation
228.5	General works
.6	Local, A-Z
	<u>Currents</u>
229	Congresses
.2	Dictionaries. Encyclopedias
	General works
.8	Early through 1800
231	1801-1974
.2	1975-
232	Juvenile works
233	Addresses, essays, lectures
236	Handbooks, tables, etc.
239	General special
	Methodology
.2	General works
.3	Special methods, A-Z
	.M3 Mathematical models
.5	Causes of currents
	<u>By region</u>
	Polar
240	General works
	Arctic
	Including Arctic Ocean
241	General works
	Barents Sea
.2	General works
.3	White Sea
.5	Greenland Sea
	Antarctic
	Including Antarctic Ocean
245	General works
.2	Weddell Sea
	Temperate
251	General works
253	North Temperate
255	South Temperate
261	Tropical. Equatorial
	<u>By ocean</u>
	<u>Atlantic Ocean</u>
271	General works
272	North Atlantic
	Cf. GC241+, Arctic region

OCEANOGRAPHY

<u>Dynamics of the ocean</u>
  <u>Currents</u>
    <u>By ocean</u>
      <u>Atlantic Ocean</u> - Continued

273	South Atlantic
	Cf. GC245+, Antarctic region
	<u>By sea or other body of water</u>
274	Baltic Sea
.2	English Channel
.3	Irish Sea
.4	Irminger Sea
275	North Sea
	Including Skagerrak and Cattegat
.2	Norwegian Sea
276	Bay of Biscay
	Mediterranean Sea
277	General works
.2	Individual parts, A-Z
	e. g. .M4 Strait of Mesina
278	Black Sea
.5	Caribbean Sea
	<u>Coastal waters</u>
279	Europe and Africa, A-Z
	e. g. .D8 Strait of Dover
281	North America, A-Z
	e. g. .F9 Bay of Fundy
	.M5 Miami Beach, Fla.
	.S2 Gulf of St. Lawrence
282	South America, A-Z
	<u>Indian Ocean</u>
283	General works
284	Red Sea
285	Persian Gulf
	<u>Pacific Ocean</u>
286	General works
287	North Pacific
288	South Pacific
	By sea
.2	Coral Sea
.5	Japan Sea
.7	Tasman Sea
	<u>Currents on inland waters</u>
290	General works
	Great Lakes
291	General works
292	Individual lakes, A-Z
	e. g. .E7 Lake Erie
293	Other lakes, A-Z
	e. g. .M4 Lake Mead
	By individual current
296	Gulf Stream
.2	Kuroshio
.8	Other, A-Z
	e. g. .G8 Guinea Current
	Water masses
297	General works
298	Local, A-Z
299	Oceanic mixing

OCEANOGRAPHY

    Dynamics of the ocean - Continued
     Tides
       Cf. QB414+, Theory of tides
         VK600+, Tide tables

300	Periodicals. Societies. Serials
.2	Congresses
.3	Dictionaries. Encyclopedias
	General works
.8	Early through 1800
301	1801-1974
.2	1975-
302	Juvenile works
.2	Addresses, essays, lectures
.3	Handbooks, tables, etc. Observers' manuals
303	General special
	Methodology
305	General works
.5	Special methods, A-Z
	.E4 Electronic data processing
	.M3 Mathematical models
306	Instruments and apparatus
	e. g. Tide predictors, gauges
307	Tide stations
	Tidal currents
308	General works
309	Local. By region, A-Z
	e. g. .B6 Boston Harbor
	.C5 Chesapeake Bay
	.M3 Massachusetts
	e. g. Narragansett Bay to Nantucket Sound
	.N7 New York Harbor
	.S27 St. Johns River
	By region
311	Arctic
	Including Arctic Ocean
313	Antarctic
	Including Antarctic Ocean
316	Temperate
321	Tropical. Equatorial
	Atlantic Ocean
331	General works
334	North Atlantic
335	South Atlantic
	By sea or other body of water
337	Baltic Sea
341	North Sea
	Including Skagerrak and Cattegat
343	English Channel
346	Bay of Biscay
	Mediterranean Sea
347	General works
348	Special parts, A-Z
	e. g. .I7 Italy
	European coast
350	General works
351	By country, A-Z

OCEANOGRAPHY

Dynamics of the ocean
  Tides
    By region
      Atlantic Ocean - Continued
        African coast
352	General works
353	By country, A-Z

        American coast
         United States

356.A1A-Z	General works
.A3-W	By state
357	By city, A-Z
358	Other special, A-Z

          e. g. .C2 Canada. Canadian coast
              .F8 Fundy, Bay of

      Indian Ocean
359	General works
361	Red Sea
364	Persian Gulf

      Pacific Ocean
367	General works
369	North Pacific
371	South Pacific

    Tides on inland waters
373	General works
374	Tides on the Great Lakes
375	Tides on other lakes, A-Z
376	Tidal bores

  Marine sediments
    Cf. GC75+, Deep-sea soundings
       GC96+, Estuarine sediments
       QE471+, Sedimentary rocks
       QE471.2, Sediments
       QE571+, Sedimentation

377	Congresses
	General works
380	1801-1974
.15	1975-
.2	Special topics, A-Z

    .A25 Acoustic properties
         Microbiology, see QR106
    .G3 Gas content
    .S4 Sediment transport
    .T4 Testing
    By region
.3	Tropical. Equatorial
.5	Arctic
	Including Arctic Ocean
.6	Antarctic
	Including Antarctic Ocean

    Atlantic Ocean
381	General works
	North Atlantic
383	General works
.2	Caribbean Sea
.5	Gulf of Mexico
385	Baltic Sea
387	North Sea
389	Mediterranean Sea
.5	Black Sea
391	South Atlantic

OCEANOGRAPHY

Marine sediments
   By region - Continued
      Indian Ocean

393   General works
.5   Arabian Sea
394   Red Sea
395   Persian Gulf
        Pacific Ocean
397   General works
          North Pacific
398   General works
.5   Bering Sea
399   South Pacific
Oceanography. By region
     Arctic Ocean
401   General works
        Western
411   General works
413   Beaufort Sea
421   Baffin Bay
431   Davis Strait
436   Denmark Strait
441   Hudson Bay
443   Hudson Strait
        Eastern
451   General works
452   Barents Sea
453   Kara Sea
454   East Siberian Sea
455   Chukchi Sea
    Coast of Antarctica. Antarctic Ocean
461   General works
462   Weddell Sea
     Atlantic Ocean
481   General works
      North Atlantic
491   General works
492   Norwegian Sea
      Western Atlantic
501   General works
502   Grand Banks of Newfoundland
503   Labrador Sea
         Coast of North America
511   General works
512   By state or province, A-Z
              e. g. .M3 Maine
521   Gulf of Mexico
531   Caribbean Sea
535   Sargasso Sea
541   Coast of South America
      Eastern Atlantic
551   General works
561   Scandinavian coasts
571   Baltic Sea. Coast of Finland
581   German coast
591   North Sea
593   Dutch coast
597   Belgian coast
601   British coast
603   Irish Sea

Oceanography.   By region
    Atlantic Ocean
       Eastern Atlantic - Continued

611	English Channel
621	French coast
631	Bay of Biscay
641	Spanish and Portuguese coasts
645	Strait of Gibralter

           Mediterranean Sea

651	General works
661	Adriatic Sea
671	Aegean Sea
681	Black Sea
685	Other parts, A-Z

                  e. g.   .A9   Azov, Sea of
                             .B58 Bocca Piccola
                             .B6   Bosporus
                             .M4   Messina, Strait of
                             .S8   Suez Canal
                             .T3   Taranto, Gulf of

       South Atlantic

691	General works
701	Gulf of Guinea
711	Cape of Good Hope
715	Caspian Sea

    Indian Ocean

721	General works
731	Arabian Sea
741	Red Sea
751	Persian Gulf
761	Bay of Bengal

    Pacific Ocean

771	General works

       North Pacific

781	General works

          Western Pacific

791	General works
801	China Sea
811	Yellow Sea
821	Japan Sea
831	Sea of Okhotsk
841	Bering Sea
845	Other, A-Z

                  e. g.   .Y6 Yŏsu Bay

          Eastern Pacific

851	General works
852	Alaskan coast
854	Canadian coast
856	United States coast
858	Mexican coast
859	Central American coast
860	Other, A-Z

                  e. g.   .C8 Costa Rica

       South Pacific

861	General works
862	Coral Sea
865	Tasman Sea
871	South American coast
880	Tropical. Equatorial
881	Temperate

OCEANOGRAPHY

	<u>Marine resources. Applied oceanography</u>
	Cf. HC92, Economic geography
	SH, Fish culture and fisheries
	TC147, Tidal power as a source of energy
	TD430+, Fresh water from seawater
	V396+, Military oceanography
	For applied oceanography in particular
	uses, <u>see</u> the field of application,
	e. g. TD898, Radioactive waste disposal
	in the sea; VK588+, Marine hydrography
1000	Periodicals. Societies. Serials
1001	Congresses
	Study and teaching. Research
1005	General works
	By region or country
.2	United States
.3	Other regions or countries, A-Z
	General works
1015	1801-1974
.2	1975-
1016	Popular works
.5	Juvenile works
1017	General special
1018	Conservation
	By region or country
	United States
1020	General works
1021	By region or state, A-Z
1023	Other regions or countries (Table I, decimally)[1]
	Mineral resources, <u>see</u> TN264
	<u>Marine pollution. Seawater pollution</u>
	Cf. QH91.8.04, Oil pollution (Marine biology)
1080	Periodicals. Societies. Serials
1081	Congresses
1085	General works
1101-1581	By region
	Subdivided like GC401-881

---

[1]

For Table I, <u>see</u> pp. 380-381

HUMAN ECOLOGY. ANTHROPOGEOGRAPHY

Including human geography
Cf. HM206, Social ecology
For conservation of natural
  resources, <u>see</u> S900+; for
  environmental policy (General),
  <u>see</u> HC79.E5; for environmental
  technology, <u>see</u> TD

1	Periodicals. Societies. Serials
3	Congresses
4	Dictionaries. Encyclopedias
.5	Terminology. Notations. Abbreviations
5	Directories
	Collected works (nonserial)
8	Several authors
9	Individual authors, A-Z
13	History
	Biography
15	Collective
16	Individual, A-Z
	Philosophy. Relation to other topics. Methodology
21	General works
23	Special methods, A-Z
	<u>Study and teaching</u>
26	General works
	By region or country
	United States
27	General works
.5	By region or state, A-Z
	Under each state:
	.x General works
	.x2 Individual schools or universities.
	By place, A-Z
28	Other regions or countries, A-Z
	Each country may be subarranged like GF27.5
	<u>General works, treatises, and textbooks</u>
	Early through 1969
31	Comprehensive works
33	Elementary textbooks
37	Popular works
	1970-
41	Comprehensive works
43	Elementary textbooks
45	Outlines, syllabi
46	Pictorial works
47	Popular works
48	Juvenile works
49	Addresses, essays, lectures
50	General special (Special aspects of the subject as a whole)
	<u>Environmental influences on man</u>
	Cf. BF353, Environmental psychology
	GN386+, Ethnology
51	General works
53	Frontiers
57	Mountains
59	Plains
61	Islands

266

HUMAN ECOLOGY.   ANTHROPOGEOGRAPHY

<u>Environmental influences on man</u> - Continued
    Bodies of water

63		Rivers
65		Oceans
67		Lakes
71		Climatic influences
75	Man's influence on the environment	
80	Moral and religious aspects	
85	Hazardous aspects of the environment	

          Cf. TD172+, Environmental pollution

| 95 | Spatial studies |

<u>Settlements</u>
    Including limits of land settlement, natural
       boundaries, etc.
    For works on demography, theory of population,
       etc., <u>see</u> HB849+; geopolitics, <u>see</u> JC319+;
       human migrations, <u>see</u> GN370

| 101 | General works |

By region or country, <u>see</u> GF500+

| 125 | Cities.   Urban geography |

    Cf. HT101+, Urban sociology
    For urban geography of individual cities, <u>see</u>
       D - F

| 127 | Rural settlements.   Rural geography |

    Cf. HT401+, Rural sociology

<u>By region or country</u>
    Under each:
    (1) General works
    (2) By region, country, state, etc., A-Z

500	<u>America</u>
501	North America
503-504	United States
511-512	Canada
516-517	Mexico
521-522	Central America
526-527.	West Indies
531-532	South America
540	<u>Europe</u>
541	Mediterranean regions
545	Alps
547	Baltic region
551	Great Britain. England (General)
552	England (Local), A-Z
555-556	Scotland
561-562	Northern Ireland
563	Ireland
565	Austria
567	Local, A-Z
568	Czechoslovakia
569	Hungary
571-572	France
576	Germany
	Including West Germany
578	West German local, A-Z
579	East Germany
581-582	Greece
586-587	Italy

HUMAN ECOLOGY.   ANTHROPOGEOGRAPHY

By region or country
Europe - Continued

591	Low countries
593-594	Netherlands
596-597	Belgium
601-602	Russia
604	Finland
611	Scandinavia
612-613	Norway
614-615	Sweden
616-617	Denmark
621-622	Spain
623-624	Portugal
631-632	Switzerland
641	Balkan Peninsula (General)
642	Individual Balkan States, A-Z
	Under each:
	.x General works
	.x2 Local, A-Z
645	Other regions or countries of Europe, A-Z
651	Asia
656-657	China
659	Korea
661-662	India
664	Pakistan
666-667	Japan
668	Southeast Asia
	Including Malay Archipelago
669	Malaysia
670	Near East
671-672	Iran
674	Afghanistan
675	Iraq
676-677	Russia in Asia. Siberia
678-679	Turkey. Asia Minor
681-682	Saudi Arabia
685-686	Palestine. Israel
687-688	Syria
696	Other regions or countries of Asia, A-Z
698	Arab countries
701	Africa
702	North Africa
703	Morocco
704	Algeria
706	Libya
711-712	Egypt
715	Sahara
720	Eastern Africa
721	Ethiopia
725	Madagascar
726	Mozambique
728	Sudan
729	Tanzania
730	Central Africa
740	West Africa
746	Gabon
747	Zaire

HUMAN ECOLOGY. ANTHROPOGEOGRAPHY

<u>By region or country</u>
<u>Africa</u> – Continued

750	Southern Africa
758	South Africa
801-802	Australia
805-806	New Zealand
851-852	Pacific islands
891	Arctic regions
	Cf. G600+, Geography
895	Tropics

1	Periodicals. Serials
2	Societies
3	Congresses
	Collected works (nonserial)
4	Several authors
6	Individual authors
11	Dictionaries. Encyclopedias
12	Terminology. Abbreviations. Notation
	Communication of information
13	Information services
17	History
	Biography
20	Collective
21	Individual, A-Z
	General works, treatises, and textbooks
23	Early through 1870
24	1871-1974
25	1975-
27	General special (Special aspects of the subject as a whole)
29	Addresses, essays, lectures
	Popular works
30	Early through 1870
31	1871-1974
.2	1975-
.5	Juvenile works
32	Pictorial works

Philosophy. Relation to other topics. Methodology
     Cf. BD450, Philosophical anthropology

33	General works
	Relation to psychology, see GN290+; GN502+
	Relation to sociology, see HM37
34	Classification
.3	Other special methods, A-Z
	.A35 Aerial photography
	.C6 Componential analysis
	.M3 Mathematical anthropology

Museums. Exhibitions
     Class here general collections only. For special
       collections, see the subject

35	General works
36	By region or country, A-Z
	Under each country:
	.x General works
	.x2 Special. By city, A-Z
	e. g. .C9 Cuba (General works); .C92H38,
	Havana. Universidad. Museo anthropológico
	Montané
41	Private collections
	Anthropologists
.6	General works
.8	Anthropology as a profession
	Biography, see GN20+

	Study and teaching. Research
42	General works
.3	Audiovisual aids
	Class catalogs of materials in .Z9A-Z
	By region or country
	Class individual institutions by state or
	country without further subdivision
	United States
43	General works
.2	By region or state, A-Z
44	Other American regions or countries, A-Z
45	Europe. By region or country, A-Z
46	Other regions or countries, A-Z

PHYSICAL ANTHROPOLOGY. SOMATOLOGY

Cf. QM, Human anatomy
QP34+, Human physiology

49	Periodicals. Societies. Serials
50	Congresses
.2	Collected works (nonserial)
.3	Dictionaries. Encyclopedias
.4	History
	Biography
.5	Collective
.6	Individual, A-Z
	Philosophy. Relation to other topics. Methodology
.8	General works
	Anthropometry
	General works
51.A2A-Z	Early works through 1800
.A3-Z	1801-
53	Instruments
54	Special methods
56	Compilations of statistical data, tables, etc.
	(General)
	For compilations of data on special topics,
	see the topic, GN62.9+
	Special anthropometric studies
	Including results of studies
	For studies limited to special topics, see
	the topic, GN62.9+
57	By race, ethnic group, etc., A-Z
	For American Indians, see E98.A55
58	By region or country, A-Z
59	By class of persons, A-Z
	Athletes, see GV435
	Children, see GN63; LB3421+
.M4	Men
.S7	Soldiers
	Including all military personnel
.S8	Students
.W6	Women

	Physical anthropology. Somatology - Continued
	Museums. Exhibitions
59.8	General works
.82	By region or country, A-Z
	Each region or country subarranged by author
60	General works
62	General special
	Man as an animal, see GN280.7
	Human variation
	Cf. GN280, Race (General)
.8	General works
	Human growth
	Cf. QP84.2+, Physiology of growth
.9	General works
63	Children. Adolescents
	Cf. LB1101+, Child development for teachers
	LB3421+, Physical measurements of school children
	RJ, Pediatrics
	Physical form and dimensions
	Head. Cephalometry
	Cf. GN71+, Craniometry
.8	General works
64	Face form and profile. Physiognomy
	Including shape of special features, e. g. nose, lips, etc.
	Cf. BF840+, Physiognomy and phrenology
	For works on the shape of the ear, see GN201
	Body dimensions and proportions
	Cf. NC765, Proportions in art
66	General works
.5	Somatotypes
67	Climate and body build
.5	Women
	Special variations
	Cf. RB140+, Growth disorders
	Giants
69	General works
	Biography
.2	Collective
.22	Individual, A-Z
	Dwarfs. Midgets
	Cf. RB140.3, Growth disorders
.3	General works
	Biography
.5	Collective
.52	Individual, A-Z
	The skeleton. Osteology
	Cf. QM101+, Anatomy of the skeleton
	For works on the skeletal remains of fossil man, see GN281+
70	General works
	By continent
	Under each:
	.A1A-Z General works
	.A2-Z Individual countries, A-Z
.5	America
.6	Europe
.7	Asia
.8	Africa
.9	Australia and Pacific islands

Physical anthropology. Somatology
Human variation
The skeleton. Osteology - Continued
The skull. Craniology. Craniometry
71   General works
72   General special
                            Including identification of skulls,
                                artificial deformation of skulls, etc.
                      By period
                        Pleistocene skulls, see GN282+
85   Ancient skulls. By country, A-Z
                      Medieval and modern skulls
87   General works
                            Including description of skulls from
                                several parts of the world
                      By continent
                        Under each:
                        (1) General works
                        (2) Individual countries, A-Z
                      e. g. GN90-93 America
                             90   General works
                             93   Individual countries,
                                  A-Z
                                    e. g. .A7 Argentina
90-93   America
100-103   Europe
110-113   Asia
120-123   Africa
125-128   Australia and Pacific islands
130   By race, A-Z
                      e. g. .M7 Mongolian
                           .N3 Negro
131   Special details (not A-Z)
                      e. g. Exostosis, eye sockets, hard palate,
                        prognathism
                    For teeth, see GN209
141   Vertebra
145   Shoulder girdle, scapula, etc.
151   Pelvis
161   Extremities
                    Including hand, foot, etc.
171   Muscular system
            Nervous system. Brain (Convolutions, etc.)
              Cf. QM455, Anatomy of the brain
181   General works
               By continent
                  Under each:
                    (1) General works
                    (2) Individual countries, A-Z
182-183   America
184-185   Europe
186-187   Asia
188-189   Africa
190-190.5   Australia and Pacific islands

Physical anthropology. Somatology
Human variation - Continued
Skin
191   General works
192   Fingerprints
Including classification, directories,
information, use, etc.
Cf. HV6074, Criminal anthropology
193   Hair
197   Color. Pigmentation
Including hair and eyes
199   Albinism
201   Sense organs
Including the shape of the external ear
Cf. QM501+, Anatomy of the sense organs
206   Internal organs
Including individual organs, e. g. heart,
lungs, etc.
209   Teeth. Dental anthropology
211   Sex organs
Physiological anthropology
Cf, QP, Physiology
221   General works
223   Basal metabolism
Physical traits
229   Strength
231   Posture. Movement
232   Sitting position
233   Left- and right-handedness
Including significance, measurement and
determination of hand preference, etc.
Cf. LB1123, Left- and right-handedness in
education
QP385, Localization of functions
(Brain)
Reproduction. Sexual functions
235   General works
236   Birth
   .5   Multiple births (Twins, triplets, etc.)
238   Puberty
241   Fertility
Hereditary functions
Cf. GN289, Population genetics
QH431, Human genetics
247   General works
251   Atavism
252   Inbreeding
Cf. HQ1026, Consanguineous marriages
HV4981, Social pathology
254   Racial crossing. Miscegenation
Cf. HQ1031, Mixed marriages
256   Degeneration
Cf. HQ750+, Eugenics
263   Blood groups

Physical anthropology. Somatology - Continued
    Race (General)
        For works on particular races, see GN537+;
          for anthropometric works on particular races,
          see GN57

269	General works
	Race psychology
	Cf. BF431+, Racial intelligence
	BF699+, Genetic psychology
	CB195+, Civilization and race
	GN502+, Psychological anthropology
	QP351+, Physiological psychology
270	General works
273	General special
	Special senses
275	Hearing
277	Vision
279	Other senses, A-Z
280.7	Man as an animal. Simian traits versus human traits
	Including man's place in nature
	Cf. GF, Human ecology

Human evolution
    Including the origin of man
    Cf. BL263, Natural theology
        QH361+, Biology

281	General works
.4	General special

Fossil man. Human paleontology
    Class here works on physical remains only,
        including particular parts of the skeleton.
        For works on physical remains and associated
        cultural remains, see GN768+

282	General works
.5	General special
	e. g. Piltdown man
	Australopithecines
283	General works
.3	Australopithecus prometheus
.5	Meganthropus paleojavanicus
.6	Paranthropus crassidens
.7	Plesianthropus transvaalensis
.8	Zinjanthropus boisei
	Homo erectus. Pithecanthropines
284	General works
.4	Homo soloensis
.6	Pithecanthropus erectus
.7	Sinanthropus pekinensis
285	Homo neanderthalensis
	Homo sapiens
286	General works
.2	Boskop
.3	Cro-Magnon
.7	Swanscombe
289	Population genetics
	Including mechanics of evolution and continuing
	evolution
	Cf. GN247, Hereditary functions
	HB848+, Population (Economic theory)
	QH455, Genetics (General)
296	Medical anthropology
	Cf. GN477, Primitive medicine

ETHNOLOGY. SOCIAL AND CULTURAL ANTHROPOLOGY

Many topics provided for here represent concepts
also encompassed by the discipline of sociology
in HM. In cases of overlap, the following
principle should normally apply, unless specific
instructions are made to the contrary. Class here
those works which deal with the nature of human
societies in general, as well as those works which
deal specifically with preliterate and/or folk
societies. For those works which deal principally
with modern civilization, see HM

Cf. CB, History of civilization
   GF, Human ecology
   GT, Manners and customs (General)
   HM+, Sociology

301	Periodicals. Societies. Serials
302	Congresses
	Collected works (nonserial)
303	Several authors
304	Individual authors
307	Dictionaries. Encyclopedias
.3	Directories
	Communication of information
.5	General works
.6	Information services
.7	Writing of ethnographies
.8	Study and teaching
.82	Audiovisual aids
.85	By region or country, A-Z
	Museums. Exhibitions, see GN35+
	History
	For the history of specific schools, see the pertinent topic, e. g. GN365+, German diffusionists
308	General works
.3	By region or country, A-Z
	Ethnologists, see GN41.6+
	General works, treatises, and textbooks
310	Through 1870
315	1871-1974
316	1975-
320	General special (Special aspects of the subject as a whole)
323	Outlines, syllabi
325	Addresses, essays, lectures
330	Popular works
333	Juvenile works
340	Pictorial works
	Philosophy. Relation to other topics. Methodology
345	General works
.2	Relation to history
	Relation to linguistics, see P35
	Relation to sociology, see HM37
.3	Classification
.5	Cultural relativism
	Cf. GN469, Value systems
	GN495.8, Ethnocentrism
	GN517, Culture shock

	Ethnology. Social and cultural anthropology
	Philosophy. Relation to other topics.
	Methodology - Continued
	Special methods
345.7	Cross cultural studies
	Fieldwork
346	General works
.3	Interviews
.4	Participant observation
347	Photography
	Culture and cultural processes
357	General works
.5	Origin of culture
358	Culture change. Social change
	Cultural evolution. Evolutionism
360	General works
.4	Neo-evolutionism
362	Structuralism. Structural anthropology
363	Functionalism
	Culture diffusion
365	General works
	Culture history
.4	General works
.6	Kulturkreis theory
.8	Cultural determinism
	Psychoanalytic approach, see GN508
	Acculturation. Culture contact
	Cf. GN380, Threatened societies
366	General works
367	Assimilation
370	Migrations of peoples (General)
372	Feral studies. Wolf children
378	Collected ethnographies

Class here works which describe two or more ethnic groups not confined to one geographic region or country. For works on individual groups not confined to one region or country, see GN537+. For works on specific groups in specific regions or countries, see the appropriate number for the group in D-F. For comprehensive works on the groups of specific regions or countries, see GN550+

	Ethnographies of special categories of peoples
380	Threatened societies

Class here ethnographies which discuss collectively the nonliterate or traditional peoples of the world whose particular way of life is being shattered by Western encroachments

386	Oceanic peoples. Maritime anthropology
	Cf. GF65, Oceanic influences on man
	GN440+, Transportation by water
387	Nomadic peoples
388	Hunting and gathering peoples
	Cf. GN407+, Food and food production
389	Fishing peoples
395	City dwellers. Urban anthropology

Ethnology. Social and cultural anthropology - Continued
  Applied anthropology
397   Periodicals. Societies. Serials
 .5   General works
  Cultural traits, customs, and institutions
      Class here general works on specific topics
        only. For works on specific topics
        pertaining to special groups or races, see
        the name of the group or race in D-F or
        GN537+. For works on topics pertaining to
        one region or country, see the region or
        country in GN550+
  Technology. Material culture
406   General works
 .5   Influence of the environment
  Food and food production. Subsistence
407   General works
  Hunting and gathering
 .3   General works
 .33   Special, A-Z
         Arrows, see GN498.B78
       .H55 Harpoons
       .T7   Traps
 .35   Fishing
        Including fishing implements
  Agriculture
 .4   General works
        Domesticated plants
 .5   General works
 .55   Horticulture
        Domesticated animals
 .6   General works
 .7   Pastoralism. Herding
 .8   Irrigation
408   Geophagy. Dirt eating
409   Cannibalism
 .5   Insects
410   Food preparation
 .5   Beverages
        Stimulants and narcotics
411 .   General works
 .5   Alcohol
  Shelter. Habitation
413   General works
 .5   Village patterns
  Dwellings
        Cf. GT170+, Manners and customs
414   General works
 .3   Special types, A-Z
       .G7   Grass huts
       .T45 Tents
  Furniture
415   General works
 .3   Special, A-Z
       .H35 Hammocks
  Fire. Light and heat
416   General works
 .5   Light and heat
417   Fire-making
        Including fire-making implements

Ethnology. Social and cultural anthropology
Cultural traits, customs and institutions
Technology. Material culture - Continued
Clothing and adornment
Cf. GT500+, Manners and customs

418	General works
	Ornaments. Jewelry
.4	General works
419	Special, A-Z
	.B4 Beads
.13	Hairstyles. Headdresses
.15	Cosmetics. Body markings
.2	Mutilations
.3	Tattooing
.5	Masks

Arts and crafts. Industries

429	General works
430	General special
	Special crafts
431	Basketmaking
432	Weaving and spinning. Textile fabrics
433	Pottery making

Special materials
Stone

434	General works
.2	Special, A-Z
	.A45 Amber
	.F55 Flint

Plant materials

.3	General works
.5	Bark
.6	Gourds
.7	Wood

Animal materials

.435	General works
.3	Bone, tooth, horn
.5	Leather. Skin dressing
.7	Shell
.9	Feathers

Metals. Metallurgy

436	General works
.2	Copper. Bronze
.3	Gold
.4	Iron

Tools. Implements

.8	General works
437	Special, A-Z

Class here works on tools made of various
materials. For works on tools made of
a special material, see the material,
GN434+. For works on tools used in a
particular activity, see the activity,
GN406+. For prehistoric tools, see GN700+

.A35 Adzes
.A9 Axes
.D7 Drilling implements
.K55 Knives
.P65 Pounders

Ethnology. Social and cultural anthropology
Cultural traits, customs, and institutions
Technology. Material culture - Continued
Transportation
Cf. GN407.6+, Domesticated animals
438 General works
.2 General special
439 Routes of communication
Including trails, roads, bridges, etc.
Transportation by water. Navigation
440 General works
.1 Boats
.2 Canoes
441 Vehicles. Wheels
442 Snowshoes. Skis
Economic organization. Economic anthropology
448 General works
.2 General special
.3 Allocation of natural resources
Division of labor. Organization of work
.5 General works
.6 Specialization
.8 Cooperation. Competition
Property. Ownership
449 General works
.3 Land tenure
Distribution of goods and services
.6 General works
Commerce and trade
450 General works
.2 Markets
Cf. HF5470+, Business (General)
.4 Barter
.5 Money
.7 Reciprocity
Intellectual life
Cf. GN502+, Psychological anthropology
For works on the arts, see the special
topic, e. g. N, Art; GV1580+, Dance;
GR72+, Folk literature; etc.
451 General works
Communication
Cf. P1+, Linguistics
452 General works
.5 Symbolism. Signs and symbols
Recreation. Sports
454 General works
.5 General special
.55 Wit and humor
Cf. PN6147+, Wit and humor (General)
.6 Gambling
.7 Play
Games and toys
.8 General works
455 Special, A-Z
.S9 String figures

<pre>
                    Ethnology. Social and cultural anthropology
                      Cultural traits, customs, and institutions
                        Intellectual life - Continued
                          Philosophy. World view
        468   General works
          .2   General special
          .4   Classification systems
                                Cf. GN476+, Science and knowledge
        469.7   Ethics
                            Values
                          Religion and ritual. Belief systems
                              For works on the religion of a particular
                                ethnic group or region, see BL. For works
                                on mythology, see BL300+
        470   General works
          .2   General special
          .5   Origin of religion
          .7   Religion and society
        471   Nature worship. Animism
          .4   Mana. Taboo
        472   Fetishism
                            Totemism, see GN489
          .4   Religious experience. Trances. Vision and ecstasy
          .5   Supernatural beings
          .6   Soul concept
                            Nativistic movements
          .7   General works
          .75   Cargo cults
          .8   Ancestor worship
                            Rites and ceremonies
        473   General works
          .3   Head hunting
          .4   Sacrifice
          .5   Blood sacrifice
        474   Religious specialists, priests, etc.
                          Magic. Witchcraft
                              Cf. BR1405+, Occult sciences
                                GR525+, Folklore
        475   General works
          .3   Magic
          .5   Witchcraft. Black magic. Sorcery
          .7   Divination
                                Cf. BF1745+, Occult sciences
                                  BL613, Religions
          .8   Curing. Medicine men. Shamanism
                          Science and knowledge
        476   General works
          .15   Mathematics. Counting and number systems
          .3   Astronomy. Calendars
                            Geography
          .4   General works
          .5   Cartography
          .6   History
                            Biology
          .7   General works
          .73   Ethnobotany
          .76   Ethnozoology
</pre>

ANTHROPOLOGY

Ethnology. Social and cultural anthropology
    Cultural traits, customs, and institutions
        Intellectual life
            Science and knowledge - Continued
                Medicine
                    Cf. GN296, Medical anthropology
                        GN475.8, Medicine men
                        GR880, Folk medicine
477   General works
                    Surgery
    .5   General works
                        Mutilation, see GN419.2
    .7   Trepanation
        Social organization
            Cf. HM1+, Sociology
478   General works
479   General special
    .5   Matriarchy
    .6   Patriarchy
            Social roles
                Sex roles
                    Cf. GN490.7, Sex-based groups
    .65   General works
    .7   Women
                Age roles, see GN490.5
                Leadership roles, see GN492.25
    .8   Social groups (General)
        Domestic groups. Family. Forms of marriage
                Cf. GN484.4, Marriage customs
                    HQ1+, Sociology
480   General works
    .2   General special
    .25   Incest
    .3   Endogamy and exogamy
            Polygamy
    .33   General works
    .35   Polygyny
    .36   Polyandry
    .4   Cross-cousin marriage
    .43   Levirate
    .5   Nuclear families
    .55   Extended families
            Residence rules
    .6   General works
    .63   Matrilocal. Uxorilocal
    .65   Patrilocal. Virilocal
        Life cycle
            Children
482   General works
                Birth
    .1   General works
    .3   Adoption
    .4   Birth control. Abortion
    .5   Infanticide
            Adolescence
483   General works
    .3   Initiations. Puberty rites
484   Circumcision

Ethnology. Social and cultural anthropology
Cultural traits, customs, and institutions
Social organization
Life cycle - Continued
Adulthood
484.2   General works
.3   Sexual behavior. Sex customs
Marriage
.4   General works
.43   Betrothal
.45   Bridewealth. Dowry
.47   Virginity. Defloration
.7   Divorce
485   Old age
.5   Death
486   Funeral and mourning customs
Cf. GT3150+, Manners and customs
Kinship systems. Regulation of descent
.5   Dictionaries. Encyclopedias
487   General works
Unilineal descent
.3   General works
.4   Matrilineal
.5   Patrilineal
.6   Double descent
.7   Special kinship groups, A-Z
.C55   Clans. Sibs
.M6   Moieties
.P45   Phratries
Cognatic descent. Nonunilineal descent
488   General works
.2   Ambilineal. Ramages
.4   Bilateral. Kindreds
489   Totemism
Associations
490   General works
.2   Institutionalized friendships. Blood brothers.
Bond friends
.3   God parents
.5   Age groups
Cf. GN483.3, Puberty rites
.7   Sex-based groups
.8   Secret societies
Social stratification
491   General works
.4   Castes
.45   Classes
.5   Professional distinctions
Cf. GN448.6, Economic specialization
.7   Territorial groups

Ethnology. Social and cultural anthropology
Cultural traits, customs, and institutions - Continued
Political organization. Political anthropology
Cf. JC20+, The primitive state (Political theory)
492   General works
.2   General special
.25   Leadership. Authority
Types of political organizations
.4   Bands
.44   Segmentary systems
.5   Tribes
.55   Chieftainships
States
.6   General works
.7   Kingships. Kings
Social control
Cf. GN471.4, Taboo
K190, Primitive law
493   General works
.3   Social norms. Behavioral conformity
.5   Deviance
494   Violation of norms. Crime
.3   Punishment. Ordeals
Disputes
.5   General works
495   Retaliation. Vendetta
.4   Societal groups. Ethnic groups
Cf. GN506, Patterns of culture
.6   Ethnicity. Ethnic identity
.8   Ethnocentrism
Cf. GN349, Cultural relativism
Intergroup relations. Diplomacy
496   General works
.5   Feuds
Warfare
497   General works
Weapons and armor
General works
.5
498   Special, A-Z
.B6   Boomerangs
.B78 Bows and arrows
.C6   Clubs
.S5   Shields
.S55 Slings
.S68 Spears
.T5   Throwing sticks
Psychological anthropology
Cf. GN290+, Race psychology
HM251+, Social psychology
502   General works
504   Culture and personality
Cf. BF698.9.C8, Psychology (General)
506   Culture patterns. Cultural configurations
Cf. BF751+, National characteristics
508   Psychoanalytic interpretations
510   Socialization. Enculturation
Cf. HQ783, Sociology
LC189.4, Educational sociology
512   Self concept. Self identity
Cf. GN495.6, Ethnic identity
514   Psychology and social change
Cf. RC451.5.A2, Ethnopsychiatry
517   Culture shock

Ethnology. Social and cultural anthropology - Continued
 Ethnic groups and races
   Cf. CB195+, Civilization and race
    GN269+, Race (General)
  Groups not limited to particular regions
   Including works on certain European groups
   found in several countries

537	Caucasian. White races (General)
539	Aryan. Indo-European
543	Mediterranean
547	Semitic. Jewish
548	Mongolian races (General)
	Negro races (General), see GN645
549	Other, A-Z

    .A7 Arabs
    .B3 Basques
    .B9 Budini
    .C3 Celts
      For works on Celtic antiquities, see D70
    .F5 Finno-Ugrians
    .G4 Germanic tribes
     Gypsies, see DX
    .P3 Pelasgi
    .P9 Pygmies
    .S6 Slavs
    .T4 Teutonic peoples. Nordic peoples
  By region or country
   Class here comprehensive works on the preliterate
   or folk societies of particular regions or
   countries (including works on certain individual
   large groupings, e. g. Bantus, Melanesians,
   Australian aborigines, etc.) even in the case of
   works limited to special topics or aspects. For
   works on particular societies or groups, including
   works on specific topics pertaining to those
   groups, see the society or group in D-F, e. g.
   DT878, Zulus; DU423, Maoris. For works on prehistoric archaeology, including prehistoric
   remains of particular regions or countries, see
   GN700+
   Class catalogs of audiovisual material under the
   appropriate subject number with the Cutter .Z9,
   e. g. GN665.Z9, catalogs of audiovisual materials
   on the Australian aborigines
  North America
   For works on Indians of North America, see E51+
   and local divisions in F

550	General works
560	By region or country, A-Z

  Central and South America
   For works on Indians of Central and South America,
   see E65 and local divisions in F

562	General works
564	By region or country, A-Z

  Europe

575	General works
585	By region or country, A-Z
590	Parts of Asia, Africa, and Oceania (Collectively)

<u>Ethnology. Social and cultural anthropology</u>
  <u>Ethnic groups and races</u>
    <u>By region or country</u> - Continued
      <u>Asia</u>

625	General works
635	By region or country, A-Z

        e. g. .A75 Southeastern Asia
                .B6   Borneo
                .I65 Indonesia
                .M35 Malay Archipelago
                .M4   Malaysia
                .N42 Near East. Southwestern Asia
                       New Guinea, <u>see</u> GN671.N5
                       Philippine Islands, <u>see</u> GN671.P5
                .R9   Ryukyu Islands
                .S5   Siberia
                .T4   Thailand

      <u>Africa</u>

643	Periodicals. Societies. Serials
645	General works
	Including Negroes in general

       <u>North Africa</u>

646	General works
648	Egypt
649	Other regions or countries, A-Z
	.M65 Morocco

       <u>Northeast Africa</u>

650	General works
.5	By region or country, A-Z
	.E8 Ethiopia
	.S65 Somalia

       <u>Central Africa. Sahara</u>
          Including French-speaking West Africa and
            the Sudan region

651	General works
652	By region or country, A-Z
	.C44 Central African Republic
	.C5 Chad
	.M25 Mali
	.S93 Sudan

       <u>West Africa</u>
          For works on French-speaking West Africa,
            <u>see</u> GN651+

.5	General works
653	Nigeria
	Including the Niger area (General)
	Zaire
	Including the Congo area (General)
654.A1A-Z	Periodicals. Societies. Serials
.A5-Z	General works
655	Other regions or countries, A-Z
	.A5 Angola
	.C3 Cameroon
	.G3 Gabon
	.G74 Equatorial Guinea
	.G76 Portuguese Guinea
	.I9 Ivory Coast
	.L5 Liberia
	.S3 Senegal
	.S5 Sierra Leone

ANTHROPOLOGY

Ethnology. Social and cultural anthropology
  Ethnic groups and races
    By region or country
      Africa - Continued
        Southern Africa. South Africa
656   General works
657   By region or country, A-Z
              .R4 Northern Rhodesia. Zambia
              .R5 Southern Rhodesia
              .S6 Southwest Africa
        Eastern Africa
658   General works
659   By region or country, A-Z
              .B78 Burundi
                    Ethiopia, see GN650.5.E8
              .K4   Kenya
              .M6   Mozambique
              .R85 Rwanda
              .T3   Tanzania
              .U3   Uganda
661   Islands, A-Z
              .C2 Canary Islands
              .M2 Madagascar
        Australia and Pacific islands
662   General works
663   General special
            By country, island, or island group
              Australia
665   General works
666   General special
667   By region or state, A-Z
   .5   New Zealand
                    For works on Maoris, see DU423+
668   Melanesia (General)
669   Micronesia (General)
670   Polynesia (General)
671   Other islands or island groups, A-Z
                    Class individual islands and small island
                      groups with the larger island group,
                      e. g. the island Mindanao is to be classed
                      in GN671.P5, Philippine Islands
                .B5   Bismark Archipelago
                .C3   Caroline Islands
                .C5   Chatham Islands
                .E2   Easter Island
                .F5   Fiji Islands
                .G35 Gambier Islands. Mangareva
                .H3   Hawaiian Islands
                .M25 Manihiki Islands
                .M27 Marianas Islands
                .M3   Marquesas Islands
                .N35 New Caledonia
                .N5   New Guinea
                .N6   Hew Hebrides
                .P5   Philippine Islands
                .S2   Samoa Islands

Ethnology. Social and cultural anthropology
   Ethnic groups and races
     By region or country
       Australia and Pacific islands
         By country, island, or island group

671   Other islands or island groups, A-Z - Continued
             .S55 Society Islands
             .S6   Solomon Islands
             .T4   Portuguese Timor
             .T46 Tokelau Islands
             .T5   Tonga Islands
             .T6   Torres Straits
             .T8   Tubuai Islands
             .W3   Wallis Islands
673   Arctic regions
         For works on Eskimos, see E99.E7

PREHISTORIC ARCHAEOLOGY

For works dealing with a particular period, including
works dealing with a particular period also limited
in coverage to a particular topic and/or geographic
area, see the period, GN768+. For works on a particular
topic and geographic area without regard to the period,
see the area, GN803+

700   Periodicals. Societies. Serials
701   Congresses
705   Collected works (nonserial)
710   Dictionaries. Encyclopedias
     Philosophy. Relation to other topics. Methodology,
       see CC73+
     Study and teaching. Research, see GN761
     Museums. Exhibitions, see GN800+
720   History
     Biography, see CC110+
     General works, treatises, and textbooks
733   Early through 1800
735   1801-1869
738   1870-1950
739   1951-1974
740   1975-
741   General special
743   Popular works
744   Juvenile works
     Lost continents
        Including Atlantis, Lemuria, Mu, etc.
750   Periodicals. Societies. Serials
751   General works
755   Subterranean civilization
761   Study and teaching. Research
766   Addresses, essays, lectures

ANTHROPOLOGY

<u>Prehistoric archaeology</u> - Continued
    <u>By period division</u>
        For works which are limited in scope to the
          physical remains of Early man, <u>see</u> GN282+
        <u>Stone age</u>

768	General works
	By region or country, <u>see</u> GN803+

        <u>Archeolithic. Eolithic</u>

769	General works
770	General special

          By continent
            Under each continent:
              (1)
                  .A1A-Z General works
                  .A5-Z   Special cultures, peoples, etc., A-Z
              (2)   By region or country, A-Z
                            Prefer classification by
                              special cultures

            America, <u>see</u> E-F

770.2-.22	Europe
.3-.32	Asia
.4-.42	Africa
.5-.52	Australia and Pacific islands

        <u>Paleolithic</u>

771	General works
772	General special
.2-.52	By continent

            Subarranged like GN770.2-.52
            Under each continent:
              (1)
                  .A1A-Z General works
                  .A5-Z   Special cultures, peoples, etc., A-Z

	.A53 Acheulian
	.A8 Aurignacian
	.C3 Capsian
	.M3 Magdalenian
	.M6 Mousterian
	.P4 Perigordian
	Reindeer, <u>see</u> .M3
	.S6 Solutrean

              (2)   By region or country, A-Z
                            Prefer classification by
                              special cultures

        <u>Mesolithic</u>

773	General works
774	General special
.2-.52	By continent

            Subarranged like GN770.2-.52
            Under each continent:
              (1)
                  .A1A-Z General works
                  .A5-Z   Special cultures, peoples, etc., A-Z

	.S6 Smithfield
	.T3 Tardenoisian
	.W5 Wilton

              (2)   By region or country, A-Z
                              Prefer classification by
                              special cultures

<u>Prehistoric archaeology</u>
  <u>By period division</u>
    <u>Stone age</u> - Continued
      <u>Neolithic</u>

775   General works
776   General special
  .2-.52   By continent
          Subarranged like GN770.2-.52
          Under each continent:
          (1)
            .A1A-Z General works
            .A5-Z Special cultures, peoples, etc.,
                A-Z
              .B4 Beaker
              .C6 Corded ware
              .D3 Danilo
              .F8 Funnel-beaker
              .G5 Ghassul
              .H6 Horgen
              .J6 Jomon
              .L4 Lengyel-Jordansmühl
              .M5 Michelsberg
              .V5 Vinča
              .Y3 Yayoi
         (2)   By region or country, A-Z
               Prefer classification by
                 special cultures

      <u>Copper and bronze ages</u>
777   General works
778   General special
  .2-.52   By continent
          Subarranged like GN770.2-.52
          Under each continent:
          (1)
            .A1A-Z General works
            .A5-Z Special cultures, peoples, etc., A-Z
              .B3 Baden
              .K5 Knoviz
              .L3 Lausitz
         (2)   By region or country, A-Z
               Prefer classification by special
                 cultures

      <u>Iron age</u>
779   General works
780   General special
  .2-.52   By continent
          Subarranged like GN770.2-.52
          Under each continent:
          (1)
            .A1A-Z General works
            .A5-Z Special cultures, peoples, etc., A-Z
              .H3 Hallstatt
              .L3 La Tene
              .V5 Villanovans
         (2)   By region or country, A-Z
               Prefer classification by special
                 cultures

Prehistoric archaeology - Continued
By special topic
For works on special topics in special
geographic areas, see the area, GN803+
Caves and cave dwellers
Cf. GB601+, Caves (Physical geography)

783		General works
		General special
.3		Artificial caves
.5		Other (not A-Z)
785		Lake dwellings and lake dwellers
787		Kitchen middens
789		Fortifications. Earthworks
790		Megalithic monuments

Including menhirs, dolmens, cromlechs, etc.

795		Mounds, tumuli, etc.
799		Other special topics, A-Z
	.A4	Agriculture

Cf. S421, Origin of agriculture

	.A5	Amber
		Art, see N5310+
	.A8	Astronomy
	.B7	Bronzes
	.B8	Buildings
	.C45	Commerce
	.C5	Costume
	.C9	Cyclons
	.E4	Economics
	.F5	Fishing
	.F6	Food
	.G6	Gold
	.M4	Metallurgy
	.N3	Navigation
	.P4	Petroglyphs. Rock paintings
	.P5	Pins and needles
	.P6	Pottery
	.P74	Psychology
	.R4	Religion
		Rock paintings, see .P4
	.S4	Sculpture
	.S5	Skis
	.S9	Symbolism
	.T6	Tools
	.T7	Toys
	.W3	Weapons

Including arrowpoints, daggers, spearheads,
swords

	.W4	Weaving
	Museums. Exhibitions (General)	

Class here works on general collections or
exhibitions only. For works on collections or
exhibitions representative of particular
periods, topics, or places, or combinations
thereof, see the appropriate number, e. g.
GN768+, Particular periods; GN803+, Partiuclar
places

800	General works
802	Private collections

<u>Prehistoric archaeology</u> - Continued
     By region or country
         Under each country:
            (1)
                .A1A-Z   Periodicals.   Societies
                .A3A-Z   Museums.   Exhibitions
                         Subarranged by name of city
                .A5-Z   General works
            (2)   Local, A-Z
     America, <u>see</u> E-F
     Greenland, <u>see</u> E99.E7
     <u>Europe</u>

803	General works
805-806	Great Britain
807-808	Austria
811-812	France
813-814	Germany
	Including West Germany
814.5-.6	East Germany
815-816	Greece
817-818	Italy
819-820	Netherlands
821-822	Belgium
823-824	Russia
	For Russia in Asia, <u>see</u> GN855.R9
825	Scandinavia
826-827	Denmark
828-829	Norway
830-831	Sweden
835-836	Spain
837-838	Portugal
841-842	Switzerland
845	Other regions or countries, A-Z
	.F5 Finland
	.P7 Poland

     <u>Asia</u>

851	General works
855	By region or country, A-Z
	e. g. .R9 Russia in Asia. Siberia
	.T83 Turkey

     <u>Africa</u>

861	General works
865	By region or country, A-Z

     <u>Australia and Pacific islands</u>

871	General works
875	By country, island, or group of islands, A-Z

Folklore may be defined as the study of those products
of the human spirit created outside of the written
record and kept alive by oral transmission, including
folk literature, custom and festival, and material
culture

Class here works which discuss these traditions compre-
hensively. For works which are limited in scope to
the study of custom, festival, or material culture,
see the appropriate numbers of the classification system, e. g. GN301+, Ethnology; GT, Manners and customs;
or special class numbers for social life and customs
or for specific ethnic groups in D-F, e. g. DT131,
Egypt; DT764.H6, Hottentots

Also class here works which discuss folk literature com-
prehensively, as well as works which discuss specifically the following forms: folktales, legends, (except
legends of medieval European origin), fairy tales and
nursery rhymes. For works which discuss folk literature solely from the standpoint of literary history and
criticism, see PN905+; or the folk literature area of
special literatures, e. g. PT881+, German folk literature. For works which deal with other specific forms
not designated above, see the specific form; i. e., for
folk songs (lyrics) and poetry, ballads (lyrics), drama,
fables, proverbs, riddles, jokes, toasts, etc., see the
appropriate number in P, e. g. PT1287+, German folk
drama; for folk music, see ML3545+; for mythology, see
BL300+. For legends, romances, sagas, etc., of medieval European origin, see P, e. g., PT915+, German
legends

Class collections representative of special literary forms
in the same general locations as indicated above for
discussions of those forms. That is, class here comprehensive collections of folk literature, as well as separate collections of tales, legends, fairy tales, etc.
For separate collections of folk songs, poetry, ballads,
drama, fables, riddles, etc., as well as comprehensive
collections limited to these special forms, see P

Cf. AZ999, Popular errors, delusions
    BF1001+, Parapsychology
    GV1743, Folk dances
    M1627+, Folk music scores
    PZ8+, Juvenile folk literature

1   Periodicals. Societies. Serials
10   Congresses
        Collected works (nonserial)
15   Several authors
20   Individual authors
35   Dictionaries. Encyclopedias
37   Directories
40   Philosophy. Relation to other topics. Methodology
42   Relation to psychology
43   Relation to special classes of persons, A-Z
            .C4 Children
44   Special methods, A-Z
            .C3 Cartography
            .S7 Structural analysis

FOLKLORE

<table>
<tr><td></td><td colspan="2">Study and teaching. Research</td></tr>
<tr><td>45</td><td colspan="2">General works</td></tr>
<tr><td>.5</td><td colspan="2">Fieldwork</td></tr>
<tr><td></td><td colspan="2">By region or country</td></tr>
<tr><td>46</td><td colspan="2">United States</td></tr>
<tr><td>47</td><td colspan="2">Other regions or countries, A-Z</td></tr>
<tr><td></td><td colspan="2">Museums. Exhibitions, see GN35+</td></tr>
<tr><td>48</td><td colspan="2">History</td></tr>
<tr><td></td><td colspan="2">Folklorists</td></tr>
<tr><td>49</td><td colspan="2">Folklore as a profession</td></tr>
<tr><td></td><td colspan="2">Biography</td></tr>
<tr><td>50</td><td colspan="2">Collective</td></tr>
<tr><td>55</td><td colspan="2">Individual, A-Z</td></tr>
<tr><td></td><td colspan="2">General works, treatises, and textbooks</td></tr>
<tr><td>60</td><td colspan="2">Early through 1800</td></tr>
<tr><td>65</td><td colspan="2">1801-1974</td></tr>
<tr><td>66</td><td colspan="2">1975-</td></tr>
<tr><td>67</td><td colspan="2">General special (Special aspects of the subject as a whole)</td></tr>
<tr><td>68</td><td colspan="2">Outlines, syllabi</td></tr>
<tr><td>.5</td><td colspan="2">Popular works</td></tr>
<tr><td>69</td><td colspan="2">Juvenile works</td></tr>
<tr><td>71</td><td colspan="2">Addresses, essays, lectures</td></tr>
</table>

Folk literature (General)

> For studies or collections of folk literature from a particular region, country, or ethnic group, including folk literature from a particular region, etc., on a specific topic, see GR95+. For folk literature on a specific topic not limited to a particular region, etc., see GR440+
>
> For medieval literature, see PN661+; PQ-PT

72   General works
73   Collections of texts

By form
     Fable, see PN980+
     Folk drama, see PN6120.F6; etc.
     Folk poetry, see PN1341; PN6110.F7; etc.

Folktales
> For fairy tales, see GR550; juvenile folktales, see PZ8+

74   General works

Themes, motives, etc.
     .4   General works
     .6   Classification, indexes, etc.
     75   Individual folktale themes and motives, A-Z
> Including collections of variant tales found in more than one region or country

.B3   Basil maiden
.B6   Book of the book
.C4   Cinderella
.C8   Cupid
.G6   Grateful dead
.H3   Halfchick
.M3   Maiden without hands
.O4   Oldenburger Horn
.O9   Our Lady's child
.P3   Pai she chuan
.P5   Pent Cuckoo
.P53   Perseus

Folk literature (General)
  By form
    Folktales
      Themes, motives, etc.
75   Individual folktale themes and motives, A–Z – Continued
        .P6   Polyphemus
        .S67 Sorcerer's apprentice
        .S8   Swan maidens
        .T5   Three stolen princesses
        .W3   Wandering Jew
             Cf. PN57.W3, Wandering Jew as theme in
                 literature
76   Collections of texts
          For collections of tales on a single theme from more
            than one region or country, see GR75
      Jokes, see PN6147+
      Legends
78   General works
79   Collections of texts
      Nursery rhymes, see GR487
      Proverbs, see PN6400+
      Riddles, see PN6366+
81   Folk beliefs, superstitions, etc. (General)
  By race or group not limited to special places
      For folklore of individual races or groups in specific
        regions or countries, see GR100+
    Celtic, see GR137+
    Christian, see BR135+
    Gypsy, see DX157
95   Indo-European. Aryan
97   Semitic
     Jewish
.8   Periodicals. Societies. Serials
98   General works
By hemisphere
99   Northern
.2   Southern
.4   Eastern
    Western, see GR100+
By region or country
    Class here works on the folklore of specific places, in-
      cluding the folklore of specific places on specific topics
100   America
  North America
101   General works
    American Indians, see E98.F6
103   Afro-American peoples. Negroes
     Cf. GR108, The South
  United States
105   General works
.5   Collections of texts (General)
106   New England
108   The South
109   The West
110   By state, A-W
     Cf. GR385, Hawaiian Islands
112   Insular possessions (General)
113 Canada

FOLKLORE

By region or country - Continued
Latin America
- 114   General works
- 115   Mexico
      Central America
- 117   General works
- 118   By region or country, A-Z
      West Indies
- 120   General works
- 121   By island, etc., A-Z
          e. g. .B3 Bahamas
                .D6 Dominican Republic
                .H3 Haiti
                .P8 Puerto Rico
      South America
- 130   General works
- 133   By region or country, A-Z
     Europe
- 135   General works
    By race or group not limited to one country
- 136   Miscellaneous combinations of races or groups
         e. g. Slavs and Magyars
- 137   Celtic
- 138   Slavic
- 139   Nordic
- .3   By region not limited to one country, A-Z
      .A4 Alps
        Balkan Peninsula, see GR250
        Scandinavia, see GR205
    Great Britain. England
- 140   Periodicals. Societies. Serials
- 141   General works
- 142   England (Local), A-Z
- 143-145   Scotland[1]
- 146-148   Northern Ireland[1]
- 149-151   Wales[1]
- 153   Other divisions, A-Z
        e. g. .G9 Guernsey
              .M3 Man, Isle of
- .5   Ireland
- 154   Czechoslovakia
- .5   Hungary
    Austria
- 155   Periodicals. Societies. Serials
- 156   General works
- 159   Local, A-Z
- 160-162 France[1]
    Germany
      Including West Germany
- 165   Periodicals. Societies. Serials
- 166   General works
- 167   Local (West Germany), A-Z
        Cf. DD801.R72, Rhine legends, etc.
- 168   East Germany
- 170   Greece (Modern)

---

[1]   Divided like GR140-142

By region or country
Europe - Continued

175-177	Italy[1]
178	Malta
179	Monaco
180-182	Netherlands[1]
185	Belgium
188	Luxemburg

Poland

195	General works
196	Local, A-Z
.2	By tribe or ethnic group, A-Z

Finland

200	General works
201	Local, A-Z
.2	By tribe or ethnic group, A-Z

Russia

Cf. GR345, Russia in Asia

202	General works
203	Local, A-Z
.2	By tribe or ethnic group, A-Z
	.C5 Chukchi
	.G3 Gagauzi

Scandinavia

205	General works
210	Denmark
213	Faeroe Islands
214	Greenland

For works on Eskimo folklore, see E99.E7

215	Iceland
220-222	Norway[1]
224-226	Sweden[1]

Spain

229	Periodicals. Societies. Serials
230	General works
233	Moorish folklore
237	Local, A-Z
238	Portugal
240-242	Switzerland[1]

Cf. DQ92, Tell and Rütli legends

Balkan States.   Southern Slavs

250	General works
251	Albania
253	Bulgaria
257	Romania
259	Yugoslavia
263	Other European countries, A-Z

Asia.   The Orient

265	General works
268	By race or group not limited to one country, A-Z
	.K2 Kalmucks

Near East

270	General works
275	Saudi Arabia
280	Turkey
285	Israel. Palestine
290	Iran
293	Syria
295	Other, A-Z
	e. g. .C9 Cyprus

---

[1]   Divided like GR140-142

FOLKLORE

<pre>
                By region or country
                  Asia. The Orient - Continued
300   Central Asia. Turkestan
                    South Asia
302   General works
                      Pakistan
303   General works
304   Local, A-Z
   .5   Bangladesh
                        India
305   General works
   .5   Local, A-Z
306   Sri Lanka
307   Other, A-Z
                    Southeastern Asia
308   General works
309   Burma
310   Cambodia
311   Laos
312   Thailand
313   Vietnam
                      Malaysia
315   General works
316   Local, A-Z
                      Indonesia
320   General works
323   Borneo
324   Other local, A-Z
                      Philippine Islands
325   General works
326   Local, A-Z
330   Eastern Asia. Far East
334-336   China1
337   Tibet
338   Taiwan
339-341   Japan1
342   Korea
345   Siberia. Russia in Asia
                Africa
350   General works
                  By region or country
                    Under each country (unless otherwise provided for):
                      (1) General works
                      (2) Local or individual groups, A-Z
                    West Africa
   .3   General works
   .32   By group not limited to one country, A-Z
                        .M33 Mandingo
                      Cameroon
351   General works
   .2   Local or individual groups, A-Z
                          e. g.   .M63 Mongo
                                  .N75 Nso
</pre>

1
   Divided like GR140-142

298

FOLKLORE

<pre>
                    By region or country
                      Africa
                        By region or country
                          West Africa - Continued
                            Nigeria
        351.3   General works
           .32   Local or individual groups, A-Z
                                    e. g. .H34 Hausa
                                           .Y56 Yoruba
           .4-.42   Dahomey
           .5-.52   Togo
                            Ghana
           .6   General works
           .62   Local or individual groups, A-Z
                                    e. g. .A83 Ashanti
                                           .G83 Gurma
                                           .M33 Mamprusi
                            Upper Volta
           .7   General works
           .72   Local or individual groups, A-Z
                                    e. g. .M63 Mossi
           .8-.82   Ivory Coast
   352-352.2   Liberia
                            Sierra Leone
        352.3   General works
           .32   Local or individual groups, A-Z
                                    e. g. .L53 Limba
           .5-.52   Portuguese Guinea
           .7-.72   Senegal
                          North Africa
        353   General works
           .2   By group not limited to one country, A-Z
                                .B43 Berber
                                .K33 Kabyle
           .3-.32   Morocco
           .4-.42   Algeria
           .5-.52   Tunisia
   355-355.2   Egypt
                            Chad
        355.5   General works
           .52   Local or individual groups, A-Z
                                    e. g. .Z33 Zaghawa
                          Eastern Africa
           .6   General works
           .62   By group not limited to one country, A-Z
                                .S93 Swahili
                            Sudan
           .8   General works
           .82   Local or individual groups, A-Z
                                    e. g. .D53 Dinka
   356-356.2   Ethiopia
           .3-.32   Somalia
</pre>

FOLKLORE

<pre>
                    By region or country
                      Africa
                        By region or country
                          Eastern Africa - Continued
                            Kenya
        356.4   General works
           .42   Local or individual groups, A-Z
                                    e. g. .B83 Bukusu
                                           .K53 Kikuyu
                                           .L83 Luo
                                           .W33 Wachaga
                            Uganda
           .5   General works
           .52   Local or individual groups, A-Z
                                    e. g. .B33 Bairo
                                           .L34 Lango
                            Tanzania
        356.7   General works
           .72   Local or individual groups, A-Z
                                    e. g. .B84 Burungi
                                           .W33 Wachaga
                                           .W34 Wambulu
     357-357.2   Madagascar
                        Central Africa
           .3   General works
           .32   By group not limited to one country, A-Z
                          .M35 Mbete
                          Gabon
           .6   General works
           .62   Local or individual groups, A-Z
                                 e. g. .F34 Fan
                          Zaire
           .8   General works
           .82   Local or individual groups, A-Z
                                    e. g. .B33 Bakongo
                                           .M64 Mongo
                        Southern Africa
        358   General works
           .2   By group not limited to one country, A-Z
                          .B33 Bantu
                          .B83 Bushmen
                          .H64 Hottentot
           .3-.32   Angola
                          Zambia
           .4   General works
           .42   Local or individual groups, A-Z
                                 e. g. .B43 Bemba
                          Southern Rhodesia
           .6   General works
           .62   Local or individual groups, A-Z
                                    e. g. .M34 Mashona
                                           .M35 Matabele
           .7-.72   Botswana
           .8-.82   South West Africa
</pre>

	By region or country
	Africa
	By region or country
	Southern Africa - Continued
	South Africa
359	General works
.2	Local or individual groups, A-Z

                              e. g. .B63 Boer
                                       .S95 Swazi
      .T45 Thonga
      .V43 Venda
      .X64 Xosa
      .Z83 Zulu

	Lesotho
.5	General works
.52	Local or individual groups, A-Z

                e. g. .B34 Basuto

	Other, A-Z
360	Other, A-Z

                e. g. .C3 Cape Verde Islands
      .F4 Fernando Pó
      .S3 São Thomé

365	Australia
370	Tasmania
375	New Zealand
	Including Maori tales, etc.
	Pacific islands
380	General works
385	By island or groups of islands, A-Z
	e. g. .H3 Hawaiian Islands
390	Arctic regions (General)

	By subject
	For works on special subjects limited to a special region or country, see GR100+
	Costume. Dress
420	General works
425	Jewelry. Rings
	Cf. GR805, Gems
	Folklore relating to private life
430	General works
435	Dreams
	Cf. BF1074+, Parapsychology
	Birth, love, marriage, and death
440	General works
450	Birth
455	Death
460	Love
465	Marriage
467	Rebirth
470	Women
473	Brothers and sisters

By subject
   Folklore relating to private life - Continued
      Children and childhood

475	General works
480	Games
485	Counting-out rhymes
486	Alphabet rhymes
487	Nursery rhymes
	For collections of nursery rhymes, see PZ8.3; etc.
489	Human body and its parts. Blood
	Dwellings
490	General works
495	Fire. Hearth
496	Lanterns
497	Beds
498	Eating. Drinking

Supernatural beings and forces
      Cf. BL473, Religions
          GR825, Mythical monsters

500	General works
505	Sacred places. Churches
	Cf. BL580+, Worship (Religions)
506	Cemeteries
507	Sepulchral and perpetual lamps
510	Gods
515	Heroes
	Cf. BL325.H46, Mythology
520	Kings
	Cf. BL325.K5, Mythology
	DG124, Cult of emperors
	JC374, Origins, myth, magic, etc., of monarchy
523	Fools. Jesters

Demonology
      Cf. BF1501+, Occult sciences
          BL480, Religious doctrines (General)

525	General works
530	Witches
535	Sorcerers
540	Incantations. Invocations. Exorcisms

Fairies
      Including brownies, elves, gnomes, jinn, etc.
      Cf. BF1552, Occult sciences
          GR785, Wood nymphs, dryads

549	General works

Fairy tales
      Cf. PN3437; PN6071.F15; etc., Literature
      For fairy tales of special regions or countries, see
          GR100+

550	General works
552	Collections of texts (General)
	Cf. PZ8; etc., Juvenile literature
555	Dwarfs
560	Ogres. Giants
580	Ghosts. Specters. Apparitions
	Cf. BF1445+, Occult sciences
	Evil eye, see BF1553

By subject - Continued
    Charms. Talismans. Amulets. Spells
        Cf. BF1561, Occult sciences
          GN475+, Primitive religion

600	General works
	Special topics
605	Elixirs. Elixir of life
	Love potions, see GR460
610	Pentacles
615	Wishes
	Cosmic phenomena
620	General works
625	Sun. Moon. Stars
630	Thunder and lightning
635	Weather lore. Meteorology
	Cf. QC998, Weather forecasting
	Astrology, see BF1651+
	Alchemy, see QD13; QD23.3+
	Geographical topics
650	General works
655	Earth
660	Mountains
	Cf. GR940, Mythical mountains
665	Caves
	Seas, see GR910
675	Islands
	Cf. GR940, Mythical islands
	Waters
678	General works
680	Rivers. Streams
690	Springs. Wells
	Animals, plants, and minerals
700	General works
	Animals. Animal lore
705	General works
710	Language of animals
	Special kinds of animals
715	Horses
720	Dogs
725	Cats
730	Other mammals, A-Z
	.A6 Apes
	.A8 Asses
	.B3 Badgers
	.B4 Bears
	.B8 Bulls
	.D4 Deer
	.F6 Foxes
	.H3 Hares
	.M6 Monkeys
	.R3 Rams
	.S4 Seals
	.S9 Swine
	.W5 Wild boar
	.W6 Wolves

<u>By subject</u>
  <u>Animals, plants, and minerals</u>
    <u>Animals.   Animal lore</u>
      <u>Special kinds of animals</u> - Continued

735	Birds. Eggs
740	Reptiles
745	Fishes
750	Insects
755	Spiders
760	Other animals, A-Z

          .B3   Barnacles
          .O27 Octopuses
          .T6   Toads

<u>Plants.   Plant lore</u>.
    Cf. QK834, Botany

780	General works
785	Trees

      Including wood nymphs, dryads

790	Special kinds of plants, A-Z

      .E3 Edelweiss
      .F5 Fig
      .G3 Garlic
      .G5 Ginseng
      .L4 Lemon
      .M3 Mandrakes
      .R6 Roses
      .S4 Sesame

<u>Minerals and rocks.   Folklore of stones</u>

800	General works
805	Precious stones. Gems
810	Metals

<u>Mythical animals, plants, and minerals</u>

820	General works

  <u>Mythical animals.   Monsters</u>

825	General works
830	Special, A-Z

      .B3 Basilisk
      .D7 Dragon
      .J3 Jayhawk
      .P4 Phoenix
      .S3 Salamander
      .T3 Tengu
      .U6 Unicorn
      .V3 Vampire
          Cf. BF1556, Occult sciences
      .W4 Werewolf

  Mythical plants

840	General works
845	Special, A-Z
860	Mythical minerals

    Cf. QD25, Philosopher's stone

<u>Transportation and travel</u>
    Cf. GR910, Seafaring

865	General works

  <u>Vehicles</u>

867	General works
869	Automobiles
870	Railroads

By subject — Continued
  Commerce
872   General works
873   Markets
874   Money
880   Medicine. Folk medicine
        Cf. GN477+, Ethnology
           GR489, Folklore of the body, blood, etc.
           R133; R706, Curiosities, delusions, etc.
885   Music. Dancing
    Occupations
890   General works
895   Agriculture
         Including planting, harvesting, etc.
896   Blacksmithing
897   Executioners. Executions
898   Hunting
900   Mining. Mines
905   Sandmen
910   Seafaring. Folklore of the sea
        Cf. PN57.F6, Flying Dutchman as theme in literature
930   Special days, months, seasons, etc.
    Signs and symbols
        Cf. AZ108, Symbols and their use
931   General works
932   Special, A-Z
        .C5 Circle
        .S66 Square
933   Special numbers
940   Mythical places
        Including mythical islands, mountains, etc.
        Cf. G555, Voyages touching unidentified places
           GN751, Lost continents
943   Treasure troves
950   Miscellaneous implements, utensils, etc., A-Z
        .B3 Balance (Scales)
        .G5 Girdle. Cincture
        .K6 Knots
        .S9 Swords

Class here comprehensive works on social life
and customs, as well as works on certain
specific customs. For general works on the
broader topic of civilization, i. e., the
aggregate of characteristics displayed in
the collective life of literate peoples, including intellectual life, the arts, etc., as
well as social life and customs, see CB. For
general works on the social life and customs
of literate peoples in specific countries, see
D-F. For general works on the social life and
customs of preliterate and folk societies, see
GN301+. For works on the social life and customs of particular ethnic groups, see the name
of the group in D-F
Cf. BJ1801+, Social usages. Etiquette
    GR, Folklore
    HM-HX, Sociology

1	Periodicals. Societies. Serials
3	Congresses
	Collected works (nonserial)
19	Several authors
23	Individual authors
31	Dictionaries. Encyclopedias
	Museums. Exhibitions, see GN35+; D-F
41	History of the study of manners and customs
	Biography
51	Collective
53	Individual, A-Z
61	Philosophy. Relation to other topics. Methodology
	General works, treatises, and textbooks
70	Early through 1850
75	1851-1974
76	1975-
80	Pictorial works
85	Juvenile works
90	Addresses, essays, lectures
95	General special (Special aspects of the subject as a whole)
	By period
	Class here works on Europe as a whole for the period ending with 1944. For works on Europe dealing with later periods and works on other regions or countries of any period, see D-F
110	Ancient
	Classical, see DE-DG
120	Medieval
129	Modern
130	Renaissance
135	16th century
140	17th century
143	18th century
146	19th century
150	20th century
	Houses. Dwellings
	Including the history of dwellings
	Cf. GT3550, Castles and castle life
	NA7100+, Domestic architecture
170	General works
171	Popular works

MANNERS AND CUSTOMS (GENERAL)

Houses. Dwellings - Continued

172	Juvenile works
	By period
175	Ancient
	Cf. DF99, Greek dwellings
	DG97, Roman dwellings
180	Medieval
185	Renaissance
190	16th-18th centuries
195	1801-
	By region or country
	Under each country (unless otherwise provided for):
	(1) General works
	(2) Local, A-Z
201	America
	North America
203	General works
	United States
205	General works
	By period
206	Colonial period. 18th and early 19th century
207	19th century
208	20th century
	By region
210	New England
211	South
214	Central
217	West
219	Pacific States
225	By state, A-W
227	By city, A-Z
228-229	Canada
	Latin America
230	General works
231-232	Mexico
	Central America
233	General works
235-236	Belize. British Honduras
237-238	Costa Rica
239-240	Guatemala
241-242	Honduras
243-244	Nicaragua
245-245.5	Panama
246-246.5	Salvador
	West Indies
247	General works
249-250	Bahamas
251-252	Cuba
253-254	Haiti
255-256	Jamaica
257-257.5	Puerto Rico
258	Other, A-Z
	South America
259	General works
261-262	Argentina
263-264	Bolivia
265-266	Brazil
267-268	Chile
269-270	Colombia
271-272	Ecuador
273-274	Guianas

MANNERS AND CUSTOMS (GENERAL)

Houses. Dwellings
  By region or country
    Latin America
      South America - Continued

275-276	Paraguay
277-278	Peru
279-280	Uruguay
281-282	Venezuela
	Europe
283	General works
	Great Britain. England (General)
285	General works
287	England (Local), A-Z
289-290	Scotland
291-292	Northern Ireland
293-294	Wales
294.5-.6	Ireland
295-296	Austria
296.5-.6	Hungary
297-298	France
298.5	North Sea region
	Germany
	Including West Germany
.9	General works
299	West Germany (Local, A-Z)
300-300.5	East Germany
301-302	Greece
303-304	Italy
	Low Countries
305	General works
307-308	Netherlands
309-310	Belgium
311-312	Russia
	Cf. GT371+, Russia in Asia
	Scandinavia
313	General works
315-316	Denmark
317-318	Iceland
319-320	Norway
321-322	Sweden
323-324	Spain
325-326	Portugal
327-328	Switzerland
	Balkan States
331	General works
332-332.5	Albania
333-334	Bulgaria
337-338	Romania
339-340	Yugoslavia
341	Other, A-Z
342	Other European regions or countries, A-Z
	Asia. The Orient
343	General works
	Near East
.5	General works
344-344.2	Syria
345-346	Turkey
346.5-.6	Iraq
347-348	Iran
349-350	Central Asia

MANNERS AND CUSTOMS (GENERAL)

Houses. Dwellings
    By region or country
        Asia. The Orient - Continued

350.5	South Asia
351-352	India
352.5-.6	Sri Lanka
	Southeast Asia
353	General works
355-356	Thailand
357-358	Malaysia
359-360	Indonesia
361-362	Philippine Islands
	East Asia
363	General works
365-366	China
366.5-.6	Taiwan
367-368	Japan
369-370	Korea
371-372	Siberia. Russia in Asia
	Africa
373	General works
375-376	Egypt
377	Other regions or countries, A-Z
379-380	Australia
381-382	New Zealand
	Pacific islands
383	General works
384	By island or group of islands, A-Z
	Special topics
420	Heating. Hearths. Fireplaces
440	Lighting
445	Lamps, lanterns, etc.
450	Furniture
470	House marks
471	House names
472	Sanitation
474	Sanding. Sandhouses
480	Household arts
	Cf. TT700+, Sewing, needlework
	TX645+, Cookery
482	Laundering
	Cf. TT980+, Laundry work
485	Churches and church going
	Cf. BR, Church history
	BV4523, Christian life
	NA4800+, Christian architecture

Costume. Dress. Fashion
    Class here descriptive and historical studies,
      and publications of historical interest
    Cf. NK4700+, Costume and its accessories (Art)
      TT490+, Clothing manufacture

500	Periodicals. Societies. Serials
	For current fashion periodicals, see TT500
503	Exhibitions
505	Collections of costumes (General)
	Cf. NK4702+, Museums and collections (Art)
507	Dictionaries. Encyclopedias
	General works
509	Early through 1800
510	1801-1974
511	1975-

MANNERS AND CUSTOMS (GENERAL)

Costume. Dress. Fashion - Continued

513	Pictorial works
518	Juvenile works
520	Addresses, essays, lectures
521	Philosophy. Relation to other topics
	Cf. TT507, Art of dress (Dressmaking and tailoring)
522	Relation to aesthetics
523	Relation to art
	Relation to ethics, see BJ1697
524	Relation to psychology
525	Relation to sociology. Social aspects
	Laws, regulations, etc., concerning dress
527	General works
528	By region or country, A-Z
	By class (age, sex, occupation, etc.), see GT1710+, GT5910+
	By period
530	Ancient
533	Egyptian
535	Other Near Eastern: Babylonian, Assyrian, Persian, etc.
537	South Asian
538	Far Eastern
	Including Japanese and Chinese
540	Hebrew
	Cf. BS680.C65, Religious aspects, symbolism, etc. of Biblical costume
545	Classical
550	Greek
555	Roman
560	Other ancient
575	Medieval
580	Modern
585	1500-1789
589	1790-1815
595	1816-1899
596	1900-
	By region or country
	America
601	General works
	North America
603	General works
	United States
605	General works
607	Colonial period. 18th and early 19th century
610	19th century
615	20th century
617	Local, A-Z
620	Canada
	Latin America
623	General works
625	Mexico
	Central America
630	General works
633	Belize. British Honduras
636	Costa Rica
639	Guatemala
641	Honduras
644	Nicaragua
646	Panama
648	Salvador

MANNERS AND CUSTOMS (GENERAL)

Costume. Dress. Fashion
By region or country
Latin America - Continued
West Indies
655	General works
658	Bahamas
661	Cuba
664	Haiti
667	Jamaica
670	Puerto Rico
673	Other, A-Z

South America
675	General works
678	Argentina
681	Bolivia
684	Brazil
687	Chile
690	Colombia
693	Ecuador

Guianas
695	General works
698	Guyana
701	Surinam
704	French Guiana
707	Paraguay
710	Peru
713	Uruguay
716	Venezuela
720	Europe

By ethnic group not limited to one country
721	Basque
725	Slavic

Great Britain. England (General)
730	General works
	By period
731	Ancient
732	Medieval
733	Modern
734	15th-16th centuries
735	17th century
736	18th century
737	19th century
738	20th century
	England (Local)
741	By region or country, A-Z
742	By city, A-Z
750-762	Scotland[1]
	For Tartans, see DA880.H76
770-782	Northern Ireland[1]
790-802	Wales[1]
805	Other local, A-Z
	e. g. .J4 Jersey
	Ireland
806	General
807	Local, A-Z

[1] Divide like GT730-742

Costume. Dress. Fashion
  By region or country
    Europe - Continued

810-818	Austria
	Divided like GT730-738
820	By division, A-Z
821	By city, A-Z
	Hungary
825	General works
831	By division, A-Z
833	By city, A-Z
835-843	Czechoslovakia
	Divided like GT825-833
	France
850	General works
	By period
851	Ancient
852	Medieval
853	Modern
855	15th-16th centuries
857	17th century. Reign of Louis XIV
860	18th century. Early 19th century
863	Reign of Louis XV
865	Reign of Louis XVI
867	French Revolution
869	Directory
871	19th century
873	First Empire
875	Second Empire
880	20th century
885	By region or department, A-Z
	By city
887	Paris
889	Other cities, A-Z
	Germany
	Including West Germany
900	General works
	By period
901	Ancient
902	Medieval
903	Modern
905	15th-16th centuries
907	17th century
909	18th century
910	19th century
911	20th century
	West Germany (Local)
	By region or state
918	Baden-Württemberg
919	Bavaria
920	Black Forest
921	Hesse
923	Lower Saxony
924	North Rhine-Westphalia
925	Rhineland-Palatinate
926	Saarland
928	Schleswig-Holstein
931	By city, A-Z

MANNERS AND CUSTOMS (GENERAL)

Costume. Dress. Fashion
By region or country
Europe - Continued
East Germany

932	General works
933	Local, A-Z
940-952	Greece (Modern)[1]
960-972	Italy[1]
975	Vatican
	Low Countries
980	General works
1000-1012	Netherlands[1]
1020-1032	Belgium[1]
1040-1052	Russia[1]
	Cf. GT1447, Turkestan
	GT1570, Russia in Asia
1060	Poland
1080	Finland
	Scandinavia
1100	General works
1120-1132	Denmark[1]
1140	Iceland
1150-1162	Norway[1]
1170-1182	Sweden[1]
1190	Spain and Portugal
1200-1212	Spain[1]
1220-1232	Portugal[1]
1240-1252	Switzerland[1]
	Balkan States
1280	General works
1285	Albania
1290	Bulgaria
1310	Romania
1325	Yugoslavia
1330	Other European regions or countries, A-Z
	Mediterranean islands
	For islands belonging to particular Mediterranean countries, see the special divisions of those countries, e. g. Balearic Islands (Spain), GT1211; Sardinia (Italy), GT971
1350	Cyprus
1360	Malta
	Asia
1370	General works
	Near East
1380	General works
1390	Arabia
1400	Turkey
1405	Iraq
1410	Syria
1420	Iran
1430	Other regions or countries, A-Z
	West Central Asia
1440	General works
1443	Afghanistan
1447	Turkestan
1450	Other regions or countries, A-Z

---
[1] Divided like GT730-742

MANNERS AND CUSTOMS (GENERAL)

Costume. Dress. Fashion
  By region or country
    Asia. The Orient - Continued
      South Asia. Southeast Asia

1455	General works
	India
1460	General works
1470	By region or state, A-Z
1475	By city, A-Z
1476	Nepal
1478	Pakistan
1479	Sri Lanka
	Indochina
1490	General works
1495	Vietnam
1498	Cambodia
1501	Laos
1520	Thailand
1522	Burma
1530	Malaysia
	Indonesia
1535	General works
1539	By island, A-Z
	Philippine Islands
1540	General works
1544	By island, A-Z
1545	Other regions or countries, A-Z
	East Asia
1550	General works
1555	China
1556	Taiwan
1560	Japan
1565	Korea
1570	Siberia. Russia in Asia
	Africa
1580	General works
1581	North Africa
1582	Morocco
1583	Algeria
1585	Egypt
.5	Ethiopia
1586	Kenya
.5	Tanzania
1587	Zaire
1588	South Africa
1589	Other African regions or countries, A-Z
	Australia
1590	General works
1593	By state or territory, A-Z
1595	New Zealand
	Pacific islands
1597	General works
1599	By island or group of islands, A-Z
1605	Arctic regions
	By class (Age, sex, birth, etc.)
	For industries, trades, see GT5910+; professional classes, see GT6110+; sport costumes, see GV; academic dress, see LB2389
1710	Men
1720	Women
1730	Children

Costume. Dress. Fashion
 Materials and articles of clothing. Details and accessories - Continued
  Hairdressing. Coiffures
2290   General works
2310   Use of false hair. Wigs
2318   Mustaches
2320   Beards
2340   Cosmetics, perfumes, etc.
    Cf. RA773+, Personal hygiene
      TP983, Chemical technology
2345   Tattooing
    Cf. GN419.3, Ethnology
2350   Other (not A-Z)
2370   Spectacles, eyeglasses, opera glasses, etc.
Customs relative to private life
  Cf. GR440+, Folklore
   HQ, Sociology
2400 General works
2420 Family life. Home life
 Children
2450   General works
2460   Birth customs, baptism, etc.
    Cf. GT5080, Ceremonies of royalty
2470   Circumcision
     Cf. BM705, Judaism
      GN484, Ethnology
2480   Amusements. Games. Play
    Cf. GV182.9, Recreation for children
     GV1203+, Children's amusements
 Adolescence. Maturation
   Including coming of age rites and ceremonies, initiations
   Cf. GN483.3, Coming of age rites (Ethnology)
2485   General works
2486   General special (Special aspects of the subject as a whole)
2487   By region or country, A-Z
2520 Women
2540   Young women. Girls
 Love. Courtship. Marriage. Sex customs
   For works dealing with sex customs specifically, see GN484.3+; HQ12+
2600   General works
  By period
2610   Ancient
2620   Medieval
2630   Modern
2640   Kissing
2650   Courtship. Betrothal
2651   Bundling
  Marriage customs
    Cf. GT5070, Royal marriages
   General works
2660   Early through 1800
2665   1801-
   By period
2670   Ancient
2680   Medieval
2690   Modern

MANNERS AND CUSTOMS (GENERAL)

Customs relative to private life
   Love. Courtship. Marriage. Sex customs
      Marriage customs - Continued

2695	By ethnic group, A-Z
	Class here only individual groups not located in particular regions or countries. For groups located in particular regions or countries, see the group in D-F
	.J4 Jews
	Cf. BM713, Judaism
	.M8 Muslims
	By region or country
	Under each one number country:
	.A2A-Z General works
	.A3A-Z Provinces, regions, etc.
	.A4-Z Cities, towns, etc.
2701	America
	North America
2702	General works
	United States
2703	General works
	By region
2705	New England
2706	South
2707	Central
2708	West
2709	Pacific States
2710	By state, A-W
2711	By city, A-Z
2703	Canada
	Latin America
.5	General works
2714	Mexico
	Central America
2715	General works
2716	Belize. British Honduras
2717	Costa Rica
2718	Guatemala
2719	Honduras
2720	Nicaragua
2721	Panama
2722	Salvador
	West Indies
2723	General works
2724	Bahamas
2725	Cuba
2726	Haiti
2727	Jamaica
2728	Puerto Rico
2729	Other, A-Z
	South America
2730	General works
2731	Argentina
2732	Bolivia
2733	Brazil
2734	Chile
2735	Colombia
2736	Ecuador
2737	Guianas
2738	Paraguay
2739	Peru
2740	Uruguay
2741	Venezuela

MANNERS AND CUSTOMS (GENERAL)

<u>Customs relative to private life</u>
 <u>Love. Courtship. Marriage. Sex customs</u>
  <u>Marriage customs</u>
   <u>By region or country</u>[1]- Continued
    <u>Europe</u>

2742	General works
	<u>Great Britain. England (General)</u>
2743	General works
2744	England (Local), A-Z
2745	Scotland
2746	Northern Ireland
2747	Wales
.5	Ireland
2748	Austria
.5	Hungary
2749	France
2750	Germany
	Including West Germany
.5	East Germany
2751	Greece
2752	Italy
	Low Countries
2753	General works
2754	Netherlands
2755	Belgium
2756	Russia
	Cf. GT2785, Russia in Asia
	<u>Scandinavia</u>
2757	General works
2758	Denmark
2759	Iceland
2760	Norway
2761	Sweden
2762	Spain
2763	Portugal
2764	Switzerland
	<u>Balkan States</u>
2766	General works
2767	Bulgaria
2769	Romania
2770	Yugoslavia
2771	Other European regions or countries, A-Z
	.C9 Czechoslovakia
	.F5 Finland
	.P6 Poland
	<u>Asia</u>
2772	General works
	Near East
2773	General works
.5	Turkey. Asia Minor
2774	Iran
2775	Central Asia
2776	South Asia. India
	<u>Southeast Asia</u>
.5	General works
2777	Indochina

---

[1]
For subarrangement, <u>see</u> p. 317

MANNERS AND CUSTOMS (GENERAL)

<u>Customs relative to private life</u>
  <u>Love. Courtship. Marriage. Sex customs</u>
    <u>Marriage customs</u>
      <u>By region or country</u>[1]
        <u>Asia</u>
          <u>Southeast Asia</u> - Continued

2779	Malaysia
2780	Indonesia
2781	Philippine Islands
	<u>East Asia</u>
2782	General works
2783	China
.5	Taiwan
2784	Japan
2785	Siberia. Russia in Asia
2786	Other Asian regions or countries, A-Z
	<u>Africa</u>
2787	General works
2788	Egypt
2789	Other regions or countries, A-Z
	<u>Australia</u>
2790	General works
2791	By state or territory, A-Z
2793	New Zealand
	Pacific islands
2795	General works
2796	By island or group of islands, A-Z
2800	Wedding anniversaries
2810	Girdles of chastity
	Celibacy (General), <u>see</u> HQ800; celibacy of the clergy, <u>see</u> BV4390
2845	Bathing customs
	Cf. RA780, Bathing (Personal hygiene)
	RM819+, Baths (Physical therapy)

<u>Eating and drinking customs</u>
    Cf. GT3770+, Inns and taverns

2850	General works
2853	By region or country, A-Z
	<u>Foods and beverages</u>
	Cf. BJ2021+, Etiquette of entertaining
	TX15+, History and antiquities of home economics
	TX631+, Gastronomy
2855	General works
2860	Foods
	Cf. TX341+, Home economics
2870	Condiments. Salt, etc.
	Cf. TX819, Cookery
	<u>Beverages</u>
	Cf. TX815+, Cookery
2880	General works
2883	By region or country, A-Z
2884	<u>Alcoholic beverages</u>
2885	Wines
2887	Sake
2890	Ale and beer

---

[1]
  For subarrangement, <u>see</u> p. 317

MANNERS AND CUSTOMS (GENERAL)

<u>Customs relative to private life</u>
  <u>Eating and drinking customs</u>
    <u>Foods and beverages</u>
      <u>Beverages</u>
        <u>Alcoholic beverages</u> - Continued
          <u>Distilled liquors</u>

2893	General works
2894	Brandy
2895	Whiskey
2896	Gin
2897	Rum

<u>Tea</u>
  Cf. RM240+, Diet therapy

2905	General works
2910	<u>Japanese tea ceremony</u>
	Tea masters
2911.A1A-Z	Collective
.A2-Z	Individual, A-Z
2912	Special schools, A-Z
	.M8 Mushanokōji Senke
	.O4 Omote Senke
	.S55 Sōhen school
	.U7 Ura Senke
	Gardens, <u>see</u> SB458; SB466.J34
2915	Utensils, etc.
2916	Aesthetics, psychology, etc.
	Kaiseki, <u>see</u> TX724.5.J3
2918	Coffee
	Cf. RM240+, Diet therapy
2920	Other, A-Z
	e. g. .C3 Chocolate
2930	Drinking of healths

<u>Drinking vessels</u>
  Cf. NK4895, Decorative arts

2940	General works
	Special
2945	By form, material, etc., A-Z
	Cf. NK7218, Gold and silver plate
2947	By region or country, A-Z
2948	Tableware
2950	Spoons
2952	Toothpicks
2955	Picnics
	Sleeping customs
3000.3	General works
.4	By region or country
3010	Narcotics
3015	Betel. Betel nut
3020	Tobacco. Smoking
3030	Snuff
3032	Japanese incense ceremony
3050	Salutations, courtesies, etc.
	Cf. GT2640, Kissing
3055	Scatology
3080	Swearing. Profanity
3100	Treatment of the aged

<u>Burial and funeral customs. Treatment of the dead</u>
  Cf. BF789.F8, Funerals (Psychology)
      RA619+, Public health

3150	General works

Customs relative to private life
Burial and funeral customs.   Treatment of
the dead - Continued
By period

3170	Ancient
3180	Medieval
3190	Modern
3201-3296	By region or country

Divided like GT2701-2796

3320	Interment. Burial
3330	Incineration. Cremation
3335	Urns
3340	Embalming. Mummies

For works limited to Egyptian mummies, see
DT62.M7

3350	Exposure
3353	Body snatching

Special funeral customs

3360	Wakes
3370	Suttee. Widow suicide

Cf. GT3276, India
GT3330, Incineration, cremation

3380	Ship burial
3390	Mourning customs

Customs relative to public and social life
For recreation, amusements, sports, games,
dances, etc., see GV; popular dramatic
representations, broadcasts, motion
pictures, the theater, etc., see PN1720+

3400	General works
3405	By region or country, A-Z

Entertaining. Hospitality
Cf. BJ2021+, Etiquette of entertaining
GV1470+, Parties
TX731, Cookery

3410	General works. History
3415	By region or country, A-Z

Town life
Cf. HT101+, Urban sociology

3420	General works
3430	Fashionable life. High life
3433	Snobs

Dandies, see GT6720

3440	Street life
3450	Street cries

London cries, see DA688
New York City cries, see F128.37

3452	Street decoration
3470	Country life

Cf. HT401+, Rural sociology
S521, Farm life

3490	Mountain life

Court and castle life
Cf. GT5010+, Official ceremonies
GV1747, Court and state balls

3510	General works

By period

3520	Medieval
3530	Modern

By region or country, see D-F

3550	Castle life

MANNERS AND CUSTOMS (GENERAL)

<u>Customs relative to public and social life</u>
<u>Festivals. Holidays</u> - Continued

3940	<u>Public rejoicing. Spectacles. Fêtes</u>
3980	Processions. Pageants
4001-4096	By region or country[1]
4180	Carnivals. Mardi gras
4201-4296	By region or country[1]
4380	Harvest festivals
4401-4496	By region or country[1]
4580	Fairs. Kermisses
4601-4696	By region or country[1]
4801-4896	By region or country[1]

<u>Special days</u>
  Cf. TT900, Decorations for special events
    TX739, Cookery for special occasions

4905	New Year's Day
	Cf. BV135.N5, Religious observance
4915	Twelfth Night. Epiphany
	Cf. BV50.E7, Religious observance
4925	St. Valentine's Day
4935	Easter
	Cf. BV55, Religious observance
4945	May Day
4965	Halloween
4975	Thanksgiving Day
	Cf. BV75, Religious observance
	E162, United States (Descriptive works, 1607-1764)
	F7, New England before 1775

<u>Christmas</u>
  Cf. BV45, Religious observance

4985	General works
	By region or country
	Prefer classification by special custom
	United States
4986.A1A-Z	General works
.A2-Z	By region or state, A-Z
4987	Other regions or countries. (Table I, decimally)[2]
	Special customs
4990	Pistol shooting
4995	Other days, A-Z
.A4	All Souls' Day
.A6	April Fools Day
.A8	Ascension Day
.C6	Corpus Christi
.D5	Dingaan's Day
.F6	Fools, Feast of
.G4	St. George's Day
.J6	John the Baptist's Day
.J66	St. Joseph's Day
.L8	St. Lucy's Day
.M3	St. Martin's Day
.N5	St. Nicholas Day
.P3	St. Patrick's Day
.P8	Purim
.V4	Vernal equinox

---

[1] Divided like GT2701-2796

[2] For Table I, <u>see</u> pp. 380-381

MANNERS AND CUSTOMS (GENERAL)

<u>Customs relative to public and social life</u> - Continued
<pre>
5010·   <u>Official ceremonies of royalty, nobility, etc.</u>
                Cf. CR3499+, Titles of honor, rank, precedence, etc.
                    GT5350+, Customs of royalty and nobility
                    JX1678+, Diplomatic ceremonials and precedence
                For works on the official ceremonies of individual
                    countries, see the country, D - F
5020   Heralds, trumpeters, etc.
5030   Triumphs. Triumphal entries
                Cf. DG89, Military and naval antiquities (Rome)
5050   Coronations
5070   Marriages
                Cf. GT2660+, Marriage customs
5080   Baptisms
5090   Visits of royalty, etc.
5150   Customs relative to use of trees and plants
                Cf. GR780+, Folklore of plants
                    GT5897+, Cultivated plants
                    SD363, Arbor Day
        Customs relative to use of flowers, leaves, etc.
                Cf. GR780+, Folklore of plants, language of flowers
                    SB449, Use of flowers in decoration
5160   General works
5164   Herbs
5170   Customs relative to use of precious metals
        <u>Customs relative to transportation and travel</u>
                Cf. BJ2137+, Etiquette of travel
                    G149+, Voyages and travels
                    G540+, Seafaring life
                    GT6490, Customs relating to wayfarers
                    HE, Transportation
5220   General works
            By period
5230   Ancient
5240   Medieval
5250   Modern through 1800
5260   1801-
            Vehicles. Chariots. Cars
5280   General works
5285   Sleighs and sledges
            Horses, see GT5885
        <u>Customs relative to special classes. By birth, rank, etc.</u>
                Cf. CR3499+, Titles of honor, rank, precedence, etc.
                    GT1710+, Costumes of special classes
                    HT641+, Sociology
5320   General works
            Special groups
              <u>Royalty</u>
                Cf. GT3510+, Court life
                    GT5010+, Official ceremonies
                    JC385, Theory of kingship
                For the customs of royalty in particular countries,
                    see the country, D - F
5350   General works
              By period
5360   Ancient.
5370   Medieval
5380   Modern through 1800
5390   1801-
</pre>

MANNERS AND CUSTOMS (GENERAL)

Customs relative to special classes. By birth, rank, etc.
  Special groups - Continued
    Nobility
        Cf. HT647+, Sociology
            JC411+, Political theory
        For the customs of the nobility in particular
          countries, see the country, D - F
5450   General works
            By period
5460   Ancient
5470   Medieval
5480   Modern through 1800
5490   1801-
    Burghers
5550   General works
            By period
5560   Medieval
5570   Modern through 1800
5580   1801-
    Peasants
        Cf. HD1521+, Agricultural laborers (Economic
                history)
5650   General works
            By period
5660   Medieval
5670   Modern through 1800
5680   1801-
Customs relative to special classes. By occupation
        Cf. HT675+, Sociology
5750   General works
          By period
5760   Ancient
5770   Medieval
5780   Modern through 1800
5790   1801-
    Agriculture and hunting
        Cf. GN402+, Primitive customs
            GT3470, Country life
            HD1506+, Agricultural classes (Economic history)
            SK31+, Hunting sports
5810   General works
          By period
5820   Ancient
5830   Medieval
5840   Modern through 1800
5850   1801-
          By region or country
            United States
5855   General works
5856   By region or state, A-Z
    .15-.995 Other regions or countries (Table I)[1]

---

[1]
  For Table I, see pp. 380-381

MANNERS AND CUSTOMS (GENERAL)

<u>Customs relative to special classes. By occupation</u>
    <u>Agriculture and hunting - Continued</u>
       <u>Domestic animals and cultivated plants</u>

5870	General works
	<u>Domestic and otherwise useful animals</u>
	Cf. SF, Animal culture
5880	General works
	Horses and riding
5885	General works
5888	Harness, bits, spurs, etc.
	Cf. S720, Use on farms
	TS1030+, Leather industry
5890	Dogs
5895	Other animals, A-Z
	.R4 Reindeer
	<u>Cultivated plants</u>
	Cf. GT5150, Customs relative to the use
	of plants
	SB, Plant culture
5897	General works
5899	Individual plants, A-Z
	.R5 Rice
	.S5 Sisal hemp
	.W5 Wheat
5904	Fishing
	<u>Industries. Trades</u>
	Including costumes
	Cf. GN429+, Primitive industries
	HD9000+, Economic history
5910	General works
	By period
5920	Ancient
5930	Medieval
5940	Modern through 1800
5950	1801-
5960	Special, A-Z
	.B8 Building trades
	.M5 Miners
	.T2 Tailors
	<u>Commercial occupations</u>
	Cf. HF, Commerce
6010	General works
	Special
6070	Muleteers
	<u>Professions</u>
	Including costumes
6110	General works
	Church, clergy, <u>see</u> BR - BX
	Law. Judges, lawyers, etc.
6230	General works
	By period
6240	Ancient
6250	Medieval
6260	Modern through 1800
6270	1801-
6280	Special topics (not A-Z)
	e. g. Swearing by kissing the Bible, New
	Testament or Gospels

MANNERS AND CUSTOMS (GENERAL)

Customs relative to special classes. By occupation
  Professions - Continued
    Medicine. Physicians, surgeons, etc., see R707
(6380)   Apothecaries. Pharmacists, see RS122.5
    Soldiers, see U
6390   Other professions, A-Z
Customs relative to other classes
6490 Wayfarers
  Outlaws. The underworld
    Cf. HV6201+, Criminal classes (Social pathology)
6550   General works
   By period
6560   Ancient
6570   Medieval
6580   Modern through 1800
6590   1801-
6601-6696 By region or country
    Divided like GT2701-2796
  Prosecutions and punishments
    Cf. HV8501+, Penology
6710   General works
6715   Prosecutions and punishments of animals
    Cf. HV4701+, Protection of animals
6720 Dandies. Dandyism
    For the biography of dandies, see CT9985+
Miscellaneous implements, utensils, etc., illustrative
  of former customs
7050 General works
7055 By region or country, A-Z
7070 Special, A-Z
   .D5 Distaffs
   .L6 Locks

2

RECREATION. LEISURE

Including amusement in general, play, etc.
Cf. BV1620+, Recreation in the church
    GN454+, Cultural anthropology
    HT281, Urban sociology
    HT469, Rural sociology
    LB1137, Play in education
    LB3031, Recreation in school management
    LC5201+, Adult education
    NX, The arts
    TT, Handicrafts
    Z1003, Books and reading

1	Periodicals. Serials
3	Societies
4	Congresses
	Collected works (nonserial)
7	Several authors
8	Individual authors
9	Questions and answers. Quiz books
11	Dictionaries. Encyclopedias
12	Directories (General and international)

For individual regions or countries, see GV51+
14   Philosophy. Relation to other topics
            Cf. GV706+, Philosophy of sports
  .3   Relation to character and character building
            Relation to Christian life, see BV4597
  .35   Relation to ethics
            For ethics of leisure only, see BJ1498
  .4   Relation to psychology
            Cf. BF717, Play (Developmental psychology)
  .45   Relation to sociology
  .5   Study and teaching. Research
  .6   Audiovisual aids
       Museums. Exhibitions
  .7   General works
  .8   By region or country, A-Z
            Under each country:
              .x   General works
              .x2 Special. By city, A-Z
       History
            Cf. GV571+, History of athletic sports
15   General works
            Ancient. Classical games, etc.
                Cf. GV213, History of physical training
                    GV573, History of athletic sports
17   General works
19   Oriental
            Greek
21   General works
23   Olympic games
                Cf. GV721.18+, Olympic revivals
            Roman
31   General works
33   Chariot racing
34   Circus
35   Gladiators, etc.
41   Medieval

RECREATION. LEISURE

<u>History</u> - Continued
    <u>Modern</u>

45	General works
47	State policy, finance, etc. (General)

      <u>By region or country</u>
        Including history, conditions, policy,
          finance, calendars, etc.
        Under each country (unless otherwise provided for):
          (1) General works
          (2) Local, A-Z
      <u>America</u>
        Cf. E59.G3, Games of Indians

51	General works
	United States
53	General works
54	By region or state, A-Z

          .A1-195 By region (Table IV)[1]
          .A2-W   By state
                Under each:
                  .x   General works
                  .x2 Local, A-Z
                        Including regions,
                          counties, river
                          valleys, cities, etc.

55-56	Canada
	<u>Latin America</u>
57	General works
	Mexico
58.A1A-Z	General works
.A2-Z	Local, A-Z
59-60	Central America
61-62	West Indies
	<u>South America</u>
63	General works
65-66	Argentina
67-68	Brazil
69-70	Chile
71	Other South American regions or countries, A-Z

        Under each country (using three successive
          Cutter numbers):
          .x   General works
          .x2 By state, province, etc., A-Z
          .x3 By city, A-Z
      <u>Europe</u>

73	General works
	<u>Great Britain</u>
75	General works
76	By division

        Subarranged like GV71
      .E5-7 England
      .N6-8 Northern Ireland
      .S4-6 Scotland
      .W3-5 Wales

.5-.6	Ireland
77-78	Austria
79-80	France

---

[1]

For Table IV, <u>see</u> p. 382

RECREATION.   LEISURE

	History
	Modern
	By region or country[1] - Continued
145-146	Australia
149-150	New Zealand
	Pacific islands
157	General works
158	By island or group of islands, A-Z
	Subarranged like GV71
	For Hawaii, see GV54.H3
	Recreation specialists
160	Recreation as a profession
	Biography
	For biographies within special recreational subjects,
	see the subject, e. g. GV697, Athletics
161	Collective
163	Women
165	Individual, A-Z
	General works, treatises, and textbooks
171	American, through 1975
173	English, through 1975
174	American and English, 1976-
177	French
179	German
181	Other (not A-Z)
.15	Pictorial works
.2	Program handbooks
	Class here comprehensive guides offering suggestions
	and ideas for special programs, activities, parties,
	games, fun, etc.
	Cf. GV181.43, Program planning
	GV1199+, Games and amusements
	Addresses, essays, lectures, see GV191
.3	General special (Special aspects of the subject
	as a whole)
	Recreation leadership
.35	Study and teaching
.4	General works
.43	Program planning and supervising
.46	Recreation surveys
	Class here works on methodology only
	For results of particular surveys, see GV51+
	Administration of recreation services. Community
	recreation
.5	General works
.55	Evaluation of services

---

[1]

   For subarrangement, unless otherwise provided, see p. 329, above GV51

RECREATION. LEISURE

Recreational areas and facilities. Recreation centers
　　　Cf. GV401+, Sports facilities, playgrounds, etc.
　　　　HN41+, Community centers, social centers
　　　　HS2581, Country clubs
　　　　HT485, Social centers in the country
　　　　HV4175+, Social settlements
　　　　LC223, Schools as community centers
　　　　NA6800+, Buildings for recreation (Architecture)
　　　　SB481+, Parks and reserves
　　　　TH4711, Construction of recreation buildings

182	General works
	Personnel, see GV159+
.15	Financial and business aspects
.2	Public relations
	Cf. GV714, Sports
.3	Facility planning. Standards
.4	Maintenance and repair
.5	Equipment and supplies
	Including catalogs

Recreation for special classes of persons
.8	Families
.9	Children

　　　Cf. GV1203+, Games and amusements
　　　　RJ242, Children in hospitals
　　　For works discussing the significance of play
　　　　in the life of the child, see HQ782
　　Youth, see GV1+
　　Students, see LB3608

183	Girls and women
	Handicapped

　　　Cf. GV445, Physical training
　　　　HV1765+, Recreation for the blind

.5	General works
.7	Mentally handicapped
.9	Socially handicapped
	Invalids, see GV1231; RM737
	Mentally ill, see RC489.R4
	Industrial workers, see HD7395.R4
	Military personnel (Armed Forces), see UH800+
184	The aged. Retirees
	Special occasions
186	Vacations

　　　Cf. G149+, Voyages and travel
　　　　HD5261+, Labor economics
　　　　LC5701+, Vacation schools

191	Addresses, essays, lectures. Light literature

　　For light literature of sports only, see GV707

RECREATION. LEISURE

	Outdoor life. Outdoor recreation
	Camping - Continued
198.9	Ice and snow camping
	Canoe cruising and camping, see GV789+
	Hiking. Pedestrian tours
	Cf. GV1044+, Bicycle hiking
	GV1071, Walking matches
199	Periodicals. Societies. Serials
	By region or country
	Class here works on the technical
	aspects of hiking, climbing, etc.,
	in particular places. For works
	of description and travel, see D - F,
	e. g. DQ820+, Alps
	United States
.4	General works
.42	By region or state, A-Z
.44	Other regions or countries, A-Z
.5	General works
.6	Backpacking
.7	Packhorse camping
	Mountaineering
.8	Periodicals. Societies and clubs. Serials
	Collected works (nonserial)
.82	Several authors
.83	Individual authors
.85	Dictionaries. Encyclopedias
.87	Directories
.89	History
	By region or country, see GV199.4+
	Biography
.9	Collective
.92	Individual, A-Z
200	General works
	Rock climbing
	By region or country, see GV199.4+
.2	General works
	Ice and snow climbing
	By region or country, see GV199.4+
.3	General works
.4	Orientation
.5	Wilderness survival
	Cf. TL553.7, Survival after airplane accidents

PHYSICAL EDUCATION AND TRAINING

	Cf. BV4598, Physical education
	and Christianity
	RA781, Personal hygiene
	RM719+, Mechanotherapy:
	Massage, exercise, etc.
201	Periodicals. Serials
	Societies. Clubs. Turnvereins, etc.
	Cf. GV391, Organization of athletic clubs and societies
	GV563, Sports clubs and societies
202	International
203	United States

RECREATION. LEISURE

Physical education and training
   Societies. Clubs. Turnvereins, etc. - Continued
204   Other regions or countries, A-Z
          Under each country (using three sucessive
            Cutter numbers):
            .x   General works
            .x2 Local, A-Z
                Including regions, provinces, river
                  valleys, cities, etc.
            .x3 Special societies, etc. By name, A-Z
205   Congresses
        Collected works (nonserial)
206   Several authors
  .5   Individual authors
207   Dictionaries. Encyclopedias
        Communication of information
  .3   General works
  .4   Documentation
208   Directories
        Philosophy. Relation to other topics, see GV342+
        History
211   General works
          By period
213   Ancient
215   Medieval
127   Modern
          By region or country
            Under each country (unless otherwise provided for):
            (1) General works
            (2) Local, A-Z
          America
221   General works
           United States
223   General works
224.A1A-Z   By state, A-W
  .A2-Z   By city, A-Z
           Canada
225.A1A-Z   General works
  .A2-Z   Local, A-Z
          Latin America
226   General works
227   Mexico
            Subarranged like GV225
228-229   Central America
230-231   West Indies
           South America
233   General works
235-236   Argentina
237-238   Brazil
239-240   Chile
241   Other South American regions or countries, A-Z
            Under each country (using three
              successive Cutter numbers):
            .x   General works
            .x2 By state, province, etc., A-Z
            .x3 By city, A-Z

RECREATION. LEISURE

Physical education and training
  History
    By region or country[1] - Continued
      Europe

243	General works
245	Great Britain
	Including England
246	By division, A-Z
	Subarranged like GV241
	.N6-8 Northern Ireland
	.S4-6 Scotland
	.W3-5 Wales
.5-.6	Ireland
247-248	Austria
249-250	France
251-252	Germany
	Including West Germany
252.5-.6	East Germany
253-254	Greece
255-256	Italy
	Low Countries
257	General works
259-260	Belgium
261-262	Netherlands
263-264	Russia
	Cf. GV299+, Russia in Asia
	Scandinavia
265	General works
267-268	Denmark
269-270	Norway
271-272	Sweden
273-274	Spain
275-276	Portugal
277-278	Switzerland
	Balkan States
279	General works
281-282	Bulgaria
285-286	Romania
287-287.5	Yugoslavia
288	Other European regions or countries, A-Z
	Subarranged like GV241
	.C9-93 Czechoslovakia
	.P6-63 Poland
	Asia
289	General works
291-292	China
293-294	India
295-296	Japan
297-298	Iran
299-300	Russia in Asia. Siberia
301-302	Turkey. Asia Minor
303	Other Asian regions or countries, A-Z
	Subarranged like GV241
	.I5-53 Indonesia
	.I75-77 Israel
	.K6-63 Korea

-----

[1]

   For subarrangement, unless otherwise provided, see p. 336, above
GV221

RECREATION. LEISURE

Physical education and training
   Physical education facilities. Sports facilities - Cont.
      By region or country
        United States

429.A1A-Z	Periodicals. Societies. Associations
.A2-Z	General works
430	By state, A-W
431	By city, A-Z

           Under each:
             .x   General works
             .x2 Individual facilities. By name, A-Z
                For individual stadiums, see GV416

433	Other regions or countries, A-Z

          Under each country (using three successive
             Cutter numbers):
             .x   General works
             .x2 States, provinces, etc., A-Z
             .x3 Cities, etc., A-Z

435	Physical measurements

      Including anthropometric manuals and tables
      Cf. LB3421+, School children
    Physical tests, etc. Fitness tests
      Including tests for motor ability, physical
        aptitude, capacity, and efficiency;
        achievement scales and standards; etc.

436	General works
.5	Evaluation of performance
437	Clothing for athletics and gymnastics

      Cf. GV441, Dress for women and girls
    Diet, see TX361.A8
Physical education and training for special classes
    of persons

438	Individuals

    Women and girls
      Cf. GV464, Gymnastics for women
          GV482, Exercises for women
          GV709, Sports for women

439	General works
441	Dress
443	Children

      Class here general works on the physical education
        of children at the elementary level. For
        education at the secondary and higher levels,
        see GV201+. For physical education programs
        of particular places or school systems, any
        level, see GV221+
      Cf. BV1640, Physical culture for the young in the
        church
        GV464.5, Gymnastics for children
        GV709.2, Sports for children
        HV9083, Physical education for juvenile
          delinquents

445	Handicapped persons

      Cf. HV1767, Physical education for the blind

447	The aged

    Sailors, see V260
    Soldiers, see U320

RECREATION. LEISURE

Physical education and training
  Gymnastics. Gymnastic exercises
    Heavy exercises - Continued
525   High kick
527   Horizontal bars
529   Jumping exercises
            Cf. GV1073+, Sports
          Parallel bars
535   General works
536   Uneven parallel bars
537   Pyramids and Roman ladders
539   Rings
541   Rope climbing, pole climbing, ladders
543   Rowing machines, etc.
545   Tumbling and mat work
546   Weight lifting
547   Other (not A-Z)
            e. g. Wheels
    Acrobatics. Trapeze work. Rope and wire walking
        Cf. GV854.9.A25, Ski acrobatics
551   General works
553   General special
            Including hand balancing, triple somersault, etc.
555   Trampolining

                         SPORTS

        Cf. GV199.8+, Mountaineering
            RC1200+, Sports medicine
            SF277+, Horse racing, riding,
              and driving
            SH401+, Angling
            SK, Hunting
            U327+, Military sports
            V267+, Navy sports

561   Periodicals. Serials
          Cf. GV741, Sporting annuals
563   Societies. Clubs. Leagues
          Cf. GV202+, Physical education societies
            GV391, Organization of athletic clubs and societies
          For clubs for individual sports, see the sport,
            e. g. GV793, Rowing. For programs of special
            sports events, see GV721+
        Collected works (nonserial)
565   Several authors
    .2   Individual authors
567   Dictionaries. Encyclopedias
        Philosophy. Relation to other topics, see GV706+
        Communication of information
          General works
    .5
568   Information services
        Study and teaching, see GV201+

RECREATION. LEISURE

Sports - Continued
  History
571   General works
          By period
            Preliterate, see GN454+
573   Ancient
575   Medieval
576   Modern
          By region or country
            For sports in individual schools and colleges,
              see GV691+
            Under each country (unless otherwise provided for):

2 nos.	1 no.	Cutter	
1	1	.x	General works
2	1.3	.x3	By state, province, etc., A-Z
2.5	1.5	.x5	By city, A-Z

          America
581   General works
            United States
583   General works
584   By state, A-W
  .5   By city, A-Z
            Canada
585   General works
  .3   By province, A-Z
  .5   By city, A-Z
            Latin America
586   General works
587-588.5   Mexico
589-590.5   Central America
591-592.5   West Indies
              South America
593   General works
595-596.5   Argentina
597-598.5   Brazil
599-600.5   Chile
601   Other South American regions or countries, A-Z
          Europe
            Great Britain
              Including England
605   General works
  .2   Scotland
  .3   Wales
  .5   Northern Ireland
  .6   By county, A-Z
  .7   By city, A-Z
606.5-.55   Ireland
607-608.5   Austria
609-610.5   France
611-612.5   Germany
                Including West Germany
612.6-.65   East Germany
613-614.5   Greece
615-616.5   Italy
            Low Countries
617   General works
619-620.5   Belgium
621-622.5   Netherlands

RECREATION. LEISURE

Sports
  History
    By region or country[1]
     Europe - Continued

623-624.5	Russia
	Cf. GV659+, Russia in Asia
	Scandinavia
625	General works
627-628.5	Denmark
629-630.5	Norway
631-632.5	Sweden
633-634.5	Spain
635-636.5	Portugal
637-638.5	Switzerland
	Balkan States
639	General works
641-642.5	Bulgaria
645-646.5	Romania
647-647.5	Yugoslavia
	Subdivided like GV585-585.5
648	Other European regions or countries, A-Z
	Asia
649	General works
651-652.5	China
653-654.5	India
655-656.5	Japan
657-658.5	Iran
659-660.5	Russia in Asia. Siberia
661-662.5	Turkey. Asia Minor
663	Other Asian regions or countries, A-Z
	.T3-35 Taiwan
	Africa
665	General works
667	South Africa
669	Egypt
671	Morocco
673	Other African regions or countries, A-Z
	.E7-75 Ethiopia
675-676.5	Australia
679-680.5	New Zealand
	Pacific islands
687	General works
688	By island or group of islands, A-Z
	Individual schools and colleges
	Cf. GV367+, Schools of physical education
	and training
	For general college athletics, see GV347
691	American. By name, A-Z
693	Other. By name, A-Z
	Biography of athletes
	Cf. CT9997, Strong men
	For biography in individual sports, see the
	sport, e. g. GV850, Skating; GV865, Baseball; etc.
697.A1A-Z	Collective
.A2-Z	Individual, A-Z

---

[1]
  For subarrangement, unless otherwise provided, see table, p. 343,
above GV581

RECREATION. LEISURE

<table>
<tr><td></td><td>Sports - Continued</td></tr>
</table>

	Sports - Continued
	General works
701	American, through 1975
703	English, through 1975
704	American and English, 1976-
705	Other languages (not A-Z)
706	Philosophy. Relation to other topics
.3	Relation to ethics. Fair play. Sportsmanship
.4	Relation to psychology. Sport psychology
.45	Relation to scholastic achievement
.5	Relation to sociology
.55	Relation to success
.8	General special (Special aspects of the subject as a whole)
707	Addresses, essays, lectures. Light literature
	Sports for special classes of persons
708	Individuals
709	Women
	Cf. GV439+, Physical training for women
	For biography of women athletes, see GV697
.2	Children
	For sports for youth, see GV561+
.7	Travelers. Deck sports
	Cf. GV1099, Shuffleboard
	GV1206, Games for travelers
710	Intramural sports (General)
	Cf. GV346, School athletics
	GV347+, College athletics
711	Coaching
	Athletic contests. Sports events
712	General works
713	Organization and administration
	Cf. GV343.5, Physical education and training
714	Public relations
715	Spectator control
716	Financial and business aspects
717	Betting
	Cf. GV1301+, Games of chance
	SF331, Horse racing
718	Broadcasting
	Sports journalism, see PN4784.S6
	Biography of sports writers, broadcasters, etc.
719.A2A-Z	Collective
.A3-Z	Individual, A-Z
	Special contests and events
	International
721	General works
	Olympic games (Modern revivals)
	For Olympic games in ancient Greece, see GV23. For Olympic winter games, see GV841.5+
	Biography of trustees, etc.
.18	Collective
.2	Individual, A-Z
.3	International Olympic Committee
.4	National committees. By country, A-Z
.5	General works
.6	Philosophy. Ethics. Olympic ideal
.7	Light literature. Wit and humor
722	Individual contests. By year

RECREATION. LEISURE

<pre>
                Sports - Continued
                  Air sports
                        Cf. TL500+, Aeronautics
  750   Periodicals. Serials
  751   Societies. Clubs
  752   Dictionaries
                    History
  753   General works
  754   By region or country, A-Z
  755   General works
  756   General special
  757   Addresses, essays, lectures. Light literature
                    Airplane flying
                          Cf. TL721.4, Private flying
  758   General works
  759   Racing
                          Cf. TL721.5+, Air meets
                      Models
                          Cf. TL770+, Model airplane construction
  760   General works
  761   Competitions
    .5   Racing
                    Balloon flying
  762   General works
  763   Racing
                    Gliding and soaring
  764   General works
  765   By region or country, A-Z
  766   Racing
                    Kiteflying
                          Cf. TL759+, Aeronautics
  767   General works
  768   By region or country, A-Z
  769   Competitions
  770   Parachuting. Skydiving
                  Water sports
                        Cf. GV200.6, Water oriented recreation
    .3   Periodicals. Societies and clubs. Serials
    .4   By region or country, A-Z
    .5   General works
    .6   Safety measures
    .7   Water sports facilities
                        Including resources, planning, etc.
                    Boats and boating (General)
  771   Periodicals. Serials
  775   General works
                      By region or country·
                        United States
  776.A2A-Z   General works
    .A3-Z   By region or state, A-Z
                            Under each state:
                              .x   General works
                              .x2 Local, A-Z
    .15-.995   Other regions or countries (Table I)[1]
                            Under each country:
                              .A2A-Z General works
                              .A3-Z Local, A-Z
</pre>

---

[1]
  For Table I, see pp. 380-381

RECREATION. LEISURE

Sports
  Water sports
    Boats and boating (General) - Continued

777	Societies and clubs
	Cf. GV823, Yacht clubs
.3	Light literature
.4	Boats and equipment (General). Catalogs
.5	Seamanship. Boat handling
	Cf. VK541+, Merchant marine
.55	Safety measures. Rescue work
	Cf. VK200, Merchant marine
.57	Boating for women
.6	Small boats. Dinghies
	Cf. GV811.6, Dinghy sailing
780	Rafting
	Including use of inflatable boats

    Canoeing
      Including kayaking

781	Periodicals. Serials
783	General works
784	Light literature
785	Societies and clubs
788	White-water running

      Cruising. Tripping

789	General works
790	Camping

      By region or country, see GV776-776.995

    Rowing
      Cf. GV543, Rowing machines
      Biography

.9	Collective
.92	Individual, A-Z
791	General works
793	Societies and clubs

      College, school, and club rowing
        By country

795	England
796	United States
797	Other countries, A-Z

        Special races
        England

798	Henley regattas
799	University boat races (Oxford and Cambridge)
800	Other English races. By place, A-Z

        United States

801	New London
	Including all Harvard-Yale races
803	Poughkeepsie
804	Saratoga
805	Other races. By place, A-Z
806	Other countries. By country, A-Z

        At individual institutions

807	American
	e. g. .C6 Cornell
	.H3 Harvard
.5	Other
	e. g. .E8 Eton
	.O9 Oxford

RECREATION. LEISURE

Sports
  Water sports
    Yachting - Continued
      Motorboats and motorboating. Launches
        Cf. VM340+, Motorboat construction
833.5   Periodicals. Serials
834   Societies and clubs
835   General works
                      By region or country
                        United States
  .18   General works
  .2   By region or state, A-Z
  .3   Other regions or countries, A-Z
  .7   Light literature
  .8   Outboard motorboating
  .9   Motorboat racing
836   Houseboats and houseboating
                      Cf. VM335, Houseboat construction
    Swimming. diving, etc.
837   General works
  .13   Swimming pools
                        Cf. RA606, Sanitation
                          TH4763, Swimming pool construction
  .15   Certification and examinations for lifeguards, etc.
                      For special classes
  .2   Children
  .4   Handicapped persons
  .6   Juvenile works
                      Biography
  .9   Collective
838   Individual, A-Z
  .4   By region or country, A-Z
839   Water polo
840   Other water sports, A-Z
                        Angling, fly casting, etc., see SH401+
  .J6   Jousting
  .S5   Skiing
          Skindiving, see .S78
  .S78   Submarine diving. Skindiving
            Including underwater spear fishing
            Cf. GB602.5, Cave diving.
          Surfing. Surf riding
  .S8   General works
  .S82   By region or country, A-Z
    Winter sports
  .7   By region or country, A-Z
841   General works
  .2   Winter sports facilities
                      Winter olympic games
  .5   General works
842   Individual contests. By year
843   Iceboating
845   Curling
                    Ice hockey
846   Periodicals. Societies. Serials
  .5   History
                      Biography, see GV848.5
847   General works
  .2   Addresses, essays, lectures
  .25   Juvenile works
  .4   Financial and business aspects

RECREATION. LEISURE

Sports
    Winter sports
        Ice hockey - Continued

847.5	Rules. Records. Programs. Schedules
.7	International contests. Stanley Cup
.8	Special leagues, conferences, etc. By name, A-Z
848	Individual clubs, teams, etc. By name, A-Z
.25	Coaching
.4	By region or country, A-Z
.5	Biography
	.A1A-Z Collective
	.A2-Z Individual, A-Z

        Ice skating
           Cf. GV859+, Roller skating

.9	Directories
849	General works
.01-.995	By region or country (Table I, decimally)[1]
	Under each country:
	.A2A-Z General works
	.A3-Z Local, A-Z
	Biography
850.A2A-Z	Collective
.A3-Z	Individual, A-Z
.3	Speed skating
	Figure skating
.4	General works
.45	Pair skating. Ice dancing
	Events and competitions
.5	General works
.55	Special, A-Z
	.I25 Ice Capades
.6	Judging
.7	Facilities. Ice rinks
852	Equipment and supplies
	Including skates, costumes, etc.
853	Snowshoeing

      Skiing

854.A1A-Z	Periodicals. Societies. Serials
.A2A-Z	Directories
.A3-Z	General works
.1	History
.2	Biography
	.A1A-Z Collective
	.A2-Z Individual, A-Z
.3	Light literature
	By region or country
	United States
.4	General works
.5	By region or state, A-Z
.6	By resort, A-Z
.7	Switzerland
.8	Other regions or countries, A-Z
.85	Training. Conditioning. Exercises
.87	Rules, records, etc.
.88	Alpine combined contests
.89	Nordic combined contests

---

[1]
  For Table I, see pp. 380-381

<u>Sports</u>
   <u>Winter sports</u>
      <u>Skiing</u> - Continued

854.9	Other special topics, A-Z
	.A25 Acrobatics
	.C7 Cross-country skiing
	.E6 Equipment and supplies
	.J8 Jumping
	.R3 Racing, Downhill
	.S6 Slalom
855	Bobsledding. Tobogganing
857	Other winter sports, A-Z
	Automobile racing on ice, <u>see</u> GV1029.9.I25
	.S47 Skibobbing
	.S5 Sleighing
	.S6 Snowmobiling

   <u>Roller skating</u>

859	General works
.6	Roller derbies
.7	Roller polo. Roller skate hockey

   <u>Ball games</u>

861	General works
.01-.995	By region or country (Table I, decimally)[1]
	Under each country:
	.A2A-Z General works
	.A3-Z Local, A-Z

   <u>Baseball</u>

862	Periodicals. Societies. Serials
	History
.5	General works
	United States
863.A1A-Z	General works
.A2-Z	By region or state, A-Z
	Under each state:
	.x General works
	.x2 Local, A-Z
.15-.995	Other regions or countries (Table I)[1]
	Under each country:
	.A1A-Z General works
	.A2-Z Local, A-Z
	Biography
865.A1A-Z	Collective
.A2-Z	Individual, A-Z
	e. g. .G4 Gehrig, Lou
	.R8 Ruth, George ("Babe Ruth")
867	General works
.3	General special
.5	Juvenile works
868	Base running
869	Batting
870	Fielding
871	Pitching
872	Catching
873	Light literature

---

[1]
  For Table I, <u>see</u> pp. 380-381

RECREATION. LEISURE

       Sports
         Ball games
           Baseball - Continued
             Leagues, clubs, etc.
                Cf. GV880.5, Little League baseball

875.A1A-Z	General works
.A15A-Z	American League of Professional Baseball Clubs
.A3A-Z	National League of Professional Baseball Clubs
.A4-Z	Individual clubs. By name, A-Z

                  e. g. .B7 Brooklyn Dodgers
                         .C6 Chicago Cubs
                         .N4 New York Yankees
                         .T4 Texas Rangers
                         .W3 Washington Senators

.2	Insignia, buttons, pins, etc.
.3	Baseball cards
.5	Coaching
.7	Managing
876	Umpiring
877	Rules, records, etc. "Guides"
879	Scoring, scorebooks, schedules, etc.
880	Financial and business aspects
.5	Little League baseball
881	Softball. Indoor baseball

          Basketball

882	Periodicals. Societies. Serials
883	History
	Biography
884.A1A-Z	Collective
.A2-Z	Individual, A-Z
885	General works
.1	Juvenile works
.2	Officiating

                Including biographical works

.3	Coaching
.35	Training
	Amateur
.4	General works
.42	Individual clubs. By place, A-Z
.43	In special institutions, A-Z
.45	Rules. Records. Programs. Schedules
.47	Managing
.49	Tournaments and special games, A-Z
	Professional
.5	General works
.515	Special leagues, conferences, divisions, etc.
	By name, A-Z
.52	Individual clubs. By place, A-Z
.55	Rules. Records. Programs. Schedules
.59	Championship contests, special games, etc., A-Z
	By region or country
	United States
.7	General works
.72	By region or state, A-Z
.73	By city, A-Z
.8	Other regions or countries, A-Z
886	Girls' basketball
	Other special topics
888	Defensive play
889	Offensive play
.6	Netball

RECREATION. LEISURE

<pre>
              Sports
                Ball games
                  Football games
                    Special games
                      Rugby - Continued
945.5   International contests
    .55   Special leagues, conferences, etc. By name, A-Z
    .6   Individual clubs, teams, etc. By name, A-Z
    .7   In special institutions, A-Z
    .75   Coaching
    .8   Training
    .9   By region or country, A-Z
947   Australian football
                        For biography, see GV939
948   Canadian football
                        For biography, see GV939
    .5   Florentine football
                        For biography, see GV939
                      American football
                        Periodicals. Societies. Serials, see GV937
950   History
                        Biography, see GV939
    .5   Light literature
    .6   Spectator's guides. How to enjoy the game
                          as a spectator
    .7   Juvenile works
                        General works
951   Strategies and techniques. Playbooks
    .15   General works
    .18   Defensive play (General)
    .2   Line play
    .25   End play
    .3   Backfield play. Quarterbacking
    .5   Passing
    .7   Kicking. Punting
    .8   Offensive play (General)
    .9   T formation
    .95   Wingback formation
                        Variants, etc.
952   Touch football
953   Six-man football
    .4   Selection of players. Scouting
    .5   Training
    .6   Safety measures
                        Professional
                          History
954   General works
    .2   By season
                                Subdivided by date, e. g.
                                  GV954.2 1970 (by author, A-Z)
                            General works, see GV954
    .3   Financial and business aspects
    .35   Officiating
    .4   Coaching
955   Rules. Records. Programs. Schedules
    .5   Special leagues, conferences, divisions,
                              etc. By name, A-Z
956   Individual clubs, teams, etc. By name, A-Z
    .2   Special games, A-Z
                              .S8 Super Bowl game
</pre>

RECREATION. LEISURE

Sports
  Ball games
    Football games
      Special games
        American football - Continued
          Amateur
            History, see GV950

956.3	By season
	Subdivided by date, e. g.
	GV956.3 1970 (by author, A-Z)
	General works, see GV951
.4	Financial and business aspects
.6	Coaching
.8	Rules. Records. Programs. Schedules
957	Special games, A-Z
	.B55 Blue-Gray game
	.R6 Rose Bowl game
	.S5 Shrine East-West game
	.S8 Sugar Bowl game
958	In special institutions, A-Z
.5	Special conferences, etc. By name, A-Z
959	Miscellaneous topics (not A-Z)
960	Other football games, A-Z
	.B4 Beeball

Golf

961	Periodicals. Societies. Serials
962	Directories
963	History
	Biography
964.A1A-Z	Collective
.A2-Z	Individual, A-Z
	e. g. .J6 Jones, Robert ("Bobby Jones")
965	General works
966	Women's playing
967	Light literature
969	Associations, clubs, etc. By name, A-Z
	Cf. HS2581, Country clubs
	e. g. .R6 Royal and Ancient Golf Club
	of St. Andrews
	.W5 Western Golf Association
970	Tournaments, etc.
	e. g. Canadian Open
971	Scorebooks, scoring, rules, etc.
	Special topics
975	Golf courses, greens, etc.
976	Other equipment
977	Caddies
979	Other special topics, A-Z
	.E9 Exercises
	.G7 Grip
	.H3 Hand action
	.P7 Professionals
	.P75 Psychological aspects
	.P8 Putting
	.S9 Swing
	.T7 Trophies

RECREATION. LEISURE

<u>Sports</u>
  <u>Ball games</u>
    <u>Tennis and related games</u> - Continued

1005.5	Tamburello
1006	Paddle tennis

        Including playground paddle tennis
          and platform paddle tennis
      Paddleball, <u>see</u> GV1017.P17
      Handball, <u>see</u> GV1017.H2

1007	Badminton

    <u>Polo</u>
      Cf. GV839, Water polo
         GV859.7, Roller polo
         GV1017.W6, Wicket polo
         GV1058, Bicycle polo

1010	Periodicals. Societies. Serials
1011	General works
1017	Other ball games, A-Z
	.A5 America
	.B33 Battle ball
	.B4 Belle coquette. Lawn billiards
	.C4 Cercle
	.C45 Changers
	.C5 Chivalrie
	.D5 Dix
	.F5 Fieldball. Field handball
	.H2 Handball. Fives
	.H7 Hockey. Field hockey

         Cf. GV846+, Ice hockey
           GV1099, Ring hockey

	.H8 Hurling
	Jai alai, <u>see</u> .P4
	.K3 Kang
	.K4 Kemari
	.L3 Lapta
	Lawn billiards, <u>see</u> .B4
	.L48 Lawn tempest
	Medicine ball, <u>see</u> GV496
	.M6 Minton
	.N4 Newcomb
	.N7 Nine pockets
	.P17 Paddleball
	.P3 Pato
	.P4 Pelota. Jai alai
	.P5 Pize-ball
	.P7 Po-lo-lo
	.P9 Pushball
	.R3 Racquetball
	.R6 Rounders
	.R9 Ruse
	.S2 Schlagball
	.S3 School
	.S5 Silver chimes
	.S58 Speed-a-way
	.S6 Speedball
	.S7 Sphero
	.S8 Stoolball
	.T27 Balle au tamis
	.T3 Tan-to
	.T7 Trapball
	.V6 Volleyball

RECREATION. LEISURE

<u>Sports</u> - Continued
1035   Sailing on land. Sand yachting
                 <u>Cycling. Bicycling</u>
                     Cf. TL400+, Cycles
1040   Periodicals. Serials
   .5   History
1041   General works
1043   Light literature
   .5   Juvenile works
   .7   General special
                 <u>Bicycle hiking, touring, etc.</u>
1044   General works
                     Tour guide books. Route books
                         Class here technical works only; for descriptive
                             works of travel in particular places, <u>see</u> D - F
                         United States
1045   General works
   .5   By region or state, A-Z
1046   Other regions or countries, A-Z
                 Clubs
   .9   Collective
1047   Individual. By name, A-Z
                         e. g. .L4 League of American Wheelmen
                                .W3 Washington Cycling Club, Chicago
1048   Training for cycling
1049   Racing
                     Including six-day bicycle races, Tour de
                         France, etc.
                 Biography
1051.A1A-Z   Collective
    .A2-Z   Individual, A-Z
1053   Records, etc.
1054   Equipment, costume, etc.
1055   Safety measures
1057   Cycling for women
1058   Bicycle polo
                 <u>Motorcycling</u>
                     Cf. TL440+, Motorcycles
1059.5   General works
                 Racing
1060   General works
   .13   Racing on ice
   .15   Motorcycle soccer
   .2   Biography
                     .A1A-Z Collective
                     .A2-Z   Individual, A-Z
                 <u>Track and field athletics</u>
                     For special contests and meets, <u>see</u> GV721+
   .5   General works
                 By region or country
                     United States
   .6   General works
   .62   By region or state, A-Z
   .65   Other regions or countries, A-Z
   .67   Rules, records, etc.
   .7   All-round athletics. Decathlon. Pentathlon
   .8   Women's track

RECREATION.   LEISURE

        <u>Sports</u>
          <u>Track and field athletics</u> - Continued
            <u>Foot racing.   Running</u>

1061	General works
.5	Training
	<u>Distance running</u>
1062	General works
1063	Cross-country runs
	Cf. GV200.4, Orientation
1065	Marathon running
1066	Relay races
1067	Hurdle racing
1069	Sprinting
1071	Walking
	Cf. GV199+, Walking as recreation
	<u>Jumping</u>
	Cf. GV529, Exercises
1073	General works
1075	High jump
1077	Broad jump. Long jump
1078	Triple jump. Hop, step, and jump
	Vaulting
1079	General works
1080	Pole vaulting
	<u>Throwing games and sports</u>
	Cf. GV861+, Ball games
1091	General works
	<u>Weight throwing</u>
1093	General works
	Biography
.9	Collective
1094	Individual, A-Z
.3	Discus throwing
.5	Hammer throwing
.6	Javelin throwing
.8	Shot-putting
1095	Quoits. Horseshoe pitching
1096	Knife throwing
1097	Other throwing games, A-Z
.B7	Brist
	Darts, <u>see</u> GV1565
.F7	Frisbee
.R5	Ringtoss
1098	Tug of war
1099	Other athletic sports
	e. g. Ring hockey, shuffleboard, stilt walking
	<u>Fighting sports</u>
1101	General works
	<u>Animal fighting</u>
1103	General works
1105	Bear and badger baiting
	<u>Bullfighting</u>
	Cf. SF199.F5, Fighting bull culture
1107	General works
.5	Pictorial works
	Biography
1108.A1A-Z	Collective
.A2-Z	Individual, A-Z
.2	Costume
.4	Running to the pens. El encierro

```
                  Sports
                    Fighting sports
                      Animal fighting - Continued
                        Cockfighting, see SF503
1109                    Dogfighting
                      Human fighting.  Hand-to-hand fighting
                        Including self defense
                        Cf. GV35, Gladiators
1111                    General works
    .5                  Self defense for women
                        Oriental hand-to-hand fighting
1112                      General works
                          Biography
1113.A2A-Z                  Collective
    .A3-Z                    Individual, A-Z
1114                        Jiu-jitsu.  Judo
    .3                      Karate
                              Cf. GV1142.6, Nunchaku
                                  GV1150.6, Sai
    .7                      Kempo
                        Boxing.  Prize fighting
                          Cf. HV6733, Gambling in prize fighting
1115                      Periodicals.  Serials
1116                      Rules and regulations.  By country, A-Z
1117                      Clubs
1118                      Dictionaries.  Encyclopedias
                          History
1121                        General works
1123                        England
1125                        United States
1127                        Other regions or countries, A-Z
                          Biography
1131                        Collective
1132                        Individual, A-Z
                              e. g.  .L6  Louis, Joe
                                     .S95 Sullivan, John
1133                      General works
1135                      Light literature
1136                      Juvenile works
    .5                    Moral and religious aspects
1137                      Records.  Programs.  Schedules
    .3                    Refereeing.  Judging
    .6                    Training
                        Stick fighting
1141                      General works
    .2                    Single stick, quarter staff, etc.
                          Kendo
    .3                      Study and teaching
    .5                      History
                            Biography
    .7                        Collective
    .72                       Individual, A-Z
1142                        General works
    .4                      Pictorial works
    .6                    Nunchaku
```

RECREATION. LEISURE

Sports
　Fighting sports
　　Human fighting. Hand-to-hand fighting - Continued
　　　Fencing
　　　　Class here general works on western or
　　　　　European fencing including fencing
　　　　　with foils
　　　　Cf. PN2071.F4, Stage fencing
　　　　　U850+, Swords and daggers (Military science)

1143	Periodicals. Societies. Serials
.15	Congresses
.2	Dictionaries. Encyclopedias
.4	Study and teaching
.6	History
	Biography
1144	Collective
.2	Individual, A-Z
	General works
1145	Early through 1800
1146	1801-1900
1147	1901-
1148	Pictorial works
	Cf. N8217.F4, Fencing in art
.4	Addresses, essays, lectures
1149	Rules. Records, etc.
	Special
	Oriental fencing
1150	General works
.4	Naginata
.6	Sai
	Dueling, see CR4571+
	Wrestling, see GV1195

　　Shooting
　　　Cf. SK37+, Hunting sports

1151	Periodicals. Serials
1152	Dictionaries. Encyclopedias
1153	General works
	Biography
1156	Collective
1157	Individual, A-Z
	e. g. .03 Oakley, Annie
1163	Clubs (Rifle, revolver, etc.)
	Contests
1167	International
	United States
1169	National. Interstate
1171	Local, A-Z
1172	Other regions or countries, A-Z
1173	Scores, scorebooks, rules, etc.

　　　Guns and pistols
　　　　Cf. TS535+, Gun making
　　　　　UD380+, Infantry firearms
　　　　　UE400+, Cavalry firearms

1174	General works
1175	Pistols and revolvers
	Cf. GT4990, Christmas shooting
	UD410+, Military science
1177	Rifles
	Cf. UD390+, Military science
1179	Shotguns

Games and amusements - Continued
    Children's games and amusements
        Cf. GV182.9, Recreation, play, for children
           LB3031, School games
      History, see GV1200

1203	General works
1204	By region or country (Table I)[1]
	Games for special classes of children
.3	Boys
.4	Girls
	Handicapped children, see LC4026
	Invalids, see GV1231
	Mentally handicapped children, see LC4611
1205	Children's parties

        Class here general works on children's parties,
           including menus, decorations, costumes, games,
           etc. For works consisting solely of party
           games, see GV1203+

1206	Auto games. Games for travelers
1207	Chasing games, blindman's buff, etc.
	Counting-out rhymes, see GR485
1211	Kissing games
1213	Marbles
1215	Singing and dancing games

        Cf. GV1771, Play-party
           LB1177, Songs, games, etc., in kindergarten
           M1993, Action and drill songs in schools

1216	Games of skill and action
	e. g. Diablo
1217	How to play Indians. Scouting games, etc.
1218	Other, A-Z
.B6	Building with blocks, etc.
	Circuses, Children's, see GV1838
.C7	Cutting out pictures
.F5	Finger games
.M3	Masks
.P3	Paper work
.P5	Pinatas
.S5	Shodow pictures
.S8	String figures
	Cf. GN455.S9, Ethnology
.T5	Tops
.T55	Toy soldiers

    Toys
        Cf. GN799.T7, Prehistoric toys
           LB1029.T6, Educational toys
           NK9509+, Decorative arts
           TS2301.T7, Toy manufacture
           TT174+, Handicrafts

.5	General works
	Dolls
	Cf. NK4892+, Decorative arts
1219	General works
1220	Dollhouses
	Cf. NK4892+, Decorative arts
.7	Teddy bears

----

[1]
  For Table I, see pp. 380-381

RECREATION. LEISURE

Games and amusements - Continued
Indoor games and amusements
Cf. GV1470+, Party games and stunts
1221	Museums. Exhibitions
	History
1223	General works
1225	By region or country, A-Z
	General works
1227	Through 1800
1229	1801-
1231	Games for invalids, shut-ins, etc.
	Cf. RJ242, Children in hospitals
	Card games
1232	Dictionaries. Encyclopedias
1233	History
1235	Collections of playing cards. Illustrations of old cards
	Including playing card collecting
1236	Museum catalogs. By city and museum, A-Z
1239	Light literature
	General works
	Including Hoyle's rules
1241	Through 1800
1243	1801-
1244	Juvenile works
1245	Ethics of card playing
1247	Card sharping. Beating the game. Gamblers' tricks
	Cf. HV6708+, Criminology
	Card tricks in parlor magic, etc., see GV1549
	Cartomancy: fortune-telling by cards, see BF1876+
1249	Euchre
	Poker
1251	General works
1253	Light literature
1257	Skat
1261	Solitaire. Patience
	Whist
1271	Periodicals. Societies. Serials
1273	Congresses
	Biography
1274.9	Collective
1275	Individual, A-Z
1277	General works
	Bridge (Bridge whist)
1281.A1A-Z	Periodicals. Societies. Serials
.A4-Z	General works
.5	Light literature
1282	Auction bridge
.3	Contract bridge
.7	Solitaire bridge
.9	Other, A-Z
1283	Duplicate whist
1285	Progressive whist
1287	Short whist
1289	Solo whist. Boston

RECREATION. LEISURE

Games and amusements
Indoor games and amusements
Card games
Whist - Continued
1291   Other varieties, A-Z
.A8 Auction whist
.D7 Drive whist
.L7 Living whist
.P8 Preference. Swedish whist
.S6 Social whist
.T8 Triplicate whist
1295   Other card games, A-Z
Argentine rummy, see .C2
.A8 Auction piquet
.B3 Baccarat
Basket rummy, see .C2
.B5 Bezique
.B55 Blackjack
.C15 Calypso
.C2 Canasta
Cf. GV1295.S3, Samba
Cinch, see .P3
.C6 Cooncan (Conquian)
.C9 Cribbage
.E3 Écarté
.F5 Five hundred
.F6 Football poker
.F7 Forty-five
Gin rummy, see .R8
.H4 Hearts
High five, see .P3
.H6 Hollywood bridge
.J3 Jass
.O4 Oklahoma
.O5 Ombre (Quadrille)
.P17 Panguingue (Pan)
.P3 Pedro (Cinch, High five)
.P6 Pinochle
.P7 Piquet
.R8 Rummy (Gin rummy)
.R9 Russian bank
.S3 Samba
.S4 Scopa
.S6 Solo-sixty
.T7 Tressette
1297   Game counters, score sheets, etc.
1299   Games with other than regulation cards, A-Z
.I7 Iroha karuta
.M3 Mah jong
.M6 Money game
.R6 Rook
Lotteries, see HG6105+
Gambling. Chance and banking games
Cf. HV6708+, Criminology
1301   General works
1302   Probabilities, betting systems, etc.
1303   Dice and dice games
1305   Faro
1306   Keno
1307   Monte
1308   Trente et quarante. Rouge et noir

RECREATION. LEISURE

Games and amusements
  Indoor games and amusements
    Gambling. Chance and banking games - Continued

1309	Roulette
1311	Other, A-Z
	.B5 Bingo
	.L6 Lotto
	.P5 Pinball machines
	.T73 Triboulet
	Board games. Move games
1312	General works
	Chess
	Cf. NK4696, Chessmen
1313	Periodicals. Serials
1314	Societies, clubs, etc.
.5	Dictionaries. Encyclopedias
	History
1315	Collected works (nonserial)
1317	General works
1318	General special
	By period
1319	Origin
1320	Middle Ages through 1600
1321	1601-1850
1322	1851-
	By region or country
	United States
1323	General works
1325	By city, A-Z
1330	Other regions or countries, A-Z
	Biography
1438	Collective
1439	Individual, A-Z
	Also class here the collected games of individual players, treating such works as autobiographies, e. g. .F5A3, Fischer, Bobby. Games of chess
	General works
1442	Early to Philidor
1444	Philidor (1726-1795) to Tarrash, 1894
1445	1894-
1446	Chess for beginners. Juvenile works
1447	Miscellany and curiosa
1448	Psychology
1449	Light literature. Wit and humor
	Strategies and tactics
.5	General works
	Openings
1450	General works
.2	Individual openings, A-Z
.3	Middle games. Combinations
.7	End games. Studies
1451	Problems
.2	Fairy chess
.5	Moves of particular men, A-Z
	.K5 King
	.K6 Knight
	.P3 Pawn
1452	Collections of games
	For the collected games of an individual player, see GV1439

Games and amusements
   Parties. Party games and stunts
      Puzzles

1507	Other, A-Z - Continued
	.S9 Syzygies
	.T3 Tangrams
	.T47 Tic-tac-toe
	.T5 Time games
	.W8 Word games and puzzles
	.W9 Word lists
1511	Other party games, A-Z
1521	Miniature theaters
	For marionettes, Punch and Judy shows,
	etc., see PN1970+

Parlor magic and tricks
   Including conjuring, juggling, etc.
   Cf. BF1405+, Occult sciences
      Q164, Scientific recreations

1541	Periodicals. Societies. Serials
1542	Collected works (nonserial)
.5	Dictionaries. Encyclopedias
1543	History
	Biography
1545.A2A-Z	Collective
.A3-Z	Individual, A-Z
	e. g. .H6 Herrmann, Carl
	.H8 Houdini, Harry
	.R7 Robert-Houdin, Jean Eugène
	.T5 Thurston, Howard
	General works
1546	Through 1800
1547	1801-
1548	Juvenile works
1549	Card tricks
	Cf. GV1247, Card sharping, gamblers' tricks
	Fortune-telling, see BF1845+
1553	Second sight, mind reading, etc.
	Shadow pictures, see GV1218.S5
	Slate writing, see BF1343
1555	Sleight of hand
1556	Pocket tricks
1557	Ventriloquism
1559	Other tricks (not A-Z)
	e. g. Tricks with balls, cigarettes, coins,
	hats, matchsticks, paper, rope, etc.
1560	Magic patents
1561	Magicians' supplies, etc.
1565	Darts
1570	Model car racing

RECREATION. LEISURE

DANCING

Cf. HV1664.D3, Education of
the blind
ML3400+, Music
RC489.D3, Dance therapy
RJ505.D3, Dance therapy
(Pediatrics)

1580	Periodicals. Societies. Serials
1583	Congresses
1585	Dictionaries. Encyclopedias
1587	Terminology. Abbreviations. Notation
	Philosophy. Relation to other topics
1588	General works
.3	Relation to aesthetics
.4	Relation to education
	Relation to ethics, see GV1740+
.5	Relation to psychology
.6	Relation to society
	Study and teaching, see GV1753.5+; GV1788
	General works
1590	Early through 1850
1593	1851-1974
1594	1975-
1595	General special (Special aspects of the subject as a whole)
1596	Pictorial works
.5	Juvenile works
	Cf. GV1799, Children's dances
1597	Dancing as a profession
1599	Addresses, essays, lectures
1600	Dance criticism. Appreciation
	History
	General works
	Early through 1850, see GV1590
1601	1851-
1603	General special
1605	Preliterate (General)
	For particular ethnic groups in particular countries, see the country, GV1621+
	By period
	Ancient
1607	General works
1609	Oriental
1611	Classical
	Cf. GV1783, Revival of classical dancing
1613	Other ancient. Egyptian, etc.
1615	Medieval
	Modern
1617	General works
1618	15th-18th centuries
1619	19th-20th centuries

RECREATION. LEISURE

Dancing
  History
    By region or country
      Europe - Continued

1675-1676	Portugal
1677-1678	Switzerland
	Balkan States
1679	General works
1681-1682	Bulgaria
1685-1686	Romania
1687-1687.5	Yugoslavia
1688	Other European regions or countries, A-Z

          e. g. .C9-92 Czechoslovakia
                .F5-52 Finland
                .H8-82 Hungary

      Asia

1689	General works
1691-1692	China
1693-1694	India
1695-1696	Japan
1697-1698	Iran
1699-1700	Russia in Asia. Siberia
1701-1702	Turkey. Asia Minor
1703	Other Asian regions or countries, A-Z

          e. g. .B95-952 Burma
                .C3-32   Cambodia
                .I5-52   Indochina
                .I53-532 Indonesia
                .I75-752 Israel

      Africa

1705	General works
1709-1710	Egypt

          Cf. GV1613, Ancient Egyptian dancing

1713	Other African regions or countries, A-Z
1715-1716	Australia
1719-1720	New Zealand
	Pacific islands
1727	General works
1728	By island or group of islands, A-Z

          For Hawaii, see GV1624

1735	Apparatus and equipment
	Ethics. Dancing and the Church
1740	Early works through 1800
1741	1801-
1743	National dances. Folk dances and dancing (General)

          Cf. GT3930+, Festivals, holidays (Manners and customs)
             PN3203+, Spectacles, tableaux, pageants, etc.
          For individual countries, see GV1621+. For
            special dances, see GV1796

Social dancing. Ballroom dancing
  Balls. Dance parties
    Including college proms, school dances, etc.
    Cf. GV1757, Cotillion
        PN1992.8.D3, Television dance parties
    For local history, see D - F

1746	General works
1747	Court and state balls, etc.
1748	Public balls
1749	Mask and fancy-dress balls
1750	Programs, german cards, etc.

RECREATION. LEISURE

<u>Dancing</u>
    Social dancing. Ballroom dancing - Continued
      <u>Technique (General)</u>

1751	General works
1753	General special
	e. g. Revival of old dances
	Study and teaching. Research
.5	General works
1754	Individual schools, A-Z
	<u>Round dances</u>
1755	General works
1757	German. Cotillion
	Special dances
1761	Waltz
	Other, <u>see</u> GV1796
	<u>Square dances. Quadrilles. Country dances</u>
1763	General works
1767	Call books
	Special dances, <u>see</u> GV1796
1771	Play-party
1779	Dancing in motion pictures, television, etc.
	Cf. PN1992.8.D3, Television dance parties
	<u>Theatrical dancing</u>
1781	General works
1782	Production and staging
	For costumes, <u>see</u> GT1740+
.3	Safety measures. Accident prevention
	Cf. GV1789, Ballet
.5	Choreography
1783	Modern or expressionistic dancing. Revival of
	classical dancing
.5	Religious dancing
	Incidental dances in specific dramas, <u>see</u>
	PA - PS, e. g. PR3034, Shakespeare
	Biography
1785.A1A-Z	Collective
.A2-Z	Individual, A-Z
	e. g. .D5 Diagilev, Sergei
	.D8 Duncan, Isadora
	.F63 Fonteyn, Margot
	.L5 Lifar, Serge
	.N6 Nijinsky, Waslaw
	.P3 Pavlova, Anna
1786	Special groups or companies. By name, A-Z
	<u>Ballet</u>
	Cf. ML3460, Ballet music (History and criticism)
	Dictionaries. Encyclopedias, <u>see</u> GV1585
	Biography, <u>see</u> GV1785
1787	General works
.5	Juvenile works
.6	Addresses, essays, lectures. Light literature
1788	Technique. Instruction
1789	Safety measures. Accident prevention
	Ballets
	Cf. ML520+, Music scores
	ML52, Librettos
1790.A1A-Z	Collected
	Class here individual ballets
	discussed collectively
.A3-Z	Individual. By title
	e. g. .G5 Giselle
	.R4 Red Shoes Ballet

Dancing
 Theatrical dancing - Continued
1791   Buck and wing
1793   Clog and jig
1794   Tap dancing
1795   Miscellaneous theatrical dances (not A-Z)
1796   Special dances, A-Z
    .B25 Bailecito
    .B3 Baseda
    .B4 Bharata Natyam
    .C13 Calandria
    .C14 Candombe
       Cante hondo, see .F55
    .C2 Cha-cha
    .C39 Chamarrita
    .C4 Charleston
    .C57 Condición
    .C6 Conga
    .E8 Escondido
    .F55 Flamenco. Cante hondo
    .F6 Fox trot
    .F7 Frevo
    .H2 Halling
    .H75 Huella
    .H8 Hula
    .J6 Jitterbug
       Kagura, see BL2224.25.K3
    .K6 Kolo
    .K7 Krakowiak
    .L5 Lindy
    .M32 Manzai
    .M33 Margamkali
    .M34 Mariquita
       Maypole, see GT4945
    .M36 Maxixe
    .M45 Merengue
    .M5 Minuet
    .M7 Morris dance
    .P24 Pajarillo
    .P55 Polka
    .R3 Rapper
    .R6 Rock and roll
    .R8 Rumba
    .S23 Sajuriana
    .S25 Samba
    .S3 Sardana
    .S9 Sword dance
    .T2 Tamunangue
    .T3 Tango
    .T9 Two-step
       Waltz, see GV1761
1797   Drills, parades, etc.
     Cf. GV495, Marching (Calisthenics)
   Gymnastic dancing. Rhythmic exercises
1798   General works
 .5   Belly dancing
1799 Children's dances. Dances for schools

RECREATION. LEISURE

CIRCUSES, SPECTACLES, ETC.

<u>Circuses</u>
1800	Periodicals. Societies. Serials
	History
1801	General works
	By region or country
1803	United States
1805	Other regions or countries, A-Z
1807	Museums. Exhibitions
1808	Vocational guidance
	Biography
	Including circus clowns
1811.A1A-Z	Collective
.A2-Z	Individual, A-Z

     e. g. .B3 Barnum, P.T.
       .F7 Fratellini Brothers
       .H2 Hagenbeck, Carl

1815	General works
1816	Pictorial works
1817	Juvenile works
1818	Addresses, essays, lectures. Light literature
1821	Special shows, A-Z
	Including circulars, programs, etc.

     e. g. .B8 Buffalo Bill's Wild West Show
       .H3 Hagenbeck-Wallace Circus
       .R5 Ringling Brothers and Barnum and
          Bailey Circus

	Equipment and supplies
1823	Wagons
	Management, conduct, etc.
1825	General works
1826	General special
1827	Collecting living animals for exhibition purposes
	Cf. QL61+, Zoological specimens
1828	Clowning. Clown acts
	For biography of clowns, <u>see</u> GV1811

<u>Training of animals</u>
1829	General works
1831	Special. By name of animal, A-Z
	.B4 Bear
	.E4 Elephant
	.H8 Horse
	.L5 Lion
	.P6 Pig
1833	Wild West shows
	For special shows, <u>see</u> GV1821

<u>Rodeos</u>
1834	General works
.5	Local. By city, A-Z
	e. g. .C3 Calgary, Alta. Calgary Stampede
1835	Carnivals. Side shows. Freaks, wonders, etc.
	Including biographies of freaks
	Cf. QM690+, Teratology (Human anatomy)
1836	Waxworks
	e. g. Madame Tussaud's
	Cf. NK9580+, Wax modeling
1838	Amateur circuses, carnivals, etc.

RECREATION. LEISURE

Circuses, spectacles, etc. - Continued
    Spectacles, "Son et lumière", etc.
        Cf. GT3930+, Festivals, carnivals, Mardi gras
           PN3203+, Tableaux, pageants, "Happenings", etc.
           (Dramatic representation)
        For local history, <u>see</u> D - F

1841	General works
1843	Local. By city, A-Z

    Amusement parks, resorts, gardens, etc.

1851.A3A-Z	Periodicals. Societies. Serials
.A35A-Z	History
.A4-Z	General works
1853	Local. By city, etc., A-Z
	e. g. .C6 Coney Island, N.Y.
	.C62 Coney Island Amusement Park, Ohio
	.D5 Disneyland
1860	Amusement devices, A-Z
	.M4 Merry-go-round

TABLES OF GEOGRAPHICAL SUBDIVISIONS

I   II

COUNTRY SUBDIVISIONS

.01	America	
.12	United States[1]	
.13	By region or state, A-Z	
.15	Canada	29-30
.16	Mexico	31-32
.17	Central America	33
.18	British Honduras	35-36
.19	Costa Rica	37-38
.2	Guatemala	39-40
.21	Nicaragua	41-41.5
.215	Panama	42-42.5
.22	Salvador	43-43.5
.23	West Indies	45
.24	Bahamas	47-48
.25	Cuba	49-50
.26	Haiti	51-52
.27	Jamaica	53-54
.28	Puerto Rico	55-56
.29	Other islands, A-Z	57
.3	South America	58
.31	Argentina	59-60
.32	Bolivia	61-62
.33	Brazil	63-64
.34	Chile	65-66
.35	Colombia	67-68
.36	Ecuador	69-70
.365	French Guiana	70.5-.6
.37	Guyana	71-72
.38	Paraguay	73-74
.39	Peru	75-76
.395	Surinam	76.5-.6
.4	Uruguay	77-78
.41	Venezuela	79-80
.42	Europe	81
.425	Special regions, international bodies of water, A-Z	82
.43	Great Britain	83
.44	England	85-86
.45	Scotland	87-88
.46	Northern Ireland	89-89.5
.465	Wales	90-90.5
.467	Ireland	90.7-.8
.47	Austria	91-92
	Belgium, see Low Countries	
	Denmark, see Scandinavia	
.48	France	93-94
.49	Germany	95-96
	Including West Germany	
.495	East Germany	96.5-.6

---

[1]
    Unless otherwise provided for

TABLES OF GEOGRAPHICAL SUBDIVISIONS

<table>
<thead>
<tr><th>I</th><th></th><th>II</th></tr>
</thead>
<tbody>
<tr><td></td><td>Europe - Continued</td><td></td></tr>
<tr><td>.5</td><td>Greece ——————————————————————————————</td><td>97–98</td></tr>
<tr><td>.51</td><td>Italy ——————————————————————————————</td><td>99–100</td></tr>
<tr><td>.52</td><td>Low Countries ——————————————————————</td><td>101</td></tr>
<tr><td>.53</td><td>Belgium ————————————————————————————</td><td>103–104</td></tr>
<tr><td>.54</td><td>Netherlands ————————————————————————</td><td>105–106</td></tr>
<tr><td></td><td>Norway, see Scandinavia</td><td></td></tr>
<tr><td>.55</td><td>Russia —————————————————————————————</td><td>107–108</td></tr>
<tr><td></td><td>For Siberia, see Russia in Asia</td><td></td></tr>
<tr><td>.56</td><td>Scandinavia ————————————————————————</td><td>109</td></tr>
<tr><td>.57</td><td>Denmark—————————————————————————————</td><td>111–112</td></tr>
<tr><td>.58</td><td>Iceland ————————————————————————————</td><td>113–114</td></tr>
<tr><td>.59</td><td>Norway —————————————————————————————</td><td>115–116</td></tr>
<tr><td>.6</td><td>Sweden —————————————————————————————</td><td>117–118</td></tr>
<tr><td>.61</td><td>Spain ——————————————————————————————</td><td>119–120</td></tr>
<tr><td>.62</td><td>Portugal ———————————————————————————</td><td>121–122</td></tr>
<tr><td></td><td>Sweden, see Scandinavia</td><td></td></tr>
<tr><td>.63</td><td>Switzerland ————————————————————————</td><td>123–124</td></tr>
<tr><td>.635</td><td>Balkan States ——————————————————————</td><td>124.5</td></tr>
<tr><td>.65</td><td>Bulgaria ———————————————————————————</td><td>127–128</td></tr>
<tr><td>.66</td><td>Romania ————————————————————————————</td><td>129–130</td></tr>
<tr><td>.67</td><td>Yugoslavia —————————————————————————</td><td>131–132</td></tr>
<tr><td>.68</td><td>Other divisions of Europe, A–Z —————</td><td>133</td></tr>
<tr><td>.69</td><td>Asia ———————————————————————————————</td><td>135</td></tr>
<tr><td>.7</td><td>China ——————————————————————————————</td><td>137–138</td></tr>
<tr><td>.71</td><td>India ——————————————————————————————</td><td>139–140</td></tr>
<tr><td>.72</td><td>Southeast Asia —————————————————————</td><td>141</td></tr>
<tr><td>.73</td><td>Vietnam ————————————————————————————</td><td>143–144</td></tr>
<tr><td>.74</td><td>Indonesia ——————————————————————————</td><td>145–146</td></tr>
<tr><td>.76</td><td>Philippine Islands —————————————————</td><td>149–150</td></tr>
<tr><td>.77</td><td>Japan ——————————————————————————————</td><td>151–152</td></tr>
<tr><td>.78</td><td>Iran ———————————————————————————————</td><td>153–154</td></tr>
<tr><td>.79</td><td>Russia in Asia. Siberia ——————————</td><td>155–156</td></tr>
<tr><td>.795</td><td>Taiwan —————————————————————————————</td><td>156.5–.52</td></tr>
<tr><td>.8</td><td>Turkey. Asia Minor ————————————————</td><td>157–158</td></tr>
<tr><td>.81</td><td>Other divisions of Asia, A–Z ———————</td><td>159</td></tr>
<tr><td>.82</td><td>Africa —————————————————————————————</td><td>161</td></tr>
<tr><td>.83</td><td>Egypt ——————————————————————————————</td><td>163–164</td></tr>
<tr><td>.84</td><td>South Africa ———————————————————————</td><td>165–166</td></tr>
<tr><td>.85</td><td>Algeria ————————————————————————————</td><td>167–168</td></tr>
<tr><td>.86</td><td>Tanzania ———————————————————————————</td><td>169–170</td></tr>
<tr><td>.87</td><td>Angola —————————————————————————————</td><td>171–172</td></tr>
<tr><td>.88</td><td>Other African divisions, A–Z ——————</td><td>173</td></tr>
<tr><td></td><td>e. g.   .E7   Ethiopia</td><td></td></tr>
<tr><td></td><td>   .Z3   Zaire</td><td></td></tr>
<tr><td></td><td>   .Z36   Zambia</td><td></td></tr>
<tr><td>.89</td><td>Australia ——————————————————————————</td><td>175–176</td></tr>
<tr><td>.91</td><td>New Zealand ————————————————————————</td><td>179–180</td></tr>
<tr><td>.98</td><td>Pacific islands, A–Z ———————————————</td><td>193</td></tr>
<tr><td>.99</td><td>Arctic regions —————————————————————</td><td>195–196</td></tr>
<tr><td>.993</td><td>Greenland ——————————————————————————</td><td>196.5–.6</td></tr>
<tr><td>.995</td><td>Antarctic regions ——————————————————</td><td>197–198
or
197–197.5</td></tr>
</tbody>
</table>

TABLE III

STATES IN THE UNITED STATES

Alabama	.A2	Montana	.M9
Alaska	.A4	Nebraska	.N2
Arizona	.A6	Nevada	.N3
Arkansas	.A8	New Hampshire	.N4
California	.C2	New Jersey	.N5
Colorado	.C6	New Mexico	.N6
Connecticut	.C8	New York	.N7
Delaware	.D3	North Carolina	.N8
District of Columbia	.D6	North Dakota	.N9
Florida	.F6	Ohio	.O3
Georgia	.G4	Oklahoma	.O5
Hawaii	.H3	Oregon	.O7
Idaho	.I2	Pennsylvania	.P4
Illinois	.I3	Rhode Island	.R4
Indiana	.I6	South Carolina	.S6
Iowa	.I8	South Dakota	.S8
Kansas	.K2	Tennessee	.T2
Kentucky	.K4	Texas	.T4
Louisiana	.L8	Utah	.U8
Maine	.M2	Vermont	.V5
Maryland	.M3	Virginia	.V8
Massachusetts	.M4	Washington	.W2
Michigan	.M5	West Virginia	.W4
Minnesota	.M6	Wisconsin	.W6
Mississippi	.M7	Wyoming	.W8
Missouri	.M8		

TABLE IV

REGIONS (UNITED STATES)

.A1-19	Regions
.A11	New England
.A115	Northeastern States
.A12	Middle Atlantic States
.A124	Potomac Valley
.A13	South
.A135	Tennessee Valley
.A137	Osark Mountain region
.A14	North Central States
	Including Great Lakes region and Old Northwest
.A145	Northwestern States
.A15	Mississippi Valley
.A16	Ohio Valley
.A165	Southwest
.A17	West
.A172	Missouri Valley
.A175	Pacific Southwest
.A18	Pacific coast
.A19	Pacific Northwest
.A195	Columbia Valley

INDEX

Geographic names are indexed only for the atlases and maps sections (G1001-9980) and with the following limitation: for the United States, Canada, and Great Britain entries have been made for the states, provinces, constituent countries, and larger regions; for the rest of the world the index includes only names of countries and larger or international regions

A

Abbreviations (Cartography): GA102.2
Abortion (Ethnology): GN482.4
Abyssinia, see Ethiopia
Accessories (Costume): GT2050+
Accident prevention, see Safety measures
Accreditation (Camps): GV198.A38
Acculturation (Ethnology): GN366+
Acheulian culture
  By continent, see table below GN772.2+, e. g. GN772.4.A53 (Africa)
Achievement scales and standards (Physical education and training): GV436+
Acoustic properties
  of
    marine sediments: GC380.2.A25
Acrobatics: GV551+
  Skiing: GV854.9.A25
Action, Children's games of: GV1216
Adamus Bremensis: G69.A2
Aden, see Yemen (People's Democratic Republic)
Administration (Camps): GV198.A4
Adolescence
  Ethnology: GN483+
  Human variation: GN63
  Manners and customs: GT2485+
Adoption (Ethnology): GN482.3
Adornment (Ethnology): GN418+
Adulthood (Ethnology): GN484.2+
Adventure and adventurers: G521+
Adventure playgrounds: GV424
Advocates, see Lawyers
Adzes (Ethnology): GN437.A35
Aerial cartography: GA109
Aerial geography: G142
Aerial photography
  Glaciers: GB2401.72.A37
  Groundwater: GB1001.72.A37
  Ice: GB2401.72.A37
  Ice sheets: GB2401.72.A37
  in
    anthropology: GN34.3.A35
    geomorphology: GB400.42.A35
    hydrogeology: GB1001.72.A37
    hydrology: GB656.2.A37
    hydrometeorology: GB2801.72.A37
    limnology: GB1601.72.A37
  Lagoons: GB2201.72.A37
  Lakes: GB1601.72.A37
  Ponds: GB1801.72.A37
  Rivers: GB1201.72.A37
  Sea ice: GB2401.72.A37

Aerial photography - Continued
  Snow: GB2601.72.A37
  Snow surveys: GB2601.72.A37
  Stream measurements: GB1201.72.A37
  Waterfalls: GB1401.72.A37
Aerology, see Meteorology
Aeronautical sports, see Air sports
Aeronautics
  Glaciers: GB2401.72.A38
  Groundwater: GB1001.72.A38
  Ice: GB2401.72.A38
  Ice sheets: GB2401.72.A38
  in
    hydrogeology: GB1001.72.A38
    hydrometeorology: GB2801.72.A38
    limnology: GB1601.72.A38
    oceanography: GC10.4.A3
  Lagoons: GB2201.72.A38
  Lakes: GB1601.72.A38
  Ponds: GB1801.72.A38
  Rivers: GB1201.72.A38
  Sea ice: GB2401.72.A38
  Snow: GB2601.72.A38
  Snow surveys: GB2601.72.A38
  Stream measurements: GB1201.72.A38
  Waterfalls: GB1401.72.A38
Aesthetics
  and
    costume: GT522
    dancing: GV1588.3
Afars and Issas, see French Territory of the Afars and Issas
Afghanistan
  Atlases: G2265+
  Maps: G7630+
Africa
  Atlases: G1780+; G2445+
  Maps: G5670+; G8200+
African Americans, see Afro-Americans
Afro-Americans
  and
    dancing: GV1624.7.N4
  Folklore: GR103
Age groups (Ethnology): GN490.5
Aged, The
  Physical education and training: GV447
  Recreation: GV184
  Treatment of (Manners and customs): GT3100
Agriculture
  Ethnology: GN407.4+
  Folklore: GR895
  Manners and customs: GT5810+
  Prehistoric archaeology: GN799.A4

Agronomy, see Agriculture
Air-age geography, see Aerial geography
Air-sea interaction, see Ocean-atmosphere
   interaction
Air sports: GV750+
Aircraft
   for
      polar exploration: G599
Airplane flying (Sports): GV758+
Alabama
   Atlases: G1340+
   Maps: G3970+
Alaska
   Atlases: G1530+
   Maps: G4370+
Albania
   Atlases: G2005+
   Maps: G6830+
Alberta
   Atlases: G1165+
   Maps: G3500+
Albinism (Human variation): GN199
Alchemy: QD13; QD23.3+
Alcohol
   Ethnology: GN411.5
   Manners and customs: GT2884+
Ale (Manners and customs): GT2890
Algeria
   Atlases: G2465+
   Maps: G8240+
All-England Club, Wimbledon, England,
   see Wimbledon, England. All-England
   Club
All Fool's Day, see April Fools' Day
All Hallow's Eve, see Halloween
All-round athletics: GV1060.7
All Souls' Day (Manners and customs):
   GT4995.A4
Alleys, Bowling, see Bowling alleys
Allocation of natural resources
   (Ethnology): GN448.3
Alluvial fans (Natural landforms):
   GB591+
Alphabet rhymes (Folklore): GR486
Alpine combined contests (Skiing):
   GV854.88
Alps
   Atlases: G1890+
   Maps: G6035+
Amateur basketball: GV885.4+
Amateur carnivals: GV1838
Amateur circuses: GV1838
Amateur football: GV956.3+
Amber
   Ethnology: GN434.2.A45
   Prehistoric archaeology: GN799.A5
Ambilineal descent (Ethnology): GN488.2
America (Ball game): GV1017.A5
American Automobile Association: GV1027
American football: GV950+
American Indians: E-F

American League of Professional
   Baseball Clubs: GV875
America's cup races: GV829+
Amulets (Folklore): GR600+
Amundsen, Roald: G585.A6
Amusement (General): GV
Amusement devices: GV1860
Amusement parks, etc.: GV1851+
Anagrams (Game): GV1507.A5
Analogies, Electromechanical, see
   Electromechanical analogies
Analysis, Componential, see Componential
   analysis
Ancestor worship (Ethnology): GN472.8
Ancient and medieval atlases: G1001+
Ancient costumes: GT530+
Ancient dancing: GV1607+
Ancient geographers: G83+
Ancient manners and customs: GT110
Ancient sports, games, etc.: GV17+;
   GV573
Ancient voyages: G88
Andorra
   Atlases: G1970+
   Maps: G6660+
Angling, see Fishing
Anglo-Egyptian Sudan, see Sudan
Angola
   Atlases: G2595+
   Maps: G8640+
Anguilla (Maps): G5045+
Animal fighting: GV1103+
Animal lore: GR705+
Animal materials (Ethnology): GN435+
Animal trials and punishment, see
   Animals, Prosecution and punishment of
Animals (Folklore): GR700+
Animals, Circus
   Collecting for exhibition purposes:
      GV1827
   Training: GV1829+
Animals, Domestic, see Domestic animals
Animals, Language of, see Language of
   animals
Animals, Mythical, see Mythical animals
Animals, Prosecution and punishment of
   (Manners and customs): GT6715
Animism (Ethnology): GN471
Anniversaries, Wedding, see Wedding
   anniversaries
Anniversary parties (General): GV1472
Annuals, Sporting, see Sporting annuals
Antarctic oceanography: GC461+
   Currents: GC245+
   Marine sediments: GC380.6
   Tides: GC313
Antarctica
   Atlases: G3100+
   Exploration, etc.: G575+
   Hydrology: GB839
   Maps: G9800+

Anthropogeography: GF
Anthropological sociology: HM107
Anthropologists: GN41.6+
Anthropology: GN
  as a profession: GN41.8
Anthropology, Applied, see Applied
  anthropology
Anthropology, Cultural, see Cultural
  anthropology
Anthropology, Dental, see Dental
  anthropology
Anthropology, Mathematical, see
  Mathematical anthropology
Anthropology, Medical, see Medical
  anthropology
Anthropology, Philosophical, see
  Philosophical anthropology
Anthropology, Physical, see Physical
  anthropology
Anthropology, Physiological, see
  Physiological anthropology
Anthropology, Psychological, see
  Psychological anthropology
Anthropology, Social, see Social
  anthropology
Anthropology, Structural, see Structural
  anthropology
Anthropology, Urban, see Urban
  anthropology
Anthropometric manuals and tables
  (Physical education and training):
  GV435
Anthropometry
  Physical anthropology: GN51+
  Physical education and training: GV435
    School children: LB3421+
Anthropophagy, see Cannibalism
Antiqua (Maps): G5050+
Antiquities, Prehistoric, see Prehistoric
  archaeology
Apes (Folklore): GR730.A6
Apothecaries (Manners and customs):
  RS122.5
Appalachian Mountains (Maps): G3707.A6
Appalachian Trail (Maps): G3709.32.A6
Apparatus, Oceanographic (General), see
  Oceanographic instruments and
  apparatus (General)
Apparatus
  for
    playgrounds: GV426
  See also Equipment and supplies
Apparitions (Folklore): GR580
Applied anthropology: GN397+
Applied oceanography: GC1000+
Applied science, see Technology
Appreciation of dancing, see Dance
  appreciation
April Fools' Day (Manners and customs):
  GT4995.A6
Aquafers, see Aquifers

Aquatic sports, see Water sports
Aquifers (Groundwater): GB1199+
Arabia and Arabian Peninsula
  Atlases: G2245+
  Maps: G7520+
Arabs
  Anthropogeography: GF698
  Costume: GT1390
  Ethnology: GN549.A7
  Folklore: GR275
  Geographers: G93
  Human ecology: GF698
Archaeology, Prehistoric, see
  Prehistoric archaeology
Archeolithic age (Prehistoric
  archaeology): GN769+
Archery: GV1183+
Architecture (Gymnasiums): GV405
Arctic Ocean
  Atlases: G3050+
  Maps: G9780+
  Oceanography: GC401+
    Currents: GC241+
    Marine sediments: GC380.5
    Tides: GC311
Arctic regions
  Anthropogeography: GF891
  Exploration, etc.: G575+
  Hydrology: GB835
  Human ecology: GF891
  Maps: G3270+
Areca nut, see Betel nut
Arenas (Sports): GV415+
Areometers, see Hydrometers
Argentina
  Atlases: G1755+
  Maps: G5350+
Argentine rummy (Card game), see
  Canasta
Arid regions
  Geomorphology: GB611+
  Hydrology: GB841
  Physical geography: GB398
Arizona
  Atlases: G1510+
  Maps: G4330+
Arkansas
  Atlases: G1355+
  Maps: G4000+
Arkansas River and Valley (Maps):
  G4052.A7
Arm exercises: GV508
Armillae (Manners and customs): GT2270
Arrow making, see Bow and arrow making
Arrowpoints (Prehistoric archaeology):
  GN799.W3
Art
  and
    costume: GT523
  Prehistoric archaeology: N5310+

Artificial caves (Prehistoric archaeology): GN783.3

Arts and crafts (Ethnology): GN429+

Aryan groups (Ethnology): GN539

Ascension Day (Manners and customs): GT4995.A8

Ashantis (Folklore): GR351.62.A83

Asia
  Atlases: G2200+
  Maps: G7400+

Asia and Europe, see Eurasia

Asia Minor
  Atlases: G2210+
  Maps: G7430+

Asian Games: GV722.5.A7

Asses (Folklore): GR730.A8

Assimilation (Ethnology): GN367

Association football: GV942+

Assyrian costume: GT535

Astrology: BF1651+

Astronautics
  Glaciers: GB2401.72.A83
  Groundwater: GB1001.72.A83
  Ice: GB2401.72.A83
  Ice sheets: GB2401.72.A83
  in
    geomorphology: GB400.42.A8
    hydrogeology: GB1001.72.A83
    hydrometeorology: GB2801.72.A83
    limnology: GB1601.72.A83
    oceanography: GC10.4.A8
  Lagoons: GB2201.72.A83
  Lakes: GB1601.72.A83
  Ponds: GB1801.72.A83
  Rivers: GB1201.72.A83
  Sea ice: GB2401.72.A83
  Snow: GB2601.72.A83
  Snow surveys: GB2601.72.A83
  Stream measurements: GB1201.72.A83
  Waterfalls: GB1401.72.A83

Astronomy
  Ethnology: GN476.3
  Prehistoric archaeology: GN799.A8

Atavism (Physiological anthropology): GN251

Athletic clubs and societies, see Clubs, Athletic and sports

Athletic contests: GV712+

Athletic equipment and supplies, see Equipment and supplies for athletics and sports

Athletic fields: GV411+

Athletics, All-round, see All-round athletics

Athletics
  in
    college, see Intramural and inter-scholastic athletics (Physical education and training) - College

Athletics
  in - Continued
    school, see Intramural and inter-scholastic athletics (Physical education and training) - School

Atlantic Ocean
  Atlases: G2805+
  Maps: G9100+

Atlantic States (United States)
  Maps: G3709.3+

Atlantis (Prehistoric archaeology): GN750+

Atlases: G1000.3+

Atlases, Historical, see Historical atlases

Atlases, World, see World atlases

Atlatl, see Throwing sticks (Weapons)

Atmosphere-ocean interaction, see Ocean-atmosphere interaction

Atomic energy
  in
    oceanography: GC10.4.N8

Attorneys, see Lawyers

Auction bridge: GV1282

Auction piquet: GV1295.A8

Auction whist: GV1291.A8

Audiovisual aids
  Anthropology: GN42.3
  Ethnology: GN307.82
  Geography: G76
  Oceanography: GC31.2
  Physical education and training: GV364
  Recreation and leisure: GV14.6

Augury, see Divination

Aurignacian culture
  By continent, see table below GN772.2+, e. g. GN772.2.A8 (Europe)

Austral Islands (Maps): G9650+

Australasia
  Atlases: G2740+
  Maps: G8950+

Australia
  Atlases: G2750+
  Maps: G8960+

Australian football: GV947

Australopithecines (Fossil man): GN283+

Australopithecus prometheus (Fossil man): GN283.3

Austria
  Atlases: G1935+
  Maps: G6490+

Austria-Hungary
  Atlases: G1930+
  Maps: G6480+

Authority (Ethnology): GN492.25

Authors (Game): GV1483

Auto games: GV1206

Autographs (Games): GV1507.A75

Automatic data processing, see Electronic data processing

Automation
  Glaciers: GB2401.72.A9
  Groundwater: GB1001.72.A9
  Ice: GB2401.72.A9
  Ice sheets: GB2401.72.A9
  in
    hydrogeology: GB1001.72.A9
    hydrology: GB656.2.A9
    hydrometeorology: GB2801.72.A9
    limnology: GB1601.72.A9
  Lagoons: GB2201.72.A9
  Lakes: GB1601.72.A9
  Ponds: GB1801.72.A9
  Rivers: GB1201.72.A9
  Sea ice: GB2401.72.A9
  Snow: GB2601.72.A9
  Snow surveys: GB2601.72.A9
  Stream measurements: GB1201.72.A9
  Waterfalls: GB1401.72.A9
Automobile racing on ice, see Ice
  racing - Automobiles
Automobile travel: GV1020+
Automobiles
  Folklore: GR869
  Manners and customs: GT5280
Automobiling, see Automobile travel
Avalanches: QC929.A8
Aviation
  and
    cartography, see Aerial cartography
    geography, see Aerial geography
    photography, see Aerial photography
  See also Aeronautics
Axes (Ethnology): GN437.A9
Azores
  Atlases: G2815+
  Maps: G9130+

                    B

BMR, see Basal metabolism
"Babe Ruth" (George Ruth): GV865.R8
Babylonian costume: GT535
Baccarat: GV1295.B3
Backfield play (Football): GV951.3
Backgammon: GV1469.B2
Backpacking: GV199.6
Baden culture
  By continent, see table below GN778.2+,
    e. g. GN778.2.B3 (Europe)
Badgers
  Badger baiting (Sport): GV1105
  Folklore: GR730.B3
Badminton: GV1007
Bahama Islands (Bahamas)
  Atlases: G1635+
  Maps: G4980+
Bahrein
  Atlases: G2249.85+
  Maps: G7590+
Bailecito (Dance): GV1796.B25

Bairo (Folklore): GR356.52.B33
Baiting, Animal, see Animal fighting
Baiting, Badger, see Badgers - Badger
  baiting
Baiting, Bear, see Bears - Bear baiting
Bakongo (Folklore): GR357.82.B33
Balance (Scales)
  Folklore: GR950.B3
Balance beam exercises: GV512
Balancing apparatus: GV513
Balkan Peninsula
  Atlases: G1995+
  Maps: G6800+
Ball games: GV861+
Ball tricks: GV1559
Balle au tamis (Game): GV1017.T27
Ballet: GV1787+
  Ballet dancers: GV1785
Ballets: GV1790
Balloon flying (Sports): GV762+
Ballroom dancing: GV1746+
Balls (Calisthenics): GV484
Balls, dance parties, etc.: GV1746+
Balolo, see Mongo
Baltic States
  Atlases: G2120+
  Maps: G7020+
Banaba, see Ocean Island
Bands (Political anthropology): GN492.4
Bangladesh
  Atlases: G2275+
  Maps: G7645+
Banking games, see Chance and banking
  games
Banks Islands (Maps): G9310+
Bansaw, see Nso
Bantu (Folklore): GR358.2.B33
Baptism customs: GT2460+
  of
    royalty, nobility, etc.: GT5080
Bar bell exercises: GV485
Barbados (Maps): G5140+
Barbary corsairs, see Pirates
Barbary States
  Atlases: G2455+
  Maps: G8220+
Bark (Ethnology): GN434.5
Barkov, Aleksandr Sergeevich: G69.B35
Barnacles (Folklore): GR760.B3
Barnum, P.T.: GV1811.B3
Barnum and Bailey Circus: GV1821.R5
Barristers, see Lawyers
Barter (Ethnology): GN450.4
Basal metabolism (Physiological
  anthropology): GN223
Base flow, see Groundwater flow
Base running (Baseball): GV868
Baseball: GV862+
Baseball cards, see Cards, Baseball
Baseball guides, see Guides, Baseball
Baseball leagues and clubs, see Leagues
  and clubs, Baseball

Basil maiden (Folktale): GR75.B3
Basilisk (Folklore): GR830.B3
Basket rummy (Card game), see Canasta
Basketball: GV882+
Basketball, Girls', see Women and
  girls - Girls' basketball
Basketmaking (Ethnology): GN431
Basques
  Costume: GT721
  Ethnology: GN549.B3
Basuto (Folklore): GR359.52.B34
Basutoland, see Lesotho
Bathing
  Hydrotherapy: RM819+
  Manners and customs: GT2845
  Personal hygiene: RA780
Batting (Baseball): GV869
Battle-ax culture, see Corded ware
  culture
Battle ball (Game): GV1017.B33
Bawenda, see Venda
Beach cusps (Coastal landform): GB454.B3
Beachcombing: G532+
Beaches (Geomorphology): GB450+
Beaker cultures
  By continent, see table below GN776.2+,
    e. g. GN776.2.B4 (Europe)
Beards
  Ethnology: GN419.B4
  Manners and customs: GT2320
Bears
  Bear baiting (Sport): GV1105
  Folklore: GR730.B4
  Trained bears: GV1831.B4
Beating the game (Card games): GV1247
Bechuanaland, see Botswana
Beds (Folklore): GR497
Beeball (Football game): GV960.B4
Beer (Manners and customs): GT2890
Behaim, Martin: G69.B4
Behavioral conformity (Ethnology):
  GN493.3
Belief systems (Ethnology): GN470+
Belgian Congo, see Zaire
Belgian East Africa, see Ruanda-Urundi
Belgium
  Atlases: G1865+
  Maps: G6010+
Belize
  Atlases: G1560+
  Maps: G4820+
Belle coquette (Ball game): GV1017.B4
Belly dancing: GV1798.5
Bemba (Folklore): GR358.42.B43
Benelux countries
  Atlases: G1850+
  Maps: G5990+
Beniseed, see Sesame
Berbers (Folklore): GR353.2.B43
Bermuda
  Atlases: G2810+
  Maps: G9120+

Berri, see Zaghawa
Beseda (Dance): GV1796.B3
Betel (Manners and customs): GT3015
Betel nut (Manners and customs): GT3015
Betrothal
  Ethnology: GN484.43
  Manners and customs: GT2650+
Betting (Sports): GV718
Betting systems (Gambling): GV1302
Beverages
  Ethnology: GN410.5
  Manners and customs: GT2855+
Bezique: GV1295.B5
Bharata Natyam (Dance): GV1796.B4
Bhutan
  Atlases: G2299.5+
  Maps: G7780+
Bible games and puzzles: GV1507.B5
Bible lands
  Atlases: G2230+
  Maps: G7480+
Biblical costume: GT540
Bicycle clubs, see Clubs, Bicycle
Bicycle polo: GV1058
Bicycling: GV1040+
Bilateral descent (Ethnology): GN488.4
Billiards: GV891+
Billiards, Lawn, see Lawn billiards
Bingo: GV1311.B5
Bio-geography, see Anthropogeography
Biographical games, see Authors (Game)
Biology (Ethnology): GN476.7+
Biology, Marine, see Marine biology
Birds (Folklore): GR735
Birth
  Ethnology: GN482.1+
  Folklore: GR440+
  Manners and customs: GT2460+
  Physiological anthropology: GN236+
Birth control (Ethnology): GN482.4
Birthday parties: GV1472.7.B5
Births, Multiple, see Multiple births
Bits (Harness)
  Manners and customs: GT5888
Black Americans, see Afro-Americans
Black art, see Witchcraft
Black magic (Ethnology): GN475.5
Blackjack (Card game): GV1295.B55
Blacksmithing (Folklore): GR896
Blind persons
  Physical education and training:
    HV1767
  Recreation and leisure: HV1765+
Blindman's buff: GV1207
Block diagrams (Cartography): GA138
Blocks, Building (Children's games):
  GV1218.B6
Blood (Folklore): GR489
Blood brothers (Ethnology): GN490.2
Blood feuds, see Vendetta
Blood groups (Physiological anthropology):
  GN263

Blood sacrifice (Ethnology): GN473.5
Blue-Gray game: GV957.B55
Blue Ridge Mountains (Maps): G3872.B6
Boar, Wild, see Wild boar
Board games: GV1312+
Boat handling, see Handling of boats
Boating on ice, see Iceboating
Boats, Small, see Small boats
Boats and boating
    Ethnology: GN440.1
    Sports: GV771+
"Bobby Jones" (Robert Jones): GV964.J6
Bobsledding: GV855
Bodies of water (Environmental
    influences on man): GF63+
Body, Human, see Human body
Body dimensions and proportions (Human
    variation): GN66+
Body markings (Ethnology): GN419.15
Body mechanics, see Posture
Boer (Folklore): GR359.2.B63
Bogs (Geomorphology): GB621+
Bolivia
    Atlases: G1745+
    Maps: G5320+
Bond friends (Ethnology): GN490.2
Bone (Animal materials)
    Ethnology: GN435.3
Book of the book (Folktale): GR75.B6
Books (Recreation and leisure), see
    Reading for pleasure
Boomerangs (Ethnology): GN498.B6
Boots (Manners and customs): GT2130
Bores (Tidal waves), see Tidal bores
Bosjesmen, see Bushmen
Boskop (Fossil man): GN286.2
Bosnia and Herzegovina (Maps): G6860+
Boston (Card game): GV1289
Boston Harbor (Tidal currents):
    GC309.B6
Botswana
    Atlases: G2579.7+
    Maps: G8600+
Bottom deposits (Oceanography), see
    Marine sediments
Bottom relief, Ocean, see Submarine
    topography
Boundaries, Natural, see Natural
    boundaries
Bow and arrow making: GV1189.5
Bowling alleys: GV907
Bowling games: GV901+
Bowling greens: GV910
Bowling on the green: GV909+
Bowls (Bowling games): GV909+
Bows and arrows (Ethnology): GN498.B78
Box lacrosse: GV989
Boxing: GV1115+
Bracelets (Manners and customs): GT2270
Brain (Human variation): GN181+
Brandy (Manners and customs): GT2894

Brazil
    Atlases: G1775+
    Maps: G5400+
Bridewealth (Ethnology): GN484.45
Bridge (Card game): GV1281+
Bridge whist, see Bridge (Card game)
Bridges (Ethnology): GN439
Brist (Game): GV1097.B7
British Columbia
    Atlases: G1170+
    Maps: G3510+
British Commonwealth Games: GV722.5.B7
British East Africa
    Atlases: G2529.3+
    Maps: G8400+
British Empire
    Atlases: G1805+
    Maps: G5730+
British Guiana, see Guyana
British Honduras, see Belize
British Indian Ocean Territory (Maps):
    G9195+
British Isles
    Atlases: G1807+
    Maps: G5740+
British Somaliland, see Somalia
British South Africa
    Atlases: G2560+
    Maps: G8480+
British West Africa
    Atlases: G2690+
    Maps: G8830+
Broad jump: GV1077
Broadcasters, Sports, see Sports
    broadcasters
Broadcasting (Sports): GV718
Bronze (Ethnology): GN436.2
Bronze age (Prehistoric archaeology):
    GN777+
Bronzes (Prehistoric archaeology):
    GN799.B7
Brooches (Manners and customs):
    GT2280
Brooklyn Dodgers: GV875.B7
Brothers and sisters (Folklore):
    GR473
Brownies (Folklore): GR549+
Buccaneers: G535+
Buck and wing (Theatrical dancing):
    GV1791
Buck vaulting exercises: GV519
Buckles (Manners and customs): GT2281
Budini (Ethnology): GN549.B9
Buffalo Bill's Wild West Show:
    GV1821.B8
Building blocks, see Blocks, Building
Building trades (Manners and customs):
    GT5960.B8
Buildings (Prehistoric archaeology):
    GN799.B8

Buildings, facilities, etc. (Camps): GV198.L3
Bukusu (Folklore): GR356.42.B83
Bulgaria
  Atlases: G2040+
  Maps: G6890+
Bullfighting: GV1107+
Bulls (Folklore): GR730.B8
Bundling: GT2651
Burghers
  Costume: GT1800
  Manners and customs: GT5550+
Burial customs: GT3150+
Buried treasure: G521+
  Folklore: GR943
Burma
  Atlases: G2285+
  Maps: G7720+
Burnt offering, see Sacrifice
Burungi (Folklore): GR356.72.B84
Bushmen (Folklore): GR358.2.B83
Business, Choice of, see Vocational guidance
Buttons, Baseball: GV875.2
Byrd, Richard Evelyn: G585.B8

C

Cadastral mapping: GA109.5
Caddies, Golf: GV977
Caicos and Turks Islands, see Turks and Caicos Islands
Calandria (Dance): GV1796.C13
Calcio fiorentino (Game), see Florentine football
Calculation
  of
    geographical areas: GA23
Calendars (Ethnology): GN476.3
Calgary, Alberta. Calgary Stampede: GV1834.5.C3
California
  Atlases: G1525+
  Maps: G4360+
Calisthenics: GV481+
Call books (Square dances): GV1767
Calmucks, see Kalmucks
Calypso (Card game): GV1295.C15
Cambodia
  Atlases: G2374.3+
  Maps: G8010+
Cambridge-Oxford boat races, see Oxford-Cambridge boat races
Cambridge University Cricket Club: GV921.C2
Cameroon
  Atlases: G2635+
  Maps: G8730+
Camp counselors, see Counselors, Camp
Camp decoration, see Decoration (Camps)

Campfire programs, see Recreational programs (Camps)
Campground construction, see Construction of campgrounds
Campground maintenance, see Maintenance and repair of campgrounds
Camping: GV191.68+
  Canoe camping: GV790
Camps, Church, see Church camps
Camps, Music, see Music camps
Camps, Summer, see Summer camps
Canada
  Atlases: G1115+
  Maps: G3400+
Canadian football: GV948
Canadian Open (Golf tournament): GV970
Canal Zone
  Atlases: G1590+
  Maps: G4880+
Canary Islands
  Atlases: G2825+
  Maps: G9150+
Canasta: GV1295.C2
  Three-deck canasta, see Samba - Card game
Candombe (Dance): GV1796.C14
Canes (Manners and customs): GT2220
Cannibalism: GN409
Canoes and canoeing
  Camping, see Camping - Canoe camping
  Ethnology: GN440.2
  Sports: GV781+
Cante hondo, see Flamenco dancing
Capacity tests (Physical education and training): GV436+
Cape Verde Islands
  Atlases: G2830+
  Maps: G9160+
Capital cities (Geography): G140
Capsian culture
  By continent, see table below GN772.2+, e. g. GN772.2.C3 (Europe)
Card games: GV1232+
Card playing and ethics, see Ethics and card playing
Card sharping: GV1247
Card tricks
  Gamblers' tricks: GV1247
  Parlor tricks: GV1549
Cardinal points: G108.5.C3
Cards, Baseball: GV875.3
Cargo cults (Nativistic movements): GN472.75
Caribbean area
  Atlases: G1535+
  Maps: G4390+
Caribbees, see Lesser Antilles
Carnivals
  Manners and customs: GT4180+
  Recreation and leisure: GV1835
Carnivals, Amateur, see Amateur carnivals

Caroline Islands
  Atlases: G2920+
  Maps: G9420+
Carousel, see Merry-go-round
Cars (Automobiles), see Automobiles
Cartographers: GA197.5+
Cartography: GA101+
  as a profession: GA197.5
  Ethnology: GN476.5
  Folklore: GR44.C3
  See also Mapping
Cartography, Marine: GA359+
Cascade Range (Maps): G4232.C3
Castes (Ethnology): GN491.4
Castle life (Manners and customs):
  GT3510+
Cat-worship, see Cats
Catalogs
  Athletic and sporting goods: GV747
  Boats: GV777.4
    Sailboats: GV811.2
  Playing cards (Museum catalogs):
    GV1236
Catamarans: GV811.63.C3
Catching (Baseball): GV872
Cats (Folklore): GR725
Caucasian race (Ethnology): GN537
Cave diving (Geomorphology): GB602.5
Cave dwellers (Prehistoric
  archaeology): GN783+
Cave exploration: GB602+
Caverns, see Caves
Caves
  Folklore: GR665
  Geomorphology: GB601+
  Prehistoric archaeology: GN783+
Caves, Artificial, see Artificial caves
Caves, Marine, see Marine caves
Cayman Islands (Maps): G4965+
Celestial globes: G3160
Celestial maps: G3190+
Celibacy (General): HQ800
Celts
  Ethnology: GN549.C3
  Folklore: GR137+
Cemeteries (Folklore): GR506
Central Africa
  Atlases: G2590+
  Maps: G8630+
Central Africa Protectorate, see Malawi
Central African Republic
  Atlases: G2625+
  Maps: G8710+
Central America
  Atlases: G1550+
  Maps: G4800+
Central Europe
  Atlases: G1880+
  Maps: G6030+
Cephalometry: GN63.8+
Ceramics (Art), see Pottery

Cercle (Ball game): GV1017.C4
Cerebrum, see Brain
Ceremonies (Religion and ritual), see
  Rites and ceremonies (Religion and
  ritual)
Certification and examinations, see
  Examinations and certification
Ceylon, see Sri Lanka
Cha-cha (Dance): GV1796.C2
Chad
  Atlases: G2630+
  Maps: G8720+
Chamarrita (Dance): GV1796.C39
Champions, Athletic and sports: GV741
Chance and banking games: GV1301+
Changers (Ball game): GV1017.C45
Character building
  and
    recreation and leisure: GV14.3
Chariot racing, Roman: GV33
Chariots (Manners and customs): GT5280
Charleston (Dance): GV1796.C4
Charms (Folklore): GR600+
Chartography, see Cartography.
Chasing games: GV1207
Chastity belts, see Girdles of chastity
Checkers (Game): GV1461+
Chemical oceanography: GC109+
Chesapeake Bay
  Maps: G3842.C5
  Tidal currents: GC309.C5
Chess: GV1313+
Chess clubs, see Clubs, Chess
Chessmen, Moves of: GV1451.5
Chest weight exercises: GV515
Chesterfield Archipelago (Maps): G9370+
Chicago. Washington Cycling Club:
  GV1047.W3
Chicago Cubs: GV875.C6
Chieftainships (Ethnology): GN492.55
Children
  Costume: GT1730
  Dances: GV1799
  Ethnology: GN482+
  Folklore: GR43.C4; GR475+
  Games: GV1203+
  Gymnastics: GV464.5
  Handicapped children's camps, see
    Handicapped persons - Children's
    camps
  Handicapped children's games, see
    Handicapped persons - Children's
    games
  Human variation: GN63
  Manners and customs: GT2450+
  Parties, see Parties - Children's
    parties
  Physical education and training: GV443
  Recreation and leisure: GV182.9
    in hsopitals: RJ242
  Sports: GV709.2
  Swimming: GV837.2

Chile
  Atlases: G1750+
  Maps: G5330+
Chimarrita (Dance), see Chamarrita
  (Dance)
China
  Atlases: G2305+
  Maps: G7820+
Chinese chess: GV1458.C5
Chinese Empire
  Atlases: G2305+
  Maps: G7810+
Chivalrie (Ball game): GV1017.C5
Chivalry (Manners and customs): GT3600+
Chocolate (Drinking customs): GT2920.C3
Choice of profession, see Vocational
  guidance
Choreography (Theatrical dancing):
  GV1782.5
Christening customs, see Baptism
  customs
Christian folklore: BR135+
Christian life
  and
    recreation and leisure: BV4597
Christmas
  Manners and customs: GT4985+
  Religious observance: BV45
Christmas parties: GV1472.7.C5
Chukchi folklore: GR203.2.C5
Church
  and
    dancing: GV1740+
    travel: G156.5.C5
Church camps: BM135; BV1650
Church going (Manners and customs):
  GT485
Church gynasiums, see Gymnasiums -
  Church gymnasiums
Churches
  Folklore: GR505
  Manners and customs: GT485
    Professional customs: BR - BX
Churchyards, see Cemeteries
Cigarette tricks: GV1559
Cinch (Card game), see Pedro (Card game)
Cincture (Folklore): GR950.G5
Cinderella (Folktale): GR75.C4
Cipher stories (Games): GV1507.C5
Circle (Folklore): GR932.C5
Circuit training (Physical education
  and training): GV462
Circulation (Ocean), see Ocean
  circulation
Circumcision
  Ethnology: GN484
  Manners and customs: GT2470
Circumnavigations (Expeditions): G419+
Circus, Roman: GV34
Circus animals, see Animals, Circus
Circus wagons: GV1823
Circuses: GV1800+

Circuses, Amateur, see Amateur
  circuses
Cities (Human ecology): GF125
Cities and towns (Collectively)
  of
    the United States (Maps): G3704
    the world
      Atlases: G1028
      Geography: G140
City dwellers (Ethnographies): GN395
Clans (Ethnology): GN487.7.C55
Clasps (Jewelry)
  Manners and customs: GT2280
Classes (Social stratification)
  Ethnology: GN491.45
Classical costume: GT545+
Classical dancing: GV1611
  Revival of: GV1783
Classical games, etc.: GV17+
Classical geographers: G87
Classification
  Glaciers: GB2401.72.C55
  Groundwater: GB1001.72.C55
  Ice: GB2401.72.C55
  Ice sheets: GB2401.72.C55
  in
    hydrogeology: GB1001.72.C55
    hydrometeorology: GB2801.72.C55
    limnology: GB1601.72.C55
  Lagoons: GB2201.72.C55
  Lakes: GB1601.72.C55
  Ponds: GB1801.72.C55
  Rivers: GB1201.72.C55
  Sea ice: GB2401.72.C55
  Snow: GB2601.72.C55
  Snow surveys: GB2601.72.C55
  Stream measurements: GB1201.72.C55
  Waterfalls: GB1401.72.C55
Classification systems (Philosophy)
  Ethnology: GN468.4
Clay modeling, see Modeling
Clergy (Manners and customs): BR - BX
Climatic geomorphology: GB447
Climatic influences on man: GF71
Climbing structures (Playgrounds):
  GV426
Clog (Theatrical dancing): GV1793
Clothing
  Ethnology: GN418+
  for
    athletics and gymnastics: GV437
      Women and girls, see Women and
        girls - Clothing for athletics
        and gymnastics
  See also Costume
Clown acts: GV1828
Clowns, Circus: GV1811
Clubs (Weapons)
  Ethnology: GN498.C6
Clubs, Athletic and sports: GV563
  Organization: GV391

Clubs, Baseball, see Leagues and
clubs, Baseball
Clubs, Bicycle: GV1046.9+
Clubs, Chess: GV1314
Clubs, Physical education and
training: GV202+
Coaching: GV711
Baseball: GV875.5
Basketball: GV885.3
Football
Amateur: GV956.6
Professional: GV954.4
Ice hockey: GV848.25
Rugby: GV945.75
Soccer: GV943.8
Coastal landforms: GB454
Coasting, see Bobsledding
Coasts and coast changes (Geomorphology):
GB450+
Cockfighting: SF503
Cocos Islands (Maps): G9205+
Coffee (Manners and customs): GT2918
Cognatic descent (Ethnology): GN488+
Coiffures (Manners and customs):
GT2290+
Coin tricks: GV1559
Cold regions
Geomorphology: GB641+
Physical geography: GB398.5
Coliseums (Sports): GV415+
College athletics, see Intramural and
interscholastic athletics (Physical
education and training) - College
College proms: GV1746+
College sports: GV691+
Colombia
Atlases: G1730+
Maps: G5290+
Colonial costume (United States): GT607
Color
of
eyes: GN197
hair: GN197
skin: GN197
Colorado
Atlases: G1500+
Maps: G4310+
Colorado River and Valley (Maps):
G4302.C6
Columbia River and Valley (Maps):
G4232.C62
Coming of age rites (Manners and
customs): GT2485+
Commerce and trade
Ethnology: GN450+
Folklore: GR872+
Prehistoric archaeology: GN799.C45
Commercial geography, see Economic
geography
Commercial occupations (Manners and
customs): GT6010+

Commonwealth of Nations
Atlases: G1805+
Maps: G5730+
Communication (Ethnology): GN452+
Communication, Routes of, see Routes
of communication
Communication of information
Anthropology: GN13
Ethnology: GN307.5+
Hydrography: GB657+
Oceanography: GC37+
Physical education and training:
GV207.3+
Sports: GV567.5+
Community recreation: GV181.5+
Community recreation centers: HN41+
Comoro Islands (Maps): G9210+
Companies, Dance: GV1786
Compass card, see Cardinal points
Compass rose, see Cardinal points
Competition (Economic anthropology):
GN448.8
Competitions
Kiteflying: GV769
Model airplanes: GV761
Componential analysis (Anthropology):
GN34.3.C6
Computer control, see Automation
Computer programs
in
hydrology: GB656.2.C63
Condición (Dance): GV1796.C57
Condiments (Eating customs): GT2870
Conditioning, see Training
Coney Island, N.Y. (Amusement park):
GV1853.C6
Coney Island Amusement Park, Ohio:
GV1853.C62
Confederate States of America
Atlases: G1280+
Maps: G3860+
Conga (Dance): GV1796.C6
Congo (Brazzaville)
Atlases: G2620+
Maps: G8700+
Congo (Democratic Republic), see Zaire
Conjuring (Parlor magic): GV1541+
Connecticut
Atlases: G1240+
Maps: G3780+
Conquian, see Cooncan (Card game)
Conservation
of
marine resources: GC1018
Construction
of
campgrounds: GV191.72
playgrounds: GV425.5
Contests, Shooting: GV1167+
Continental margins (Submarine
topography): GC84+

Continental shelves (Submarine
topography): GC85+
Continental slopes (Submarine
topography): GC86+
Contract bridge: GV1282.3
Contract golf: GV986
Conventional signs and symbols
(Cartography): GA155
Convolutions of the brain (Human
variation): GN181+
Cook Islands (Maps): G9600+
Cooncan (Card game): GV1295.C6
Cooperation (Economic anthropology):
GN448.8
Copper (Ethnology): GN436.2
Copper age (Prehistoric archaeology):
GN777+
Corded Ware culture
By continent, see table below GN776.2+,
e. g. GN776.2.C6 (Europe)
Cornell University rowing: GV807.C6
Coronations (Manners and customs):
GT5050
Corpus Christi festival (Manners and
customs): GT4995.C6
Corsets (Manners and customs): GT2075
Cosmetics
Ethnology: GN419.15
Manners and customs: GT2340
Cosmic phenomena (Folklore): GR620+
Cosmographies: GA6
Costa Rica
Atlases: G1580+
Maps: G4860+
Costume
by
class (Manners and customs): GT1710+
occupation (Manners and customs):
GT5910+
Folklore: GR420+
for
bullfighters: GV1108.2
cycling: GV1054
ice skating: GV852
Manners and customs: GT500+
Prehistoric archaeology: GN799.C5
See also Clothing
Costumes, Court, see Court costumes
Costumes, Theatrical, see Theatrical
costumes
Cotillion (Dance): GV1757
Counselors, Camp: GV198.C6
Counting (Ethnology): GN476.15
Counting-out rhymes (Folklore): GR485
Country clubs: HS2581
Country dances: GV1763+
Country life
Farm life: S521
Manners and customs: GT3470
Rural sociology: HT401+

Court balls: GV1747
Court costumes: GT1754+
Diplomatic court: JX1681+
Court fools
Folklore: GR523
Manners and customs: GT2130
Court life (Manners and customs):
GT3510+
Court tennis: GV1003
Courtesies (Manners and customs):
GT3050
Courts, Tennis, see Tennis courts
Courtship (Manners and customs):
GT2600+
Cousins marrying cousins, see Cross-
cousin marriage
Cowboy sports, see Rodeos
Crafts, see Arts and crafts
Craniology (Human variation): GN71+
Craniometry (Human variation): GN71+
Cremation customs: GT3330+
Cribbage: GV1295.C9
Cricket (Ball game): GV911+
Cries, Street, see Street cries
Crime (Ethnology): GN494
Criminals, see Outlaws
Crinoline (Manners and customs):
GT2075
Crna Gora, see Montenegro
Cro-Magnon (Fossil man): GN286.3
Croatia
Atlases: G2030+
Maps: G6870+
Crockery, see Pottery
Cromlechs (Prehistoric archaeology):
GN790
Croquet: GV931+
Cross-country runs: GV1063
Cross-country skiing: GV854.9.C7
Cross-cousin marriage (Ethnology):
GN480.4
Cross-sums (Games): GV1507.C68
Crossbow shooting: GV1190
Crossword puzzles: GV1507.C7
Cruises
in
time of peace: G549
Cruising (Canoeing): CV789+
Cryptograms (Games): GV1507.C8
Cuba
Atlases: G1605+
Maps: G4920+
Cultivated plants (Manners and customs):
GT5897+
Cults, Messianic, see Nativistic
movements
Cultural anthropology: GN301+
Cultural configurations (Psychological
anthropology): GN506
Cultural determinism (Ethnology):
GN365.8

Cultural evolution (Ethnology): GN360+
Cultural processes (Ethnology): GN357+
Cultural relativism (Ethnology):
  GN345.5
Cultural traits (Ethnology): GN406+
Culture (Ethnology): GN357+
Culture and personality (Psychological
  anthropology): GN504
Culture change (Ethnology): GN358
Culture contact (Ethnology): GN366+
Culture diffusion (Ethnology): GN365+
Culture patterns (Psychological
  anthropology): GN506
Culture shock (Psychological
  anthropology): GN517
Cupid (Folktale): GR75.C8
Curing (Magic)
  Ethnology: GN475.8
Curling (Winter sports): GV845
Currency, see Money
Currents, Ocean: GC229+
  By region or ocean: GC240+
Currents, Tidal, see Tidal currents
Customs (Ethnology): GN406+
Customs and manners (General), see
  Manners and customs (General)
Cutting out pictures (Children's
  games): GV1218.C7
Cycle, Hydrologic, see Hydrologic cycle
Cycling: GV1040+
Cyclons (Prehistoric archaeology):
  GN799.C9
Cyclopean remains, see Megalithic
  monuments
Cyprus
  Atlases: G2215+
  Maps: G7450+
Czechoslovakia
  Atlases: G1945+
  Maps: G6510+

                    D

Dactylography, see Fingerprints
Daggers (Prehistoric archaeology):
  GN799.W3
Dahomey
  Atlases: G2650+
  Maps: G8750+
Dalmatia (Atlases): G2025+
Dance appreciation: GV1600
Dance companies, see Companies, Dance
Dance notation, see Notation - Dance
  movements
Dancers: GV1785
Dancing: GV1580+
  as a profession: GV1597
  Folklore: GR885
  on
    ice, see Ice dancing

Dancing, Ballroom, see Ballroom dancing
Dancing, Gymnastic, see Gymnastic
  dancing
Dancing, Social, see Social dancing
Dancing, Theatrical, see Theatrical
  dancing
Dancing and aesthetics, see Aesthetics
  and dancing
Dancing and the church, see Church
  and dancing
Dancing and education, see Education
  and dancing
Dancing and ethics, see Ethics and
  dancing
Dancing and psychology, see Psychologi-
  cal aspects of dancing
Dancing and society, see Society and
  dancing
Dancing games, see Singing and dancing
  games
Dancing schools: GV1754
Dandies
  Biography: CT9985+
  Manners and customs: GT6720
Danilo culture
  By continent, see table below GN776.2+,
    e. g. GN776.2.D3 (Europe)
Darts: GV1565
Davis cup (Tennis tournament): GV999
Day camps: GV197.D3
Days
  Festive days, see Festive days
  Folklore: GR930
Dead, Exposure of the, see Exposure of
  the dead
Dead, Treatment of the: GT3150+
Death
  Ethnology: GN485.5+
  Folklore: GR440+
Decathlon: GV1060.7
Deck sports: GV709.7
Decoration (Camps): GV198.D4
Deep diving vehicles, see Oceanographic
  submersibles
Deep-sea deposits, see Marine
  sediments
Deep-sea research vessels, see Oceano-
  graphic submersibles
Deep-sea soundings: GC75+
  Sounding apparatus in navigation:
    VK584.S6
Deep submergence vehicles, see Oceano-
  graphic submersibles
Deer (Folklore): GR730.D4
Defensive play
  Basketball: GV888
  Football: GV951.18
Defloration (Ethnology): GN484.47
Degeneration
  Eugenics: HQ750+
  Physiological anthropology: GN256

Deities, see Gods
Delaware
   Atlases: G1265+
   Maps: G3830+
Delaware River and Valley (Maps):
   G3792.D44
Delsarte system of exercises: GV463
Deltas (Natural landforms): GB591+
Demonology (Folklore): GR525+
Denmark
   Atlases: G2055+
   Maps: G6920+
Denmark and colonies
   Atlases: G2053+
   Maps: G6915+
Density
   of
      seawater: GC151
Dental anatomy, see Teeth
Dental anthropology (Human variation):
   GN209
Deposits, Deep-sea, see Marine
   sediments
Descent, Regulation of (Ethnology):
   GN486.5+
Deserts (Geomorphology): GB611+
Design, see Planning and design
Detective and mystery puzzles: GV1507.D4
Deutschland, see Germany
Development education, see Acculturation
Deviance (Ethnology): GN493.5
Devilfish, see Octopuses
Diabolo (Game): GV1216
Diaghilev, Sergeĭ: GV1785.D5
Dice and dice games: GV1303
Diet for athletes: TX361.A8
Diffusion, Culture, see Culture diffusion
Dimensions, Physical, see Physical form
   and dimensions
Dingaan's Day (Manners and customs):
   GT4995.D5
Dinghies (Sports): GV777.6
   Sailing: GV811.6
Dinka (Folklore): GR355.82.D53
Dionysius Periegetes: G87.D5+
Diplomacy (Ethnology): GN496+
Dirt eating (Ethnology): GN408
Disasters, Natural, see Natural disasters
Discoveries (Geography): G200+
Discus throwing: GV1094.3
Disneyland: GV1853.D5
Disputes (Ethnology): GN494.5+
Distaffs (Manners and customs): GT7070.D5
Distance running: GV1062+
Distances, Tables of (Geography): G109+
Distilled liquors (Manners and customs):
   GT2893+
Distribution of goods and services
   (Ethnology): GN449.6+
District of Columbia
   Atlases: G1275+
   Maps: G3850+

Div-a-let (Games): GV1507.D6
Diversions, see Recreation and leisure
Divination (Ethnology): GN475.7
Diving (Sports): GV837+
Diving, Cave, see Cave diving
Diving, Submarine, see Submarine diving
Division of labor (Ethnology): GN448.5+
Divorce (Ethnology): GN484.7
Dix (Ball game): GV1017.D5
Doctors, see Physicians
Dogfighting: GV1109
Dogs
   Folklore: GR720
   Manners and customs: GT5890
Dokhmas, see Exposure of the dead
Dollhouses: GV1220
Dolls: GV1219+
Dolmens (Prehistoric archaeology):
   GN790
Domestic animals
   Ethnology: GN407.6+
   Folklore, see Animal lore
   Manners and customs: GT5870+
Domestic groups (Ethnology): GN480+
Domesticated plants (Ethnology):
   GN407.5+
Dominica (Maps): G5100+
Dominican Republic
   Atlases: G1620+
   Maps: G4950+
Domino bridge: GV1468
Dominoes (Games): GV1467+
Double-crostics (Game): GV1507.D65
Double descent (Kinship systems)
   Ethnology: GN487.6
Doubles (Tennis): GV1002.8
Down, see Feathers
Downhill racing (Skiing): GV854.9.R3
Dowry (Ethnology): GN484.45
Drag racing: GV1029.3
Dragons (Folklore): GR830.D7
Drainage (Hydrology): GB980+
Draughts (Game): GV1461+
Draw poker, see Poker (Card game)
Dreams (Folklore): GR435
Dress, see Costume
Drilling implements (Ethnology): GN437.D7
Drills, see Marching and drills
Drinking
   Folklore: GR498
   Manners and customs: GT2850+
Drinking of healths: GT2930
Drinking vessels (Manners and customs):
   GT2940+
Drive whist: GV1291.D7
Druggists, see Pharmacists
Dryads (Folklore): GR785
Duckpins (Bowling): GV910.5.D8
Dueling: CR4571+
Dumbbell exercises: GV487
Duncan, Isadora: GV1785.D8
Dune buggy racing: GV1029.9.D8

Dunes (Geomorphology): GB631+
Duplicate whist: GV1283
Duricrusts (Geomorphology): GB649.D8
Dutch Guiana, see Surinam
Dutch West Indies, see Netherlands
  Antilles
Dwarfs
  Body dimensions and proportions:
    GN69.3+
  Folklore: GR555
Dwellings
  Ethnology: GN414+
  Folklore: GR490+
  See also Houses
Dynamics
  of
    the ocean: GC200+
      Hydrodynamics: QA911+

E

Ear, Shape of external (Human
  variation): GN201
Earth (Folklore): GR655
Earth, Effect of man on, see Man's
  influence on the environment
Earth movements: QE598+
Earth pillars, see Earth pyramids
Earth pyramids (Geomorphology): GB649.E3
Earthenware, see Pottery
Earthquakes: QE521+
Earthworks (Prehistoric archaeology):
  GN789
East Africa Protectorate, see Kenya
East Germany
  Atlases: G1915+
  Maps: G6090+
East Indies, see Indonesia
East North Central States (United States)
  Atlases: G1390+
  Maps: G4070+
East Pakistan, see Bangladesh
East South Central States (United States)
  Atlases: G1325+
  Maps: G3940+
Easter
  Manners and customs: GT4935
  Religious observance: BV55
Easter Island (Maps): G9665+
Eastern Canada (Maps): G3405+
Eastern Europe
  Atlases: G2080+
  Maps: G6965+
Eastern Hemisphere
  Atlases: G1780+
  Maps: G5670+
Eastern United States, 1870-
  Atlases: G1205+
  Maps: G3705+

Eating
  Folklore: GR498
  Manners and customs: GT2850+
Ecarté: GV1295.E3
Ecology, Human, see Human ecology
Economic anthropology: GN448+
Economic geography: HF1021+
Economic organization (Ethnology):
  GN448+
Economics (Prehistoric archaeology):
  GN799.E4
Ecstasy (Religion and ritual)
  Ethnology: GN472.4
Ecuador
  Atlases: G1735+
  Maps: G5300+
Edelweiss (Folklore): GR790.E3
Education
  and
    dancing: GV1588.4
    travel: LC6681
Educational games, see Instructive
  games
Efficiency tests (Physical education
  and training): GV436+
Eggs (Bird)
  Folklore: GR735
Egypt
  Atlases: G2490+
  Maps: G8300+
Egyptian costume (Ancient): GT533
Egyptian dancing (Ancient): GV1613
Eire
  Atlases: G1830+
  Maps: G5780+
Electromechanical analogies
  Glaciers: GB2401.72.E42
  Groundwater: GB1001.72.E42
  Ice: GB2401.72.E42
  Ice sheets: GB2401.72.E42
  in
    hydrogeology: GB1001.72.E42
    hydrology: GB656.2.E42
    hydrometeorology: GB2801.72.E42
    limnology: GB1601.72.E42
  Lagoons: GB2201.72.E42
  Lakes: GB1601.72.E42
  Ponds: GB1801.72.E42
  Rivers: GB1201.72.E42
  Sea ice: GB2401.72.E42
  Snow: GB2601.72.E42
  Snow surveys: GB2601.72.E42
  Stream measurements: GB1201.72.E42
  Waterfalls: GB1401.72.E42
Electronic data processing
  Glaciers: GB2401.72.E45
  Groundwater: GB1001.72.E45
  Ice: GB2401.72.E45
  Ice sheets: GB2401.72.E45
  in
    cartography: GA102.4.E4

Electronic data processing
in - Continued
geography: G70.2
geomorphology: GB400.42.E4
hydrogeology: GB1001.72.E45
hydrology: GB656.2.E43
hydrometeorology: GB2801.72.E45
limnology: GB1601.72.E45
Lagoons: GB2201.72.E45
Lakes: GB1601.72.E45
Ponds: GB1801.72.E45
Rivers: GB1201.72.E45
Sea ice: GB2401.72.E45
Snow: GB2601.72.E45
Snow surveys: GB2601.72.E45
Stream measurements: GB1201.72.E45
Tides: GC305.5.E4
Waterfalls: GB1401.72.E45
Elementary map drawing and reading:
GA130
El encierro, see Running to the pens
(Bullfighting)
Elephants, Trained: GV1831.E4
Elixir of life (Folklore): GR605
Elixirs (Folklore): GR605
Ellice Islands (Maps): G9510+
Ellsworth, Lincoln: G585.E6
El Salvador
Atlases: G1570+
Maps: G4840+
Elves (Folklore): GR549+
Embalming (Manners and customs):
GT3340
Encroachment, Saltwater, see Saltwater
encroachment
Enculturation (Psychological
anthropology): GN510
End games
of
chess: GV1450.3
go: GV1460.4
End play (Football): GV951.25
Endogamy (Ethnology): GN480.3
Endrumpf, see Peneplains
Engineering cybernetics, see Automation
England
Atlases: G1815+
Maps: G5750+
English university boat races: GV799
Entertainers, Private: GV1472.5
Entertaining (Manners and customs):
GT3410+
Entertainment, see Recreation and
leisure
Environment, Effect of man on, see
Man's influence on the environment
Environment, Hazardous aspects of the,
see Hazardous aspects of the
environment
Environment, Human, see Human ecology
Environmental influences on man:
GF51+

Environmental perception, see
Geographical perception
Eolithic age (Prehistoric archaeology):
GN769+
Epiphany
Manners and customs: GT4915
Religious observance: BV50.E7
Equal area projection: GA115
Equatorial Africa, see Central Africa
Equatorial Guinea
Atlases: G2605+
Maps: G8660+
Equatorial Islands, see Line Islands
Equatorial oceanography: GC880
Currents: GC261
Marine sediments: GC380.3
Tides: GC321
Equestrianism, see Horsemanship
Equinox, Vernal, see Vernal equinox
Equipment and supplies
for
athletics and sports: GV743+
billiards and pool: GV899
boats and boating: GV777.4
Sailboats: GV811.4+
camping: GV191.76
circuses: GV1823
cycling: GV1054
dancing: GV1735
golf: GV976
gymnasiums: GV409+
ice skating: GV852
magicians: GV1561
playgrounds: GV426.5
recreational areas and centers:
GV182.5
skiing: GV854.9.E6
tennis: GV1002.5
See also Apparatus
Escondido (Dance): GV1796.E8
Eskimos: E99.E7
Esther, Feast of, see Purim
Estonia
Atlases: G2125+
Maps: G7030+
Estuarine oceanography: GC96+
Estuarine sediments (Oceanography):
GC97.7+
Ethics
and
card playing: GV1245
costume: BJ1697
dancing: GV1740+
the Olympic games: GV721.6
recreation and leisure: GV14.35
sports: GV706.3
Ethnology: GN468.7
Ethiopia
Atlases: G2505+
Maps: G8330+
Ethnic groups and races: GN495.4+;
GN537+

Ethnic revivals, see Nativistic
  movements
Ethnicity: GN495.6
Ethnobotany (Ethnology): GN476.73
Ethnocentrism: GN495.8
Ethnographies: GN378+
Ethnology: GN301+
Ethnozoology: GN476.76
Eton College rowing: GV807.5.E8
Euchre: GV1249
Eurasia
  Atlases: G1780+
  Maps: G5670+
Europa Cup (Soccer): GV943.52+
Europe
  Atlases: G1791+
  Maps: G5700+
Europe, Western, see Western Europe
Europe and Asia, see Eurasia
European Athletic Championships:
  GV722.5.E9
Evil eye: BF1553
Evil spirits, see Demonology
Evolution, Cultural, see Cultural
  evolution
Evolution, Human, see Human evolution
Evolutionism (Ethnology): GN360+
Examinations and certification
  for
    lifeguards: GV837.15
Exchange (Barter), see Barter
Exchange of oceanographic information:
  GC38
Executioners (Folklore): GR897
Executions (Folklore): GR897
Exercises, Golf, see Golf exercises
Exercises, Group, see Group exercises
Exercises, Gymnastic, see Gymnastics
Exercises, Heavy, see Heavy exercises
Exercises, Reducing, see Weight
  reducing exercises
Exercises, Rhythmic, see Rhythmic
  exercises
Exercises
  for
    skiiers: GV854.85
Exhibitions, see Museums and exhibitions
Exorcisms (Folklore): GR540
Exogamy (Ethnology): GN480.3
Exostosis (Human variation): GN131
Expeditions, Oceanographic: GC63
Expeditions, Scientific: Q116
Expletives (Oaths), see Profanity
Exploration, Cave, see Cave exploration
Exploration, Underwater, see Underwater
  exploration
Explorations: G200+
Exposure of the dead (Manners and
  customs): GT3350
Expressionistic dancing: GV1783
Extended families (Ethnology): GN480.55

Extremities (Human variation): GN161
Eye sockets (Human variation): GN131
Eyeglasses (Manners and customs): GT2370
Eyes, Color of, see Color of eyes

F

Fabrics, Textile, see Textile fabrics
Face form and profile (Physical form
  and dimensions): GN64
Facial exercises: GV508
Facilities, Physical education and
  training: GV401+
Facsimiles, Atlases of: G1025+
Fair play
  and
    sports: GV706.3
Fairies (Folklore): GR549+
Fairs (Manners and customs): GT4580+
Fairy chess: GV1451.2
Fairy tales (Folklore): GR550+
Falkland Islands
  Atlases: G2835+
  Maps: G9175+
False hair (Manners and customs): GT2310
Family (Ethnology): GN480+
Family life (Manners and customs):
  GT2420
Fan (African group)
  Folklore: GR357.62.F34
Fancy dress (Manners and customs): GT1750
Fancy-dress balls: GV1749
Fanorona (Game): GV1469.F34
Fans (Manners and customs): GT2150
Far East
  Atlases: G2300+
  Maps: G7800+
Far Eastern costume (Ancient): GT538
Far West (United States)
  Atlases: G1460+
  Maps: G4210+
Farm folklore, see Agriculture - Folklore
Farming, see Agriculture
Faro (Game): GV1305
Fashion
  Clothing manufacture: TT490+
  Manners and customs: GT500+
Fashionable life (Manners and customs):
  GT3430+
Feast of Esther, see Purim
Feast of Fools, see Fools, Feast of
Feathers (Ethnology): GN435.9
Fecundity, see Fertility
Federal Republic of Germany, see West
  Germany
Feet, see Foot
Fencing: GV1143+
  Military science: U850+
Fencing, Oriental, see Oriental fencing
Feral studies (Ethnology): GN372

Fertility (Physiological anthropology): GN241

Festivals: GT3925+

Festivals, Harvest, see Harvest festivals

Festive days (Manners and customs): GT4905+

Feticide, see Abortion

Fetishism (Ethnology): GN472

Field handball: GV1017.F5

Field hockey: GV1017.H7

Fieldball: GV1017.F5

Fielding (Baseball): GV870

Fieldwork
  Ethnology: GN346+
  Folklore: GR45.5
  Geography: G74.5
  Physical geography: GB25

Fig (Folklore): GR790.F5

Fighting sports: GV1101+

Figure skating: GV850.4+

Fiji
  Atlases: G2890+
  Maps: G9380+

Filibusters: G539
  West Indian buccaneers, see Buccaneers

Finger games (Children's games): GV1218.F5

Fingerprints (Human variation): GN192

Finland
  Atlases: G2075+
  Maps: G6960+

Finno-Ugrians (Ethnology): GN549.F5

Fiords (Coastal landform): GB454.F5

Fire and fire-making
  Ethnology: GN416+
  Folklore: GR495
  in
    dwellings (Manners and customs): GT420

Fireplaces (Manners and customs): GT420

Fischer, Bobby: GV1439.F5

Fishes (Folklore): GR745

Fishing: SH
  Ethnology: GN407.35
  Manners and customs: GT5904
  Prehistoric archaeology: GN799.F5

Fishing implements (Ethnology): GN407.35

Fishing peoples (Ethnographies): GN389

Fitness tests, see Physical fitness tests

Five hundred (Card game): GV1295.F5

Fives (Ball game): GV1017.H2

Fjords, see Fiords

Fjort, see Bakongo

Flag-waving exercises: GV488

Flags, codes, etc. (Yachting): GV826

Flamenco dancing: GV1796.F55

Flights around the world: G445

Flint (Ethnology): GN434.2.F55

Flood forecasting: GB1399.2

Floodplains (Natural landforms): GB561+

Floods (Hydrology): GB1399+

Florentine football: GV948.5

Florida
  Atlases: G1315+
  Maps: G3930+

Flow, Groundwater, see Groundwater flow

Flowers (Manners and customs): GT5160

Flowoff, see Runoff

Fluvial sediment transport, see Sediment transport

Flying Dutchman (Theme in literature): PN57.F6

Folk beliefs: GR81

Folk dances and dancing (General): GV1743

Folk literature: GR71+

Folk medicine: GR880

Folklore: GR
  as a profession: GR49

Folklore and children, see Children - Folklore

Folklorists: GR49+

Folktales: GR74+

Fonteyn, Margot: GV1785.F63

Food
  Camps: GV198.F6
  Ethnology: GN407+
  Manners and customs: GT2860+
  Prehistoric archaeology: GN799.F6

Food preparation (Ethnology): GN410

Food production (Ethnology): GN407+

Fools, Feast of (Manners and customs): GT4995.F6

Fools, see Court fools

Foot (Human variation): GN161

Foot racing: GV1061+

Football, Amateur, see Amateur football

Football, American, see American football

Football, Australian, see Australian football

Football, Canadian, see Canadian football

Football, Professional, see Professional sports - Football

Football, Six-man, see Six-man football

Football, Touch, see Touch football

Football games: GV937+

Football poker: GV1295.F6

Footwear (Manners and customs): GT2130

Forecasting, Hydrological, see Hydrological forecasting

Foreign trade, see Commerce and trade

Form, Physical, see Physical form and dimensions

Form puzzles: GV1501

Formosa, see Taiwan

Fortifications (Prehistoric archaeology): GN789

Fortune telling: BF1845+

Forty-five (Card game): GV1295.F7

Fossil man (Human evolution): GN282+

Fox trot (Dance): GV1796.F6

Foxes (Folklore): GR730.F6

France
 Atlases: G1837+
 Maps: G5830+
Franklin, Sir John: G660+
Franklin Search: G660+
Franz Josef Land
 Atlases: G3055+
 Maps: G9785+
Fratellini Brothers: GV1811.F7
Freaks, wonders, etc. (Circuses):
 GV1835
Free exercises: GV489
Free Foresters (Cricket club): GV921.F8
Freezing and opening
 of
  lakes, see Ice on lakes
  rivers, see Ice on rivers
French Cameroons, see Cameroon
French Congo, see French Equatorial
 Africa
French Empire
 Atlases: G1835
 Maps: G5820+
French Equatorial Africa
 Atlases: G2610+
 Maps: G8680+
French Guiana
 Atlases: G1720+
 Maps: G5270+
French Guinea, see Guinea
French Indochina
 Atlases: G2365+
 Maps: G8005+
French Oceania (Maps): G9610+
French Somaliland, see French Territory
 of the Afars and Issas
French Sudan, see Mali
French Territory of the Afars and Issas
 Atlases: G2520+
 Maps: G8360+
French Togoland, see Togo
French Union
 Atlases: G1835
 Maps: G5820+
French West Africa
 Atlases: G2645+
 Maps: G8740+
French West Indies
 Atlases: G1660+
 Maps: G5060+
Fresh-air fund camps: HV931+
Fresh water from seawater: TD430+
Frevo (Dance): GV1796.F7
Friendly Islands, see Tonga
Friendships, Institutionalized (Eth-
 nology): GN490.2
Frisbee (Game): GV1097.F7
Frontiers (Environmental influences on
 man): GF53
Frozen ground (Geomorphology): GB641+

Fruits of gold (Folktale), see Three
 stolen princesses (Folktale)
Functionalism (Culture and cultural
 processes): GN363
Funeral customs
 Ethnology: GN486
 Manners and customs: GT3150+
Funnel-beaker culture
 By continent, see table below GN776.2+,
  e. g. GN776.2.F8 (Europe)
Fur (Manners and customs): GT2070
Furniture
 Ethnology: GN415+
 for
  gymnasiums: GV407
 Manners and customs: GT450
Futuna Islands (Maps): G9525+

G

GANEFO Games (Games of the New Emerging
 Forces): GV722.5.G3
Gabon
 Atlases: G2615+
 Maps: G8690+
Gaels, see Celts
Gagauzi folklore: GR203.2.G3
Gambia
 Atlases: G2710+
 Maps: G8870+
Gamblers' card tricks, see Card tricks -
 Gamblers' tricks
Gambling: GV1301+
 Ethnology: GN454.6
Game-counters for card games: GV1297
Games: GV1199+
 Ethnology: GN454.8+
 Folklore: GR480+
Games, Instructive, see Instructive
 games
Games of the New Emerging Forces, see
 GANEFO Games (Games of the New
 Emerging Forces)
Ganefo Games, see GANEFO Games (Games
 of the New Emerging Forces)
Gardens, Amusement, see Amusement
 parks, etc.
Garlic (Folklore): GR790.G3
Gases
 in
  marine sediments: GC380.2.G3
  seawater: GC141
Gathering (Ethnology): GN407.3+
Gathering peoples, see Hunting and
 gathering peoples
Gazetteers, Geographical: G101+
Gehrig, Lou: GV865.G4
Gems (Folklore): GR805
Generation, see Reproduction

Geo-codes, see Geographical location codes
Geographers: G65+
Geographers, Ancient, see Ancient geographers
Geographers, Arab, see Arabs - Geographers
Geographers, Classical, see Classical geographers
Geographers, Medieval, see Medieval geographers
Geographers, Popes as, see Popes as geographers
Geographic names: G104+
Geographic surveys, see Surveys, Geographic
Geographic terms: G107.8+
Geographical areas, Calculation of, see Calculation of geographical areas
Geographical location codes: G108.7
Geographical perception: G71.5
Geographical positions: G109+
Geographical research, see Research, Geographical
Geography: G1+
  as a profession: G65
  Ethnology: GN476.4+
Geography, Aerial, see Aerial geography
Geography, Historical, see Historical geography
Geography, Mathematical, see Mathematical geography
Geography, Physical, see Physical geography
Geography, Social, see Anthropogeography
Geography and geopolitics, see Geopolitics and geography
Geography and religion, see Religion and geography
Geography and sociology, see Sociology and geography
Geography games: GV1485
Geology, Submarine, see Submarine geology
Geology
  of
    the Atlantic and Pacific Oceans: QE350.2+
Geomorphic geology, see Geomorphology
Geomorphology: GB400+
Geophagy: GN408
Geophysics: QC801+
Geopolitics
  and
    geography: JC319+
Georgia (United States)
  Atlases: G1310+
  Maps: G3920+
Geothermal resources (Groundwater): GB1199.5+
German (Dance): GV1757

German Cameroons, see Cameroon
German cards (Dances): GV1750
German Democratic Republic, see East Germany
German East Africa, see Tanzania
German Empire
  Atlases: G1905+
  Maps: G6070+
German gymnastics: GV465
German horse exercises, see Horse, Vaulting
German Southwest Africa, see Southwest Africa (Namibia)
Germanic tribes (Ethnology): GN549.G4
Germany
  Atlases: G1907+
  Maps: G6080+
Geysers (Groundwater): GB1198.5+
Ghana
  Atlases: G2700+
  Maps: G8850+
Ghassul culture
  By continent, see table below GN776.2+, e. g. GN776.3.G5 (Asia)
Ghosts (Folklore): GR580
Giants
  Body dimensions and proportions: GN69+
  Folklore: GR560
Gilbert and Ellice Islands Colony (Maps): G9475+
Gilbert Islands (Maps): G9480+
Gin (Drinking customs): GT2896
Gin rummy, see Rummy (Card game)
Ginseng (Folklore): GR790.G5
Girdle (Folklore): GR950.G5
Girdle, Shoulder, see Shoulder girdle
Girdles of chastity (Manners and customs): GT2810
Girls, see Women and girls
Giselle (Ballet): GV1790.G5
Glacial landforms: GB581+
Glaciated terrain, see Glacial landforms
Glaciers (Hydrology): GB2401+
Gladiatorial contests, Roman: GV35
Gladiators, Roman: GV35
Glasgow. Queen's Park Football Club: GV943.6.G67
Gliding (Sports): GV764+
Globe gores, Terrestrial, see Terrestrial globe gores
Globe making: GA260+
Globes: G3160+
Gloves (Manners and customs): GT2170
Gnomes (Folklore): GR549+
Go (Game): GV1459+
Goblins, see Fairies
God parents (Ethnology): GN490.3
Gods (Folklore): GR510
Gold
  Ethnology: GN436.3
  Prehistoric archaeology: GN799.G6

Gold Coast, see Ghana
Golf: GV961+
Golf, Contract, see Contract golf
Golf, Miniature, see Miniature golf
Golf courses, greens, etc.: GV975
Golf exercises: GV979.E9
Gourds (Ethnology): GN434.6
Government policy, see State policy, etc.
Graffiti (Manners and customs): GT3912+
Grand Prix racing: GV1029+
Grass huts (Ethnology): GN414.3.G7
Grateful dead (Folktale): GR75.G6
Graveyards, see Cemeteries
Great Britain, see British Isles
Great Lakes
  Currents: GC291+
  Tides: GC374
Great Lakes Aggregation
  Atlases: G1107.G7
  Maps: G3310+
Great Plains (United States)
  Maps: G4052.G75
Great Smoky Mountains (Maps): G3902.G69+
Greater Antilles (Maps): G4910+
Greece
  Atlases: G2000+
  Maps: G6810+
Greek classical games, etc.: GV17+
Greek costume (Ancient): GT550
Greenland
  Atlases: G1110+
  Maps: G3380+
Greetings, see Salutations
Grenada (Maps): G5130+
Grids (Cartography): GA116
Grip (Golf): GV979.G7
Grottoes, see Caves
Groundwater (Hydrology): GB1001+
Groundwater exploration: GB1197.6
Groundwater flow: GB1197.7
Group exercises: GV481+
Guadeloupe (Maps): G5070+
Guam
  Atlases: G2910+
  Maps: G9415+
Guatemala
  Atlases: G1555+
  Maps: G4810+
Guessing games: GV1473
Guianas
  Atlases: G1705+
  Maps: G5240+
Guidance, Vocational, see Vocational
  guidance
Guides, Baseball: GV877
Guinea
  Atlases: G2670+
  Maps: G8790+
Guinea-Bissau
  Atlases: G2730+
  Maps: G8890+

Guinea Current: GC296.8.G8
Gulf Stream: GC296
Gun clubs: GV1163
Guns (Shooting sports): GV1174+
Gurmas (Folklore): GR351.62.G83
Guyana
  Atlases: G1710+
  Maps: G5250+
Gymnasiums: GV403+
  Church gymnasiums: BV1645
  Roman gymnasiums: NA325.G9
Gymnastic dancing: GV1798+
Gymnastics: GV460+
Gypsies: DX

H

Habitation (Ethnology): GN413+
Hagenbeck, Carl: GV1811.H2
Hagenbeck-Wallace Circus: GV1821.H3
Hair, Color of, see Color of hair
Hair, False, see False hair
Hairdressing (Manners and customs):
  GT2290+
Hairstyles (Ethnology): GN419.13
Haiti
  Atlases: G1615+
  Maps: G4940+
Hakluyt, Richard: G69.H2
Halfchick (Folktale): GR75.H3
Hall Islands (Maps): G9435+
Halling (Dance): GV1796.H2
Halloween (Manners and customs): GT4965
Hallstatt culture
  By continent, see table below GN780.2+,
    e. g. GN780.2.H3 (Europe)
Hammer throwing: GV1094.5
Hammocks (Ethnology): GN415.3.H35
Hand (Human variation): GN161
Hand action (Golf): GV979.H3
Hand balancing (Acrobatics): GV553
Hand preference (Physiological
  anthropology): GN233
Hand-to-hand fighting (Sports): GV1111+
Handbags (Manners and customs): GT2180
Handball (Game): GV1017.H2
Handball, Field, see Field handball
Handicapped persons
  Children's camps: GV197.H3
  Children's games: LC4026
  Physical education and training: GV445
  Recreation and leisure: GV183.5+
  Swimming: GV837.4
  See also Mentally handicapped; Social-
    ly handicapped
Handkerchiefs (Manners and customs):
  GT2135
Handling
  of
    boats: GV777.5
      Sailboats: GV811.5

Hares (Folklore): GR730.H3
Harness (Manners and customs): GT5888
Harpoons (Ethnology): GN407.33.H55
Harvard University rowing: GV807.H3
Harvard-Yale boat races: GV801
Harvest festivals (Manners and customs):
  GT4380+
Harvesting (Folklore): GR895
Hat tricks: GV1559
Hats (Manners and customs): GT2110+
Hausa (Folklore): GR351.32.H34
Hawaii
  Atlases: G1534.2+
  Maps: G4380+
Hazardous aspects
  of
    the environment: GF85
Head (Physical form and dimensions):
  GN63.8+
Head hunting: GN473.3
Headdresses (Ethnology): GN419.13
Headgear (Manners and customs): GT2110+
Healths, Drinking of, see Drinking of
  healths
Hearing (Race psychology): GN275
Heart (Human variation): GN206
Hearth
  Folklore: GR495
  Manners and customs: GT420
Hearts (Card game): GV1295.H4
Heat and heating
  Ethnology: GN416+
  Manners and customs: GT420
Heaths (Geomorphology): GB621+
Heavy exercises: GV511+
Hebrew costume (Ancient): GT540
Hebrews, see Jews
Henley regattas: GV798
Heralds (Manners and customs): GT5020
Herbs (Manners and customs): GT5164
Herding (Ethnology): GN407.7
Hereditary functions (Physiological
  anthropology): GN247+
Heroes (Folklore): GR515
Herrmann, Carl: GV1545.H6
Herzegovina, see Bosnia and Herzegovina
Hexagonal chess: GV1458.H4
Hibernia, see Ireland
High five (Card game), see Pedro (Card
  game)
High jump: GV1075
High kicking exercises: GV525
High life (Manners and customs): GT3430+
Hiking: GV199+
Hiking, Bicycle: GV1044+
Himalaya Mountains
  Atlases: G2202.H5
  Maps: G7402.H5
Hispaniola
  Atlases: G1610+
  Maps: G4930+

Historical atlases: G1030+
Historical geography: G141
History (Ethnology): GN476.6
History games: GV1487
Hobbies: GV1201.5
Hockey: GV1017.H7
Hockey, Ice, see Ice hockey
Hockey, Ring, see Ring hockey
Hockey, Roller skate, see Roller
  skate hockey
Hogoleu Islands, see Truk Islands
Hogs, see Swine
Holidays: GT3925+
  See also names of special days, e. g.
    Christmas, May Day
Hollywood bridge (Card game): GV1295.H6
Holy Roman Empire (Maps): G6080+
Home life (Manners and customs): GT2420
Homes, see Dwellings
Homo capensis (Fossil man), see Boskop
  (Fossil man)
Homo erectus (Fossil man): GN284+
Homo neanderthalensis (Fossil man):
  GN285
Homo sapiens (Fossil man): GN286+
Homo soloensis (Fossil man): GN284.4
Honduras
  Atlases: G1565+
  Maps: G4830+
Hongkong (Crown colony)
  Maps: G7940+
Hon'inbō (Go tournament): GV1460.75
Hoods (Costume): GT2110+
Hoop exercises: GV490
Hoorn Islands, see Futuna Islands
Hop, step, and jump (Track and field
  event): GV1078
Horgen culture
  By continent, see table below GN776.2+,
    e. g. GN776.2.H6 (Europe)
Horizontal bar exercises: GV527
Horn (Animal materials)
  Ethnology: GN435.3
Horse, Vaulting (Heavy exercises):
  GV517+
Horsemanship: SF309+
  Manners and customs: GT5885+
Horses
  Folklore: GR715
  Manners and customs: GT5885+
  Trained horses: GV1831.H8
Horseshoe pitching: GV1095
Horticulture (Ethnology): GN407.55
Horu Shoto, see Hall Islands
Hosiery (Manners and customs): GT2128
Hospitality (Manners and customs):
  GT3410+
Hot springs (Groundwater): GB1198+
Hotels (Manners and customs): GT3770+
Hottentots (Folklore): GR358.2.H64
Houdini, Harry: GV1545.H8

House marks (Manners and customs): GT470
House names (Manners and customs): GT471
Houseboats and houseboating (Sports): GV836
Household arts (Manners and customs): GT480+
Household sanitation (Manners and customs): GT472
Houses (Manners and customs): GT170+
　See also Dwellings
Hoyle's rules: GV1241+
Hrvatska, see Croatia
Huella (Dance): GV1796.H75
Hula (Dance): GV1796.H8
Human body (Folklore): GR489
Human ecology: GF
Human evolution (Physical anthropology): GN281+
Human fighting (Sports): GV1111+
Human geography, see Anthropogeography
Human growth (Physical anthropology): GN62.9+
Human paleontology (Human evolution): GN282+
Human traits versus simian traits, see Simian traits versus human traits
Human variation (Physical anthropology): GN62.8+
Hungary
　Atlases: G1940+
　Maps: G6500+
Hunting
　Ethnology: GN407.3+
　Folklore: GR898
　Manners and customs: GT5810+
　Sports: SK
Hunting and gathering peoples (Ethnographies): GN388
Hurdle racing: GV1067
Hurling (Ball game): GV1017.H8
Hurricane waves, see Storm surges
Huts, Grass, see Grass huts
Hydrogeology: GB1001+
Hydrologic cycle: GB848
Hydrologic models: GB656.2.H9
Hydrological forecasting: GB845
Hydrology (Physical geography): GB651+
Hydrometeorology: GB2801+
Hydrometers (Oceanography): GC155
Hypsometry: QC895

I

Iberian Peninsula
　Atlases: G1960+
　Maps: G6540+

Ice
　and
　　snow camping: GV198.9
　　snow climbing: GV200.3
　Hydrology: GB2401+
　on
　　lakes: GB1798.2+
　　rivers: GB1398.2+
Ice Capades: GV850.55.I25
Ice dancing: GV850.45
Ice hockey: GV846+
Ice racing
　Automobiles: GV1029.9.I25
　Motorcycles: GV1060.13
Ice rinks: GV850.7
Ice sheets (Hydrology): GB2401+
Ice skates: GV852
Ice skating: GV848.9+
Iceboating: GV843
Iceland
　Atlases: G2060+
　Maps: G6930+
Idaho
　Atlases: G1480+
　Maps: G4270+
Ilhas do Cabo Verde, see Cape Verde Islands
Illinois
　Atlases: G1405+
　Maps: G4100+
Illumination, see Lighting
Illustrations
　of
　　old playing cards: GV1235
　　yachts: GV821+
Imaginary voyages: G560
Impenetrable secret (Games): GV1507.I5
Implements (Ethnology): GN436.8+
Inbreeding
　Physiological anthropology: GN252
　Social pathology: HV4981
Incantations (Folklore): GR540
Incense ceremonies, Japanese, see Japanese incense ceremonies
Incest (Ethnology): GN480.25
Incineration (Funeral customs): GT3330+
India
　Atlases: G2280+
　Maps: G7650+
Indian Ocean
　Atlases: G2850+
　Maps: G9180+
Indiana
　Atlases: G1400+
　Maps: G4090+
Indians, Games of: E59.G3
Indians, How to play: GV1217
Individuals
　Physical education and training: GV438
　Sports: GV708

Indian club exercises: GV491+
Indo-Europeans
  Ethnology: GN539
  Folklore: GR95
Indochina, see Southeast Asia
Indonesia
  Atlases: G2400+
  Maps: G8070+
Indoor baseball: GV881
Indoor games and amusements: GV1221+
Indoor soccer: GV943.9.I6
Industries
  Ethnology: GN429+
  Manners and customs: GT5910+
Infanticide (Ethnology): GN482.5
Inflatable boats (Sports): GV780
Influence of the environment
  (Technology): GN406.5
Information services
  Anthropology: GN13
  Ethnology: GN307.6
  Hydrology: GB657.2
  Oceanography: GC37.5
Initiations (Adolescence)
  Ethnology: GN483.3
  Manners and customs: GT2485+
Inns (Manners and customs): GT3770+
Insects
  Ethnology: GN409.5
  Folklore: GR750
Insignia, Baseball: GV875.2
Institutions (Ethnology): GN406+
Instructive games: GV1480+
Instruments, Oceanographic (General),
  see Oceanographic instruments and
  apparatus (General)
Integrated data processing, see
  Electronic data processing
Intellectual life (Ethnology): GN451+
Intergroup relations (Ethnology):
  GN496+
Interior valleys (Geomorphology): GB609
Interment customs: GT3320
Internal organs (Human variation):
  GN206
International Map Committee: GA323
International Olympic Committee: GV721.3
International sports and athletic
  contests: GV721+
  Rugby: GV945.5+
  Soccer: GV943.45+
International Stoke Mandeville Games:
  GV722.5.I42
International trade, see Commerce and
  trade
Internationaler Sportkongress: GV722.5.I5
Interpretive dancing, see Expressionistic
  dancing
Interscholastic athletics, see Intramural
  and interscholastic athletics
Interviews (Ethnology): GN346.3

Intramural and interscholastic athletics
  (Physical education and training)
  College: GV347+
  School: GV346
Intramural sports: GV710
Intrusion, Saltwater, see Saltwater
  encroachment
Inundations, see Floods
Invalids, Games for: GV1231
Invocations (Folklore): GR540
Iowa
  Atlases: G1430+
  Maps: G4150+
Iran
  Atlases: G2255+
  Maps: G7621+
Iraq
  Atlases: G2250+
  Maps: G7610+
Ireland
  Atlases: G1830+
  Maps: G5780+
Irish Free State, see Eire
Iroha karuta (Card game): GV1299.I7
Iron (Ethnology): GN436.4
Iron age (Prehistoric archaeology):
  GN779+
Irrigation (Ethnology): GN407.8
Islamic World
  Atlases: G1785+
  Maps: G5680+
Islands
  Environmental influences on man: GF61
  Folklore: GR675
  Geomorphology: GB471+
  of
    the world (Atlases): G1029
Islands, Mythical, see Mythical islands
Islas Malvinas, see Falkland Islands
Isle de Bourbon, see Réunion
Isolated areas, Travels in: G503
Isotopic indicators, see Radioactive
  tracers
Israel
  Atlases: G2235+
  Maps: G7500+
Italian Empire
  Atlases: G1980+
  Maps: G9705+
Italian Somaliland, see Somalia
Italy
  Atlases: G1983+
  Maps: G6710+
Ivory Coast
  Atlases: G2665+
  Maps: G8780+

J

Jai alai (Ball game): GV1017.P4

Jamaica
  Atlases: G1625+
  Maps: G4960+
Japan
  Atlases: G2355+
  Maps: G7960+
Japanese chess, see Shōgi
Japanese Empire
  Atlases: G2353+
  Maps: G7950+
Japanese incense ceremony: GT3032
Japanese tea ceremony: GT2910+
Japanese wrestling: GV1197
Jass (Card game): GV1295.J3
Javelin throwing: GV1094.6
Jayhawk (Folklore): GR830.J3
Jesters
  Folklore: GR523
  Manners and customs: GT3670
Jewelry
  Ethnology: GN418.4+
  Folklore: GR425
  Manners and customs: GT2250+
Jews
  Ethnology: GN547
  Folklore: GR97.8+
  Marriage customs: GT2695.J4
Jig (Theatrical dancing): GV1793
Jigsaw puzzles: GV1507.J5
Jinn (Folklore): GR549+
Jitterbug dancing: GV1796.J6
Jiu-jitsu: GV1114
Jogging: GV494
John the Baptist's Day (Manners and
  customs): GT4995.J6
John the bear (Folktale), see Three
  stolen princesses (Folktale)
Jōmon culture
  By continent, see table below GN776.2+,
    e. g. GN776.3.J6 (Asia)
Jordan
  Atlases: G2240+
  Maps: G7510+
Jōseki (Go): GV1460
Journalism, Sports: PN4784.S6
Jousting (Water sport): GV840.J6
Jousts (Modern revivals): GV1191
Judges (Manners and customs): GT6230+
Judging
  Boxing: GV1137.3
  Ice skating: GV850.6
Judo: GV1114
Juegos Deportivos Centro-Americanos y del
  Caribe: GV722.5.J8
Juggling: GV1541+
Jumping (Track and field event): GV1073+
Jumping, Ski: GV854.9.J8
Jumping exercises: GV529
Jumping rope: GV498
Jurists, see Judges

Juvenile voyages and travels: G570

K

Kabyle (Folklore): GR353.2.K33
Kagura (Dance): BL2224.25.K3
Kalmucks (Folklore): GR268.K2
Kamerun, see Cameroon
Kang (Ball game): GV1017.K3
Kansas
  Atlases: G1455+
  Maps: G4200+
Karate: GV1114.3
Karst landforms (Geomorphology): GB599+
Karting (Automobile racing): GV1029.5
Kayaking (Sports): GV781+
Keeling Islands, see Cocos Islands
Kemari (Ball game): GV1017.K4
Kempo: GV1114.7
Kendo (Fighting sports): GV1141.3+
Keno (Game): GV1306
Kentucky
  Atlases: G1330+
  Maps: G3950+
Kenya
  Atlases: G2530+
  Maps: G8410+
Kermadec Islands (Maps): G9590+
Kermisses (Manners and customs): GT4580+
Khmer Republic, see Cambodia
Kicking (Football): GV951.7
Kicking exercises, see High kicking
  exercises
Kiki-kō, see Japanese incense ceremony
Kikuyu (Folklore): GR356.42.K53
Kindreds (Ethnology): GN488.4
Kings
  Chess: GV1451.5.K5
  Ethnology: GN492.7
  Folklore: GR520
Kingships (Ethnology): GN492.7
Kingsmill Islands, see Gilbert Islands
Kinship systems (Ethnology): GN486.5+
Kissing (Manners and customs): GT2640
Kissing games: GV1211
Kissing the Bible (Legal custom): GT6280
Kitchen middens (Prehistoric archaeology)
  GN787
Kiteflying (Sports): GV767+
Kleine Bosco (Games): GV1507.K5
Knife throwing: GV1096
Knight (Chess): GV1451.5.K6
Knives (Ethnology): GN437.K55
Knots (Folklore): GR950.K6
Knoviz culture
  By continent, see table below GN778.2+,
    e. g. GN778.2.K5 (Europe)
  See also Lausitz culture
Knowledge (Ethnology): GN476+

Kōdō, see Japanese incense ceremony
Kolo (Dance): GV1796.K6
Korea
   Atlases: G2330+
   Maps: G7900+
Krakowiak (Dance): GV1796.K7
Kulturkreis theory (Culture diffusion):
   GN365.6
Kumiko, see Japanese incense ceremony
Kuroshio: GC296.2
Kuwait
   Atlases: G2249.9+
   Maps: G7600+

L

Labor, Division of, see Division of labor
Labrador
   Atlases: G1190+
   Maps: G3610+
Labyrinths (Games), see Maze puzzles
Lacrosse: GV989
Ladder exercises: GV541
Lagoon Islands, see Ellice Islands
Lagoons (Hydrology): GB2201+
Lake dwellings and lake dwellers (Pre-
   historic archaeology): GN785
Lake temperatures: GB1798.6+
Lakes
   Environmental influences on man: GF67
   Hydrology: GB1601+
Lambert's projection: GA115
Lamps (Manners and customs): GT445
Lamso, see Nso
Land drainage, see Drainage
Land settlement, Limits of, see Limits
   of land settlement
Land subsidences, see Subsidences
Land tenure (Ethnology): GN449.3
Land yachts, see Sand yachting
Landforms (Geomorphology): GB400+
Landforms, Coastal, see Coastal landforms
Lango (Folklore): GR356.52.L34
Language of animals (Folklore): GR710
Lanterns
   Folklore: GR496
   Manners and customs: GT445
Laos
   Atlases: G2374.5+
   Maps: G8015+
Lapland (Maps): G6912.L3
Lapta (Ball game): GV1017.L3
La Tene culture
   By continent, see table below GN780.2+,
     e. g. GN780.2.L3 (Europe)
Latin America (General)
   Atlases: G1540+
   Maps: G3292.L3
Latitude and longitude (Cartography):
   QB224.5+

Latvia
   Atlases: G2130+
   Maps: G7040+
Launches (Sports): GV833.5+
Laundering (Manners and customs): GT482
Lausitz culture
   By continent, see table below GN778.2+,
     e. g. GN778.2.L3 (Europe)
Lava tubes (Geomorphology): GB649.L3
Law (Manners and customs): GT6230+
Lawn billiards: GV1017.B4
Lawn bowls (Bowling games): GV909+
Lawn tempest (Ball game): GV1017.L48
Lawn tennis: GV991+
Laws concerning dress: GT527+
Lawyers (Manners and customs): GT6230+
Leadership (Ethnology): GN492.25
League of American Wheelmen: GV1047.L4
Leagues, Sports: GV563
Leagues and clubs, Baseball: GV875
Leather (Ethnology): GN435.5
Leaves (Manners and customs): GT5160
Lebanon
   Atlases: G2225+
   Maps: G7470+
Leeward Islands
   Atlases: G1650+
   Maps: G5030+
Left- and right-handedness
   Education: LB1123
   Physiological anthropology: GN233
Legal profession (Manners and customs):
   GT6230+
Legends: GR78+
Leisure time activities, see Recreation
   and leisure
Lemon (Folklore): GR790.L4
Lemuria (Prehistoric archaeology):
   GN750+
Lenglen, Suzanne: GV994.L4
Lengyel-Jordansmühl culture
   By continent, see table below GN776.2+,
     e. g. GN776.2.L4 (Europe)
Lesotho
   Atlases: G2579.3+
   Maps: G8580+
Lesser Antilles (Maps): G5000+
Levant
   Atlases: G2205+
   Maps: G7420+
Leveling: TA606+
Levirate (Ethnology): GN480.43
Libraries, Map, see Map collections
Libya
   Atlases: G2475+
   Maps: G8260+
Liechtenstein
   Atlases: G1900+
   Maps: G6050+
Lifar, Serge: GV1785.L5
Life cycle (Ethnology): GN482+

Lifeguards, Certification and examina-
tions for, see Examinations and
certification for lifeguards
Lifting weights, see Weight lifting
Light (Ethnology): GN416+
Light, Underwater, see Underwater light
Lighting (Manners and customs): GT440+
Lightning (Folklore): GR630
Limbas (Folklore): GR352.32.L53
Limits of land settlement (Human
ecology): GF101+
Limnology: GB1601+
Lindbergh hop, see Lindy (Dance)
Lindy (Dance): GV1796.L5
Line Islands (Maps): G9530+
Line play (Football): GV951.2
Lions, Trained: GV1831.L5
Lips (Physical form and dimensions):
GN64
Literary games: GV1491+
Lithuania
    Atlases: G2135+
    Maps: G7050+
Little League baseball: GV880.5
Liturgical dancing, see Religious
dancing
Living whist: GV1291.L7
Location codes, Geographical, see
Geographical location codes
Locks (Manners and customs): GT7070.L6
London
    Arsenal Football Club: GV943.6.L6
    Queen's Park Rangers Football Club:
      GV943.6.L67
Long-horse exercises: GV521
Long jump: GV1077
Long-nosed goblin, see Tengu
Longitude, see Latitude and longitude
Losap Atoll (Maps): G9445+
Lost continents (Prehistoric archaeology):
GN750+
Lotto (Game): GV1311.L6
Louis, Joe: GV1132.L6
Louisiana
    Atlases: G1360+
    Maps: G4010+
Love
    Folklore: GR440+
    Manners and customs: GT2600+
Love potions (Folklore), see Love –
Folklore
Low Archipelago, see Tuamoto Archipelago
Low Countries, see Benelux countries
Loyalty Islands (Maps): G9350+
Lucayos, see Bahama Islands (Bahamas)
Luciafest, see St. Lucy's Day
Lunar globes: G3165+
Lungs (Human variation): GN206
Luo (Folklore): GR356.42.L83
Lusatian culture, see Lausitz culture
Lusitania, see Portugal

Luxemburg
    Atlases: G1870+
    Maps: G6020+

M

Macao (Colony and city)
    Maps: G7945+
Macedonia (Federated Republic)
    Maps: G6845+
Madagascar
    Atlases: G2555+
    Maps: G8460+
Madame Tussaud's waxworks: GV1836
Madeira Islands
    Atlases: G2820+
    Maps: G9140+
Magdalenian culture
    By continent, see table below GN772.2+,
      e. g. GN772.2.M3 (Europe)
Magic (Ethnology): GN475+
Magic, Parlor: GV1541+
Magyar and Slavic folklore, see Slavic
and Magyar folklore
Mah jong: GV1299.M3
Maiden without hands (Folktale): GR75.M3
Maine
    Atlases: G1215+
    Maps: G3730+
Maintenance and repair
    of
      campgrounds: GV191.72
      sailboats: GV811.3
Make-up (Cosmetics), see Cosmetics
Malagasy Republic, see Madagascar
Malawi
    Atlases: G2579.9+
    Maps: G8610+
Malay Archipelago
    Atlases: G2385+
    Maps: G8050+
Malay Peninsula
    Atlases: G2380+
    Maps: G8030+
Malaya
    Atlases: G2380+
    Maps: G8030+
Malaysia
    Atlases: G2380+
    Maps: G8030+
Maldives (Maps): G9215+
Mali
    Atlases: G2675+
    Maps: G8800+
Malta
    Atlases: G1992.3+
    Maps: G6790+
Malvinas, Islas, see Falkland Islands
Mamprusi (Folklore): GR351.62.M33

Man, Climatic influences on, see
  Climatic influences on man
Man, Fossil, see Fossil man
Man, Prehistoric, see Prehistoric
  archaeology
Man as an animal (Physical anthropology):
  GN280.7
Mana (Ethnology): GN471.4+
Management
  Baseball: GV875.7
  Basketball: GV885.47
  Circuses: GV1825+
  Playgrounds: GV427
Manchuria
  Atlases: G2310+
  Maps: G7830+
Mandeville, Sir John: G370.M2
Mandingo (Folklore): GR350.32.M33
Mandrakes (Folklore): GR790.M3
Manitoba
  Atlases: G1155+
  Maps: G3480+
Manned exploration devices, see Oceano-
  graphic submersibles
Manned underwater stations: GC66
Manners and customs (General): GT
Manners and customs, Modern, see Modern
  manners and customs
Man's influence on the environment: GF75
Manzai (Dance): GV1796.M32
Maori folktales: GR375
Map collections (Cartography): GA192+
Map drawing and reading, Elementary, see
  Elementary map drawing and reading
Map engraving: GA150+
Map grids, see Grids (Cartography)
Map libraries, see Map collections
Map photocopying: GA150.7
Map printing: GA150+
Map reading: GA151
Map reproduction: GA150.7
Map scales: GA118
Mapping, Cadastral, see Cadastral
  mapping
Mapping, Statistical, see Statistical
  mapping
Mapping
  Glaciers: GB2401.72.M32
  Groundwater: GB1001.72.M32
  Ice: GB2401.72.M32
  Ice sheets: GB2401.72.M32
  in
    geomorphology: GB400.42.M3
    hydrogeology: GB1001.72.M32
    hydrometeorology: GB2801.72.M32
    limnology: GB1601.72.M32
    oceanography: GC10.4.M33
  Lagoons: GB2201.72.M32
  Lakes: GB1601.72.M32
  Ponds: GB1801.72.M32
  Rivers: GB1201.72.M32

Mapping - Continued
  Sea ice: GB2401.72.M32
  Snow: GB2601.72.M32
  Snow surveys: GB2601.72.M32
  Stream measurements: GB1201.72.M32
  Waterfalls: GB1401.72.M32
Maps: G3200+
  for
    the visually handicapped, see Visually
      handicapped, Maps for the
  in
    boundary disputes: GA203
Maps, World, see World maps
Marathon running: GV1065
Marbles (Game): GV1213
Marching and drills
  Calisthenics: GV495
  Dancing: GV1797
Mardi gras (Manners and customs):
  GT4180+
Margamkali (Dance): GV1796.M33
Mariana Islands
  Atlases: G2905+
  Maps: G9410+
Marine biology: QH91+
Marine cartography, see Cartography,
  Marine
Marine caves (Geomorphology): GB601.8
Marine deposits, see Marine sediments
Marine disasters, see Shipwrecks
Marine fauna: QL121+
Marine flora: QK103; QK108+
Marine pollution: GC1080+
  By region: GC1101+
Marine resources: GC1000+
  Economic geography: HC92
Marine sediments: GC377+
  By region or ocean: GC380.3+
Mariquita (Dance): GV1796.M34
Maritime anthropology (Ethnographies):
  GN386
Maritime atlases: G1059+
Maritime Provinces (Canada)
  Atlases: G1120+
  Maps: G3410+
Markets
  Ethnology: GN450.2
  Folklore: GR873
Marks, House, see House marks
Marquesas Islands (Maps): G9620+
Marriage
  Ethnology: GN484.4+
  Folklore: GR440+
  Manners and customs: GT2600+
    Royalty, nobility, etc.: GT5070
Marriage forms (Ethnology): GN480+
Mars
  Atlases: G1000.5.M3
  Globes: G3167.M3
  Maps: G3182.M3

Marshall Islands
  Atlases: G2930+
  Maps: G9460+
Marshes (Geomorphology): GB621+
Martinique (Maps): G5080+
Maryland
  Atlases: G1270+
  Maps: G3840+
Marylebone Cricket Club: GV921.M3
Mashona (Folklore): GR358.62.M34
Mask balls: GV1749
Masks
  Children's games: GV1218.M3
  Ethnology: GN419.5
  Manners and customs: GT1747
Massachusetts
  Atlases: G1230+
  Maps: G3760+
  Tidal currents: GC309.M3
Masses, Water, see Water masses
Mat work (Heavy exercises): GV545
Matabele (Folklore): GR358.62.M35
Matadors: GV1108
Matchstick tricks: GV1559
Material culture (Ethnology): GN406+
Mathematical anthropology: GN34.3.M3
Mathematical games: GV1491+
Mathematical geography: GA1+
Mathematical models
  Currents: GC239.3.M3
  Glaciers: GB2401.72.M35
  Groundwater: GB1001.72.M35
  Ice: GB2401.72.M35
  Ice sheets: GB2401.72.M35
  in
    geomorphology: GB400.42.M33
    hydrogeology: GB1001.72.M35
    hydrology: GB656.2.M33
    hydrometeorology: GB2801.72.M35
    limnology: GB1601.72.M35
    oceanography: GC10.4.M36
  Lagoons: GB2201.72.M35
  Lakes: GB1601.72.M35
  Ponds: GB1801.72.M35
  Rivers: GB1201.72.M35
  Sea ice: GB2401.72.M35
  Snow: GB2601.72.M35
  Snow surveys: GB2601.72.M35
  Stream measurements: GB1201.72.M35
  Tides: GC305.5.M3
  Waterfalls: GB1401.72.M35
  Waves: GC213.7.M3
Mathematics
  Ethnology: GN476.15
  in
    geomorphology: GB400.42.M34
    physical geography: GB21.5.M33
Matriarchy (Ethnology): GN479.5
Matrilineal descent (Ethnology): GN487.4
Matrilocal (Ethnology): GN480.63
Maturation (Manners and customs): GT2485+

Mauritania
  Atlases: G2685+
  Maps: G8820+
Mauritius (Maps): G9185+
Maxixe (Dance): GV1796.M36
May Day (Manners and customs): GT4945
Maze puzzles: GV1507.M3
Mbete (Folklore): GR357.32.M35
Measurement
  of
    yachts: GV828
Measurements, Physical, see Anthropometry
Medical anthropology: GN296
Medical folklore, see Folk medicine
Medicine
  Ethnology: GN477+
  Folklore: GR880
  Manners and customs: R707
Medicine ball: GV496
Medicine men (Ethnology): GN475.8
Medieval costume: GT575
Medieval dancing: GV1615
Medieval geographers: G89+
Medieval manners and customs: GT120
Medieval sports, games, etc.: GV41;
  GV575
Mediterranean groups (Ethnology): GN543
Megalithic monuments (Prehistoric
  archaeology): GN790
Meganthropus paleojavanicus (Fossil man):
  GN283.5
Meijinsen (Go tournament): GV1460.75
Melanesia
  Atlases: G2870+
  Maps: G9260+
Men (Anthropometry): GN59.M4
Men-of-war (Peacetime cruises): G549
Menhirs (Prehistoric archaeology): GN790
Men's costume: GT1710
Mental maps, see Geographical perception
Mentally handicapped, Recreation for:
  GV183.7
Mercator-Hondius atlases: G1007
Mercator's projection: GA115
Merengue (Dance): GV1796.M45
Merry-go-round: GV1860.M4
Mesolithic age (Prehistoric archaeology):
  GN773+
Mesopotamia, see Iraq
Messianic cults, see Nativistic movements
Metallurgy
  Ethnology: GN436+
  Prehistoric archaeology: GN799.M4
Metals
  Ethnology: GN436+
  Folklore: GR810
Metals, Precious, see Precious metals
Meteorology (Folklore): GR635
Mexico
  Atlases: G1545+
  Maps: G4410+

Michelsberg culture
  By continent, see table below GN776.2+,
    e. g. GN776.2.M5 (Europe)
Michigan
  Atlases: G1410+
  Maps: G4110+
Micronesia
  Atlases: G2900+
  Maps: G9400+
Middens, Kitchen, see Kitchen middens
Middle Atlantic States (United States)
  Atlases: G1245+
  Maps: G3790+
Middle Congo, see Congo (Brazzaville)
Middle East
  Atlases: G2205+
  Maps: G7420+
Middle games
  of
    chess: GV1450.3
    go: GV1460.3
Midget auto racing: GV1029.5
Midgets, see Dwarfs
Migrations of peoples (Ethnology): GN370
Military chess: GV1458.M5
Military grid systems, see Grids
  (Cartography)
Military oceanography: V396+
Military personnel
  Anthropometry: GN59.S7
  Recreation: UH800+
  See also Sailors; Soldiers
Mind reading (Parlor magic): GV1553
Mineral resources (Oceanography): TN264
Minerals (Folklore): GR700+
Minerals, Mythical, see Mythical
  minerals
Miners (Manners and customs): GT5960.M5
Mines and mining (Folklore): GR900
Miniature golf: GV987
Miniature theaters: GV1521
Minnesingers (Manners and customs):
  GT3650
Minnesota
  Atlases: G1425+
  Maps: G4140+
Minstrels (Manners and customs): GT3650
Minton (Ball game): GV1017.M6
Minuet (Dance): GV1796.M5
Miscarriage, see Abortion
Miscegenation (Physiological
  anthropology): GN254
Mississippi
  Atlases: G1345+
  Maps: G3980+
Mississippi River and Valley
  Atlases: G1375+
  Maps: G4042.M5
Missouri
  Atlases: G1435+
  Maps: G4160+

Missouri River and Valley (Maps):
  G4052.M5
Mixing, Oceanic, see Oceanic mixing
Model airplane flying: GV760+
Model car racing, see Racing - Automo-
  biles - Model cars
Modeling (Cartography): GA145
Modern costume: GT580+
Modern dancing: GV1617+; GV1783
Modern manners and customs: GT129+
Moieties (Ethnology): GN487.7.M6
Monaco
  Atlases: G1845+
  Maps: G5980+
Money
  Ethnology: GN450.5
  Folklore: GR874
Money game (Card game): GV1299.M6
Mongo (Folklore): GR351.2.M63;
  GR357.82.M64
Mongolia (Mongolian People's Republic)
  Atlases: G2329.3+
  Maps: G7895+
Mongolian race
  Craniology: GN130.M7
  Ethnology: GN548
Monkeys (Folklore): GR730.M6
Monopoly (Game): GV1469.M65
Monsters (Folklore): GR825+
Monstrosities, see Monsters
Montana
  Atlases: G1470+
  Maps: G4250+
Monte (Game): GV1307
Montenegro
  Atlases: G2020+
  Maps: G6855+
Months (Folklore): GR930
Montserrat (Maps): G5055+
Moon
  Atlases: G1000.3+
  Folklore: GR625
  Globes: G3167.M6
  Maps: G3195+
Moorish folklore: GR233
Moors (Geomorphology): GB621+
Moral and religious aspects
  of
    boxing: GV1136.5
    human ecology: GF80
Moral philosophy, see Ethics
Morocco
  Atlases: G2460+
  Maps: G8230+
Morris dance: GV1796.M7
Mortlock Islands (Maps): G9450+
Mossi (Folklore): GR351.72.M63
Motion picture dancing: GV1779
Motion pictures
  in
    physical education and training:
      GV364

Motor ability tests: GV436+
Motorboats and motorboating (Sports): GV833.5+
Motorcycle racing on ice, see Ice racing - Motorcycles
Motorcycle soccer: GV1060.15
Motorcycling: GV1059.5+
Motoring: GV1020+
Mototokko Islands, see Truk Islands
Mounds (Prehistoric archaeology): GN795
Mountain climbing, see Mountaineering
Mountain life (Manners and customs): GT3490
Mountain passes (Geomorphology): GB515
Mountain States (United States), see Pacific and Mountain States (United States)
Mountaineering: GV199.8+
Mountains
  Environmental influences on man: GF53
  Folklore: GR660
  Geomorphology: GB500+
Mountains, Mythical, see Mythical mountains
Mourning
  Ethnology: GN486
  Manners and customs: GT3390
Moustaches, see Mustaches
Mousterian culture
  By continent, see table below GN772.2+, e. g. GN772.2.M6 (Europe)
Mouth protectors (Sports): GV749.M6
Move games: GV1312+
Movement (Physiological anthropology): GN231+
Moves of chessmen, see Chessmen, Moves of
Mozambique
  Atlases: G2550+
  Maps: G8450+
Mu (Prehistoric archaeology): GN750+
Muffs (Manners and customs): GT2190
Mule drivers, see Muleteers
Mule skinners, see Muleteers
Muleteers (Manners and customs): GT6070
Multiple births (Physiological anthropology): GN236.5
Mummies
  Burial customs: GT3340
  Egyptology: DT62.M7
Muscat and Oman
  Atlases: G2249.7+
  Maps: G7560+
Muscular system (Human variation): GN171
Museums and exhibitions
  Anthropology: GN35+
    Physical anthropology: GN59.8+
    Prehistoric archaeology: GN800+
  Cartography: GA190
  Circuses: GV1807

Museums and exhibitions - Continued
  Ethnology: GN35+
  Folklore: GN35+
  Geography: G77.8+
  Hydrology: GB659.4+
  Manners and customs (General): GN35+; D - F
  Oceanography: GC35+
  Physical education and training: GV381
  Physical geography: GB27
  Recreation and leisure: GV14.7+
Mushanokōji Senke (Japanese tea ceremony): GT2912.M8
Music (Folklore): GR885
Music camps: MT
Muslims (Marriage customs): GT2695.M8
Mustaches (Manners and customs): GT2318
Mutilations (Ethnology): GN419.2
Mystery boxes (Playgrounds): GV426
Mystery puzzles, see Detective and mystery puzzles
Mythical animals (Folklore): GR820+
Mythical islands (Folklore): GR940
Mythical minerals (Folklore): GR820+
Mythical mountains (Folklore): GR940
Mythical places (Folklore): GR940
Mythical plants (Folklore): GR820+

N

Naginata: GV1150.4
Names, Geographic, see Geographic names
Nantucket Sound (Tidal currents): GC309.M3
Narcotics
  Ethnology: GN411+
  Manners and customs: GT3010
Narragansett Bay (Tidal currents): GC309.M3
National dances: GV1743
National League of Professional Baseball Clubs: GV875
Nativistic movements (Ethnology): GN472.7+
Natural boundaries (Human ecology): GF101+
Natural disaster warning systems, see Warning systems, Natural disaster
Natural disasters (Physical geography): GB5000+
Natural resources, Allocation of, see Allocation of natural resources
Natural water chemistry: GB855+
Nature, Effect of man on, see Man's influence on the environment
Nature worship (Ethnology): GN471
Nauru (Maps): G9490+
Navigation
  Ethnology: GN440+
  Prehistoric archaeology: GN799.N3

Navodo, see Nauru
Near East
    Atlases: G2205+
    Maps: G7420+
Nebraska
    Atlases: G1450+
    Maps: G4190+
Neck exercises: GV508
Necklaces (Manners and customs): GT2260
Neckties (Manners and customs): GT2120
Neckwear (Manners and customs): GT2120
Needles, see Pins and needles
Negro race
    Craniology: GN130.N3
    Ethnology: GN645
Negroes, see Afro-Americans
Neo-evolutionism (Cultural evolution):
    GN360.4
Neolithic age (Prehistoric archaeology):
    GN775+
Nepal
    Atlases: G2295+
    Maps: G7760+
Nervous system (Human variation):
    GN181+
Netball: GV889.6
Netherlands
    Atlases: G1860+
    Maps: G6000+
Netherlands Antilles
    Atlases: G1690+
    Maps: G5165+
Netherlands Indies, see Indonesia
Netherlands Union
    Atlases: G1858+
    Maps: G5995+
Nets, Tennis, see Tennis nets
Network analysis (Geography): G70.25
Nevada
    Atlases: G1520+
    Maps: G4350+
New Brunswick
    Atlases: G1130+
    Maps: G3430+
New Caledonia
    Atlases: G2885+
    Maps: G9340+
New England
    Atlases: G1210+
    Maps: G3720+
New Guinea
    Atlases: G2440+
    Maps: G8140+
New Hampshire
    Atlases: G1220+
    Maps: G3740+
New Hebrides
    Atlases: G2880+
    Maps: G9295+
New Jersey
    Atlases: G1255+
    Maps: G3810+

New London regattas: GV801
New Mexico
    Atlases: G1505+
    Maps: G4320+
New Southwest (United States)
    Atlases: G1495+
    Maps: G4300+
New Year's Day
    Manners and customs: GT4905
    Religious observances: BV135.N5
New York. Racket and Tennis Club:
    GV997.R3
New York (City). Yankee Stadium, see
    Yankee Stadium
New York (State)
    Atlases: G1250+
    Maps: G3800+
New York Harbor (Tidal currents):
    GC309.N7
New York Yankees (Baseball club):
    GV875.N4
New Zealand
    Atlases: G2795+
    Maps: G9080+
Newcomb (Ball game): GV1017.N4
Newfoundland
    Atlases: G1185+
    Maps: G3600+
Nicaragua
    Atlases: G1575+
    Maps: G4850+
Niger
    Atlases: G2660+
    Maps: G8770+
Nigeria
    Atlases: G2695+
    Maps: G8840+
Nijinsky, Waslaw: GV1785.N6
Nine pockets (Ball game): GV1017.N7
Ninepins (Bowling): GV910.5.N5
Nitrogen (Chemical oceanography):
    GC117.N5
Niue (Maps): G9580+
Nobility
    Baptisms, see Baptism customs of
      royalty, nobility, etc.
    Ceremonies, Official: GT5010+
    Costume: GT1760
    Court and castle life: GT3510+
    Heraldry: CR3499+
    Manners and customs: GT5450+
    Marriage, see Marriage - Manners and
      customs - Royalty, nobility, etc.
Nomadic peoples (Ethnographies): GN387
Nomoi Islands, see Mortlock Islands
Nonunilineal descent (Ethnology):
    GN488+
Nordic combined contests (Skiing):
    GV854.89
Nordic peoples
    Ethnology: GN549.T4
    Folklore: GR139

Norms, Violation of (Ethnology): GN494
North Africa
  Atlases: G2455+
  Maps: G8220+
North America
  Atlases: G1105+
  Maps: G3300+
North Carolina
  Atlases: G1300+
  Maps: G3900+
North Central States (United States)
  Atlases: G1385+
  Maps: G4060+
North Dakota
  Atlases: G1440+
  Maps: G4170+
North Korea
  Atlases: G2334.3+
  Maps: G7905+
North Polar regions, see Arctic regions
North Vietnam, see Vietnam
Northeast Africa
  Atlases: G2500+
  Maps: G8220+
Northeastern States (United States)
  Atlases: G1205+
  Maps: G3710+
Northern Asia
  Atlases: G2170+
  Maps: G7270+
Northern Europe
  Atlases: G2050+
  Maps: G6910+
Northern Hemisphere
  Atlases: G1050
  Maps: G3210+
Northern Ireland
  Atlases: G1829.2+
  Maps: G5790+
Northern Rhodesia, see Zambia
Northwest Territories (Canada)
  Atlases: G1180+
  Maps: G3530+
Northwest Territory (United States)
  Atlases: G1390+
Northwestern States (United States)
  Atlases: G1420+
Norway
  Atlases: G2065+
  Maps: G6940+
Nose (Physical form and dimensions): GN64
Notation
  Cartography: GA102.2
  Dance movements: GV1587
Noughts and crosses, see Tic-tac-toe
Nova Scotia
  Atlases: G1125+
  Maps: G3420+
Nso (Folklore): GR351.2.N75
Nuclear energy, see Atomic energy
Nuclear families (Ethnology): GN480.5

Nudism: GV450
Number rhymes, see Counting-out rhymes
Number systems (Ethnology): GN476.15
Numbers (Folklore): GR933
Nunchaku: GV1142.6
Nursery rhymes, History of: GR487
Nyasaland, see Malawi

O

Oakley, Annie: GV1157.03
Oaths (Legal customs): GT6280
Observation, Participant, see Participant
  observation
Occupation, Choice of, see Vocational
  guidance
Occupations
  Folklore: GR890+
  Manners and customs: GT5750+
Ocean, Dynamics of the, see Dynamics
  of the ocean
Ocean-atmosphere interaction: GC190+
Ocean basin: GC87+
Ocean bottom: GC87+
Ocean circulation: GC228.5+
Ocean currents, see Currents, Ocean
Ocean floor, see Ocean bottom
Ocean Island (Maps): G9485+
Ocean pollution, see Marine pollution;
  Seawater pollution
Ocean travel: G540+
Oceanic mixing: GC299
Oceanic peoples (Ethnographies): GN386
Oceanographic expeditions, see
  Expeditions, Oceanographic
Oceanographic information, Communication
  of, see Communication of information -
  Oceanography
Oceanographic instruments and
  apparatus (General): GC41
Oceanographic research, see Research,
  Oceanographic
Oceanographic submersibles: GC67
Oceanography: GC
  as a profession: GC30.5
  By region: GC401+
Oceanography, Applied, see Applied
  oceanography
Oceanography, Chemical, see Chemical
  oceanography
Oceanography, Military, see Military
  oceanography
Oceanography, Optical, see Optical
  oceanography
Oceanology, see Oceanography
Oceans (General)
  Atlases: G2800+
  Environmental influences on man: GF65
  Maps: G9095+
Octopuses (Folklore): GR760.027

Odontography, <u>see</u> Teeth
Offensive play
  Basketball: GV889
  Football: GV951.8
Official ceremonies
  of
    nobility, <u>see</u> Nobility - Ceremonies,
      Official
    royalty, <u>see</u> Royalty - Ceremonies,
      Official
Officiating, Sports: GV735
Ogres (Folklore): GR560
Ohio
  Atlases: G1395+
  Maps: G4080+
Ohio River and Valley
  Atlases: G1207.03
  Maps: G3707.05
Oirots, <u>see</u> Kalmucks
Oklahoma
  Atlases: G1365+
  Card game: GV1295.04
  Maps: G4020+
Old age (Ethnology): GN485
Old Northwest (United States)
  Atlases: G1390+
  Maps: G4070+
Old Southwest (United States)
  Atlases: G1350+
  Maps: G3990+
Oldenburger Horn (Folktale): GR75.04
Olympic Games
  Greek classical games: GV23
  Modern revivals: GV721.18+
    Winter games: GV841.5+
Olympic ideal: GV721.6
Oman
  Atlases: G2249.7+
  Maps: G7560+
Ombre (Card game): GV1295.05
Omote Senke (Japanese tea ceremony):
  GT2912.04
Omweso (Game): GV1469.04
Ontario
  Atlases: G1145+
  Maps: G3460+
Opera glasses (Manners and customs):
  GT2370
Optical oceanography: GC177.6+
Oral literature, <u>see</u> Folk literature
Ordeals (Ethnology): GN494.3
Oregon
  Atlases: G1490+
  Maps: G4290+
Oregon Trail (Maps): G4127.07
Organization of work (Ethnology): GN448.5+
Organized camping: GV192+
Organs, Internal, <u>see</u> Internal organs
Organs, Sense, <u>see</u> Sense organs
Organs, Sex, <u>see</u> Sex organs
Oriental costume: GT1370+
Oriental fencing: GV1150+

Oriental hand-to-hand fighting: GV1112+
Oriental houses: GT343+
Oriental sports, games, etc. (Ancient):
  GV19
Orientation (Outdoor recreation):
  GV200.4
Origin
  of
    culture (Ethnology): GN357.5
    man (Physical anthropology): GN281+
    religion (Ethnology): GN470.5
Ornaments, Personal
  Ethnology: GN418.4+
  Manners and customs: GT2250+
Orography: GB500+
Ortelius, Abraham
  Atlases: G1006
Orthomorphic projection: GA115
Osteology (Human variation): GN70+
Otjisewa (Fossil man), <u>see</u> Boskop
  (Fossil man)
Ottoman Empire
  Atlases: G2210+
  Maps: G7430+
Our Lady's child (Folktale): GR75.09
Outboard motorboating: GV835.8
Outdoor life and recreation: GV191.2+
  Nature books: QH81
Outer Mongolia, <u>see</u> Mongolia (Mongolian
  People's Republic)
Outlaws (Manners and customs): GT6550+
Ownership (Economic anthropology):
  GN449+
Oxford-Cambridge boat races: GV799
Oxford University rowing: GV807.5.09
Ozark Mountains (Maps): G4002.09

P

Pachisi: GV1469.P17
Pacific and Mountain States (United
  States)
  Atlases: G1460+
  Maps: G4210+
Pacific Northwest (United States)
  Atlases: G1465+
  Maps: G4240+
Pacific Ocean
  Atlases: G2860+
  Maps: G9230+
Packhorse camping: GV199.7
Paddle tennis: GV1006
Paddleball (Game): GV1017.P17
Pageants, <u>see</u> Processions and pageants
Pai she chuan (Folktale): GR75.P3
Paintings, Rock, <u>see</u> Rock paintings
Pair skating (Ice skating): GV850.45
Pajarillo (Dance): GV1796.P24
Pakistan
  Atlases: G2270+
  Maps: G7640+

Pala-pala (Dance), see Mariquita (Dance)
Palate, Hard (Human variation): GN131
Palau Islands (Maps): G9425+
Paleolithic age (Prehistoric archaeology): GN771+
Paleontology, Human, see Human paleontology
Palestine, see Israel
Pan (Card game), see Panguingue (Card game)
Pan American Games: GV722.5.P3
Panama
    Atlases: G1585+
    Maps: G4870+
Panguingue (Card game): GV1295.P17
Paper tricks: GV1559
Paper work (Children's games): GV1218.P3
Parachuting (Sports): GV770
Parade dancing: GV1797
Paraguay
    Atlases: G1770+
    Maps: G5380+
Parallel bar exercises: GV535+
Paranthropus crassidens (Fossil man): GN283.6
Parasols (Manners and customs): GT2210
Parks, Amusement, see Amusement parks, etc.
Parlor magic, see Magic, Parlor
Parlor tricks, see Tricks, Parlor
Partially seeing, Maps for the, see Visually handicapped, Maps for the
Participant observation (Ethnology): GN346.4
Parties: GV1470+
    Children's parties: GV1205
Party games and stunts: GV1470+
Passenger life (Ocean travel): G550
Passes, see Mountain passes
Passing (Football): GV951.5
Pastimes, see Recreation and leisure
Pastoralism (Ethnology): GN407.7
Patents, Magic: GV1560
Patience (Card game): GV1261
Pato (Ball game): GV1017.P3
Patriarchy (Ethnology): GN479.6
Patrilineal descent (Ethnology): GN487.5
Patrilocal (Ethnology): GN480.65
Pavlova, Anna: GV1785.P3
Pawn (Chess): GV1451.5.P3
Peary, Robert Edwin: G635.P4
Peasants
    Costume: GT1850
    Manners and customs: GT5650+
Peatbogs (Geomorphology): GB621+
Pedestrian tours: GV199+
Pedro (Card game): GV1295.P3
Pelasgi (Ethnology): GN549.P3
Pelew Islands, see Palau Islands
Pelota (Ball game): GV1017.P4
Pelvis (Human variation): GN151

Peneplains (Natural landforms): GB571+
Pennsylvania
    Atlases: G1260+
    Maps: G3820+
Pent cuckoo (Folktale): GR75.P5
Pentacles (Folklore): GR610
Pentathlon: GV1060.7
People's Republic of China, see China
Perfumes (Manners and customs): GT2340
Perigordian culture
    By continent, see table below GN772.2+, e. g. GN772.2.P4 (Europe)
Permafrost, see Frozen ground
Perpetual lamps, see Sepulchral and perpetual lamps
Perseus (Folktale): GR75.P53
Persia, see Iran
Persian costume: GT535
Personality and culture, see Culture and personality
Perspective projection: GA115
Peru
    Atlases: G1740+
    Maps: G5310+
Perukes, see Wigs
Petanque (Bowling): GV910.5.P4
Petermann, August: G69.P4
Petroglyphs (Prehistoric archaeology): GN799.P4
Pharmacists (Professional customs): RS122.5
Phenomena, Cosmic, see Cosmic phenomena
Philippines
    Atlases: G2390+
    Maps: G8060+
Philidor: GV1444
Philosophical anthropology: BD450
Philosophy (Ethnology): GN468+
Philosophy, Moral, see Ethics
Phobos (Globes): G3167.P5
Phoenix (Folklore): GR830.P4
Phoenix Islands (Maps): G9540+
Photocopying of maps, see Map photocopying
Photography
    Ethnology: GN347
    in
        oceanography: GC10.4.P5
Photography, Aerial, see Aerial photography
Phratries (Ethnology): GN487.7.P45
Physical anthropology: GN49+
Physical aptitude tests: GV436+
Physical education and training: GV201+
Physical education and training clubs, see Clubs, Physical education and training
Physical education and training facilities, see Facilities, Physical education and training
Physical education teachers, Training of: GV361+

Physical fitness programs: GV481+
Physical fitness tests: GV436+
Physical form and dimensions (Human variation): GN63.8+
Physical geography: GB
Physical measurements, see Anthropometry
Physical oceanography: GC150+
Physical tests: GV436+
Physical traits (Physiological anthropology): GN229+
Physicians (Professional customs): R707
Physiognomy: GN64
Physiological anthropology (Human variation): GN221+
Picnics (Manners and customs): GT2955
Picture puzzles: GV1507.P47
Piedmonts (Natural landforms): GB571+
Pigmentation (Human variation): GN197
Pigs, see Swine
Pile dwellings and pile dwellers, see Lake dwellings and lake dwellers
Piltdown man (Fossil man): GN282.5
Pinang, see Betel nut
Pinatas (Children's games): GV1218.P5
Pinball machines: GV1311.P5
Ping-pong, see Table tennis
Pinochle (Card game): GV1295.P6
Pins, Baseball: GV875.2
Pins (Jewelry)
  Manners and customs: GT2280
Pins and needles (Prehistoric archaeology): GN799.P5
Pinwheel puzzles: GV1507.P5
Piquet (Card game): GV1295.P7
Pirates: G535+
Pistol shooting
  Christmas custom: GT4990
  Sports: GV1174+
Pitcairn (Island and colony)
  Maps: G9660+
Pitching (Baseball): GV871
Pitching horseshoes, see Horseshoe pitching
Pithecanthropines (Fossil man): GN284+
Pithecanthropus erectus (Fossil man): GN284.6
Pize-ball (Game): GV1017.P5
Places, Mythical, see Mythical places
Plains
  Environmental influences on man: GF57
  Natural landforms: GB571+
Planets
  Atlases: G1000.5
  Globes: G3165+
Planning and design
  of
    athletic fields and playing fields: GV413
    gymnasiums: GV405
    playgrounds: GV425
Plant lore: GR780+
Plant materials (Ethnology): GN434.3+

Planting (Folklore): GR895
Plants
  Folklore: GR700+
  Manners and customs: GT5150
Plants, Cultivated, see Cultivated plants
Plants, Domesticated, see Domesticated plants
Plants, Mythical, see Mythical plants
Plateaus (Natural landforms): GB571+
Platform burial, see Exposure of the dead
Platform paddle tennis: GV1006
Play (Recreation and leisure): GV
  Ethnology: GN454.7
  Manners and customs (Children): GT2480
Play spaces, see Playgrounds
Play-party: GV1771
Playbooks (Football): GV951.15+
Players, Selection of (Football): GV953.4
Playground paddle tennis: GV1006
Playgrounds: GV421+
  School playgrounds: LB3251
Playgrounds, Adventure, see Adventure playgrounds
Playing card collections: GV1235
Playing card games, see Card games
Playing fields: GV411+
  Cricket: GV927
  See also Golf courses, greens, etc.; Tennis courts; etc.
Pleasant (Island), see Nauru
Plesianthropus transvaalensis (Fossil man): GN283.7
Plural births, see Multiple births
Po-lo-lo (Ball game): GV1017.P7
Pocket tricks: GV1556
Points of the compass, see Cardinal points
Poker (Card game): GV1251+
Poker, Football, see Football poker
Poland
  Atlases: G1950+
  Maps: G6520+
Polar exploration, Aircraft for, see Aircraft for polar exploration
Polar regions
  Exploration, etc.: G757+
  Maps: G3260+
Pole climbing, see Pole exercises - Climbing poles
Pole exercises: GV497
  Climbing poles: GV541
Pole vaulting: GV1080
Political anthropology: GN492+
Political organization (Ethnology): GN492+
Political puzzles: GV1507.P7
Polje (Geomorphology): GB609
Polka (Dance): GV1796.P55
Pollution, Marine, see Marine pollution

Pollution, Seawater, see Seawater pollution
Polo: GV1010+
Polo, Bicycle, see Bicycle polo
Polyandry (Ethnology): GN480.36
Polye, see Polje (Geomorphology)
Polygámy (Ethnology): GN480.33+
Polygyny (Ethnology): GN480.35
Polynesia
  Atlases: G2970+
  Maps: G9500+
Polyphemus (Folktale): GR75.P6
Ponds (Hydrology): GB1801+
Pontifical court costume: GT975
Pool (Game): GV891+
Pool tables: GV899
Pools, Swimming, see Swimming pools
Popes
  . as
    geographers: GA203
Population genetics
  Biology: QH455
  Human evolution: GN289
Portugal
  Atlases: G1975+
  Maps: G6690+
Portuguese East Africa, see Mozambique
Portuguese Empire
  Atlases: G1973
  Maps: G6680+
Portuguese Guinea, see Guinea-Bissau
Portuguese West Africa, see Angola
Posture (Physiological anthropology): GN231+
Posture control exercises: GV505
Potomac River and Valley (Maps): G3709.32.P6
Pottery
  Ethnology: GN433
  Prehistoric archaeology: GN799.P6
Poughkeepsie regattas: GV803
Pounders (Tools)
  Ethnology: GN437.P65
Prairie Provinces (Canada)
  Atlases: G1150+
  Maps: G3470+
Precious metals (Manners and customs): GT5170
Precious stones (Folklore): GR805
Preference (Card game): GV1291.P8
Prehistoric archaeology: GN700+
Preschool children, Playgrounds for: GV424.5
Prevention of accidents, see Safety measures
Priests (Ethnology): GN474
Prince Edward Island
  Atlases: G1135+
  Maps: G3440+
The Princess without hands (Folktale), see Maiden without hands (Folktale)
Private life (Manners and customs): GT2400+

Prize fighting: GV1115+
Probabilities (Gambling): GV1302
Processions and pageants (Manners and customs): GT3980+
Production
  of
    theatrical dancing: GV1782
Profanity (Manners and customs): GT3080
Professional distinctions (Ethnology): GN491.5
Professional sports: GV734
  Football: GV954+
  Golf: GV979.P7
Professionalism in sports: GV733
Professions (Manners and customs): GT6110+
Profile, Facial, see Face form and profile
Prognathism (Human variation): GN131
Programs, Computer, see Computer programs
Programs, Dance: GV1750
Programs, Recreational, see Recreational programs
Progressive whist: GV1285
Projection, Map: GA110+
Projections (Cartography): G3201.B72
Proms: GV1746
Properties, Acoustic, see Acoustic properties
Property (Ethnology): GN449+
Prophetistic movements, see Nativistic movements
Proportions of the body, see Body dimensions and proportions
Prosecutions and punishments
  Ethnology: GN494.3
  Manners and customs: GT6710+
Psychoanalytic interpretations (Psychological anthropology): GN508
Psychological anthropology: GN502+
Psychological aspects
  of
    camping (Organized): GV198.P74
    chess: GV1448
    costume: GT524
    dancing: GV1588.5
    golf: GV979.P75
    prehistoric archaeology: GN799.P74
    recreation and leisure: GV14.4
    soccer: GV943.9.P7
    social change: GN514
    sports: GV706.4
    tennis: GV1002.9.P75
Psychological recreations (Games): GV1507.P9
Ptolemy (Ptolemaeus, Claudius)
  Ptolemy's atlases: G1005
Puberty (Physiological anthropology): GN238
Puberty rites (Ethnology): GN483.3
Public balls: GV1748

Public life (Manners and customs): GT3400+
Public relations.(Sports): GV714
Puerto Rico
  Atlases: G1630+
  Maps: G4970+
Punishments, see Prosecutions and punishments
Punting (Football): GV951.7
Purim (Manners and customs): GT4995.P8
Pushball (Game): GV1017.P9
Putting (Golf): GV979.P8
Putting the shot, see Shot-putting
Puzzles: GV1491+
Puzzles, Form, see Form puzzles
Pygmies (Ethnology): GN549.P9
Pyramid exercises: GV537
Pyramids, Earth, see Earth pyramids

Q

Qatar
  Atlases: G2249.8+
  Maps: G7580+
Quadrille (Card game), see Ombre (Card game)
Quadrilles (Dances): GV1763+
Quarter staff (Fighting sports): GV1141.2
Quarterbacking (Football): GV951.3
Quebec (Province)
  Atlases: G1140+
  Maps: G3450+
Queen Charlotte Islands, see Santa Cruz Islands
Quiz books: GV1507.Q5
Quiz shows: GV1507.Q5
Quoits: GV1095
Quotation puzzles: GV1507.Q6

R

Race (General)
  Physical anthropology: GN269+
Race psychology (Physical anthropology): GN270+
Races of man, see Ethnology
Racetracks (Automobile races): GV1033.5+
Racial crossing (Physiological anthropology): GN254
Racing: GV1018+
  Airplanes: GV759
    Model airplanes: GV761.5
  Automobiles: GV1029+
    Model cars: GV1570
  Balloons: GV763
  Cycling: GV1049
  Gliders: GV766
  Motorboats: GV835.9
  Motorcycling: GV1060+

Racing - Continued
  Sailboats: GV826.5+
  Skiing (Downhill racing), see Downhill racing (Skiing)
  Yachts: GV826.5+
    Model yachts: GV833
Racket and Tennis Club, New York, see New York. Racket and Tennis Club
Rackets (Ball game), see Racquets (Ball game)
Rackets, Tennis, see Tennis rackets
Racquetball (Game): GV1017.R3
Racquets (Ball game): GV1003.5
Radar
  in
    hydrology: GB656.2.R3
Radioactive isotopes, see Radioisotopes
Radioactive tracers
  in
    oceanography: GC10.4.R3
Radioactivity
  in
    seawater: GC149
Radioisotopes
  Glaciers: GB2401.72.R34
  Groundwater: GB1001.72.R34
  Ice: GB2401.72.R34
  Ice sheets: GB2401.72.R34
  in
    hydrogeology: GB1001.72.R34
    hydrology: GB656.2.R34
    hydrometeorology: GB2801.72.R34
    limnology: GB1601.72.R34
  Lagoons: GB2201.72.R34
  Lakes: GB1601.72.R34
  Ponds: GB1801.72.R34
  Rivers: GB1201.72.R34
  Sea ice: GB2401.72.R34
  Snow: GB2601.72.R34
  Snow surveys: GB2601.72.R34
  Stream measurements: GB1201.72.R34
  Waterfalls: GB1401.72.R34
Radionuclides, see Radioisotopes
Rafts and rafting (Sports): GV780
Railroads (Folklore): GR870
Ralik Chain (Maps): G9465+
Rallies (Automobile racing): GV1029.2
Ramages (Ethnology): GN488.2
Rams (Folklore): GR730.R3
Rapper (Dance): GV1796.R3
Rasmussen, Knud Johan Victor: G635.R3
Ratak Chain (Maps): G9470+
Reading for pleasure: Z1003
Rebirth (Folklore): GR467
Reciprocity (Economic anthropology): GN450.7
Records and statistics (Sports): GV741
  Automobile racing: GV1030
  Baseball: GV877
  Basketball
    Amateur: GV885.45
    Professional: GV885.55

Records and statistics (Sports) - Cont.
  Billiards and pool: GV898
  Boxing: GV1137
  Cricket: GV925
  Cycling: GV1053
  Fencing: GV1149
  Football
    Amateur: GV956.8
    Professional: GV955
  Rugby: GV945.4
  Skiing:GV854.87
  Soccer: GV943.4
  Table tennis: GV1005.4
  Track and field: GV1060.67
Recreation, Outdoor, see Outdoor life
  and recreation
Recreation and leisure: GV
  as a profession: GV160
  Books and reading, see Reading for
    pleasure
  Ethnology: GN454+
  in
    the arts: NX
    the church: BV1620+
    education: LB1137
      adult education: LC5201+
      school management: LB3031
  Modern history (By region or country):
    GV51+
Recreation and leisure, Psychological
  aspects of, see Psychological aspects
  of recreation and leisure
Recreation and leisure and character
  building, see Character building and
  recreation and leisure
Recreation and leisure and Christian
  life, see Christian life and
  recreation and leisure
Recreation and leisure and ethics, see
  Ethics and recreation and leisure
Recreation and leisure and sociology,
  see Sociology and recreation and
  leisure
Recreation centers: GV182+
  See also Gymnasiums; Playgrounds; etc.
Recreation leadership: GV181.35+
Recreation specialists: GV160+
Recreation surveys, see Surveys,
  Recreation
Recreational areas and facilities:
  GV182+
Recreational programs (Camps): GV198.R4
Recreational vehicle camping: GV198.5+
Recreations, Psychological (Games), see
  Psychological recreations (Games)
Red River and Valley (Maps): G3992.R4
Red Shoes (Ballet): GV1790.R4
Reducing exercises, see Weight reducing
  exercises
Reefs (Geomorphology): GB461+

Refereeing
  in
    basketball: GV885.2
    boxing: GV1137.3
    football: GV954.35
    soccer: GV943.9.R43
Regattas, Rowing, see Rowing regattas
Regattas, Yacht, see Yacht regattas
Regulation
  of
    costume, dress, etc.: GT527+
    descent, see Descent, Regulation of
Reincarnation, see Rebirth
Reindeer (Manners and customs): GT5895.R4
Reindeer culture, see Magdalenian culture
Relay races (Foot racing): GV1066
Relief, Submarine, see Submarine
  topography
Relief maps: GA140
Religion
  and
    geography: BL65.G4
    society (Ethnology): GN470.7
  Ethnology: GN470+
  Prehistoric archaeology: GN799.R4
Religious and military orders (Costume):
  GT1950
  Military orders: CR
  Religious orders: BX
Religious aspects, see Moral and
  religious aspects
Religious dancing (Modern): GV1783.5
Religious experience (Ethnology):
  GN472.4
Remote sensing
  Glaciers: GB2401.72.R42
  Groundwater: GB1001.72.R42
  Ice: GB2401.72.R42
  Ice sheets: GB2401.72.R42
  in
    geography: G70.4
    hydrogeology: GB1001.72.R42
    hydrometeorology: GB2801.72.R42
    limnology: GB1601.72.R42
    oceanography: GC10.4.R4
    physical geography: GB21.5.R43
  Lagoons: GB2201.72.R42
  Lakes: GB1601.72.R42
  Ponds: GB1801.72.R42
  Rivers: GB1201.72.R42
  Sea ice: GB2401.72.R42
  Snow: GB2601.72.R42
  Snow surveys: GB2601.72.R42
  Stream measurements: GB1201.72.R42
  Waterfalls: GB1401.72.R42
Renaissance manners and customs: GT130
Rennell, James: G69.R4
Repair, see Maintenance and repair
Reproduction (Physiological anthro-
  pology): GN235+

Reproduction of maps, see Map reproduction

Reptiles (Folklore): GR740

Republic of South Africa
  Atlases: G2565
  Maps: G8500+

Research, Geographical: G72+

Research, Oceanographic: GC57+
  Ships: VM453

Residence rules (Families)
  Ethnology: GN480.6+

Resorts, Amusement, see Amusement parks, etc.

Resources, Marine, see Marine resources

Retaliation (Ethnology): GN494.5

Réunion (Maps): G9190+

Revivals, Ethnic, see Nativistic movements

Revolver clubs: GV1163

Revolver shooting (Sports): GV1175

Rhine legends: DD801.R72

Rhode Island
  Atlases: G1235+
  Maps: G3770+

Rhodesia
  Atlases: G2570+
  Maps: G8550+

Rhymes (Folklore): GR485+

Rhyming alphabet, see Alphabet rhymes

Rhythmic exercises: GV1798+

Rice (Manners and customs): GT5899.R5

Rice-wine, see Sake

Riding (Horses), see Horsemanship

Rifle clubs: GV1163

Rifle shooting (Sports): GV1177

Rigging (Sailboats): GV811.45

Right-handedness, see Left- and right-handedness

Ring exercises: GV539

Ring hockey: GV1099

Ringling Brothers and Barnum and Bailey
  Circus: GV1821.R5

Rings (Jewelry)
  Folklore: GR425
  Manners and customs: GT2270

Ringtoss (Game): GV1097.R5

Rinks, Ice, see Ice rinks

Rio Grande Valley
  Atlases: G1107.R58
  Maps: G4297.R5

Ripple marks (Coastal landform): GB454.R5

Rites and ceremonies (Religion and ritual)
  Ethnology: GN473+

Ritter, Karl: G69.R6

Ritual (Ethnology): GN470+

Ritual dancing, see Religious dancing (Modern)

River basins, see Watersheds

River channels (Natural landforms): GB561+

River floodplains, see Floodplains

River temperatures: GB1398.6+

Rivers
  Environmental influences on man: GF63
  Folklore: GR680
  Hydrology: GB1201+

Road guides, Automobile: GV1024+

Roads (Ethnology): GN439

Robert-Houdin, Jean Eugène: GV1545.R7

Rock and roll dancing: GV1796.R6

Rock climbing: GV200.2

Rock paintings (Prehistoric archaeology): GN799.P4

Rocky Mountain region (United States):
  Maps: G4222.R6

Rodeos: GV1834+

Roller derbies: GV859.6

Roller polo: GV859.7

Roller skate hockey: GV859.7

Roller skating: GV859+

Roman costume: GT555

Roman Empire
  Atlases: G1980+
  Maps: G6700+

Roman gymnasiums, see Gymnasiums - Roman gymnasiums

Roman ladders (Heavy exercises): GV537

Roman sports, games, etc.: GV31+

Romania
  Atlases: G2035+
  Maps: G6880+

Rook (Card game): GV1299.R6

Rope climbing exercises: GV541

Rope jumping, see Jumping rope

Rope skipping, see Skipping rope

Rope tricks: GV1559

Rope walking: GV551+

Roque (Croquet): GV935

Rose Bowl game: GV957.R6

Roses (Folklore): GR790.R6

Rouge et noir (Game): GV1308

Roulette: GV1309

Round dances: GV1755+

Rounders (Ball game): GV1017.R6

Roundel (Calisthenics): GV499

Route books
  Automobiles: GV1024+
  Cycling: GV1045+

Routes of communication (Ethnology): GN439

Rowing (Sports): GV790.9+

Rowing machines: GV543

Rowing regattas: GV798+

Royal and Ancient Golf Club of St. Andrews: GV969.R6

Royal tennis, see Court tennis

Royalty
  Baptisms, see Baptism customs of royalty, nobility, etc.
  Ceremonies, Official: GT5010+
  Court and castle life: GT3510+

Royalty - Continued
  Insignia: CR4480+
  Manners and customs: GT5350+
  Marriage, see Marriage - Manners and
    customs - Royalty, nobility, etc.
  Titles of honor, precedence, etc.:
    CR3499+
Ruanda-Urundi
  Atlases: G2539.3+
  Maps: G8425+
Rugby football: GV944.8+
Rules: GV731
  Automobile racing: GV1030
  Baseball: GV877
  Basketball
    Amateur: GV885.45
    Professional: GV885.55
  Billiards and pool: GV897
  Bowling: GV905
  Chess: GV1457
  Cricket: GV925
  Fencing: GV1149
  Football
    Amateur: GV956.8
    Professional: GV955
  Go: GV1460.8
  Rugby: GV945.4
  Skiing: GV854.87
  Soccer: GV943.4
  Table tennis: GV1005.4
  Tennis: GV1001
  Track and field: GV1061.67
Rum (Manners and customs): GT2897
Rumba (Dance): GV1796.R8
Rummy (Card game): GV1295.R8
Running: GV1061+
Running to the pens (Bullfighting):
  GV1108.4
Runoff (Hydrology): GB980+
Rural geography (Human ecology): GF127
Rural settlements (Human ecology): GF127
Ruse (Ball game): GV1017.R9
Russia
  Atlases: G2110+
  in
    Asia
      Atlases: G2160+
      Maps: G7200+
    Europe
      Atlases: G2115+
      Maps: G7010+
  Maps: G7000+
Russian bank (Card game): GV1295.R9
Ruth, George ("Babe Ruth"), see "Babe
  Ruth" (George Ruth)

S

Sacred places (Folklore): GR505
Sacrifice (Rites and ceremonies)
  Ethnology: GN473.4+

Safety measures
  Camping: GV191.78
    Organized camping: GV198.S2
  Cycling: GV1055
  Dancing: GV1782.3
    Ballet: GV1789
  Football: GV953.6
  Physical education and training: GV344
  Water sports: GV770.6
    Boats and boating: GV777.55
Sahara
  Atlases: G2447.S2
  Maps: G8202.S2
Sai: GV1150.6
Sailing (General): GV810+
Sailing on land: GV1035
Sailors
  Physical education and training: V260
  Sports: V267+
  Uniforms: VC300+
  See also Military personnel
Sailors' folklore, see Seafaring (Folk-
  lore)
Sailors' life, see Seafaring life
Sailors' yarns: G530
Sails: GV811.45
Saint Christopher (Island)
  Maps: G5040+
St. George's Day (Manners and customs):
  GT4995.G4
Saint Helena (Colony)
  Maps: G9170+
St. John's Day, see John the Baptist's
  Day
St. Johns River, Florida (Tidal
  currents): GC309.S27
St. Joseph's Day (Manners and customs):
  GT4995.J66
Saint Kitts (Maps): G5040+
St. Lawrence River and Valley
  Atlases: G1107.S3
  Maps: G3312.S5
Saint Lucia (Maps): G5110+
St. Lucy's Day (Manners and customs):
  GT4995.L8
St. Martin's Day (Manners and customs):
  GT4995.M3
St. Nicholas Day (Manners and customs):
  GT4995.N5
St. Patrick's Day (Manners and customs):
  GT4995.P3
Saint Pierre and Miquelon Islands
  Atlases: G1195+
  Maps: G3650+
St. Valentine's Day (Manners and customs):
  GT4925
Saint Vincent (Maps): G5120+
Sajuriana (Dance): GV1796.S23
Sake (Manners and customs): GT2887
Salamander (Folklore): GR830.S3

Salinity
  Hydrogeology: GB1197.8+
  of
      seawater: GC120+
Salon soccer, see Indoor soccer
Salt (Manners and customs): GT2870
Saltwater encroachment (Hydrogeology):
  GB1197.8+
Salutations (Manners and customs): GT3050
Samba
  Card game: GV1295.S3
  Dance: GV1796.S25
Sambo wrestling: GV1197.5
Samoa Islands
  Atlases: G2980+
  Maps: G9555+
San Marino
  Atlases: G1990+
  Maps: G6780+
Sand (Coastal landform): GB454.S3
Sand dunes, see Dunes
Sand waves (Geomorphology): GB649.S3
Sand yachting: GV1035
Sandals (Manners and customs): GT2130
Sandhouses (Manners and customs): GT474
Sanding (Manners and customs): GT474
Sandmen (Folklore): GR905
Sandwich Islands, see Hawaii
Sanitation (Camping): GV191.74
  Organized camping: GV198.S3
Sanitation, Household, see Household
  sanitation
Santa Cruz Islands (Maps): G9290+
Santo Domingo, see Dominican Republic
São Tomé e Príncipe
  Atlases: G2609.3+
  Maps: G8675+
Saratoga regattas: GV804
Sardana (Dance): GV1796.S3
Saskatchewan
  Atlases: G1160+
  Maps: G3490+
Saudi Arabia
  Atlases: G2249.3+
  Maps: G7530+
Savage Island, see Niue
Scaffold burial, see Exposure of the dead
Scales (Balance), see Balance (Scales)
Scales (Cartography), see Map scales
Scandinavia
  Atlases: G2050+
  Maps: G6910+
Scapula (Human variation): GN145
Scatology (Manners and customs): GT3055
Schlagball (Game): GV1017.S2
Scholastic achievement
  and
      sports: GV706.45
School (Ball game): GV1017.S3
School athletics, see Intramural and
  interscholastic athletics (Physical ed-
  ucation and training) - School

School camps: GV197.S3
School dance parties: GV1746+; GV1799
School exercises (Calisthenics): GV483
School sports: GV691+
Schools of physical education and
  training: GV367+
Science (Ethnology): GN476+
Science, Applied, see Technology
Science, Moral, see Ethics
Scopa (Card game): GV1295.S4
Score sheets, scoring, etc.
  Baseball: GV879
  Bowling: GV905
  Card games: GV1297
  Golf: GV971
  Shooting: GV1173
  Tennis: GV1001
Scotland
  Atlases: G1825+
  Maps: G5770+
Scott, Robert Falcon: G875.S35
Scottish tartans, see Tartans
Scouting (Football): GV953.4
Scouting games: GV1217
Scrabble (Game): GV1507.S3
Sculpture
  Playgrounds: GV426
  Prehistoric archaeology: GN799.S4
Sea, Folklore of the: GR910
Sea, Science of the, see Oceanography
Sea-air interaction, see Ocean-atmos-
  phere interaction
Sea caves, see Marine caves
Sea floor, see Ocean bottom
Sea ice (Hydrology): GB2401+
Sea level (Oceanography): GC89
Sea travel, see Ocean travel
Seafaring (Folklore): GR910
Seafaring life: G540+
Seals (Folklore): GR730.S4
Seamanship: GV777.5
Seamen, see Sailors
Seamounts (Submarine topography):
  GC87.6.S4
Seas (Folklore): GR910
Seasons (Folklore): GR930
Seawater (Oceanography): GC100+
Seawater encroachment, see Saltwater
  encroachment
Seawater into fresh water, see Fresh
  water from seawater
Seawater pollution: GC1080+
  By region: GC1101+
Second sight (Parlor magic): GV1553
Secret societies (Ethnology): GN490.8
Sects, Nativistic, see Nativistic
  movements
Sediment transport
  of
      marine sediments: GC380.2.S4
Sediments, Estuarine, see Estuarine
  sediments

Sediments, Marine, see Marine sediments
Segmentary systems (Political anthropology): GN492.44
Seguiriya gitana (Dance), see Flamenco dancing
Seiches: GC217+
Seismic sea waves, see Tidal waves
Selection of players (Football), see Players, Selection of (Football)
Self concept (Psychological anthropology): GN512
Self defense (Human fighting): GV1111+
Self identity (Psychological anthropology): GN512
Semiarid regions, see Arid regions
Semitic groups
  Ethnology: GN547
  Folklore: GR97+
Senegal
  Atlases: G2680+
  Maps: G8810+
Sense organs (Human variation): GN201
Senses (Race psychology): GN275+
Sepulchral and perpetual lamps (Folklore): GR506
Serbia
  Atlases: G2015+
  Maps: G6850+
Sesame (Folklore): GR790.S4
Setting-up exercises: GV501
Settlements (Human ecology): GF101+
Sex-based groups (Ethnology): GN490.7
Sex customs: GT2600+
  Ethnology: GN484.3
Sex organs (Human variation): GN211
Sex roles (Ethnology): GN479.65+
Sexual behavior, see Sex customs
Sexual functions (Physiological anthropology): GN235+
Seychelles (Maps): G9200+
Shadow pictures (Children's games): GV1218.S5
Shamanism: GN475.8
Shawls (Manners and customs): GT2114
Shell (Animal materials)
  Ethnology: GN435.7
Shell-heaps, see Kitchen middens
Shellbacks, see Seafaring (Folklore)
Shelter (Ethnology): GN413+
Shields (Weapons)
  Ethnology: GN498.S5
Ship burial (Manners and customs): GT3380
Shipwrecks: G521+
Shoes (Manners and customs): GT2130
Shōgi: GV1458.S5
Shona, see Mashona
Shooting (Sports): GV1151+
Shooting contests, see Contests, Shooting
Shorelines (Geomorphology): GB450+
Short whist: GV1287
Shot-putting: GV1094.8

Shotgun shooting (Sports): GV1179
Shots, Billiard and pool: GV893
Shoulder girdle (Human variation): GN145
Showers (Parties): GV1472.7.S5
Shrine East-West game: GV957.S5
Shuffleboard: GV1099
Shut-ins, Games for: GV1231
Siam, see Thailand
Siberia
  Atlases: G2170+
  Maps: G7270+
Sibs (Ethnology): GN487.7.C55
Side horse exercises: GV523
Side shows: GV1835
Sierra Leone
  Atlases: G2705+
  Maps: G8860+
Sight, see Vision
Signs and symbols, Conventional, see Conventional signs and symbols
Signs, signboards, and symbols (Communication)
  Ethnology: GN452.5
  Folklore: GR931+
  Manners and customs: GT3910+
Sikkim
  Atlases: G2299.3+
  Maps: G7653.S5
Silver chimes (Ball game): GV1017.S5
Simian traits versus human traits (Physical anthropology): GN280.7
Simulation methods
  in
    geography: G70.28
    oceanography: GC10.4.S5
    physical geography: GB21.5.S55
Sinanthropus pekinensis (Fossil man): GN284.7
Singapore
  Atlases: G2384.3+
  Maps: G8040+
Singing and dancing games: GV1215
Singles (Tennis): GV1002.7
Sinkholes (Geomorphology): GB609.2
Sinks (Geology), see Sinkholes
Sisal hemp (Manners and customs): GT5899.S5
Sisters and brothers, see Brothers and sisters
Sitting position (Human variation): GN232
Six-day bicycle races: GV1049
Six-man football: GV953
Skat (Card game): GV1257
Skates, Ice, see Ice skates
Skating, Ice, see Ice skating
Skeet shooting: GV1181.3
Skeleton (Human variation): GN70+
Ski acrobatics, see Acrobatics - Skiing
Ski jumping, see Jumping, Ski
Skibobbing: GV857.S47

Skiing: GV854+
Skill, Children's games of: GV1216
Skin (Human variation): GN191+
Skin dressing (Animal materials)
   Ethnology: GN435.5
Skin, Color of, see Color of skin
Skindiving: GV840.S78
Skipping rope: GV498
Skis
   Ethnology: GN442
   Prehistoric archaeology: GN799.S5
Skulls (Human variation): GN71+
Skydiving (Sports): GV770
Slalom: GV854.9.S6
Slate writing: BF1343
Slavic and Magyar folklore: GR136
Slavs
   Costume: GT725
   Ethnology: GN549.S6
   Folklore: GR138
Sledding, see Bobsledding
Sledges, see Sleighs and sledges
Sleeping customs: GT3000.3+
Sleighing (Winter sport): GV857.S5
Sleighs and sledges (Manners and
   customs): GT5285
Sleight of hand performances: GV1555
Slings (Weapons)
   Ethnology: GN498.S55
Slopes (Geomorphology): GB448
Slovenia (Maps): G6875+
Small boats (Sports): GV777.6
   Sailing: GV811.6
Smithfield culture
   By continent, see table below
     GN774.2+, e. g. GN774.4.S6 (Africa)
Smoking (Manners and customs): GT3020+
Snobs (Manners and customs): GT3433
Snooker (Game): GV900.S6
Snow (Hydrology): GB2601+
Snow and ice-climbing, see Ice and snow
   climbing
Snow camping, see Ice and snow camping
Snow surveys (Hydrology): GB2601+
Snowmobiling: GV857.S6
Snowshoes and snowshoeing
   Ethnology: GN442
   Sports: GV853
Snuff (Manners and customs): GT3030
Soapbox racing: GV1029.7
Soaring (Sports): GV764+
Soccer: GV942+
Soccer, Motorcycle, see Motorcycle
   soccer
Social anthropology: GN301+
Social aspects
   of
     costume: GT525
Social centers: HN41+
Social change (Ethnology): GN358

Social change and psychology, see
   Psychological aspects of social change
Social control (Ethnology): GN493+
Social dancing: GV1746+
Social ecology, see Human ecology
Social geography, see Anthropogeography
Social groups (Ethnology): GN479.8
Social life (Manners and customs):
   GT3400+
Social norms (Ethnology): GN493.3
Social organization (Ethnology): GN478+
Social stratification (Ethnology):
   GN491+
Social whist: GV1291.S6
Socialization (Psychological
   anthropology): GN510
Socially handicapped, Recreation for:
   GV183.9
Societal groups (Ethnology): GN495.4+
Societies, Threatened, see Threatened
   societies
Society
   and
     dancing: GV1588.6
     religion, see Religion and society
Society for the Diffusion of Useful
   Knowledge (Maps): GA320.5.S7
Society Islands (Maps): G9640+
Sociology
   and
     geography: HM36
     recreation and leisure: GV14.45
     sports: GV706.5
Softball (Game): GV881
Sōhen school (Japanese tea ceremony):
   GT2912.S55
Soils, Frozen, see Frozen ground
Solar system (Maps): G3180+
Soldiers
   Anthropometry: GN59.S7
   Manners and customs: U
   Physical education and training: U320
   Sports: U327+
   Uniforms: UC480+
   See also Military personnel
Soldiers of fortune: G539
Solitaire
   Card game: GV1261
   Move game: GV1469.S6
Solitaire bridge: GV1282.7
Solo-sixty (Card game): GV1295.S6
Solo whist: GV1289
Solomon Islands
   Atlases: G2875+
   Maps: G9280+
Solutrean culture
   By continent, see table below
     GN772.2+, e. g. GN772.2.S6 (Europe)
Somalia
   Atlases: G2515+
   Maps: G8350+

Somaliland, see Somalia
Somatotypes (Body dimensions and
  proportions): GN66.5
Somersault, Triple, see Triple somer-
  sault
"Son et lumière": GV1841+
Soothsaying, see Divination
Sorcerers (Folklore): GR535
Sorcerer's apprentice (Folktale):
  GR75.S67
Sorcery (Ethnology): GN475.5
Sotho, see Basuto
Soul concept (Ethnology): GN472.6
Soundings, Deep-sea, see Deep-sea
  soundings
South America
  Atlases: G1700+
  Maps: G5200+
South Asia
  Atlases: G2260+
  Maps: G7625+
South Atlantic States (United States)
  Atlases: G1285+
South Carolina
  Atlases: G1305+
  Maps: G3910+
South Central Asia (Atlases): G2260+
South Central States (United States)
  Atlases: G1320+
  Maps: G3935+
South Dakota
  Atlases: G1445+
  Maps: G4180+
South Korea
  Atlases: G2330+
  Maps: G7900+
South polar regions, see Antarctica
South Vietnam, see Vietnam
Southeast Africa
  Atlases: G2529.3+
  Maps: G8400+
Southeast Asia
  Atlases: G2360+
  Maps: G8000+
Southeastern Europe
  Atlases: G1993+
  Maps: G6800+
Southeastern States (United States)
  Atlases: G1285+
  Maps: G3865+
Southern Africa
  Atlases: G2560+
  Maps: G8480+
Southern Europe
  Atlases: G1955+
  Maps: G6530+
Southern Hemisphere
  Atlases: G1052
  Maps: G3220+

Southern Rhodesia
  Atlases: G2574.3+
  Maps: G8560+
Southern States (United States)
  Atlases: G1280+
  Maps: G3860+
Southern Yemen, see Yemen (People's
  Democratic Republic)
Southwest Africa (Namibia)
  Atlases: G2580+
  Maps: G8620+
Southwestern Asia (Atlases): G2205+
Spain
  Atlases: G1965+
  Maps: G6560+
Spanish Empire
  Atlases: G1963+
  Maps: G6550+
Spanish Guinea, see Equatorial Guinea
Spanish Sahara
  Atlases: G2735+
  Maps: G8900+
Spars (Sailboats): GV811.45
Spartakiads: GV722.5.S6
Spatial studies (Human ecology): GF95
Spear fishing, Underwater: GV840.S78
Spear-throwers, see Throwing sticks
Spearheads (Prehistoric archaeology):
  GN799.W3
Spears (Ethnology): GN498.S68
Spectacles (Eyeglasses)
  Manners and customs: GT2370
Spectacles (Fêtes): GT3940+
Spectator control (Sports): GV715
Spectator stands (Sports): GV415+
Spectator's guides (Football): GV950.6
Specters (Folklore): GR580
Speed-a-way (Ball game): GV1017.S58
Speed records: GV1019
Speed skating (Ice skating): GV850.3
Speedball (Game): GV1017.S6
Speleology (Geomorphology): GB601+
Spells (Folklore): GR600+
Spelunking (Geomorphology): GB602+
Sphero (Ball game): GV1017.S7
Spiders (Folklore): GR755
Spinning (Ethnology): GN432
Spits (Coastal landform): GB454.S66
Spitsbergen, see Svalbard
Spoons (Manners and customs): GT2950
Sport psychology, see Psychological
  aspects of sports
Sporting annuals: GV741
Sporting goods, see Equipment and
  supplies for athletics and sports
Sports: GV561+
  Ethnology: GN454+
  Modern history (By region or country):
    GV581+

Sports, Intramural, see Intramural
 sports
Sports, Psychological aspects of, see
 Psychological aspects of sports
Sports, Winter, see Winter sports
Sports and ethics, see Ethics and sports
Sports and fair play, see Fair play and
 sports
Sports and scholastic achievement, see
 Scholastic achievement and sports
Sports and sociology, see Sociology and
 sports
Sports and success, see Success and sports
Sports betting, see Betting (Sports)
Sports broadcasters: GV719
Sports car events: GV1029.8
Sports clubs, see Clubs, Athletic and
 sports
Sports events: GV712+
Sports facilities: GV401+
Sports journalism, see Journalism, Sports
Sports leagues, see Leagues, Sports
Sports officiating, see Officiating,
 Sports
Sports records and statistics, see
 Records and statistics (Sports)
Sports writers: GV719
Sportsmanship: GV706.3
Sportswear, see Clothing for athletics
 and gymnastics
Springs (Groundwater): GB1198+
 Folklore: GR690
Sprinting: GV1069
Spurs (Manners and customs): GT5888
Square (Folklore): GR932.S66
Square dances: GV1763+
Squash (Ball game): GV1004+
Squash racquets (Ball game): GV1004
Squash tennis (Ball game): GV1004.5
Sri Lanka
 Atlases: G2290+
 Maps: G7750+
Stadiums (Sports): GV415+
Stage dancing, see Theatrical dancing
Staging
 of
    theatrical dancing: GV1782
Stands, Spectator, see Spectator stands
Stanley Cup: GV847.7
Stars (Folklore): GR625
State balls: GV1747
State policy, etc.
 and
    recreation (General): GV47
States (Ethnology): GN492.6+
States (Game), see Geography games
Statistical mapping: GA109.8
Statistical methods
 Glaciers: GB2401.72.S7
 Groundwater: GB1001.72.S7
 Ice: GB2401.72.S7
 Ice sheets: GB2401.72.S7

Statistical methods - Continued
 in
    geography: G70.3
    geomorphology: GB400.42.S7
    hydrogeology: GB1001.72.S7
    hydrology: GB656.2.S7
    hydrometeorology: GB2801.72.S7
    limnology: GB1601.72.S7
    oceanography: GC10.4.S7
    physical education and training:
     GV342.5.S7
    physical geography: GB21.5.S7
 Lagoons: GB2201.72.S7
 Lakes: GB1601.72.S7
 Ponds: GB1801.72.S7
 Rivers: GB1201.72.S7
 Sea ice: GB2401.72.S7
 Snow: GB2601.72.S7
 Snow surveys: GB2601.72.S7
 Stream measurements: GB1201.72.S7
 Waterfalls: GB1401.72.S7
Statistics, Sports, see Records and
 statistics (Sports)
Stefansson, Vihjalmur: G635.S7
Steppes (Natural landforms): GB561+
Stick fighting (Sports): GV1141+
Stilt walking: GV1099
Stimulants (Ethnology): GN411+
Stockings (Manners and customs): GT2128
Stone age (Prehistoric archaeology):
 GN768+
Stones
 Ethnology: GN434+
 Folklore: GR800+
Stones, Precious, see Precious stones
Stoneware, see Pottery
Stoolball (Game): GV1017.S8
Storm floods, see Storm surges
Storm surges (Oceanography): GC225+
Storm tides, see Storm surges
Storm waves, see Storm surges
Story games: GV1507.S7
Storytellers (Manners and customs):
 GT3660
Strabo: G87.S86+
Straits Settlements (Maps): G8040+
Strategies and techniques
 Chess: GV1449.5+
 Football: GV951.15+
Stream measurements (Hydrology): GB1201+
Stream sediment transport, see Sediment
 transport
Streams, see Rivers
Street cries (Manners and customs):
 GT3450
Street life (Manners and customs): GT3440
Streets
 Decorations (Manners and customs):
  GT3452
 of
    the world (Geography): G140

Strength (Physiological anthropology): GN229

Stretching exercises: GV505

String figures (Games and toys): GV1218.S8

   Ethnology: GN455.S9

Strong men: CT9997

Structural analysis (Folklore): GR44.S7

Structural anthropology: GN362

Structuralism (Culture and cultural processes): GN362

Students (Anthropometry): GN59.S8

Stunts, Acrobatic, see Acrobatics

Style in dress, see Fashion

Sub-Saharan Africa

   Atlases: G2445+

   Maps: G8200+

Submarine diving

   Sports: GV840.S78

   See also Underwater exploration

Submarine geology: QE39

Submarine research stations, Manned, see Manner underwater stations

Submarine topography: GC83+

   Submarine geology: QE39

Submersibles, Oceanographic, see Oceanographic submersibles

Subsidences: QE598+

Subsistence (Ethnography): GN407+

Subterranean civilization (Prehistoric archaeology): GN755

Success

   and

     sports: GV706.55

Sudan

   Atlases: G2495+

   Maps: G8310+

Sugar Bowl game: GV957.S8

Sugar puppet (Folktale), see Basil maiden (Folktale)

Sullivan, John L.: GV1132.S95

Summer camps: GV192+

Sumo: GV1197

Sun (Folklore): GR625

Sunbathing: GV450

Sunken treasure, see Buried treasure

Suomi, see Finland

Super Bowl game: GV956.2.S8

Supernatural beings and forces

   Ethnology: GN472.5

   Folklore: GR500+

Superstitions (General): GR81

Supplies, see Equipment and supplies

Surf riding: GV840.S8+

Surfing: GV840.S8+

Surgeons (Professional customs): R707

Surgery (Ethnology): GN477.5+

Surinam

   Atlases: G1715+

   Maps: G5260+

Surveys, Geographic: GA51+

Surveys, Recreation: GV181.46

Survival (Human ecology), see Human ecology

Survival, Wilderness, see Wilderness survival

Susquehanna River and Valley (Maps): G3792.S9

Suttee (Funeral customs): GT3370

Svalbard

   Atlases: G3060+

   Maps: G9790+

Swahili (Folklore): GR355.62.S93

Swamps (Geomorphology): GB621+

Swan maidens (Folktale): GR75.S8

Swanscombe (Fossil man): GN286.7

Swazi (Folklore): GR360.S85

Swaziland

   Atlases: G2579.5+

   Maps: G8590+

Swearing (Manners and customs): GT3080

Sweden

   Atlases: G2070+

   Maps: G6950+

Swedish gymnastics: GV467

Swedish whist: GV1291.P8

Swimming: GV837+

Swimming pools: GV837.13

Swine

   Folklore: GR730.S9

   Trained swine: GV1831.P6

Swing (Golf): GV979.S9

Swing dancing, see Jitterbug dancing

Switzerland

   Atlases: G1895+

   Maps: G6040+

Sword dance: GV1796.S9

Swords

   Folklore: GR950.S9

   Prehistoric archaeology: GN799.W3

Symbolism

   of

     animals, see Animal lore

   Prehistoric archaeology: GN799.S9

Symbols (Communication), see Signs, signboards, and symbols (Communication)

Syria

   Atlases: G2220+

   Maps: G7460+

System simulation, see Simulation methods

Syzygies (Games): GV1507.S9

T

"T" formation (Football): GV951.9

Table tennis: GV1004.9+

Tables

   of

     distances, see Distances, Tables of

     heights: QC895

Tableware (Manners and customs): GT2948+
Taboo (Ethnology): GN471.4
Tailors (Manners and customs): GT5960.T2
Taiwan
   Atlases: G2340+
   Maps: G7910+
Talismans (Folklore): GR600+
Tamburello (Ball game): GV1005.5
Tamis (Ball game), see Balle au tamis
   (Game)
Tamunangue (Dance): GV1796.T2
Tan-to (Ball game): GV1017.T3
Tanganyika, see Tanzania
Tango (Dance): GV1796.T3
Tangrams: GV1507.T3
Tanzania
   Atlases: G2540+
   Maps: G8440+
Tap dancing: GV1794
Tardenoisian culture
   By continent, see table below
     GN774.2+, e. g. GN774.2.T3 (Europe)
Tarrash, Siegbert: GV1444
Tartans: DA880.H76
Tattooing
   Ethnology: GN419.3
   Manners and customs: GT2345
Taverns (Manners and customs): GT3770+
Tchad, see Chad
Tea (Manners and customs): GT2905+
Tea ceremony, Japanese, see Japanese
   tea ceremony
Tea masters: GT2911
Teachers, Training of physical education,
   see Physical education teachers, Train-
   ing of
Technology (Ethnology): GN406+
Teddy bears: GV1220.7
Teen-age, see Adolescence
Teeth (Human variation): GN209
Television dancing: GV1779
   Television dance parties: PN1992.8.D3
Television
 in
   physical education and training: GV364
Temperate zones
   Maps: G3250+
   Oceanography: GC881
     Currents: GC251+
     Tides: GC316
Temperature
 of
   lakes, see Lake temperatures
   rivers, see River temperatures
   seawater: GC160+
Tengu (Folklore): GR830.T3
Tennessee
   Atlases: G1335+
   Maps: G3960+
Tennessee River and Valley (Maps):
   G3942.T4

Tennis: GV990+
Tennis balls: GV1002.5
Tennis courts: GV1002
Tennis nets: GV1002.5
Tennis rackets: GV1002.5
Tenpins (Bowling): GV903+
Tents (Ethnology): GN414.3.T45
Terraces (Natural landforms): GB591+
Terrain (Geomorphology): GB400+
Terrestrial globe gores: G3201.B71
Terrestrial globes: G3170+
Territorial groups (Ethnology): GN491.7
Testing
 of
   marine sediments: GC380.2.T4
Teutonic peoples (Ethnology): GN549.T4
Texas
   Atlases: G1370+
   Maps: G4030+
Texas Rangers (Baseball club): GV875.T4
Textile fabrics (Ethnology): GN432
Thailand
   Atlases: G2375+
   Maps: G8025+
Thanksgiving Day
   Manners and customs: GT4975
     United States: E162
       New England (Early): F7
   Religious observance: BV75
Theaters, Miniature, see Miniature
   theaters
Theatrical dancing: GV1781+
Theatrical costumes: GT1740+
   Art of acting: PN2067
Thematic cartography: GA103+
Thermal waters, see Geothermal resources
Thonga (Folklore): GR360.T5
Thoracic girdle, see Shoulder girdle
Threatened societies (Ethnographies):
   GN380
Three stolen princesses (Folktale):
   GR75.T5
Throwing games and sports: GV1091+
Throwing knives, see Knife throwing
Throwing sticks (Weapons)
   Ethnology: GN498.T5
Thunder (Folklore): GR630
Thurston, Howard: GV1545.T5
Tibet
   Atlases: G2325+
   Maps: G7890+
Tic-tac-toe: GV1507.T47
Ticktacktoe, see Tic-tac-toe
Tidal bores: GC376
Tidal currents: GC308+
Tidal power (Source of energy): TC147
Tidal wave warning systems, see Warning
   systems, Tidal wave
Tidal waves: GC219+
Tide gauges: GC306
Tide predictors: GC306

Tide stations: GC307
Tides: GC300+
  Theory of tides: QB414+
  Tide tables: VK600+
  By region or ocean: GC311+
Ties (Neckwear), see Neckties
Tilden, William: GV994.T5
Tillo, Alekseĭ Andreevich: G69.T55
Tilts: GV1191
Time games: GV1507.T5
Timor (Maps): G8195+
Tit-tat-toe, see Tic-tac-toe
Toads (Folklore): GR760.T6
Toasts (Drinking customs), see Drinking
  of healths
Tobacco (Manners and customs): GT3020+
Tobago, see Trinidad and Tobago
Tobogganing: GV855
Togo
  Atlases: G2655+
  Maps: G8760+
Togoland, see Togo
Tokelau Islands (Maps): G9550+
Tonga (Maps): G9570+
Tools
  Ethnology: GN436.8+
  Prehistoric archaeology: GN799.T6
Tooth (Animal materials)
  Ethnology: GN435.3
Toothpicks (Manners and customs): GT2952
Topographic drawing (Cartography): GA125
Topography, Submarine, see Submarine
  topography
Toponymy: G100.5+
Tops (Children's games): GV1218.T5
Toreadors, see Matadors
Torques (Jewelry): GT2260
Totemism (Ethnology): GN489
Touch football: GV952
Tour de France (Bicycle race): GV1049
Tour guide books (Bicycling): GV1045+
Touring, Bicycle: GV1044+
Touring Club Uruguayo: GV1027
Touring clubs, Automobile: GV1027
Tourist trade: G155+
Tournaments (Modern revivals): GV1191
Tours, Pedestrian, see Pedestrian tours
Tours around the world: G439+
Town life
  Manners and customs: GT3420+
  Urban sociology: HT101+
Toy soldiers (Children's games):
  GV1218.T55
Toys: GV1218.5+
  Ethnology: GN454.8+
  Prehistoric archaeology: GN799.T7
Tracers, Radioactive, see Radioactive
  tracers

Track and field sports and games:
  GV1060.5+
  for
    women, see Women and girls - Track
      and field athletics
Trade, see Commerce and trade
Tradesmen (Manners and customs): GT5910+
Trailer camping: GV198.5+
Trails (Ethnology): GN439
Training
  Animals (Circus), see Animals, Circus -
    Training
  Basketball: GV885.35
  Boxing: GV1137.6
  Cycling: GV1048
  Football: GV953.5
  Rugby: GV945.8
  Skiing: GV854.85
  Soccer: GV943.9.T7
  Track and field: GV1061.5
Training, Physical education and, see
  Physical education and training
Tramping, see Hiking
Trampolining (Acrobatics): GV555
Trances (Religion and ritual)
  Ethnology: GN472.4
Transport, Sediment, see Sediment
  transport
Transport phenomena, Water, see Water
  transport phenomena
Transportation
  Ethnology: GN438+
  Folklore: GR865+
  Manners and customs: GT5220+
Transportation by water, see Water
  transportation
Trapeze work: GV551+
Trapball (Game): GV1017.T7
Traps (Ethnology): GN407.33.T7
Trapshooting: GV1181+
Travel
  and
    church, see Church and travel
    education, see Education and travel
    the state: G155+
    youth, see Youth travel
  Folklore: GR865+
  Manners and customs: GT5220+
  See also Voyages and travels
Travel agents: G154+
Travel bureaus, see Travel agents
Travel clubs: G154+
Travelers, Games for: GV1206
Travelers, Sports for: GV709.7
Traveling by automobile, see Automobile
  travel
Traveling instructions: G149.9+
Treasure, Buried, see Buried treasure

Treasure hunting: GV1202.T7
Treasure troves, see Buried treasure
Trees
  Folklore: GR785
  Manners and customs: GT5150
Trente et quarante (Game): GV1308
Trepanation (Ethnology): GN477.7
Tressette (Card game): GV1295.T7
Trials of animals, see Animals, Prosecu-
  tion and punishment of
Tribes (Ethnology): GN492.5
Triboulet (Game): GV311.T73
Tricks, Parlor: GV1541+
Trimarans: GV811.63.T7
Trinidad and Tobago
  Atlases: G1680+
  Maps: G5145+
Triple jump (Track and field event):
  GV1078
Triple somersault (Acrobatics): GV553
Triplets (Physiological anthropology):
  GN236.5
Triplicate whist: GV1291.T8
Tripping (Canoeing): GV789+
Triumphal entries (Manners and customs):
  GT5030
Triumphs (Manners and customs): GT5030
Trophies, Golf: GV979.T7
Tropics
  Anthropogeography: GF895
  Atlases: G1053
  Human ecology: GF895
  Maps: G3240+
  Oceanography: GC880
    Currents: GC261
    Marine sediments: GC380.3
    Tides: GC321
  Physical geography: GB398.7
Troubadours (Manners and customs): GT3650
Trucial States, see United Arab Emirates
Truk Islands (Maps): G9440+
Trumpeters (Manners and customs): GT5020
Trust Territory of the Pacific Islands
  (Maps): G9405+
Tsonga, see Thonga
Tsunamis: GC219+
Tuamoto Archipelago (Maps): G9630+
Tubes, Lava, see Lava tubes
Tubuai Islands, see Austral Islands
Tug of war (Game): GV1098
Tumbling exercises: GV545
Tumuli (Prehistoric archaeology): GN795
Tundras (Natural landforms): GB571+
Tunisia (Tunis)
  Atlases: G2470+
  Maps: G8250+
Turkey
  Atlases: G2210+
  Maps: G7430+
Turks and Caicos Islands (Maps): G4985+
Turnvereins: GV202+

Tussaud's waxworks, see Madame Tussaud's
  waxworks
Twelfth Night (Manners and customs):
  GT4915
Twenty-one (Card game), see Blackjack
  (Card game)
Twins (Physiological anthropology):
  GN236.5
Two-step (Dance): GV1796.T9
Työväen Urheiluliitto: GV722.5.T9

                    U

U.S.S.R., see Russia
Ubangi-Shari, see Central African
  Republic
Uganda
  Atlases: G2535+
  Maps: G8420+
Ugrians, see Finno-Ugrians
Umbrellas (Manners and customs): GT2210
Umpires (Sports): GV735
Umpiring (Baseball): GV876
Underwater exploration: GC65+
  Archaeology: CC
  Diving (Marine engineering): VM975+
  Submarine photography: TR800
  See also Submarine diving
Underwater light: GC181
Underwater spear fishing, see Spear
  fishing, Underwater
Underwater stations, Manned, see Manned
  underwater stations
Underwear (Manners and customs): GT2073+
Underworld, The (Manners and customs):
  GT6550+
Uneven parallel bar exercises: GV536
Unicorn (Folklore): GR830.U6
Unidentified places, Voyages to: G555
Unilineal descent (Ethnology): GN487.3+
Union Islands, see Tokelau Islands
Union of Soviet Socialist Republics, see
  Russia
United Arab Emirates
  Atlases: G2249.75+
  Maps: G7570+
United Arab Republic, see Egypt
United States
  Atlases: G1200+
  Maps: G3700+
United States and possessions (Maps):
  G3690+
United States of Indonesia, see
  Indonesia
Universe (Maps): G3180+
Universiade: GV722.5.U5
Upper Volta
  Atlases: G2679.3+
  Maps: G8805+
Ura Senke (Japanese tea ceremony):
  GT2912.U7

Urban anthropology (Ethnographies):
GN395
Urban geography (Human ecology): GF125
Urban life, see Town life
Urns (Burial customs): GT3335
Uruguay
  Atlases: G1765+
  Maps: G5370+
Utah
  Atlases: G1515+
  Maps: G4340+
Utensils, see Implements
Uxorilocal (Ethnology): GN480.63

V

Vacations (Recreation): GV186
Valentine's Day, see St. Valentine's
  Day
Valleys (Natural landforms): GB561+
Values (Philosophy)
  Ethnology: GN469
Vampires
  Folklore: GR830.V3
  Occult sciences: BF1556
Vatican
  Atlases: G1989.24.R7:3V3
  Maps: G6714.R7:3V3
Vaulting (Track and field event):
  GV1079+
Vehicles
  Ethnology: GN441
  Folklore: GR867+
  Manners and customs: GT5280
Veils (Manners and customs): GT2112
Venda (Folklore): GR359.2.V43
Vendetta (Ethnology): GN495; GN496.5
Venezuela
  Atlases: G1725+
  Maps: G5280+
Ventriloquism: GV1557
Vermont
  Atlases: G1225+
  Maps: G3750+
Vernal equinox (Manners and customs):
  GT4995.V4
Vertebra (Human variation): GN141
Visits of royalty (Manners and customs):
  GT5090
Vessels (Utensils), see Implements
Vietnam
  Atlases: G2370+
  Maps: G8020+
Viking age (Geography): G92
Village patterns (Ethnology): GN413.5
Villanovans (Iron age people)
  By continent, see table below GN780.2+,
    e. g. GN780.2.V5 (Europe)
Vinča culture
  By continent, see table below GN776.2+,
    e. g. GN776.2.V5 (Europe)

Vingt et un (Card game), see Blackjack
  (Card game)
Viola (Folktale), see Basil Maiden
  (Folktale)
Virgin Islands
  Atlases: G1640+
  Maps: G5005+
Virginia
  Atlases: G1290+
  Maps: G3880+
Virginity (Ethnology): GN484.47
Virilocal (Ethnology): GN480.65
Vision
  Race psychology: GN277
  Religion and ritual (Ethnology):
    GN472.4
Visually handicapped, Maps for the:
  GA135
Vocational guidance (Tourist trade):
  G155.5
Volcanoes: QE521+
Volleyball: GV1017.V6
Voyages, Ancient, see Ancient voyages
Voyages, Imaginary, see Imaginary
  voyages
Voyages and travels: G149+
  Medieval: G369+
  Modern: G419+
  See also Travel

W

Wachaga (Folklore): GR356.42.W33;
  GR356.72.W33
Wakes (Manners and customs): GT3360
Wales
  Atlases: G1820+
  Maps: G5760+
Walking (Track and field event): GV1071
Walking, Rope, see Rope walking
Walking on stilts, see Stilt walking
Walking sticks (Manners and customs):
  GT2220
Wallis Islands (Maps): G9515+
Waltz: GV1761
Wambulu (Folklore): GR356.72.W34
Wand exercises: GV503
Wandering Jew (Folktale): GR75.W3
Warfare (Ethnology): GN497+
Warning systems, Natural disaster:
  GB5030
Warning systems, Tidal wave: GC223
Warwickshire County Cricket Club:
  GV921.W3
Washing and ironing clothes, see
  Laundering
Washington (State)
  Atlases: G1485+
  Maps: G4280+

Washington, D.C.
  Atlases: G1275+
  Maps: G3850+
Washington Cycling Club, Chicago, see
  Chicago. Washington Cycling Club
Washington Senators (Baseball club):
  GV875.W3
Washover apron, see Washover fans
Washover fans (Coastal landform):
  GB454.W3
Water
  Folklore: GR678+
  Physical geography: GB651+
Water, Bodies of, see Bodies of water
Water-bearing formations, see Aquifers
Water chemistry, Natural, see Natural
  water chemistry
Water cycle, see Hydrologic cycle
Water masses (Oceanography): GC297+
Water oriented recreation: GV200.6
Water polo: GV839
Water skiing: GV840.S5
Water sports: GV770.3+
  Water oriented recreation, see Water
    oriented recreation
Water transport phenomena: GB850
Water transportation (Ethnology): GN440+
Waterfalls (Hydrology): GB1401+
Watersheds
  Hydrology: GB980+
  Natural landforms: GB561+
Waves: GC205+
Waves, Sand, see Sand waves
Waxworks: GV1836
Wayfarers (Manners and customs): GT6490
Weapons and armor
  Ethnology: GN497.5+
  Prehistoric archaeology: GN799.W3
Weather lore (Folklore): GR635
Weaving
  Ethnology: GN432
  Prehistoric archaeology: GN799.W4
Wedding anniversaries (Manners and
  customs): GT2800
Weddings (Manners and customs): GT2660+
Weekend parties: GV1472.7.W4
Weight lifting: GV546
Weight reducing exercises: RA781.6
Weight throwing (Track and field event):
  GV1093+
Weights, Chest, see Chest weight exercises
Wells (Folklore): GR690
Werewolves (Folklore): GR830.W4
West, The (United States)
  Atlases: G1380+
  Maps: G4050+
West Africa
  Atlases: G2640+
  Maps: G8735+
West Germany
  Atlases: G1920+
  Maps: G6295+

West Indies
  Atlases: G1600+
  Maps: G4900+
West North Central States (United States)
  Atlases: G1420+
  Maps: G4130+
West South Central States (United States)
  Atlases: G1350+
  Maps: G3990+
West Virginia
  Atlases: G1295+
  Maps: G3890+
Western Asia (Atlases): G2205+
Western Canada (Maps): G3465+
Western Europe
  Atlases: G1800+
  Maps: G5720+
Western Golf Association: GV969.W5
Western Hemisphere
  Atlases: G1100+
  Maps: G3290+
Whaling voyages: G545
Wheat (Manners and customs): GT5899.W5
Wheel exercises: GV547
Wheels (Ethnology): GN441
Whiskey (Manners and customs): GT2895
Whist: GV1271+
White races (Ethnology): GN537
White-water running (Canoeing): GV788
Wicket (Ball game): GV1017.W5
Wicket polo: GV1017.W6
Widow suicide (Funeral customs): GT3370
Wightman cup (Tennis tournament): GV999
Wigs (Manners and customs): GT2310
Wild boar (Folklore): GR730.W5
Wild West shows: GV1833
Wilderness survival: GV200.5
Wilton culture
  By continent, see table below GN774.2+,
    e. g. GN774.4.W5 (Africa)
Wimbledon, England. All-England Club:
  GV997.A4
Windward Islands
  Atlases: G1670+
  Maps: G5090+
Wines (Manners and customs): GT2885
Wingback formation (Football): GV951.95
Winter games, Olympic, see Olympic
  Games - Modern revivals - Winter games
Winter sports: GV840.7+
Wire walking: GV551+
Wisconsin
  Atlases: G1415+
  Maps: G4120+
Wishes (Folklore): GR615
Witchcraft (Ethnology): GN475+
Witches (Folklore): GR530
Wolf children (Ethnology): GN372
Wolves (Folklore): GR730.W6
The Woman without hands (Folktale), see
  Maiden without hands (Folktale)

Women and girls
  Anthropometry: GN59.W6
  Boating: GV777.57
  Body dimensions and proportions:
    GN67.5
  Clothing for athletics and gymnastics:
    GV441
  Costume: GT1720
  Cycling: GV1057
  Ethnology: GN479.7
  Folklore: GR470
  Girls' basketball: GV886
  Girls' camps: GV197.G5
  Golf: GV966
  Gymnastics: GV464
    Calisthenics and exercises: GV482
  Manners and customs: GT2520+
  Outdoor life and recreation: GV191.64
  Physical education and training: GV439+
  Physical education teachers: GV362
  Recreation: GV183
  Self defense: GV1111.5
  Soccer: GV944.5
  Sports: GV709
  Track and field athletics: GV1060.8
Wood (Ethnology): GN434.7
Wood nymphs (Folklore): GR785
Word games and puzzles: GV1507.W8
Word lists (Games): GV1507.W9
World atlases: G1001+
World Cup (Soccer): GV943.49+
World Festival of Youth and Students for
  Peace and Friendship: GV722.5.W58
World flights, see Flights around the
  world
World maps: G3200+
World tours, see Tours around the world
World University Summer Games: GV722.5.W6
World view (Ethnology): GN468+
Wrecks, see Shipwrecks
Wrestling: GV1195+
Writers, Sports, see Sports writers
Wyoming
  Atlases: G1475+
  Maps: G4260+

X

Xosa (Folklore): GR359.2.X64

Y

Y.M.C.A. gymnastics, see Young Men's
  Christian Association gymnastics
Yacht clubs: GV823
Yacht regattas: GV827+
Yachting: GV811.8+
  Sailing: GV810+
Yachting, Sand, see Sand yachting
Yachts, Illustrations of, see Illustra-
  tions of yachts
Yale-Harvard boat races, see Harvard-
  Yale boat races
Yankee Stadium: GV416.N48
Yap (Maps): G9430+
Yayoi culture
  By continent, see table below
    GN776.2+, e. g. GN776.3.Y3 (Asia)
Yemen (People's Democratic Republic)
  Atlases: G2249.55+
  Maps: G7550+
Yemen (Yemen Arab Republic)
  Atlases: G2249.5+
  Maps: G7540+
Yoruba (Folklore): GR351.32.Y56
Young Men's Christian Association
  gymnastics: GV469
Youth travel: G156.5.Y6
Yugoslavia
  Atlases: G2010+
  Maps: G6840+
Yukon
  Atlases: G1175+
  Maps: G3520+

Z

Zaghawa (Folklore): GR355.52.Z33
Zaire
  Atlases: G2600+
  Maps: G8650+
Zambia
  Atlases: G2575+
  Maps: G8570+
Zanzibar, see Tanzania
Zinjanthropus boisei (Fossil man):
  GN283.8
Zulus (Folklore): GR360.Z8

☆ U.S. GOVERNMENT PRINTING OFFICE: 1985-462-991